# Lubbock Lake

# Lubbock Lake

## *Late Quaternary Studies on the Southern High Plains*

Edited by Eileen Johnson

TEXAS A&M UNIVERSITY PRESS
COLLEGE STATION

The paper used in this book meets the minimum requirements
of the American National Standard for Permanence
of Paper for Printed Library Materials, Z39.48-1984.
Binding materials have been chosen for durability.

*Library of Congress Cataloging-in-Publication Data*

Lubbock Lake: Late quaternary studies on the southern
  high plains.

  Bibliography: p.
  Includes index.
  1. Lubbock Lake Site (Tex.) 2. Paleoindians—Texas. 3. Excavations
(Archaeology)—Texas. 4. Indians of North America—Texas—Antiqui-
ties. 5. Texas—Antiquities. I. Johnson, Eileen McAllister.
E78.T4L82   1987     976.4'847     87-1888
ISBN 0-89096-321-5

# Contents

List of Illustrations                                         vii
List of Tables                                                ix
Preface                                                       xi


CHAPTER

1. Introduction
   Eileen Johnson and Vance T. Holliday            3

2. Geology and Soils
   Vance T. Holliday and B. L. Allen               14

3. Cultural Chronology
   Vance T. Holliday                               22

4. Modern, Historic, and Fossil Flora
   Jerome L. Thompson                              26

5. Pollen Records from Lubbock Lake
   Vaughn M. Bryant, Jr., and
   James Schoenwetter                              36

6. The Gastropods, with Notes on Other
   Invertebrates
   Harold G. Pierce                                41

7. Vertebrate Remains
   Eileen Johnson                                  49

8. Paleoenvironmental Overview
   Eileen Johnson                                  90

9. Lubbock Lake Artifact Assemblages
   Eileen Johnson and Vance T. Holliday            100

10. Cultural Activities and Interactions
    Eileen Johnson                                 120

11. Summary
    Eileen Johnson and Vance T. Holliday           159

References Cited                                   163
Contributors                                       176
Index                                              177

# Illustrations

1.1. Map of the Southern High
Plains (Llano Estacado) — 3

1.2. Topographic map of Yellowhouse Draw — 3

1.3. Map of the Southern High Plains and
physiographic provinces — 4

1.4. Aerial photograph of Lubbock Lake — 5

1.5. Topographic map of Lubbock Lake in the
reservoir area — 6

1.6. Excavations in progress in Pit C — 8

1.7. Reservoir cut showing the Texas Memorial
Museum excavation stations — 9

1.8. Generalized stratigraphic relationships of
radiocarbon ages from Lubbock Lake — 12

1.9. Aerial photograph of Lubbock Lake in the
area of the reservoir cut — 13

1.10. Matrix washing process — 13

2.1. Stratigraphic section at Lubbock Lake — 14

2.2. Geologic cross section of Yellowhouse Draw — 16

2.3. Topography with late Quaternary geology
of Yellowhouse Draw — 16

2.4. Topographic and geologic map of Lubbock
Lake in the area of the reservoir cut — 17

2.5. Stratigraphy of the late Quaternary valley
fill in Yellowhouse Draw — 18

2.6. Substratum 2A local-bed sequence — 18

2.7. Summary of the cultural chronology,
geologic history, and climatic history
of Lubbock Lake — 21

4.1. Collecting localities for modern flora along
Yellowhouse Draw — 27

4.2. Modern soil series at Lubbock Lake
Landmark — 30

4.3. Typical upland- and lowland-draw localities — 31

4.4. Typical upland- and lowland-site localities — 31

4.5. Portion of the reservoir in 1939 — 32

4.6. Fossil plant impressions from substratum 2A — 34

6.1. Climatic trends and species diversity of
invertebrate fauna — 48

7.1. Skull and shell of *Chrysemys scripta*
(pond slider) — 66

7.2. Partial carapace and anterior plastral lobe
of *Terrapene carolina putnami* (extinct
Carolina box turtle) — 67

7.3. Modern distribution and fossil localities in
Texas of *Blarina* (shrew) — 71

7.4. Modern and extralimital fossil distribution
of *Spermophilus richardsonii* (Richardson's
ground squirrel) — 73

7.5. Modern distribution and fossil localities of
*Microtus pennsylvanicus* (meadow vole) — 77

7.6. Modern distribution and fossil distribution
of *Microtus ochrogaster* (prairie vole) — 77

7.7. Modern and extralimital fossil distribution
of *Synaptomys cooperi* (southern
bog lemming) — 78

7.8. Fossil distribution of *Arctodus simus*
(short-faced bear) — 79

8.1. Hypothetical reconstruction of Lubbock
Lake local environs in Yellowhouse Draw
during Clovis period — 93

8.2. Hypothetical reconstruction of Lubbock
Lake local environs in Yellowhouse Draw
during Folsom and Plainview periods — 94

8.3. Hypothetical reconstruction of Lubbock
Lake local environs in Yellowhouse Draw
during Firstview period — 95

9.1. Composite stratigraphic column of geologic
units of eastern side of Southern High
Plains — 100

9.2. Clovis-period lithic tools from
substratum 1B — 105

9.3. Folsom period lithic tools from
substratum 2A — 106

9.4. Folsom projectile point — 107

9.5. Stratum 2 Paleoindian projectile points — 107

9.6. Stratum 2 Paleoindian lithic tools — 109

9.7. Firstview period decorated bone pieces — 110

9.8. Firstview period lithic tools — 111

9.9. Firstview period lithic tools — 111

9.10. Late Ceramic period lithic tools — 112

9.11. Protohistoric period lithic tools — 113

9.12. Protohistoric period bone tools — 114

9.13. Protohistoric and Historic period bone
tools and bone and shell decorative items — 116

9.14. Historic period projectile points — 117

9.15. Historic period bone tools — 118

10.1. Clovis-age megafaunal processing station — 121

10.2. Skinning cut lines on first phalange of
*Camelops hesternus* (extinct camel) — 122

10.3. Skinning cut lines on metacarpals of *Arctodus
simus* (short-faced bear) — 123

10.4. Helically fractured mammoth humerus — 124

10.5. Folsom period bison kill/butchering locale — 125

10.6. Cut lines on small-animal bones from
Paleoindian period — 126

10.7. Folsom period bone-reduction areas — 127

10.8. Plainview period bison kill/butchering locale — 128

10.9. Plainview period bison kill/butchering locale — 130

10.10. Firstview period complex activity area — 131

10.11. Early Archaic period bison kill/butchering
locale — 132

10.12. Middle Archaic period caliche-capped pit — 134

10.13. Later Ceramic period processing stations — 135

10.14. Later Ceramic period living floor — 136

10.15. Protohistoric period living floors 138
10.16. Protohistoric period processing station 139
10.17. Historic period processing station 141
10.18. Historic period processing station 142
10.19. Bison skeleton depicting butchering and bone treatment, Paleoindian period 146
10.20. Horse skeleton depicting butchering and bone treatment, Historic period 149
10.21. Young mammoth elements from Clovis-age processing station 150
10.22. Mammoth skeleton depicting butchering and bone treatment, Clovis period 151

# Tables

1.1. Correlations of stratigraphic terminology of all investigations at Lubbock Lake  7
1.2. Reliable radiocarbon dates  11
2.1. Generalized descriptions of strata 1 through 5  15
2.2. Classification of Holocene soils  15
4.1. Modern flora at Lubbock Lake and adjacent areas  28
4.2. Plant macrofossils recovered  33
6.1. Terrestrial gastropod faunas  44
6.2. Aquatic gastropod faunas  44
7.1. Composite faunal list by cultural period and stratigraphy  50
7.2. Measurements of ilia of *Bufo woodhousei bexarensis*  64
7.3. Maximum shell and anterior lobe measurements of *Terrapene carolina putnami* (extinct Carolina box turtle)  67
7.4. Measurements of adult *Holmesina septentrionale* (extinct giant armadillo) material  71
7.5. Measurements of *Arctodus simus* (short-faced bear) material  80
7.6. Tooth measurements of *Mammuthus columbi* (Columbian mammoth)  81
7.7. Measurements of adult *Equus mexicanus* (extinct stout-legged horse) material  82
7.8. Measurements of adult *Equus francisci* (extinct small stilt-legged horse) material  83
7.9. Measurements of adult *Camelops hesternus* (extinct camel) material  84
7.10. Measurements of tibiae and astragali of *Capromeryx* (extinct antelope)  85
8.1. Lubbock Lake Paleoindian vertebrate local faunas  91
8.2. Lubbock Lake Archaic vertebrate local faunas  95
8.3. Lubbock Lake Ceramic through Historic vertebrate local faunas  97
9.1. Projectile point measurements  101
9.2. Lubbock Lake lithic tool measurements  102
9.3. Indices of late Paleoindian projectile points, Plainview and Lubbock Lake  108
10.1 Ungulate anatomy  144

# Preface

The Southern High Plains of northeast Texas and eastern New Mexico long have been known to contain a remarkable record of late Quaternary human occupation and paleoenvironments, particularly of late Pleistocene and early Holocene times. Indeed, some of the best-known Paleoindian sites in North America are found in the region. Lubbock Lake is one of those sites, and when the Lubbock Lake Project began in 1972, the focus was on its Paleoindian record, and the goal of the research was to employ an interdisciplinary approach using up-to-date field and analytical techniques to understand better the early occupants and environments of the area. Little did anyone realize at the time that 15 years later we would still be at it. Moreover, the site surpassed all expectations by yielding substantial clues to human and natural history for most of the past 12,000 years, and every year the site continues to provide more information and many surprises.

This volume presents a good portion of the basic data recovered from the site and initial interpretations derived from those data. Some aspects of the research have been published elsewhere, and in such instances the results are summarized or, in a few instances, revised. In chapter 1, Johnson and Holliday describe the regional and local setting; outline the history of the site, including a long history of archaeological investigations; and discuss the field methods and research design of the Lubbock Lake Project. Chapter 2, by Holliday and B. L. Allen, summarizes the geologic and pedologic record of the site. Charles A. Johnson began this work in 1973 and continued it to 1975. Thomas W. Stafford continued stratigraphic investigations from 1975 to 1978, and Holliday and Allen began soil studies in 1976. Holliday took over the geologic studies in 1978, and that research continues.

Holliday presents an outline of the cultural chronology of the site in chapter 3. In chapter 4, Jerome L. Thompson presents the results of his botanical studies, conducted between 1975 and 1977. Vaughn M. Bryant and James Schoenwetter, in chapter 5, discuss the largely unsatisfactory results of pollen research at Lubbock Lake, including Bryant's work in 1973 and 1975. In chapter 6, Harold G. Pierce presents his data on the invertebrate record, recovered between 1973 and 1975. A significant aspect of the research is the vertebrate record. Johnson describes the herptile and mammalian record as of 1984 in chapter 7 and presents interpretations of that record in chapter 8. The artifact assemblages recovered at the site from 1973 through 1979 are described by Johnson and Holliday in chapter 9, and Johnson, in chapter 10, discusses the cultural interactions at the site on the basis of the features excavated during the same years. In chapter 11, Johnson and Holliday summarize the Lubbock Lake record on the basis of interpretations presented in the preceding chapters and elsewhere.

A research project with the longevity and scope of that being conducted at Lubbock Lake requires the efforts and support of numerous individuals and agencies. This book represents part of the ongoing research of the Lubbock Lake Project into cultural adaptations to ecological change on the Southern High Plains. The data base has been generated through the following granting agencies and institutions, to which we are most grateful: the National Science Foundation (SOC-14857; BNS76-12006; BNS76-12006-A01; BNS78-11155), the National Geographic Society, the Texas Historical Commission (National Register Program), the Moody Foundation (Galveston), the Center for Field Research (EARTHWATCH), Sigma Xi, the University of Colorado (Boulder), the University of Wisconsin (Madison), Texas A&M University (College Station), the City and County of Lubbock, the West Texas Museum Association, Texas Tech University (Lubbock), and the Institute of Museum Research and The Museum, Texas Tech University. We are most grateful for their generous support and continuing interest in the research at Lubbock Lake.

Technical assistance was provided primarily by April MacDowell (Collections Manager—Archaeology, The Museum, Texas Tech University), who has devoted more than ten years to the Landmark and whose unfailing efforts to manage the data and oversee production of this work are very gratefully appreciated. Mei Wan (Curatorial Assistant, The Museum) measured lithic artifacts. Shirley Burgeson (Department of Museum Science, Texas Tech University) typed drafts and the final copy. Various photographers worked for the Landmark, including Jerome L. Thompson (Iowa State Historical Department, Des Moines), June Secrist (Interpretation, Texas Parks and Wildlife Department), Gerald Urbantke (Dallas, Texas), and Nicky L. Olson (The Museum, Texas Tech University). Photographs in this publication are primarily a result of the efforts and the skill of Nicky Olson. All the photographers' services are greatly appreciated. Maps, plans, and profiles were drafted by Vance T. Holliday (Department of Geography, University of Wisconsin).

A large number of colleagues have given of their time and constructive advice and criticism, for which the authors are grateful. Particularly of thanks for their significant or sustained involvement are: Eunice Barkes (Museum of the Southwest, Midland), Peter Birkeland (Department of Geological Sciences, University of Colorado), Craig C. Black (Los Angeles County Museum of Natural History), Robson Bonnichsen (Center for the Study of Early Man, Orono, Maine), Leland Gile (Las Cruces, New Mexico), Herbert Haas (Radiocarbon Laboratory, Southern Methodist University), John Hawley (New Mexico School of Mines, Socorro), Michael J. Kaczor (Soil Conservation Service, Little Rock, Arkansas), Ernest L. Lundelius (TMM – Vertebrate Paleontology, University of Texas), C. C. Reeves, Jr. (Department of Geosciences, Texas Tech University), and Robert Stuckenrath (Radiocarbon Laboratory, Smithsonian Institution). However, interpretations and any errors are the authors'.

More than 300 persons participated in the field excavations from 1973 through 1979 as students, staff members, or community volunteers. Community support for the project has been and continues to be overwhelming. Dr. Robert Carr provided medical services each summer for the crew. A full beef was donated each summer to feed the crew by Jim Word (Floydada, Texas) and P. M. Burnet (Camp Springs, Texas). Vann's Catering (Lubbock) donated innumerable meals every summer. Both the City and the County of Lubbock provided equipment, buildings, services, and funding. County Commissioners Arch Lamb and Alton Brazell created the matrix pond and provided the water supply and Landmark road access and maintenance. All their efforts are greatly and sincerely appreciated.

Robert Nash, Alton Brazell, Jim Word, Siva Chambers, Carol Shaver, and Patti Thompson have been unfailing in their support and community campaigns on behalf of the Landmark. This book is as much a product of their efforts as it is of the authors.

Outstanding among colleagues who have offered advice and guidance are the following past researchers at Lubbock Lake: W. Curry Holden, Joe Ben Wheat, Glen L. Evans, Grayson E. Meade, and Jane Holden Kelley. In particular, Joe Ben Wheat and Glen L. Evans have shared graciously their vast knowledge of late Quaternary archaeology, geology, and vertebrate paleontology and their company on many occasions of long discussion. This book is dedicated to them because of their early efforts, which formed the basis for the Lubbock Lake Project.

# Lubbock Lake

# 1. Introduction

EILEEN JOHNSON and VANCE T. HOLLIDAY

Lubbock Lake (41LU1) is a well-stratified archaeological site within the city limits of Lubbock, Texas (33°37′13.5″ north latitude, 101°53′31.5″ west longitude), on the Southern High Plains (Llano Estacado) of northwestern Texas and eastern New Mexico (fig. 1.1). The site complex of about 120 hectares (300 acres) is designated both a State Archeological Landmark and a National Historic Landmark. The site is in valley fill in an entrenched meander of Yellowhouse Draw and contains a record of more than 11,000 years of cultural and natural history for the central Southern High Plains.

Several features of Lubbock Lake make it significant to North American archaeology and archaeological interpretation of the Southern High Plains, the Southwest, and the Great Plains. The Landmark is a complex of activity areas over an areal extent of at least 120 ha (fig. 1.2) with a virtually complete depositional, cultural, floral, and faunal

record spanning the past 11,500 years. Additionally, a series of buried and unburied soils exists within the ca. 6-m-thick deposits. The sediments and soils provide an almost complete late Quaternary geologic record to complement the archaeological, paleontological, and paleobotanical records.

Lubbock Lake Project excavations have yielded a variety of material and associated data from various cultural levels. Fieldwork attempted to integrate the various methodologies of the involved disciplines (archaeology, zooarchaeology, geology, pedology, invertebrate paleontology, palynology, paleobotany, paleoclimatology, and radiometric dating program). This book represents a first approximation at integration and interpretation of Lubbock Lake materials covering the field seasons of 1973–79 and, therefore, is basically descriptive. Geologic, radiocarbon, and vertebrate data are presented through 1984.

The Lubbock Lake cultural, depositional, and faunal sequences represent interdependent histories. Archaeological interpretation depends on the understanding of the interrela-

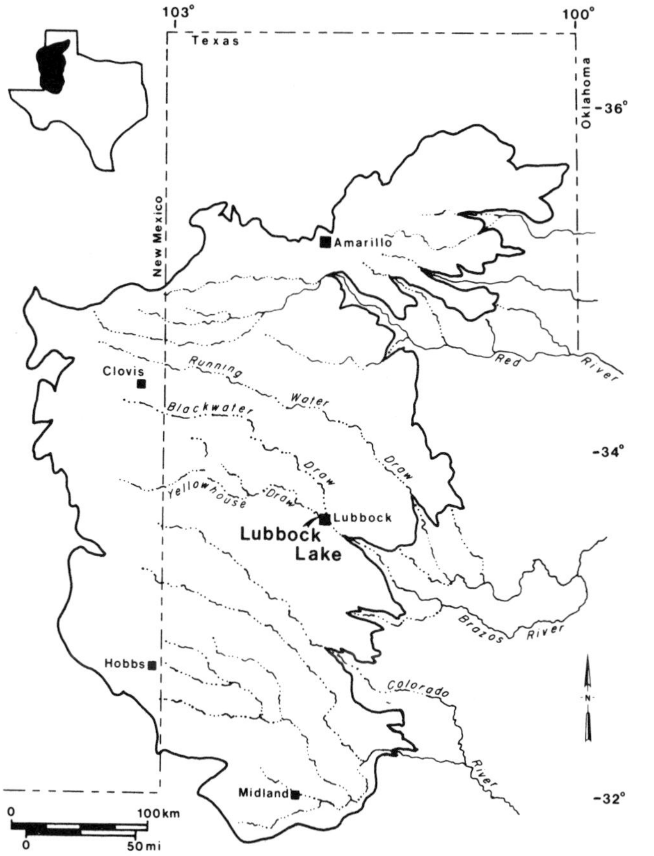

Fig. 1.1. The Southern High Plains (Llano Estacado) showing Lubbock, Lubbock Lake Landmark, and principal physiographic and cultural features.

Fig. 1.2. Topographic map of Yellowhouse Draw in the area of Lubbock Lake showing the boundaries of the Lubbock Lake Landmark (heavy line) and the location of the reservoir.

tionship of all aspects. Where there is water, there are animals; where there are animals and water, there is man. Man hunted, butchered, and processed animals along the stream or pond banks and camped along the waterway and on higher ground. Man's economy depended on the game animals that came to the site area to graze and water. Many of the rodents and rabbits were hunted by the carnivores in the area, and, in turn, both were hunted by man. The carnivores scavenged the carcasses processed by man. Changes in the draw's hydrologic system and shifting climatic conditions affected man, vegetation, and animals. The importance of Lubbock Lake to North American archaeology is its contribution toward an understanding of man's cultural response to a fluctuating climate and changing ecosystem throughout his known existence on the Southern High Plains.

## SETTING

The Southern High Plains are an extensive plateau covering approximately 80,000 km$^2$. The plateau is defined by escarpments along the west, north, and east sides (fig. 1.1). The western escarpment separates the plateau from the Pecos River Valley, and the northern escarpment separates the plateau from the Canadian River Valley. Headward erosion by tributaries of the Red, Brazos, and Colorado rivers formed the eastern escarpment. The southern portion of the Southern High Plains merges with the Edwards Plateau region of Central Texas without a distinct topographic demarcation. The latter boundary is defined by the northernmost outcrops of Edwards Limestone (Hunt, 1974).

Physiographically the Southern High Plains are the southern portion of the High Plains Section of the Great Plains Province (fig. 1.3). The southern portion of the Osage Plains Section of the Central Lowland Province is east of the eastern escarpment of the Southern High Plains. This region of north-central Texas and southwestern Oklahoma is known locally as the Rolling Plains. The Edwards Plateau and Central Texas sections of the Great Plains Province are south and southeast of the Southern High Plains. The Pecos Valley Section, another division of the Great Plains Province, is west and southwest of the Southern High Plains (Fenneman, 1931).

The Southern High Plains region, an almost featureless plain, is "the largest level plain of its kind in the United States" (NOAA, 1982:3). A regional slope on the southeast has altitudes ranging from 1,500 m in the northwest to 750 m in the southeast. The slight topographic relief is provided by a few dune fields and thousands of small depressions (playas) that dot the landscape. The basins, mainly resulting from late Quaternary wind deflation, contain the only available surface water on the Southern High Plains. Much of the water in the larger basins is highly saline, and permanent streams no longer exist. A number of northwest-southeast–trending tributaries of the Red, Brazos, and Colorado rivers are incised up to 15 m and occasionally have flowing water. Several large dune fields are present, and they often clog tributaries (Holliday, 1985a).

Fig. 1.3. Map of the Southern High Plains (Llano Estacado) and surrounding physiographic provinces, sections, and informal subsections (based on Hunt, 1974; Fenneman, 1931).

## CLIMATE

The modern climate throughout the Southern High Plains is a dry, midlatitude semidesert (Strahler and Strahler, 1983, plate C2) and remarkably uniform, apparently owing to limited topographic variation. Gradients in mean annual temperature and precipitation are relatively uniform. The precipitation gradient increases from west to east across the Southern High Plains, and the temperature gradient usually increases from northwest to southeast. Precipitation most commonly falls during spring and summer thunderstorms. However, considerable interannual variation in precipitation occurs.

## HISTORICAL PERSPECTIVE

Lubbock Lake has been known as an archaeological site since the 1930s, when the excavation of an artificial reservoir revealed its existence in Yellowhouse Draw, in northwest Lubbock, Texas (fig. 1.4). The site received its name from the reservoir. It was also known as the Lubbock Reservoir site (Green, 1962) and had a variety of other designations.

Since discovery four major archaeological projects have investigated the site. Before the Lubbock Lake Project (LLP) the only archaeological information available was contained in Sellards (1952) and Green (1962). The earlier work dealt only with the Folsom material and was a brief treatment discussed in the overall context of Early Man in

Fig. 1.4. Aerial photograph of Lubbock Lake in Yellowhouse Draw (1939, looking north). Shown are the reservoir with water, the dike created from dredge spoil, the valley walls, and the limit of the late Quaternary valley fill (denoted by the darker vegetation in the valley) (from files at The Museum, Texas Tech University, Lubbock).

North America. The latter work was a general discussion of the importance of the site, written for the public.

The early investigations are summarized with the use of the LLP geological and cultural terminology. Excavation areas are discussed with the designations of the respective excavation parties and in relation to the LLP excavation areas (fig. 1.5). All excavation programs used Singer Store Monument, west of the reservoir cut, for a primary datum. Stratigraphic correlations are presented in table 1.1.

A lake, known historically as far back as the middle 1600s, existed in the area of the reservoir cut until the 1920s. The Spanish explorers marked it on their maps as La Punta de Agua, or Place of Water. A number of springs on the west side of the reservoir cut fed a lake with a surface area of 4.05 hectares (10 acres). The water apparently was dammed downstream, but some overflow provided a continuous flow of water to the southeast. These springs and the lake were considered to be the headwaters of the Brazos River.

The first commercial establishment in Lubbock County was built by George Singer in the early 1880s near the lake in the general area of the reservoir cut (Holden, 1974:12; Conner, 1962:65–66). Its exact location is unknown. The lake was used as a watering hole for cattle until at least the turn of the century. Holden (1962a:17–18) reported that as many as 10,000 cattle were seen watering in the area in the

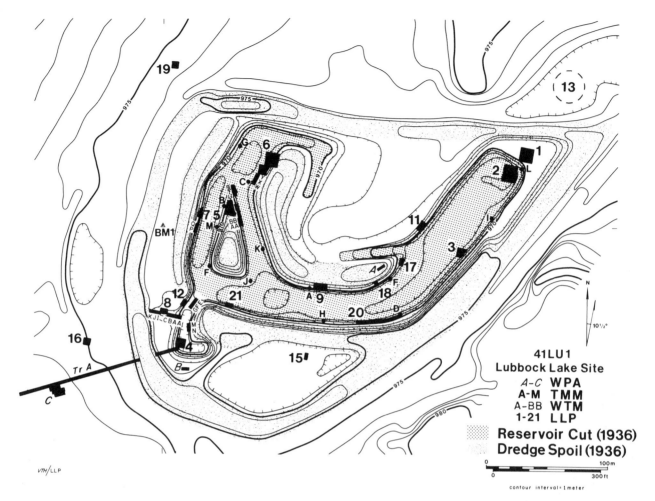

Fig. 1.5 Topographic map of Lubbock Lake in the reservoir area with locations of all known excavation areas (LLP Areas 10 and 14 are off the area covered by the map).

1880s and 1890s. In 1903 the area of the reservoir cut was owned by a homesteader who was willing to sell the land. A 38-hectare (93-acre) lot was purchased for one dollar an acre (Holden, 1974:12) as a future water supply.

During the first few decades of the twentieth century numerous water wells were drilled in the area to supply the growing population, including two wells on the 38-hectare (93-acre) tract. By 1930 irrigation was becoming common and led to the drilling of even more wells. As a consequence of this pumping activity the water table began to drop. In the early 1930s the springs in Yellowhouse Draw ceased to run, and the lake dried up. Not realizing that the water table was dropping, the local citizenry believed that the springs could be reactivated by digging them out (Holden, 1962a: 18, 1974:12).

In the middle 1930s, Works Progress Administration (WPA) funds were made available to local governments for public construction projects. In 1935, Lubbock received a large sum of WPA money, some of which was used to reactivate the springs on the 38-hectare (93-acre) tract and construct a reservoir for city fire protection. Construction began in about May, 1936. A large crew of men started the

excavations with shovels and wheelbarrows, but the water table was just below the floor of the draw, and manual excavations stopped after about 30,600 m³ (40,000 cu yd) of earth were removed. Draglines and a backhoe were used to excavate an additional 45,900 m³ (60,000 cu yd). Dragline marks from at least three different machines were found in several LLP excavation areas.

The resulting reservoir was roughly U-shaped, almost 400 m in length and averaging 6 m deep and 35 m wide. Clear water filled the reservoir to the rim. The excavated sediments and materials were deposited around the edge of the cut to form an inner dike and farther away from the cut to form an outer dike (fig. 1.4). Draglines cut down to and through the stratum 1 Clovis-age deposits in most areas.

About one week after the machinery had completed the excavation, several boys found a complete Folsom point (TTU40-36-136) beside one of the dump piles and reported it to W. C. Holden, of Texas Technological College. Remains of bison, mammoth, and horse were also found on the dump piles.

Although the importance and potential of the site were realized, it was several years before controlled excavations

Table 1.1. Correlations of Stratigraphic Terminology of All Investigators at Lubbock Lake

| Wheat, 1974 Trench A | | Sellards, 1952 | Green, 1962 | C. Johnson, 1974 | Stafford, 1981 | Holliday, 1985b |
|---|---|---|---|---|---|---|
| East | West | | | | | |
| — | — | 5 | — | 6B | 5C | 4Bℓ, 5Aℓ, 5Bℓ |
| — | — | — | — | — | S¹, S² | Singer Soil |
| I | I ⎱ | — | — | — | — | A horizon, Singer Soil |
| | II ⎰ | — | 7a, 7b | 6A | 5B | 5B |
| II | III ⎱ | — | — | — | S³, S⁴ | Apache Soil |
| | | — | — | 5C | | A horizon, Apache Soil |
| III | IV ⎰ | — | 6 | 5A, 5B | 5A | 5A |
| IVa | — | — | 5 | — | S⁵ | Lubbock Lake Soil |
| | | | | 4C | 4C | A horizon, Lubbock Lake Soil |
| IVb | — | 4 | 4b | 4B | 4B | 4B |
| | | | | 4A | 4A ⎱ | 4A (valley axis only) |
| IVc? | — | — | 4a | 3C ⎰ | 3C clay ⎰ | |
| | | | | | 3C A horizon | A horizon, Yellowhouse Soil |
| | | | | | S⁶ | Yellowhouse Soil |
| — | — | 3 | 3b | 3B | 3B | 3ℓ |
| — | — | | — | 3A | 3A | 3e |
| — | — | | — | — | S⁷ | Firstview Soil |
| — | — | | 3a | 2C | 2C | A horizon, Firstview Soil |
| — | — | | — | — | 2E | 2s |
| — | — | 2 | 2d | — | 2F | 2e |
| — | — | | 2c | 2B | 2B | 2B |
| — | — | | 2a, 2b | 2A | 2A | 2A |
| — | — | | 1b ⎰ | 1C ⎰ | 1C | Subdivisions of stratum 1 only made locally |
| | | 1 | | 1A ⎰ | 1B | |
| | | | 1a | 1B | 1A | |

SOURCE: Modified from Holliday 1985b, table 1; Johnson and Holliday 1986, table 1.

were undertaken. In the meantime the lake was used for recreational purposes. In October, 1938, the City of Lubbock Fire Department planted sapling Siberian elm (locally known as Chinese elm) around the reservoir as a beautification project.

In 1939, Holden received a grant from the WPA to conduct archaeological investigations throughout local WPA District 17. The first archaeological excavations at Lubbock Lake were supervised by Joe Ben Wheat (1974).

Most of the WPA work at Lubbock Lake took place in the late summer of 1939. Initially two pits (A and B, fig. 1.5) were opened but eventually abandoned because no cultural material was found, and the water table was encountered. Most of the work then focused on Trench A (fig. 1.5), where excavations reached the top of stratum 3. Some additional excavations were carried out in early 1941 in Pit C, excavated adjacent to Trench A (figs. 1.5, 1.6).

A considerable amount of Archaic, Ceramic, Protohistoric, and Historic cultural period material was recovered (Johnson et al., 1977; Johnson and Holliday, 1986). Trench A provided a long stratigraphic section which could be correlated with the more recent stratigraphic investigations. Finally, excavations along the western end of Trench A provided some archaeological and geological data for an area later destroyed by construction of a sewage treatment plant.

The next major excavation efforts were sponsored by Texas Memorial Museum (TMM), in Austin, under the direction of E. H. Sellards and supervised by Glen L. Evans and Grayson E. Meade. Very little of the TMM work at Lubbock Lake was published. Sellards (1952) provided a brief discussion, which is a general review of the Paleoindian material, and Evans (1949) published a description of the stratigraphy based on his first season at the site.

The TMM excavations took place in 1948, 1950, and 1951 with some additional testing and sampling in 1952, 1954, and 1955. The work was carried out along the walls of the reservoir at a series of Stations (A–O and Q, fig. 1.7; the locations of N, O, and Q are uncertain or unknown). Most of the work focused on Paleoindian material and concentrated on stratum 2.

Several Folsom points were found in situ with Bison antiquus bone beds in substratum 2A near Stations I and D (fig. 1.7). Bison antiquus bone beds also were encountered in stratum 2 at Stations E and M. A lithic tool was recovered from stratum 1 (Clovis age) near Station M, and Archaic B. bison bone beds were found in substrata 3ℓ and 4A at Station E (Johnson and Holliday, 1986). Burned bone from stratum 2 at Station M yielded a radiocarbon date of 9883 ± 350 B.P. (C-558; Libby, 1952). This date represents one of the first applications of radiocarbon dating in Paleoindian archaeology, and it was long considered to be the first date for the Folsom period (Sellards, 1952; Wormington, 1957). However, the bone bed yielding the sample is no longer considered a Folsom feature, on the basis of stratigraphy and recent redating (Holliday et al., 1983; Holliday and Johnson, 1986). Finally, because of the TMM work, Lubbock

Fig. 1.6 Excavations in progress in Pit C (1941, looking south). The overthickened A horizon of the buried Lubbock Lake Soil is obvious just above the worker with the pick. He is standing on a bench that is probably the top of the Blanco Formation, which rises rapidly to the right (southwest) (from files at The Museum, Texas Texas University).

Lake became a nationally known Paleoindian site (Sellards, 1952).

The last excavation project before the LLP was the one by F. E. Green (1962) and Jane Kelley (1974) through the West Texas Museum (WTM; now The Museum, Texas Tech University) in 1959 and 1960. Green (1967) prepared an extensive report that was never published. Kaczor (1978) analyzed much of the WTM material and correlated it with the LLP work. The work was carried out in a number of gridded and lettered "blocks" on the west side of the reservoir (fig. 1.5). All principal late Quaternary strata were investigated, and Paleoindian, Archaic, Ceramic, Protohistoric, and Historic materials were recovered. The most extensive features found were a series of Protohistoric and Historic camps (Johnson et al., 1977).

In the late 1950s and early 1960s, Lubbock Lake was one of many sites on the Southern High Plains sampled for paleobotanical and paleontological materials as part of the High Plains Paleoecology Project (Wendorf, 1961a; Wendorf and Hester, 1975). Otherwise, the period 1961–72 was the longest time between excavations at Lubbock Lake since its discovery.

## LUBBOCK LAKE PROJECT

### Research Approach

The major segment of culture being examined is the economic system within a variety of environmental settings through time. Subsistence and technology are major subsystems of the economic system that are reflected in the Lubbock Lake materials. The record is one of hunter-gatherer societies changing from a late Pleistocene adaptation for an ameliorated climate and variety of food resources to a semiarid and fluctuating setting and reduced food choices.

In general, hunter-gatherer economic and settlement systems reflect adaptive behavioral patterns (e.g., Binford, 1980). Adaptation is the means by which a group interacts with the environment, copes with constraint and stress, and sustains and perpetuates itself. Man's culture is his adaptation to and utilization of an ecosystem. Ecosystemic change places stress on a cultural system. Transformations occur to ameliorate that stress and achieve adaptation to the altered ecosystem. These transformations enact the process of adaptation. Process is taken to mean the development or method of doing something that involves a number of steps, operations, or changes. Transformation is taken to mean the act or operation of change, that is, the conversion to another form, nature, condition, or character.

A behavioral pattern is an organized, generally accepted and followed way of performing under a certain set or sets of circumstances. This systematic approach leaves a record in the ground through the material culture involved with that patterned (as opposed to random) behavior. Several behavioral patterns are involved in cultural transformations. Adaptation recombines old or conservative procedures with innovations into new patterns (cf. Bonnichsen and Young, 1980; Young and Bonnichsen, 1984).

Subsistence and technological strategies are designed to alleviate stress on the system. Within subsistence these strategies represent major organizational principles that under differing environmental conditions offer optimal security against food shortages and nutritional imbalance (cf. Binford, 1980; Speth, 1983; Speth and Spielman, 1983). A system whereby people go to the products with frequent moves of their residential bases may be characterized by opportunistic behavior within an equitable climate. A system that moves the products to the people with few residential base moves may be characterized by methodical behavior within an inequitable climate. Buffering mechanisms that modify the general subsistence strategy come into play during certain times of periodic shortages of key foods that induce nutritional stress.

The basic cultural assumption is that inferences about technology and subsistence can be made from analyses of the lithic and faunal materials. Through a combination of these inferences a plausible explanation can be derived that best fits the archaeological data. This assumption is predicated on the sealed nature of the geologic deposits; lack of disturbance through erosion, rodent burrowing, or other

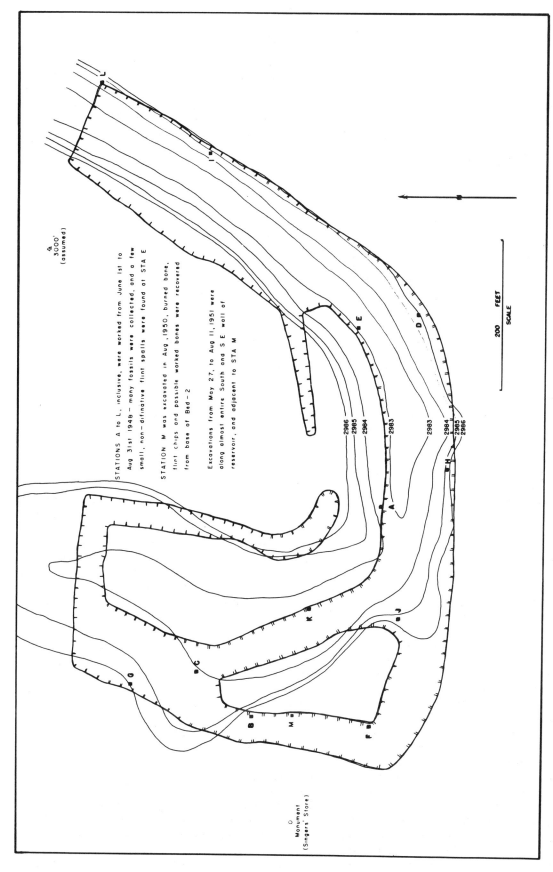

Fig. 1.7. Map of the reservoir cut, showing the location of the Texas Memorial Museum excavation stations. Stations A to L, inclusive, were worked from June 1 to August 31, 1948. Station M was excavated in August, 1950. Excavations from May 27 to August 11, 1951, were along almost the entire south and southeast wall of the reservoir, and adjacent to Station M (map prepared by Glen L. Evans, courtesy of Texas Archaeological Research Laboratory, University of Texas at Austin).

bioturbation; and rapid deposition as indicated through geologic data and minimal bone weathering. The relationship of lithics and faunal material is a primary one demonstrated by geologic data and man-induced modification to the faunal remains.

The biological and geological records provide proxy data in determining the extinct ecosystems and successive environments. The major biological assumption is that modern ecological data, environmental conditions, and range information can be used as the basis for paleoenvironmental reconstruction in dealing with late Quaternary species that are extant. For extinct forms various available data for the closest living relatives are considered pertinent (Lundelius, 1974). This assumption provides a modern framework in which to contrast changes in the past. While modern conditions are not necessarily the norm, they do provide a fixed reference point. Another assumption made was in aging dentition and postcranial material. Available eruption and wear and epiphyseal closure schedules for modern animals were considered close approximations, assuming that the rates are approximately the same between the compared forms.

Not all faunal remains are related to man's activities at the site. These noncultural remains lack man-induced modifications and represent the environmental background upon which man superimposed his activities. Large carnivores, primarily wolf (*Canis lupus*), were also bone modifiers on the site. Some of the Lubbock Lake faunal material exhibits a complex life history of both man-induced and carnivore-induced damage. Criteria were developed (cf. Johnson, 1985) to distinguish between the types of damage inflicted by these and other agencies. Questionable specimens and damage were discounted when the Lubbock Lake faunal material was analyzed for game-animal determination, bone breakage, and butchering patterns.

## Radiocarbon Dating Program

Most cultural features and all principal stratigraphic units, facies, and soils are now well dated. Throughout this volume all ages cited are expressed in years before present (B.P.) and based on a half-life of 5,568 years. Calibrations for the variations in production of atmospheric carbon 14 are presented by Holliday et al. (1983, 1985a). They are not used in this volume because calibrations are not available for the entire time span represented at Lubbock Lake.

Establishing firm age control for the Lubbock Lake record was of paramount importance. Almost 120 radiocarbon determinations (table 1.2) were secured on a variety of materials. Each assay was discussed by Holliday et al. (1983, 1985a), and other aspects of the dating program were reviewed by Haas et al. (1986). Sixty-eight radiocarbon ages were considered reliable (table 1.2, fig. 1.8). The other dates were considered questionable or unreliable (cf. Holliday et al., 1983, 1985a). A number of assays were determined either by the now-obsolete solid-carbon method or on shell and bone, both of which typically produce questionable results. Other dates were obviously in error, as shown

by stratigraphic or cultural contexts or other, overwhelming radiocarbon evidence. Some dates were determined for experimental purposes and are not included. Finally, only recently it became apparent that ages determined on samples from old exposures, even though cleaned off, produced ages younger than those from fresh exposures of the same deposit in the same area (Haas et al., 1986). Therefore, all samples from areas that had been exposed for a year or more were considered questionable.

## Methodology

The site (fig. 1.9) was instrument-surveyed, and a number of bench marks were established with known elevations relative to sea level. The area of the reservoir cut was gridded into 50 $m^2$ units, in relationship to Bench Mark 1 (BM1, Singer Store Monument). BM1 is the main horizontal and vertical datum point for all LLP excavations (fig. 1.5).

Each excavation area was gridded into meter-square units. Arbitrary levels were excavated within the smallest recognized stratigraphic unit. The standard excavation unit was 1 × 1 $m^2$, 5 cm deep, within a stratigraphic unit. Larger excavation levels may be used in sterile deposits. Material found *in situ* was recorded and drawn to scale on appropriate Museum forms, preserved if necessary, and field-documented. Materials were processed, preserved, initially identified, and cataloged in the field laboratory.

All excavated sediment from each area was bagged and tagged according to stratigraphic and excavation information and water-processed through a nested set of fine-mesh (¼-in [6 mm] and ⅟₁₆-in [1.6 mm]) screens (fig. 1.10). The washing racks are a modified version of those constructed by Guilday and McCrady (Guilday et al., 1964). This recovery method ensures retrieval of any materials (including botanical) missed during excavation. While exact provenience is unknown, a matrix item can be placed stratigraphically within a meter unit 5-cm level, determining a general relationship among associated materials.

In ten seasons the LLP has excavated less than 0.05% of the site, on the basis of 120 ha in areal extent and an average 6-m depth. The processing of all excavated sediment, although time-consuming, completes the inventory of a very small sample of what is contained in the site.

A number of cultural levels are defined within the stratigraphic framework. These levels are delineated through the designation of features in each area. Features constitute distinct units of concentrated materials or unusual occurrences, generally with relatively sterile deposits above and below them. They occur both at stratigraphic contacts and within deposits. Three general types of features are encountered: cultural (e.g., activity areas), biological (e.g., natural death), and geological (e.g., eroded surfaces with deflated or redeposited materials). The features and their stratigraphic position are the basis of correlations between areas.

Features are numbered serially in an area as they are encountered during excavations. Feature numbers are distinctive and maintained from one field season to the next. The feature designation combines an abbreviation for feature (F), excavation area number (A2), and serial number (-1). Feature layouts are produced from field records.

Catalog or accession numbers are listed for identification of specimens and reference between various chapters. The WPA material is identified by the accession number 40-36, while the accession number 892 identifies the TMM Collection. The WTM material has a catalog range of TTU-

A1 through TTU-A999 and TTU-A24500 through TTU-A24999. The materials recovered by the LLP are cataloged with numbers TTU-A1000 through TTU-A24499, TTU-A25000 through TTU-A29999, and TTU-A36000 through TTU-A49999 inclusive. The documentation and specimens from WPA, WTM, and LLP excavations are housed in the Archaeology Division of The Museum, Texas Tech University (TTU). The TMM materials are in the Texas Memorial Museum and the Texas Archaeological Research Laboratory (TARL), University of Texas at Austin.

Table 1.2. Reliable Radiocarbon Dates from Lubbock Lake

| Substratum | Lab No. | Age (Years B.P.) | Area | Material |
|---|---|---|---|---|
| 5Bℓ | SMU-716 | 210 ± 40 | 6 | Wood |
| | SMU-831f* | 390 ± 50 | 6 | Humic acid (marsh sediment) |
| | SMU-715 | 400 ± 100 | 6 | Wood |
| 5A | SMU-343 | 160 ± 60 | 7 | Humic acid (modern A horizon) |
| | SMU-314 | 720 ± 40 | 7 | Humic acid (buried A horizon) |
| | SMU-968 | 440 ± 40 | 7 | Charcoal |
| | SMU-970 | 380 ± 50 | 7 | Charcoal |
| | SMU-893f | 450 ± 50 | 7 | Charcoal |
| | SMU-345 | 300 ± 60 | 8 | Charcoal (same as SI-2700) |
| | SI-2700 | 380 ± 40 | 8 | Charcoal (same as SMU-345) |
| | SI-2701 | 505 ± 55 | 8 | Charcoal |
| | SI-3208 | 640 ± 75 | 8 | Humin (buried A horizon) |
| | SI-2704 | 315 ± 50 | 14 | Charcoal |
| | SI-2703 | 285 ± 60 | 15 | Charcoal |
| | SMU-546 | 320 ± 60 | 19 | Charcoal |
| | SMU-555 | 220 ± 50 | Tr108 | Humic acid (buried A horizon) |
| 5Aℓ | SMU-698 | 600 ± 50 | Tr108 | Humic acid (marsh sediment) |
| 4B | SMU-1090f | 1270 ± 40 | 7 | Humic acid (buried A horizon) |
| | SI-4169 | 880 ± 70 | 8 | Humin (buried A horizon) |
| | SI-3201 | 1215 ± 65 | Tr59 | Humin (buried A horizon; top) |
| | SI-4174 | 1955 ± 75 | Tr59 | Humin (buried A horizon; top) |
| | SMU-534 | 870 ± 40 | Tr108 | Humic acid (buried A horizon; top) |
| | SMU-651 | 890 ± 70 | Tr108 | Humic acid (buried A horizon; top) |
| | SMU-1177f | 1550 ± 50 | Tr108 | Humic acid (buried A horizon; top) |
| | SMU-1191f | 2070 ± 130 | Tr108 | Humic acid (buried A horizon; middle) |
| | SI-4171 | 4700 ± 65 | 16 | Ash and humin (same as SMU-492) |
| | SMU-492 | 4960 ± 50 | 16 | Ash and humic acid (same as SI-4171) |
| 4A | SMU-1200f | 5270 ± 150 | Tr116 | Humic acid (marsh sediment) |
| 4ℓ | SI-4588 | 980 ± 60 | 1 | Humin (marsh sediment) |
| | SI-4971 | 1910 ± 75 | Tr109 | Humin (marsh sediment) |
| | SI-4970 | 5010 ± 95 | Tr109 | Humin (marsh sediment) |
| | SMU-697 | 2600 ± 50 | Tr108 | Humic acid (marsh sediment) |
| | SI-4972 | 2500 ± 165 | Tr141 | Humin (marsh sediment) |
| | SI-3206 | 3925 ± 80 | Tr39 | Humin (marsh sediment) |
| | SI-3205 | 5545 ± 100 | Tr39 | Humin (marsh sediment) |
| 3ℓ | SMU-1093f | 5220 ± 50 | Tr49 | Humic acid (buried A horizon; top) |
| | SMU-531 | 4900 ± 60 | Tr108 | Humic acid (buried A horizon; top) |
| 3e | SMU-545 | 5770 ± 80 | Tr108 | Humic acid (marsh sediment) |
| 2B (upper) | SMU-1094f | 6240 ± 40 | 5 | Humic acid (buried A horizon; top) |
| | SMU-544 | 6400 ± 80 | Tr108 | Humic acid (buried A horizon; top) |
| | SI-4178 | 6705 ± 95 | 6 | Humin (buried A horizon; top) |
| | SMU-262 | 7970 ± 80 | 3 | Humic acid (buried A horizon; middle) |
| | SMU-302 | 7890 ± 100 | 3 | Humic acid (buried A horizon; bottom) |
| | SI-3204 | 7255 ± 75 | Tr90 | Humin (marsh sediment) |
| | SMU-830f | 8210 ± 240 | 6 | Humic acid (marsh sediment) |
| | SI-4177 | 8655 ± 90 | 6 | Humin (marsh sediment) |
| 2B (middle) | SMU-1089 | 8130 ± 80 | 5 | Humic acid (marsh sediment); same as SI-5499 |
| | SI-5499 | 8585 ± 145 | 5 | Humin (marsh sediment); same as SMU-1089 |
| | SMU-1116 | 9550 ± 90 | 2 | Humic acid (marsh sediment); same as SMU-1118 |
| | SMU-1118 | 9550 ± 100 | 2 | Humic acid (marsh sediment); same as SMU-1116 |

Table 1.2. *Continued*

| Substratum | Lab No. | Age (Years B.P.) | Area | Material |
|---|---|---|---|---|
| 2B (lower) | SMU-275 | 9960 ± 80 | 2 | Humic acid (marsh sediment) |
| | SMU-828 | 9870 ± 140 | 6 | Humic acid (marsh sediment) |
| | SI-4974 | 9605 ± 195 | 6 | Humin (marsh sediment) |
| | SMU-728 | 9990 ± 100 | 6 | Humic acid (marsh sediment) |
| | SI-4179 | 9075 ± 100 | 5 | Humin (marsh sediment; same as SMU-829) |
| | SMU-829*f* | 9170 ± 80 | 5 | Humic acid (same as SI-4179) |
| 2e | SMU-1192*f* | 8730 ± 240 | Tr108 | Humic acid (marsh sediment) |
| 2sLBc | SMU-699 | 9780 ± 100 | 5 | Humic acid (marsh sediment) |
| 2sLBb | SMU-1261*f* | 9950 ± 120 | 5 | Humic acid (marsh sediment) |
| 2A (upper) | SI-3203 | 10,015 ± 75 | Tr90 | Humin (marsh sediment) |
| 2ALB4 | SI-4975 | 9905 ± 140 | 6 | Humin (marsh sediment) |
| 2ALB2 | SMU-251 | 10,060 ± 70 | 3 | Humic acid (marsh sediment) |
| | SI-3200 | 10,360 ± 80 | 6 | Humin (marsh sediment) |
| | SI-4976 | 10,195 ± 165 | 6 | Humin (marsh sediment) |
| | SMU-547 | 10,540 ± 100 | Tr109 | Charcoal |
| 2ALB1 | SMU-285 | 10,530 ± 90 | 2 | Humic acid (diatomite) |
| 1B | SMU-263 | 11,100 ± 80 | 41LU26 | Wood |
| | SMU-548 | 11,100 ± 100 | 2 | Wood |

SOURCE: Modified from Haas et al. 1986.

*\*f* indicates dates corrected for fractionation.

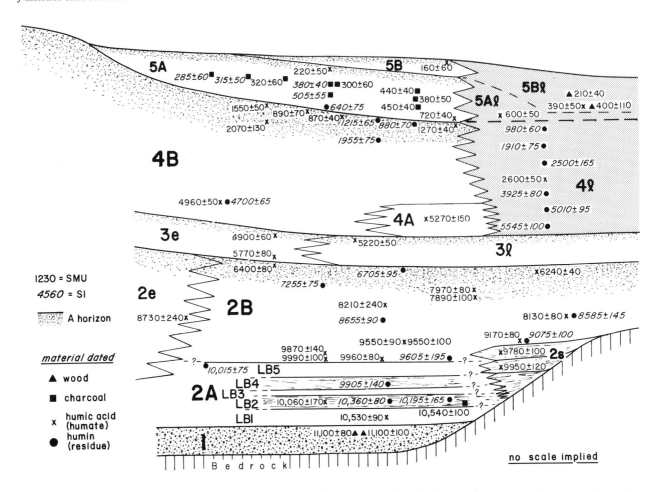

Fig. 1.8. Generalized stratigraphic relationships of the reliable radiocarbon ages from Lubbock Lake determined on wood, charcoal, and organic-rich soils and sediments from fresh exposures.

Fig. 1.9. Aerial photograph of Lubbock Lake (1975, looking northeast) in the area of the reservoir cut, which is lined with trees planted in 1938 (photograph by Jerome L. Thompson).

Fig. 1.10. The matrix washing process in operation (photograph by Jerome L. Thompson).

# 2. Geology and Soils

VANCE T. HOLLIDAY and B. L. ALLEN

Geologic investigations at Lubbock Lake have paralleled the archaeological studies since the inception of the project. The well-stratified late Quaternary deposits (fig. 2.1) in Yellowhouse Draw have aided in the correlation of archaeological materials throughout the site since the first excavation in 1939. Beyond such correlations, however, sediments provide valuable information concerning local and regional environmental conditions for the past 11,000 years.

One of the principal outgrowths of geologic research at Lubbock Lake has been the soil studies. As many as eight buried soils, in addition to the present land-surface soil, have been identified in the deposits. Soils represent periods of landscape stability following deposition or erosion. Commonly, buried soils represent longer periods of time than those represented by the geologic deposits in which the soils have developed. Pedologic investigations, which provide information on episodes between depositional events, are necessary to obtain the geologic history of a locality. They provide an important complement to stratigraphic and sedimentological studies.

Initial descriptions and interpretations of the stratigraphy of Lubbock Lake include those of Wheat (1974), Evans (1949), Green (1962), and C. Johnson (1974). Stafford (1977, 1978, 1981) conducted more extensive investigations. The following discussion is a summary of the most recent geologic and pedologic studies (Holliday, 1982, 1985a, b, c, d), which refined and revised the previous interpretations (table 1.1). Pedologic descriptions and laboratory data are presented by Holliday (1982, 1985c, d), and a summary of stratigraphic descriptions and classifications of the various soils at the site are given in tables 2.1 and 2.2, respectively.

## REGIONAL STRATIGRAPHY

The oldest rock outcrops forming the foundation of the plateau defined by the Southern High Plains are Permian and Triassic redbeds. The redbeds are overlain locally by Cretaceous limestones, shales, and sandstones (Reeves, 1970; Harbour, 1975).

Extensive Cenozoic deposits overlie these bedrock units and comprise most of the exposed sections and surficial deposits. Most Cenozoic deposits are late Tertiary alluvial and eolian sediments derived from mountains in New Mexico (Ogallala Formation). The upper part of the Ogallala has a thick pedogenic calcrete ("caliche"), known as caprock (Reeves, 1972; Hawley et al., 1976; Gustavson and Holliday, 1985).

The principal Pliocene unit is the Blanco Formation, an extensive lacustrine deposit of dolomite and some sand deposited in large east-west–trending basins cut into the Ogallala Formation (fig. 2.2). A calcrete also formed at the top of the Blanco Formation (Reeves, 1970; Meade et al., 1974; Pierce, 1974; Harbour, 1975; Hawley et al., 1976).

Throughout most of the Southern High Plains, the Ogallala Formation and, where present, the Blanco Formation are mantled by the Blackwater Draw Formation (Reeves, 1976), formerly designated Pleistocene "cover sands" by Frye and Leonard (1957, 1965). The unit consists of extensive Pleistocene eolian deposits and intercalated buried soils (Hawley et al., 1976; Gustavson and Holliday, 1985).

Various stream tributaries, such as Running Water, Blackwater, and Yellowhouse draws, probably developed during the late Pleistocene. Within these tributaries and in larger lake basins a variety of Pleistocene and Holocene lacustrine, alluvial, and eolian deposits are recognized (Holliday, 1985a, b; Reeves, 1970, 1976; Stafford, 1981).

The availability and quality of resources for tool manufacture are other important aspects of the local geology. Such considerations have an influence on the amount of lithic tools and debris found in a site, the quality and type of

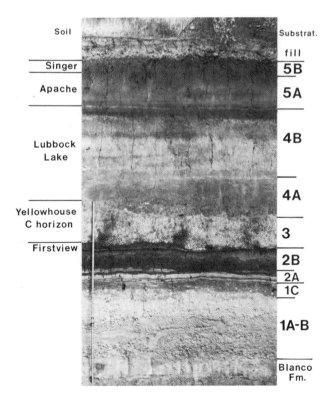

Fig. 2.1. A stratigraphic section at Lubbock Lake (trench 65, along the west wall of the reservoir cut, looking west). Strata 3 and 4 thicken considerably toward the west side of the valley, and substratum 5B becomes more distinct to the west; the leveling rod is 3 m long (photograph by Thomas W. Stafford, Jr.).

Table 2.1. Generalized Descriptions of Strata 1 through 5 at Lubbock Lake
(Facies are not necessarily time equivalents.)

| Stratum | Valley Axis Facies | Valley Margin Facies |
|---|---|---|
| 5 | Substratum 5Bℓ: up to 1 m thick; gray to very dark gray (5YR 5/1 to 3/1, dry); clay; weakly stratified | Substratum 5B: 10–25 cm thick; brown (e.g., 7.5YR 5/3, dry); sandy clay loam to sandy loam, interbedded with common sand and gravel lenses |
| | Substratum 5Aℓ: same as 5Bℓ | Substratum 5A: 30–75 cm thick; brown (e.g., 7.5YR 5/3, dry); sandy clay loam to sandy loam interbedded with few sand and gravel lenses |
| 4 | Substratum 4Bℓ: same as 5Bℓ | Substratum 4B: 1–3+ m thick; brown (e.g., 7.5YR 5/4, dry); sandy clay loam to sandy loam |
| | Substratum 4A: less than 1 m thick; olive gray (2.5YR hues); laminated to massive, often cross-bedded, well-sorted, loamy fine sand to sandy clay loam interbedded with blocky to granular, somewhat more organic, clay to clay loam | No valley margin equivalent of 4A |
| 3 | Substratum 3ℓ: 30–100+ cm thick; white (10YR 7/1, dry); massive to platy, friable, silty clay to silty clay loam | Substratum 3e: 30–100+ cm thick; light brown (7.5YR 7/3, dry); sandy loam |
| 2 | Substratum 2B: 30–80 cm thick; gray (e.g., 10YR 5/1, dry); loam to silty clay loam to clay; locally abundant silicified roots; few lenses of diatomite | Substratum 2s (facies of 2A and 2B): up to 2 m thick; gray (e.g., 2.5Y 7/2, dry); silty clay; interbedded with light gray (e.g., 2.5Y 7/2, dry) sandy clay |
| | Substratum 2A: 30–100 cm thick; light gray (10YR 7/1, dry) diatomite interbedded with gray (e.g., 10YR 5/1, dry) silt to clay | Substratum 2e (facies of 2A and 2B): up to 2 m thick; pale brown (e.g., 10YR 6/3, dry); sandy clay loam |
| 1 | Highly variable, stratigraphic subdivisions reflect local lithologic changes and can occur individually or in various combinations | |
| | Substratum 1C: up to 50 cm thick; light gray (e.g., 2.5Y 7/2, dry), massive sandy clay to clay | |
| | Substratum 1B: up to 1 m thick; light gray (e.g., 2.5Y 7/2, dry) loose, cross-bedded, sand to loamy sand, with lenses of carbonate gravel (with clasts up to 2-cm diameter) | |
| | Substratum 1A: up to 1.5 m thick; massive carbonate gravel with clasts up to 5-cm diameter and lenses of cross-bedded sand to loamy sand | |

SOURCE: Modified from Holliday, 1985b.

Table 2.2. Classification of Holocene Soils at Lubbock Lake

| Soil | Valley Margin | Valley Axis |
|---|---|---|
| Singer Soil | ———————— Ustorthent ———————— | |
| Minor 5B soil | ———————— Ustorthent ———————— | |
| Apache Soil | — Ustochrept, Haplustoll, Calciustoll, Haplustalf — | |
| Minor 5A soil | Ustipsamment, Ustorthent | Ustorthent |
| Lubbock Lake Soil | Haplustalf, Ustochrept | Calcuistoll, Haplustalf, Ustochrept |
| Yellowhouse Soil | Ustifluvent | Haplustoll |
| Firstview Soil | Ustorthent | Ustorthent, Ustifluvent |

SOURCE: Holliday 1985c, d.

tools found, and the manner in which tools were used and reused. In the Lubbock Lake area nearby lithic resources are rare, accounting for the relative scarcity of lithic tools and debris at the site (cf. Johnson and Holliday, chap. 9, and Holliday and Welty, 1981, for a review of lithic resources on the Southern High Plains).

## BEDROCK

Bedrock in the area of the Lubbock Lake Landmark consists of the Blanco Formation. These deposits are subdivided into strata 01 and 02. Stratum 01 consists of massive olive (4Y 5/4) sands with overlying dolomite. The late Quaternary deposits, which contain cultural remains, lie generally on the 01 sands, the dolomite being found at higher elevations along the buried valley walls. Stratum 02 is a fossiliferous pebbly clay overlying 01. Blancan age vertebrates found in this unit include *Stegomastodon, Nannipus,* and *Boraphagus.* Stratum 02 is either a Blancan age intraformational channel gravel or a late Blancan postlacustrine channel deposit (Stafford, 1977). Many exposures of the uppermost Blanco Formation exhibit a well-developed pedogenic calcrete.

## YELLOWHOUSE DRAW

The age of Yellowhouse Draw is uncertain, although in places it cuts through the Blackwater Draw Formation, dating the initial incision to the late Pleistocene at the earliest. Two high strath terraces are apparent on stratum 01 outcrops in the reservoir-cut area (fig. 2.3). A third, latest Pleistocene cutting stage resulted in 15 m of local relief along Yellowhouse Draw (Stafford, 1977). In the area of the reservoir cut this incision resulted in an entrenched meander (figs. 2.3, 2.4) considerably wider on the upstream end of the U.

Following the last stage of degradation, the draw began to fill intermittently with fluvial, lacustrine, paludal, eolian, and slopewash sediments. Source areas for the late Quaternary valley fill were the Blackwater Draw Formation and, to a lesser degree, the Blanco Formation.

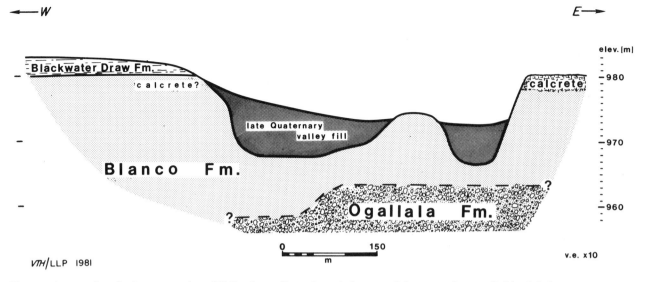

Fig. 2.2 A general geologic cross section of Yellowhouse Draw through the area of the reservoir cut at Lubbock Lake.

Fig. 2.3. Topography with late Quaternary geology of Yellowhouse Draw in the area of Lubbock Lake.

## LATE QUATERNARY STRATIGRAPHY AND SOILS

Five basic geologic units and five soils formed therein were identified at Lubbock Lake (fig. 2.5). Stratigraphic nomenclature follows a modified version of that of C. Johnson

(1974) and Stafford (1977, 1978, 1981) because considerably more sedimentological and geochronological data are now available. The five principal strata are numbered oldest to youngest. Vertical subdivisions (substrata) within each numbered unit are identified by uppercase letters, alphabetically, oldest to youngest. Principal facies within a given stratum or substratum are identified by lowercase letters ($\ell$ = lacustrine, e = eolian, s = slopewash).

Soils developed in the various strata and substrata present another problem in terminology. C. Johnson (1974) simply identified major pedologic horizons as substrata (e.g., the prominent A horizon in stratum 4 was identified as substratum 4C). This system is confusing, however, because pedologic horizons are not geologic strata. Stafford (1981) identified the soils with a numbering system, youngest to oldest. The five principal soils have now been named in lieu of Stafford's numbering scheme because numbers become difficult to use when stratigraphic units as well as soils are discussed. The use of names also eliminates chronological implications, which is often a problem with soils because they are time-transgressive features.

### Stratum 1

Stratum 1 occurs in a buried terrace and at the base of the valley fill. The sediments forming the buried terrace occur as isolated deposits averaging 2 m thick and are composed of carbonate gravel and sand. Stratum 1 at the base of the valley fill is also composed chiefly of carbonate gravel and sand and was deposited by a meandering stream (Stafford, 1977). Because of the sedimentological variability in stratum 1, substrata are identified only locally. The unit was studied most extensively and intensively in Area 2 (fig. 1.5) in association with FA2-1. Three subunits of stratum 1 were identified in Area 2. A gravel deposit (substratum 1A) extends across the floor of the valley and represents a point bar deposit. The gravel is buried by an overbank loamy sand (substratum 1B) that fines upward into clay (substratum 1C).

The age of the beginning of deposition of stratum 1 is not yet known, but the end of deposition had occurred by 11,000 B.P. Pierce (chap. 6) presents some evidence from invertebrate paleontology that deposition of stratum 1 began at least several thousand years before the end of deposition.

## Stratum 2

Stratum 2 consists primarily of lacustrine and marsh deposits. Along the axis of the channel of Yellowhouse Draw the lower 0.5 to 1 m of the unit (substratum 2A) contains beds of pure diatomite, representing periods of standing water, and interbedded peaty muds with few diatoms but abundant phytoliths, interpreted as periods when water was just below the surface. In excavation areas major beds or groups of beds (fig. 2.6) are designated "local beds" (LB). In such

areas the base of 2A is a thick (5–10 cm) bed of pure diatomite overlain by an equally thick peat lens. These two units are local beds 1 and 2, respectively. Above these beds the number and thickness of local beds vary considerably depending on location within the site. West and south of the channel axis 2A consists of interbedded, organic-rich silt and sand lenses.

Substratum 2B overlies 2A, conformably in some areas, unconformably in others. Substratum 2B is generally 0.5 to 1 m thick and consists of a homogeneous deposit of organic silt and clay with abundant phytoliths and some diatoms. Several lenses of silicified plant remains are apparent within 2B; otherwise, evidence of stratification is lacking. The zone is considered to represent a slowly aggrading boglike feature with little or no standing water.

Deposition of 2A began at about 11,000 B.P. and ended about 10,000 B.P. or slightly later. Deposition of 2B then began and continued until about 8500 B.P.

Substrata 2s and 2e are facies of both 2A and 2B. Substratum 2s is a near-shore deposit consisting of sandy

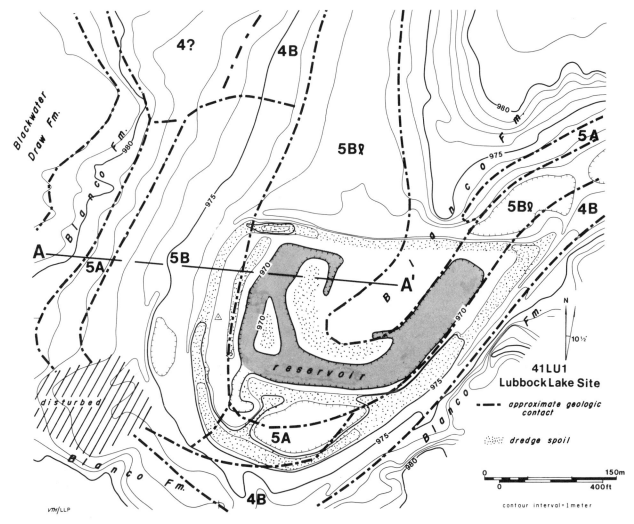

Fig. 2.4. Topographic and geologic map of Lubbock Lake in the area of the reservoir cut (contours not shown within the reservoir), with the approximate line-of-section for fig. 2.5 (A–A′).

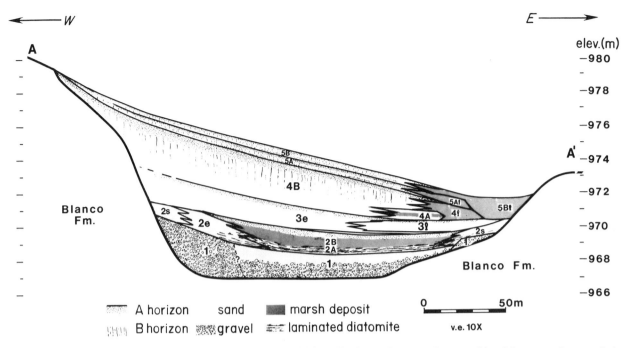

Fig. 2.5. Generalized stratigraphy of the late Quaternary valley fill in Yellowhouse Draw on the west side of the reservoir cut at Lubbock Lake (location of the section shown in fig. 2.4) (modified from Holliday, 1985b).

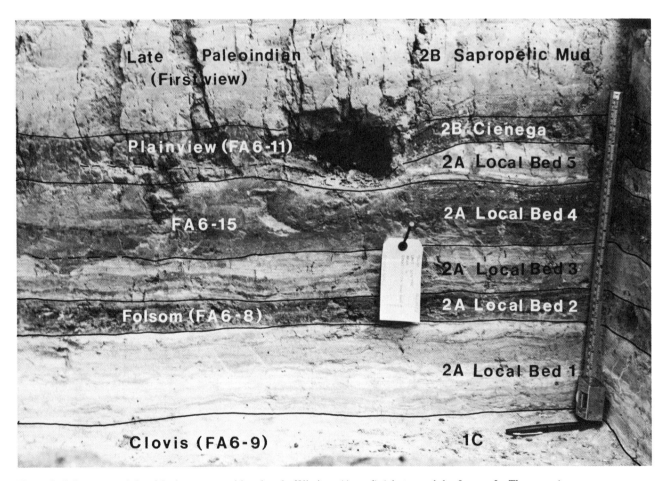

Fig. 2.6. Substratum 2A local-bed sequence with cultural affiliations (Area 6) (photograph by Jerome L. Thompson).

slopewash interbedded with lenses of lacustrine sediment from transgressions of 2A and 2B. Substratum 2e is an eolian facies common on the west side of the valley and interfingering with 2s. This eolian deposit increases in areal extent through stratum 2 times. Lenses of sediment representing transgressions of 2B are common in 2e, and locally 2e caps 2B. The eolian sediments began to accumulate as early as 9000 B.P.

The Firstview Soil formed in upper 2B and 2e from ca. 8500 to ca. 6300 B.P. The soil is divided into valley-axis and valley-margin facies. The valley-axis facies is characterized by O and A horizons with dark colors (10YR $\frac{3}{3}$ to $\frac{3}{1}$), suggestive of originally high organic-matter content. The O horizons are dominated by silicified plant remains, and amorphous silica is very common in thin section. The C horizon of the Firstview Soil is essentially unaltered 2B. Gley colors (e.g., 2.5YR $\frac{6}{2}$) in the upper C horizon suggest that the soil formed under reducing conditions. The water table probably remained at or just below the surface of the valley-axis facies of the Firstview Soil during pedogenesis. The valley-margin facies of the soil contrasts markedly with the valley-axis facies, probably because of the sandy parent material (2e and 2s) and the higher, better-drained topographic position. The valley-margin facies exhibits an A–C profile with a thin, weakly expressed A horizon and is calcareous throughout.

## Stratum 3

Stratum 3, which is up to 1 m thick, conformably overlies stratum 2 and is subdivided into substrata 3ℓ and 3e. Substratum 3ℓ is a highly calcareous, silty, friable lacustrine unit that is found along the valley axis of the draw. The lake sediments interfinger with the sandy, moderately calcareous eolian sediments of substratum 3e that are found along the western valley margin.

The Yellowhouse Soil developed in stratum 3. Where the soil formed in 3ℓ, it has a relatively organic-rich A horizon and minimal leaching of $CaCo_3$ in the highly calcareous C horizon. This situation suggests that the water table was at or just below the surface of the Yellowhouse Soil as it developed along the floor of the draw, similar to the valley-axis facies of the Firstview Soil. Where the Yellowhouse Soil developed in substratum 3e, it is oxidized and considerably lower in carbonate content. This situation reflects the parent material and probably better drainage, again similar to the Firstview Soil in the equivalent position.

Deposition of stratum 3 began about 6300 B.P. The time when deposition ended and formation of the Yellowhouse Soil began is unknown. Burial of stratum 3 and the Yellowhouse Soil was time-transgressive. Along the valley axis 3ℓ was eroded and buried by stratum 4 beginning about 5500 B.P. Along the valley margin stratum 3 and its soil were not buried until as late as 5000 B.P.

## Stratum 4

Stratum 4 consists of several types of deposits and a soil.

Substratum 4A is generally less than 1 m thick, disconformably overlies stratum 3, and is found only along the valley axis. The unit contains sandy alluvium deposited by an intermittent stream, interbedded with clayey marsh deposits. This unit is common at and downstream from Lubbock Lake but is not apparent upstream from the reservoir cut. Substratum 4B is primarily a sandy eolian deposit as much as 3 m thick. A clayey marsh facies of 4B (substratum 4Bℓ) occurs locally along the valley axis. This marsh deposit is similar to but smaller in areal extent than the marsh sediments in 4A. Apparently a marsh of varying size existed along the valley axis throughout stratum 4 deposition.

The Lubbock Lake Soil formed in substratum 4B. It is the best-developed and most widespread soil at Lubbock Lake. The A horizon is so distinctive that it was given stratigraphic designations by earlier investigators (table 1.1). The A horizon is generally dark (e.g., 7.5YR $\frac{3}{2}$, moist) and locally up to 1 m thick. The B horizon is moderately developed with good structural development and significant illuvial clay apparent in both particle-size distribution and in thin section. The C horizon can vary; along the valley axis the C horizon is substratum 4A, but along the valley margins it is unaltered 4B. Pedogenic accumulations of secondary $CaCO_3$ are common in the Lubbock Lake Soil. A well-expressed calcic horizon occurs in the lower B horizon. In those situations where the Lubbock Lake Soil is buried, a weakly developed calcic horizon occurs in the upper B horizon, immediately below the A horizon. Lenses of substratum 4Bℓ are apparent in the A horizon of the Lubbock Lake Soil in a few exposures. That occurrence and radiocarbon dates from the lenses indicate that the lowland marsh existed during the time of soil formation, periodically transgressing across the stable surface.

Substratum 4A deposition occurred between 5500 and 5000 B.P. Deposition of 4B began before 5000 B.P. and ended about 4500 B.P. The Lubbock Lake Soil then began to develop, and pedogenesis continued until less than 1000 B.P. in areas of deposition of substratum 5A. On the east side of the site stratum 4 and the Lubbock Lake Soil were never buried (fig. 2.4), and pedogenesis has continued to the present.

## Stratum 5

Stratum 5, the youngest deposit at Lubbock Lake, is divided into two substrata, 5A and 5B, each of which consists of two facies (fig. 2.5). The upslope valley-margin facies of both substrata (designated simply 5A and 5B and found only along the west and south sides of the valley) are composed of layers of slopewash sand and gravel and eolian sand, burying stratum 4. Substratum 5B is thinner than 5A and is separated from it by a soil formed in 5A. The lowland, valley-axis, lacustrine facies (5Aℓ, 5Bℓ, and 5ℓ undivided) are composed of relatively organic-rich clay. These lacustrine sediments represent a continuation of the lowland marsh deposition of stratum 4 though of considerably wider areal extent. Substratum 5Bℓ is probably related to the standing water known to have existed at the site in the late nineteenth and early twentieth centuries (Holden, 1962a).

Several soils formed in stratum 5, representing returns to landscape stability, which were interrupted by the episodic deposition of 5A and 5B. The Apache Soil formed in 5A, and the Singer Soil formed in 5B. Both soils are well drained, as indicated by oxidized colors and evidence of $CaCO_3$ translocation and accumulation. The soils differ in degree of development, stratigraphic position, and periods of development. The Apache Soil is weakly developed, though the A horizon is locally prominent and sometimes serves as a stratigraphic marker. The soil has a moderately expressed B horizon with evidence for clay translocation apparent from particle-size distribution and thin sections. Calcic horizons are locally prominent in the lower B horizon of the Apache Soil, and a C horizon is rarely apparent. Where only 5A was deposited over stratum 4, the Apache Soil is the present surface soil. The Singer Soil is very weakly developed. The soil has a thin A horizon and either a minimally expressed B horizon or a C horizon. Little evidence exists of clay or carbonate translocation in the Singer Soil.

Radiocarbon ages indicate that deposition of 5A began around 750 to 600 B.P. Deposition ceased, and the Apache Soil began forming around 450 to 300 B.P. Between 300 and 250 B.P. substratum 5A was buried by 5B in some areas (fig. 2.4). Historic European materials in 5B indicate that deposition of the unit ended and formation of the Singer Soil began about 100 years ago.

## SUMMARY AND INTERPRETATIONS

Environments of deposition varied considerably through the late Quaternary at Lubbock Lake, and most of the depositional episodes were separated by long periods of landscape stability (no erosion or deposition) and soil formation. The depositional and pedological records aid considerably in the reconstruction of local environments and suggest regional climatic conditions and trends in climate changes (fig. 2.7).

Sometime before 11,000 B.P., after Yellowhouse Draw attained maximum relief, the valley began to aggrade with alluvial sediments from a meandering stream (stratum 1). This meandering stream existed up to about 11,000 B.P. In its final stages it was graded and meandered across the valley floor. The termination of stream activity and initiation of stratum 2 deposition was apparently rather abrupt.

Deposition of stratum 2 sediments began 11,000 B.P. and continued until about 8500 B.P. From 11,000 to 10,000 B.P. episodic stands of large quiescent ponds deposited lenses of diatomite and diatomaceous earth. When water levels dropped to or below the floor of the draw, thin layers of peaty mud accumulated. Beginning about 10,000 B.P. and continuing until about 8500 B.P., the water table remained at about the level of the valley floor, and a homogeneous sapropelic mud slowly aggraded, representing a long period of marshy conditions. Eolian sediments also began to accumulate along the western valley margins during this time. From 8500 to about 6300 B.P. little deposition occurred in the draw, and a soil formed in the marsh and eolian depos-

its. Along the valley axis local geochemical conditions promoted precipitation of silica.

It is not clear how the water in the stratum 2 ponds was impounded. Evidence exists that fine-grained material from stratum 1 was reworked, perhaps by wind, and choked more constricted reaches of the draw, thus locally damming the valley.

Stratum 3 began accreting about 6300 B.P. Highly calcareous sediments were deposited along the valley axis under lake or marsh conditions as considerable eolian material was deposited along the western valley margins. By 5500 B.P. deposition had ceased, and a soil began forming in the deposits during a brief interval of nondeposition. This interval of landscape stability lasted until about 5000 B.P. along the valley margins. However, erosion of stratum 3 followed by burial by alluvial sand and marsh clays occurred along the valley axis between 5500 and 5000 B.P.

The environments of deposition of upper stratum 2 and stratum 3 indicate a warming and drying trend. The geochemical change from an environment promoting silica precipitation (stratum 2) to one favoring carbonate precipitation (stratum 3) suggests warming of the marsh waters. The increasing amounts of eolian material from stratum 2 to stratum 3 indicate that the vegetative cover of the surrounding High Plains surface was becoming reduced, thus allowing wind erosion. Such a long-term reduction in vegetation could be produced most effectively by a reduction in effective precipitation. The long period of general landscape stability associated with the Firstview Soil and thin lenses of eolian material found in the surface horizons of the soil indicate that the drying at this time was episodic. These interpretations for strata 2 and 3 are supported by evidence from the invertebrate paleontology (Pierce, chap. 6) and vertebrate paleontology (Johnson, chap. 8).

The thickness and extent of eolian sediments in strata 3 and 4, relative to the length of depositional episodes (between 500 and 1,000 years for each) document two periods of relatively intense mid-Holocene drought. A hiatus in the drought lasting about 500 years is indicated by the landscape stability associated with the Yellowhouse Soil and, along the valley axis, the erosion of upper stratum 3 and the deposition of 4A. The erosion and sedimentation are probably related to a local resurgence of spring activity rather than to regional alluviation. Springs are known to have existed in the area of the reservoir, but not upstream. Upstream from the area of the reservoir 4A has not been identified, and evidence exists for only minor erosion. The lack of eolian sedimentation during this interval and the increase in spring activity suggest an increase in effective precipitation.

The long period of nondeposition following deposition of 4B indicates the establishment of denser vegetation on the Southern High Plains surface, suggesting an increase in effective precipitation with climatic conditions probably similar to those of today. The principal exceptions to this trend occurred within the last 1,000 years. The weak calcic horizon present in the upper B horizon of the Lubbock Lake Soil where buried by stratum 5 indicates a drying trend beginning before stratum 5 deposition and perhaps culminating in reduced vegetative cover on the Southern High Plains surface and valley walls. This situation could have resulted in deposition of the slopewash and eolian sediment characteristic of substratum 5A. The landscape stability associated with the Apache Soil appears to represent a return to conditions like those of today. In Historic times there occurred another cycle of reduced effective moisture, represented by the deposition of substratum 5B.

The presence of the marsh clays of substrata 4Bℓ, 5Aℓ, and 5Bℓ indicates that throughout the last half of the Holocene at least some water was present along the floor of Yellowhouse Draw. This evidence further suggests that a

significant drop in the water table below the floor of Yellowhouse Draw did not occur during the late Quaternary until the twentieth century.

The geologic and pedologic record at Lubbock Lake appears to be generally representative for the Southern High Plains. Limited data from other draw sites and from a few dune fields and playas suggest the same general trends in late Quaternary deposition and pedogenesis (Gile, 1979, 1985; Haynes, 1975; Honea, 1980; Holliday, 1983, 1985a, e). These data further suggest that the environmental record at Lubbock Lake is representative of the region.

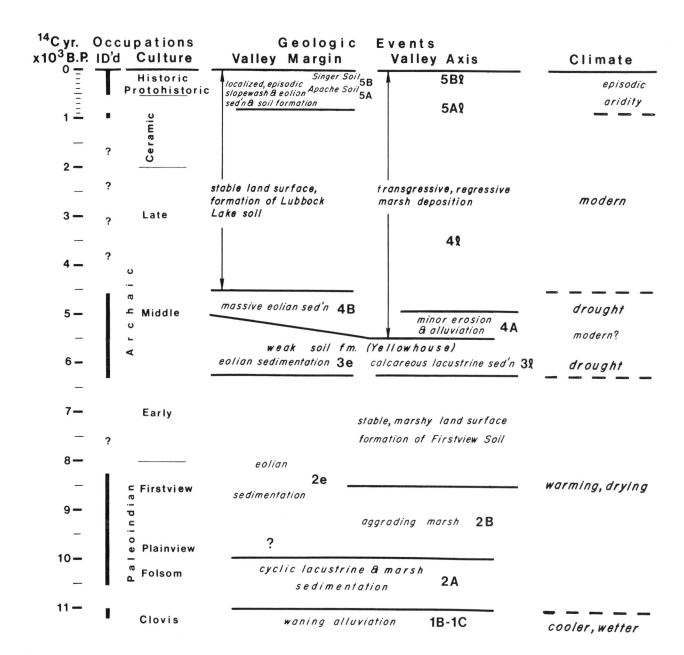

Fig. 2.7. Summary of the cultural chronology, geologic history, and inferred climatic history of Lubbock Lake. "Occupations ID'd" indicates the age range and cultures for which archaeological features were identified.

# 3. Cultural Chronology

VANCE T. HOLLIDAY

One of the ultimate goals of the Lubbock Lake Project is the study of human adaptation to ecological change. A useful if not essential tool in such an undertaking is a local cultural chronology. Several general cultural chronologies for the Southern High Plains have been presented (Kelley, 1964; Collins, 1971; Hughes and Willey, 1978) but were established without the benefit of data from well-stratified, well-dated localities with occupations spanning many cultural periods. Now, however, the outstanding stratigraphic record and age control at Lubbock Lake provide an excellent physical and temporal framework for establishing a comprehensive, local cultural chronology encompassing the last 11,000 years of human occupation. The principal difficulty in the development of such a chronology is the relative lack of diagnostic artifacts and the absence of comparable records in the region. However, the Lubbock Lake chronology serves as a first approximation for a detailed regional cultural chronology.

The Lubbock Lake cultural chronology is based primarily on diagnostic artifacts, subsistence, technological traits, and, to a lesser degree, environmental considerations. All these characteristics are compared with cultural chronologies from neighboring regions such as the Texas Panhandle (Hughes and Willey, 1978), the Central High Plains (Cassells, 1983), and Central Texas (Prewitt, 1981). Five general cultural periods are recognized at Lubbock Lake: Paleoindian (11,500 to 8500 B.P.); Archaic (8500 to 2000 B.P.); Ceramic (2000 B.P. to ca. A.D. 1450); Protohistoric (ca. A.D. 1450 to mid-1600s); and Historic (mid-1600s to late 1930s). Each period is subdivided when possible.

The Paleoindian period, occurring during the latest Pleistocene and early Holocene epochs, is characterized by hunting of now-extinct megafauna during a time of generally ameliorated climate, but a climate that was also undergoing marked change from pluvial to xeric conditions. The Archaic period, spanning the middle and early late Holocene, is characterized by exploitation of essentially modern flora and fauna during a series of xeric-mesic fluctuations in climate. The Ceramic period, the latest prehistoric cultural unit, is identified on the basis of pottery in the archaeological record. The Protohistoric period is a transitional period from just before and following the first appearance of Europeans in the area (A.D. 1541) but lacking their influence or artifacts. The Historic period is identified by the presence of European artifacts and remains of the modern horse.

The following discussion is a summary based on all archaeological data and age control available. Cultural features referred to are discussed in chapter 10, and cultural materials are described in chapter 9. All radiocarbon ages (table 1.2) are discussed and evaluated by Holliday et al. (1983, 1985a).

## THE PALEOINDIAN PERIOD

The Paleoindian is the best-known cultural period at Lubbock Lake, in contrast to the general situation in North America, where the Paleoindian is the least known or understood period. Lubbock Lake was first recognized as a Paleoindian site, and the focus of most investigations was on the Paleoindian record.

The Paleoindian period is subdivided on the basis of projectile point styles, with subdivisions created by others (Wormington, 1957; Wheat, 1972). Comparisons with Paleoindian chronologies elsewhere are facilitated by the large amount of Paleoindian research that has been carried out on the Great Plains. The Paleoindian period is subdivided into Clovis, Folsom, Plainview, and Firstview cultures. The cultures are identified by distinctive projectile points that occupy discrete time periods.

Paleoindian cultures earlier than Clovis may be present elsewhere in the Americas (e.g., Bryan, 1986) but have not been firmly identified at Lubbock Lake or on the Southern High Plains. Alexander (1978:21) suggested that pre-Clovis material was found at Lubbock Lake in "older . . . middle or early Pleistocene . . . clays," on the basis of statements made by Kelley (1974:68), who was reviewing the work of Wheat (1974). The clay referred to is the Pliocene bedrock at the site, and artifacts were recovered just below the weathered surface of the clay along the steeply sloping valley margins. The clay typically becomes very blocky and highly friable on exposure to air. The clay at the position where the artifacts were found was exposed at the surface for at least 6,000 years before burial by mid-Holocene sediments. Undoubtedly this long subaerial weathering, perhaps combined with bioturbation, resulted in the movement of late Quaternary artifacts into the Pliocene clay (Johnson and Holliday, 1986).

The Clovis culture is characterized by the distinctive Clovis point and an association with a variety of extinct late Pleistocene megafauna including mammoth, camel, horse, and bison (Haynes, 1980; Frison, 1978). Clovis-age material occurs at the contact of substrata 1A–1B. A processing station (FA2-1) contains the remains of a wide variety of megafauna and dates to about 11,100 B.P. (Johnson and Holliday, 1985). This age is well within the range of Clovis occupations on the plains (Haynes, 1980; Frison, 1978). Although Clovis points were not found *in situ,* a Clovis point was recovered from dredging spoil near the feature. The feature is quite unlike Clovis features found at other sites on the Southern High Plains, such as Blackwater Draw Locality No. 1 (Hester, 1972) and Miami (Sellards, 1938), in that it is not primarily a mammoth kill but a wide variety of animals are represented there.

Lubbock Lake is probably best known as a Folsom locality, having been identified as such by Sellards (1952) and Wormington (1957). Four Folsom points were found *in situ* during the TMM work, and a number of Folsom points were recovered from the spoil piles.

The Folsom material was found in substratum 2A associated with *Bison antiquus* bone beds. The exact nature of the TMM bone beds is unknown. However, the same bone beds remain exposed along the south and southeastern walls of the reservoir cut, and a series of small-scale kills is suggested rather than a large-scale kill or trap. Evidence of any geomorphic means of trapping the animals is lacking. The Folsom occupation at Lubbock Lake dates from 10,800 to 10,200 B.P., which is in line with other age ranges for Folsom (Frison, 1978; Haynes, 1971; Wheat, 1972).

The Plainview occupation at Lubbock Lake followed immediately after the Folsom. Plainview material at the site is found at the base of substratum 2B, just above the contact with 2A. Like the Folsom features, Plainview features contain the disarticulated remains of a few bison. The Plainview occupation at Lubbock Lake dates to 10,000 B.P., which is quite similar to the age of other Plainview sites on the Southern High Plains (Johnson et al., 1982).

Remains of the Firstview occupation at Lubbock Lake are found in upper substratum 2B. Small-scale bison kill/butchering locales continue. A different type of activity is represented by a scatter of lithic debris (Johnson and Holliday, 1981; Bamforth, 1985). The kills are generally similar to those found in the Folsom and Plainview levels. Firstview occupation dates to around 8600 B.P.

The end of the Paleoindian period is defined on the basis of environmental changes, in the absence of archaeological remains denoting the Paleoindian-Archaic transition. Considering that bison hunting continued to be a principal component of subsistence, such a transition would probably be difficult to identify. Beginning around 8500 B.P. sedimentation in the draw ceased, and a long period of landscape stability followed, represented by formation of the Firstview Soil. This event is a useful geologic marker coincident with environmental changes culminating in mid-Holocene xeric conditions. The Paleoindian-Archaic boundary is therefore placed at 8500 B.P.

## THE ARCHAIC PERIOD

Less is known about the Archaic period than about any other cultural period on the Southern High Plains, in part because few Archaic sites have been excavated, although many have been recorded (Hughes and Willey, 1978). In addition, geologic conditions during much of the Archaic on the Southern High Plains apparently were not conducive to site preservation (Johnson and Holliday, 1986). During the course of the LLP little emphasis has been on the Archaic, but enough material was recovered during the LLP and earlier investigations that an initial assessment of the Archaic at the site can be made. The following discussion is summarized from Johnson and Holliday (1986).

The Archaic period at Lubbock Lake is subdivided on the basis of limited information concerning material culture and subsistence combined with more abundant data on the environment. In areas immediately adjacent to the Southern High Plains, Archaic chronologies on which a local chronology can be based are lacking. Well-established chronologies for the Plains Archaic in regions farther away, such as eastern Oklahoma (Wyckoff, 1984) or Central Texas (Prewitt, 1981), become difficult to use because particular artifact styles may be time-transgressive over such distances.

The Archaic is subdivided into Early (8500–6300 B.P.), Middle (6300–4500 B.P.), and Late (4500–2000 B.P.), following the three general climatic stages identified for this time. The Early Archaic occurs during a time of environmental transition from the earliest Holocene warming trend into the intense xeric conditions of the middle Holocene. Geologically, the Early Archaic at Lubbock Lake is represented by the Firstview Soil and some deposition of eolian material (substratum 2e). Extinct bison existed into the Early Archaic, but was experiencing stress expressed as size diminution. The only Early Archaic feature from Lubbock Lake is a *Bison antiquus* bone bed that represents a kill of at least three animals (FA4-1). No diagnostic lithic artifacts were found with the feature.

The Middle Archaic occurs during two intense droughts (6300–5500 B.P. and 5000–4500 B.P.), represented by the eolian sediments of strata 3 and 4 and separated by a brief climatic respite represented by the Yellowhouse Soil. Some water was present along the draw during the droughts, as indicated by the marsh facies of strata 3 and 4. These droughts are considered to be the local manifestation of the Altithermal. A large Middle Archaic oven (FA16-1) was found, suggesting more reliance on plants as a food source, although several *Bison bison* bone beds were also excavated. Middle Archaic projectile points include Trinity, Ellis, and Bulverde, following the Central Texas–based classifications of Prewitt (1981) and Turner and Hester (1985).

The Late Archaic occurs during a period of more ameliorated climate compared to that of the middle Holocene droughts, a climate probably similar to the climate of the present day. Geologically, the Late Archaic is represented by the development of the Lubbock Lake Soil, which continued to develop during the Ceramic and locally during later periods. Thus the Late Archaic archaeological record is compressed into the A horizon of the Lubbock Lake Soil and can be mixed with later occupations. Considerable archaeological material was recovered from this A horizon, but no features with diagnostic artifacts of the Late Archaic were identified. The Late Archaic is, however, the best represented portion of the Archaic on the Southern High Plains.

Probably the most noteworthy aspect of the Archaic record at Lubbock Lake is that it demonstrates that the area was not abandoned, even at the height of the Altithermal. Such a near-complete, well-stratified Archaic record is unknown elsewhere on the Southern High Plains. Finally, the data from the features demonstrate that Dillehay's (1974) model of bison presence and absence is invalid at least for the Southern High Plains.

## THE CERAMIC PERIOD

The Ceramic period began about 2000 B.P., as indicated by data from sites found on the northern Southern High Plains (Willey and Hughes, 1978). Earlier workers referred to this period as Neo-American (Suhm et al., 1954; Collins, 1971) or Neo-Indian (Hughes and Willey, 1978). These terms have been abandoned in favor of Ceramic because they are not commonly used outside Texas. Ceramic technology is characteristic of this period throughout the plains and describes a dominant part of the material culture. The use of the bow and arrow also developed during this time, but evidence from the northern Southern High Plains suggests that the arrow followed the development of ceramic technology and that dart points were used well into the Ceramic period (Willey and Hughes, 1978).

Fewer data are available for the Ceramic than for any other cultural period at Lubbock Lake. The earlier Ceramic is represented geologically by the formation of the Lubbock Lake Soil and is not, therefore, found in discrete deposits. During the WPA excavations Chupadero Black-on-White pottery was recovered from the A horizon of the Lubbock Lake Soil (Wheat, 1974; Johnson and Holliday, 1986), clearly indicating interaction with southwestern cultures. Kelley (1974) briefly mentioned the testing of a feature found near the reservoir cut which produced Scallorn points, *Bison bison* remains, lithic tools and flakes, and bone beads. Hughes and Willey (1978) identify Scallorn points as characteristic of regional Plains Woodland occupations. However, the Scallorn type is common throughout most of Texas (Turner and Hester, 1985), and its relationship to classic Plains Woodland is unclear. Later Ceramic features are found in substratum 5A and its marsh facies. Therefore, these features date to less than 1000 B.P. Bison hunting continued in the area, as indicated by a processing station (FA1-3) and food debris from several camps.

## THE PROTOHISTORIC PERIOD

The Protohistoric record at Lubbock Lake, combined with the Historic record, is well stratified, well dated, and rich in archaeological remains. This situation has allowed the identification of certain artifact types that are consistently and exlusively associated with these cultural periods. Otherwise, in the absence of diagnostic artifacts and age control, compressed, nonstratified Ceramic, Protohistoric, and Historic aboriginal occupations are impossible to differentiate. The following review is based on Johnson et al. (1977).

Protohistoric features include camping areas and secondary *Bison bison* processing stations that are found in upper substratum 5A and its marsh facies. Pottery is also found in uppermost 5A and includes a thick-walled, coarsely tempered, brushed utility ware and a thin-walled, mica-tempered utility ware. The diagnostic artifact is the Garza point (Runkles, 1964; Johnson et al., 1977), a small triangular point with a basal notch. Other points found associated with Garza at Lubbock Lake and throughout the region include Harrell, Fresno, and Lott.

Archaeological data and some ethnohistoric data allow tentative speculation concerning the cultural identity of the Protohistoric groups at Lubbock Lake. The Garza occupation coincides very closely with the Apache occupation of the Southern High Plains from about A.D. 1500 to 1700 (D. Gunnerson, 1956). In addition, the early Garza levels have not produced pottery, which is consistent with the accounts by early Spanish explorers that the Apache of the time were nomadic buffalo hunters without pottery (Schlesier, 1972). However, in the middle 1600s a number of Apache groups moved onto the plains, bringing with them a micaceous pottery (Schlesier, 1972; J. Gunnerson, 1969). This situation may be represented by the later Garza occupation with pottery. The thick, coarse-tempered ware is an unrecognized type and may represent an indigenous development.

## THE HISTORIC PERIOD

The Historic occupation at Lubbock Lake included both aboriginal and European groups. In the aboriginal features the remains of modern horse (*Equus caballus*) are the principal evidence of European influence, although metal and glass also are found. This evidence first appears in the archaeological record at Lubbock Lake in the late 1600s and comes from lower substratum 5B and its marsh facies. The Historic European occupation of the area began in the later part of the nineteenth century, and remains from this time are found in upper 5B and its marsh facies.

Aboriginal Historic features include camping areas and secondary processing stations containing remains of modern bison and horse. These activity areas are characterized by the same types of artifacts as those in the Protohistoric period. However, Garza points are replaced by Washita points, small triangular points with side notches. Lott, Harrell, and Fresno points continue. Modern horse was added as a food resource, and a few tools made of glass were recovered. The second Apache population expansion across the Southern High Plains began around 1650 (Secoy, 1953).

Comanche dominated the Southern High Plains from the 1720s until 1876 (Collins, 1971). Aboriginal occupations above the Washita level were found at Lubbock Lake, but diagnostic artifacts attributable to the Comanche are lacking.

The first Anglo-American movements through the area began shortly after the Civil War, and Lubbock Lake, with its spring-fed lake, appears to have been a favorite watering place. General Ranald Mackenzie's troops probably stopped at the site to water during their campaigns against the Comanche. Buffalo hunters moved into the area in the 1870s. In 1875 a battle between buffalo hunters and Comanche took place at Lubbock Lake and downstream for several miles (Holden, 1962). The first commercial establishment in Lubbock County was constructed at Lubbock Lake by George Singer in the early 1880s (Holden, 1974; Conner, 1962). Excavations yielded artifacts probably related to the buffalo-hunting activity (heavy-caliber rifle shell casings) and the Singer Store occupation (square nails, metal cans, buttons, and a ginger-beer bottle).

## SUMMARY

Five basic cultural periods and various subperiods are outlined for Lubbock Lake. The Paleoindian period (11,500 to 8500 B.P.) is characterized by ameliorated climatic conditions during which human groups used a variety of fluted and lanceolate projectile points to hunt now-extinct animals. Subperiods, defined on the basis of projectile point styles, include Clovis (11,500 to 11,000 B.P.), Folsom (10,800 to 10,200 B.P.), Plainview (about 10,000 B.P.), and Firstview (about 8600 B.P.).

The Archaic period (8500 to 2000 B.P.) is characterized by several climatic changes. During the period hunting was supplemented by plant gathering for subsistence. The Archaic is subdivided into Early (8500 to 6300 B.P.), Middle (6300 to 4500 B.P.), and Late (4500 to 2000 B.P.) on the basis of climatic events. A decline in the human occupation of the Southern High Plains may have followed the Paleoindian period owing to climatic stress, particularly from 6300 to 4500 B.P. (the Altithermal). However, occupations continued at Lubbock Lake during this time.

The Ceramic period (2000 B.P. to A.D. 1450) is very poorly known at Lubbock Lake. Evidence for continued bison hunting was found, and both ceramics and arrow points were recovered.

The Protohistoric period (1450 to mid-1600s) covers the time when Europeans were in the area, but evidence for this is lacking in the archaeological record. Subsistence and technology are generally similar to those of the preceding period. The local Protohistoric occupants may have been various Apache groups.

During the Historic period (mid-1600s to 1930s) European presence is apparent in the archaeological record. The Historic aboriginal inhabitants probably included Apache and Comanche groups. Historic Anglo-Americans included buffalo hunters, military personnel, and settlers. This period culminated in the founding of Lubbock.

# 4. Modern, Historic, and Fossil Flora

## JEROME L. THOMPSON

In a report to Congress in 1850, Randolph B. Marcy (1850:42) described the Llano Estacado of Texas as "the Zahara of North America." In 1855, John Pope (1855:9) reported that the Llano Estacado had "no inducements to cultivation." These reports represented the cultural bias of explorers who made their homes in the eastern United States. The Southern High Plains were not a barren wasteland and had always supported plant communities.

Although Anglo-American exploration and settlement of the Southern High Plains are relatively recent events in Texas history, the Spaniards' knowledge of the area can be traced back to the explorations of Captain Francisco Vásquez de Coronado in 1541 (Holden, 1962a). Prehistorically the Southern High Plains were occupied by various native American cultures from 11,000 B.P. Mammoth, horse, camel, bison, and other vertebrates were sought by the early hunters. Until about 100 years ago modern bison and pronghorn antelope were common in the vicinity of Lubbock (Holden, 1962a). Only sketchy accounts of the historic flora exist; however, some work (Wendorf, 1961a, 1970; Wendorf and Hester, 1975; Hall, 1982) has been done to reconstruct the prehistoric flora during and since the late Pleistocene.

The research presented herein is an investigation of the late Pleistocene, Holocene, and modern flora at Lubbock Lake based on plant macrofossils, primarily seeds and seed remains. Four subjects are discussed: (1) notation of modern (1976) flora at the site, (2) information on the historic floral record, (3) analysis of plant macrofossils recovered from the site, and (4) genera that could have been of potential economic value to the past inhabitants of the locality.

## MODERN FLORA

The modern flora was identified at eight localities in Yellowhouse Draw and the Lubbock Lake Landmark (fig. 4.1). Three localities are along the draw escarpment and are designated as upland localities. Five localities are along the floor of the draw and are designated as lowland localities. Although the reservoir-cut (or basin) area of the Landmark was designated as a single locality, it contained species found in upland and lowland localities. A total of 25 families, 61 genera, and 71 species were identified. Some of the species were introduced historically. A complete list of all modern species with notations of native versus introduced species appears in table 4.1.

Each sampling locality is correlated to soil series mapped by the U.S. Soil Conservation Service (Blackstock, 1979; fig. 4.2). However, the stratigraphic and soils research conducted in Yellowhouse Draw within the Lubbock Lake Landmark (Holliday and Allen, chap. 2) indicates that the soils as mapped do not necessarily reflect pedologic or geologic reality (Holliday, 1985d).

Although the area around the Landmark has not been grazed for approximately 30 years, it has been subject to disturbance by off-road vehicles and archaeologists. According to Allred (1956), the area should be occupied by the High Plains bluestem postclimax community. Little bluestem (*Schizachyrium scoparium*) and sideoats grama (*Bouteloua curtipendula*) are the only species of this vegetation type found in the vicinity of the reservoir cut. Major species of the vegetation type noted by Allred (1956) as the mixed prairie climax are found in the area. Blue grama (*B. gracilis*), hairy grama (*B. hirsuta*), sand dropseed (*Sporobolus cryptandrus*), purple three-awn (*Aristida purpurea*), and buffalo grass (*Buchloe dactyloides*) are common at some of the localities.

Upland draw localities are distinguished by relatively steep topography and exposure of the underlying calcareous Blanco Formation bedrock (fig. 4.3a). The common soil of the three upland draw localities (figs. 4.1, 4.2) is mapped as the Potter series (Blackstock, 1979). Potter soils are in the taxonomic order of Aridisols, which are characterized by low soil-moisture content. Vegetation is characterized by grasses, forbs, cacti, and xerophytic shrubs (Soil Survey Staff, 1975). The Potter series has formed either in the bedrock exposed along the valley walls or in well-developed calcic horizons common in the Blackwater Draw Formation which overlies the bedrock (Holliday, personal communication).

Common species found at the upland draw localities include narrowleaf gromwell (*Lithospermum incisum*), brown-spine prickly pear (*Opuntia phaeacantha*), wavy-leaf thistle (*Cirsium undulatum*), stemmed bitterweed (*Hymenoxys scaposa*), perennial broomweed (*Xanthocephalum sarothrae*), sideoats grama, hairy grama, little bluestem, woolly locoweed (*Astragalus molissmus*), feather dalea (*Dalea formosa*), catclaw mimosa (*Mimosa biuncifera*), honey mesquite (*Prosopis glandulosa*), narrowleaf yucca (*Yucca angustifolia*), evening primrose (*Oenothera greggi* and *O. missouriensis*), scarlet gaura (*Gaura coccinea*), and white milkwort (*Polygala alba*).

Lowland draw localities are distinguished by relatively level topography in the bottom of the draw and the absence of exposed calcareous bedrock (fig. 4.3b). After heavy rains water may remain standing for several days. The common soils at the three lowland draw localities (figs. 4.1, 4.2) are mapped as Berda loams and Bippus clay loams (Blackstock, 1979). Berda loams are classified in the order of Inceptisols, and Bippus clay loams are classified as Mollisols. Inceptisols can support a variety of vegetation types, and Mollisols classically support grasslands in climates with seasonal dry periods (Soil Survey Staff, 1975).

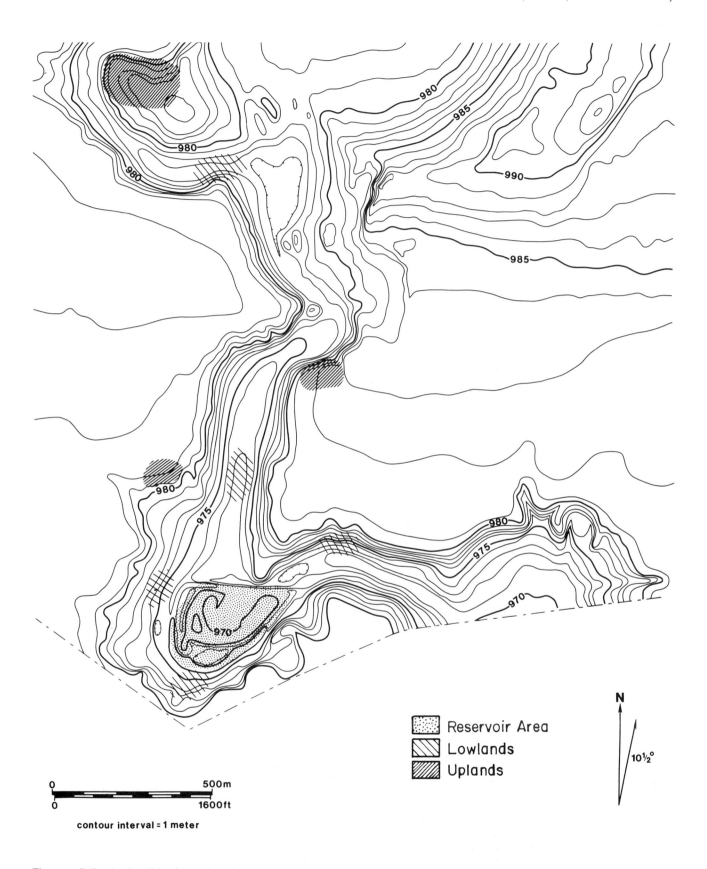

Fig. 4.1. Collecting localities for modern flora along Yellowhouse Draw at Lubbock Lake.

Table 4.1. Modern Flora at Lubbock Lake and Adjacent Areas in Yellowhouse Draw

| Family | Genus and Species | Common Name | Yellowhouse Draw | | Lubbock Lake Reservoir Area | |
|---|---|---|---|---|---|---|
| | | | Lowland | Upland | Lowland | Upland |
| Amaranthaceae | Amaranthus retroflexus L. | Redroot pigweed | × | | × | |
| Boraginaceae | Lithospermum incisum Lehm. | Narrowleaf gromwell | | × | | |
| Cactaceae | Opuntia phaeacantha Engelm | Brown-spine prickly pear | | × | | × |
| Chenopodiaceae | Chenopodium album L. | Lamb's-quarters | × | | × | |
| | Kochia scoparia (L.) Roth* | Belvedere summer cypress | × | | × | |
| | Salsola kali L.* | Russian thistle | × | × | × | × |
| Compositae | Ambrosia psilostachya D.C. | Western ragweed | × | | × | × |
| | Centaurea americana Nutt. | Thornless thistle | × | × | | |
| | Cirsium undulatum Nutt. | Wavy-leaf thistle | | × | | |
| | Conyza canadensis (L.) Cronq. | Horsetail conyza | × | | × | |
| | Grindelia squarrosa (Pursh) Dun. | Curl-cup gumweed | | × | | × |
| | Helianthus annuus L. | Annual sunflower | × | | × | |
| | Helianthus ciliaris D.C. | Blueweed sunflower | | × | | × |
| | Hymenoxys scaposa (D.C.) Parker | Stemmed bitterweed | | × | | × |
| | Liatris punctata Hook. | Dotted gayfeather | × | | × | |
| | Machaeranthera tanacetifolia (H.B.K.) Nees | Tahoka daisy | × | × | | × |
| | Prionopsis ciliata (Nutt.) Nutt. | Ironweed | | × | | × |
| | Ratibida columnaris (Sims) D. Don | Prairie coneflower | × | × | | × |
| | Tragopogon dubis Scop.* | Salsify | | | × | |
| | Vernonia baldwini Torr. | Baldwin's ironweed | × | | × | |
| | Xanthisma drummondii (T. & G.) Gray | Sleep daisy | × | × | × | × |
| | Xanthocephalum sarothrae (Pursh) Shinners | Perennial broomweed | | × | | × |
| | Xanthium strumarium L. | Cocklebur | × | | × | |
| Convolvulaceae | Convolvulus arvensis L. | Possession vine | × | | | |
| Cruciferae | Descurainia pinnata (Walt) Britt. | Tansy mustard | × | | × | |
| | Lepidium densiflorum Schrad. | Prairie pepperweed | × | | × | |
| | Lesquerella gordonii (Gray) Wats | Gordon's bladder pod | × | | | |
| | Sisymbrium altissimum L.* | Tumble mustard | × | | × | |
| | Sisymbrium irio L.* | London rocket | × | | × | |
| Cucurbitaceae | Cucurbita foetidissima H.B.K. | Buffalo gourd | × | | × | |
| Graminaeae | Aristida purpurea Nutt. | Purple three-awn | | × | | × |
| | Bouteloua curtipendula (Michx.) Torr. | Sideoats grama | | × | | × |
| | Bouteloua gracilis (H.B.K.) Griffiths | Blue grama | × | × | × | × |
| | Bouteloua hirsuta Lag. | Hairy grama | | × | | × |
| | Buchloe dactyloides (Nutt.) Engelm | Buffalo grass | × | | | × |
| | Cenchrus incertus M. A. Curtis | Coast sandbur | × | | | |
| | Chloris cucullata Bisch. | Hooded windmill grass | | × | | × |
| | Chloris verticillata Nutt. | Tumble windmill grass | | × | | × |
| | Panicum obtusum H.B.K. | Vine mesquite | × | | | |
| | Schedonnardis paniculatus (Nutt.) Trel. | Tumble grass | | × | | × |
| | Shizachyrium scoparium (Michx.) Nash | Little bluestem | | × | | |
| | Sorghum halepense (L.) Pers. | Johnson grass | × | | × | |
| | Sporobolus cryptandrus (Torr.) Gray | Sand dropseed | × | × | × | × |
| Labiate | Monarda pectinata Nutt. | Plains bee balm | | | | × |
| Leguminosae | Astragalus gracilis Nutt. | Locoweed | × | | | |
| | Astragalus mollissimus Torr. | Woolly locoweed | | × | | |
| | Astragalus praelongus Sheld. | Locoweed | × | | | |
| | Dalea formosa Torr. | Feather dalea | | × | | |
| | Hoffmanseggia jamesii T. & G. | James's rush pea | × | | × | |
| | Mimosa biuncifera Benth. | Catclaw mimosa | | × | | |
| | Prosopis glandulosa Torr. | Honey mesquite | × | × | × | × |
| Liliaceae | Yucca angustifolia Pursh | Narrowleaf yucca | × | × | | × |
| Loasaceae | Metzelia stricta (Woot & Standl) Darl | Sand lily | | × | | |
| Linaceae | Linum pratense (Nort.) Small | Meadow flax | × | | × | |
| Malvaceae | Sphaeralcea coccinea (Pursh.) Rydb. | Scarlet globe mallow | | | | × |
| | Sphaeralcea angustifolia (Cav.) D. Don | Copper mallow | × | × | × | × |
| Onagraceae | Oenothera greggii Gray | Evening primrose | | × | | × |
| | Oenothera missouriensis Sims | Evening primrose | | × | | × |
| | Gaura coccinea Pursh | Scarlet gaura | | × | | |

Table 4.1. *Continued*

| Family | Genus and Species | Common Name | Yellowhouse Draw Lowland | Yellowhouse Draw Upland | Lubbock Lake Reservoir Area Lowland | Lubbock Lake Reservoir Area Upland |
|---|---|---|---|---|---|---|
| Papaveraceae | *Argemone squarrosa* Green | Prickly poppy | × | | | |
| Plantaginaceae | *Plantago patagonica* Jacq. | Woolly plantain | × | | | |
| Polygalaceae | *Polygala alba* Nutt. | White milkwort | | × | | |
| Polygonaceae | *Eriogonum annuum* Nutt. | Annual buckwheat | × | | | |
| | *Rumex crispus* L.* | Curly dock | × | | | |
| Solanaceae | *Physalis viscosa* L. | Ground cherry | × | | × | |
| | *Solanum eleagnifolium* Cav. | Silverleaf nightshade | × | × | × | × |
| | *Solanum rostratum* Dun. | Buffalo bur | × | | × | |

*Introduced species.

Along Yellowhouse Draw the Berda series is the equivalent of the unburied Lubbock Lake Soil, developed in substratum 4B (Holliday and Allen, chap. 9; Holliday, 1985d). This soil often meets the qualifications for Ustocrept or Calciustoll (Holliday and Allen, chap. 9; Holliday, 1985d). The Bippus series is the equivalent of the unburied Lubbock Lake Soil found along the valley axis (Holliday, 1985d). This soil generally meets the qualifications for a Calciustoll (Holliday, 1985d). In some lowland localities soils are formed in substratum 5A or 5B (Apache and Singer Soils, respectively). A formal series has not been defined for these soils, and they vary from Entisols to Inceptisols to Mollisols (Holliday, 1985d). Two lowland draw localities are within areas classified as Arents owing to modern construction. However, all lowland draw localities support similar species.

The most conspicuous species are grasses. Blue grama, buffalo grass, coast sandbur (*Sorghum halapense*), and sand dropseed are common. The family Compositae (sunflower family) is well represented. Narrow-leaf yucca and honey mesquite are also found in large numbers.

Because the draw has been subjected to disturbance by off-road vehicles, pioneering species in early secondary succession, such as Belvedere summer cypress (*Kohia scoparia*), Russian thistle (*Salsola kali*), lamb's-quarters (*Chenopodium album*), redroot pigweed (*Amaranthus retroflexus*), silverleaf nightshade (*Solanum eleagnifolium*), tumble mustard (*Sisymbrium altissimum*), and goathead (*Tribulus terrestris*) are becoming dominant in the lowlands. At one draw locality (the reservoir cut) Siberian elm (*Ulmus pumila*) is dominant. These trees were introduced from Asia and were planted during the 1930s. The Siberian elms have been successfully regenerating in specific areas.

The upland area at the reservoir-cut locality (figs. 4.1, 4.4a) is situated on the Blanco Formation bedrock that crops out as the inside of the entrenched meander of Yellowhouse Draw (Holliday and Allen, chap. 9). The soil on this outcrop is mapped as the Berda loam (Blackstock, 1979; fig. 4.2). The soil is, however, an undefined series and varies from an Entisol to a Mollisol, depending on the thickness of the A horizon (Holliday, 1985d).

The upland reservoir-cut locality is dominated by grass species. The species included are purple three-awn, sideoats grama, blue grama, hairy grama, buffalo grass, hooded windmill grass (*Chloris curcullata*), tumble windmill grass

(*C. verticillata*), tumble grass (*Schendonnardis paniculatus*), and sand dropseed. Various species of Compositae, including western ragweed (*Ambrosia psilostachya*), perennial broomweed (*Xanthocephalum sarothrae*), and stemmed bitterweed, are common. Honey mesquite, narrowleaf yucca, brown-spine prickly pear, and other species are found but are not numerous. As in the lowland draw locality, disturbance in the upland reservoir-cut locality has allowed pioneering species in secondary succession to increase in dominance. Belvedere summer cypress and Russian thistle are very common.

The lowland reservoir-cut locality (fig. 4.4b) is subjected to great disturbance. This locality includes the dry reservoir basin and surrounding areas where dredge piles were dumped during the 1930s. This area was flooded briefly during heavy rains in 1972 and has since been disturbed by archaeological excavations. Although the lowland-site locality is mapped as a Bippus clay loam (Blackstock, 1979; fig. 4.2), considerable variation exists in the soil at the surface, depending on the geologic situation (Holliday and Allen, chap. 9).

Pioneer species in secondary succession (Belvedere summer cypress, Russian thistle, lamb's-quarters, tumble mustard, redroot pigweed, annual sunflower [*Helianthus annuus*], and cocklebur [*Xanthium strumarium*]) dominate all nonwoody species at the lowland reservoir-cut locality. Siberian elm, salt cedar (*Tamarix ramosisima*), and scattered honey mesquite trees are well established around the perimeter of the reservoir basin. Salsify (*Tragopogon dubius*) and salt cedar are introduced species. They are the only species unique to the lowland reservoir-cut locality. Many of the species found in the lowland reservoir-cut locality are also present in the lowland draw localities. However, the species are not as abundant in the reservoir-cut area as they are in the draw.

## HISTORIC FLORA

Little is known about the historic flora at the Landmark. A spring-fed lake existed in the reservoir-cut area in the late 1800s (Holden, 1962a). Lowering of the water table reduced the lake to a grass-covered marsh until the reservoir was dredged in the 1930s. A photograph taken of a portion

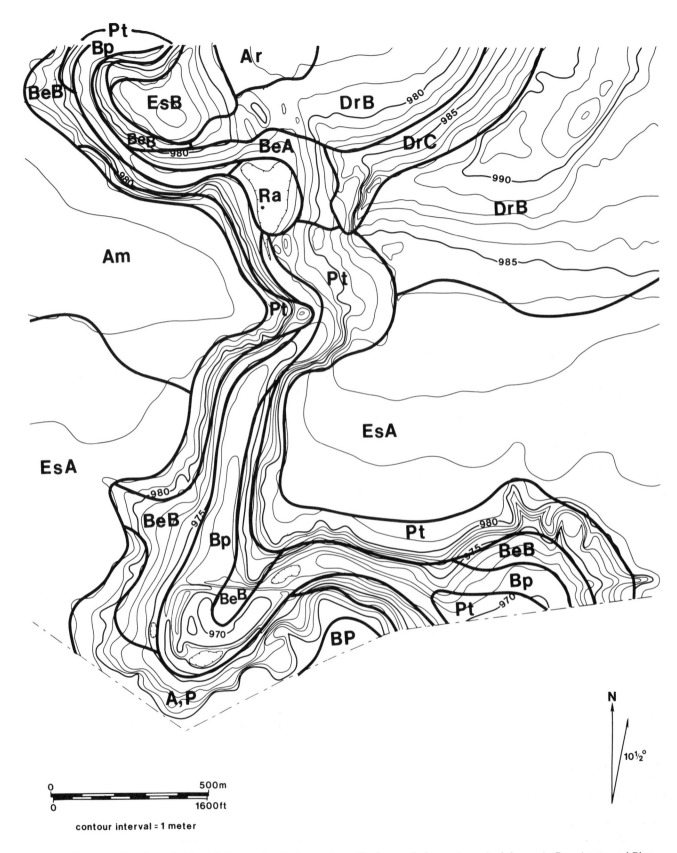

Fig. 4.2. Modern soil series at Lubbock Lake Landmark. Am = Amarillo fine sandy loam; Ar = Arch loam; A, P = Arents and Pits; Be = Berda loam; Bp = Bippus clay loam; BP = Bippus-Potter association; DrB = Drake clay loam, 1–3% slopes; DrC = Drake clay loam, 3–5% slopes; EsA = Estacado clay loam, 0–1% slopes; EsB = Estacado clay loam, 1–3% slopes; Pt = Potter loam; Ra = Randall clay; BeA = Berda loam, 1–3% slopes; BeB = Berda loam, 3–5% slopes.

Fig. 4.3. a: a typical upland-draw locality; b: a typical lowland-draw locality (photographs by Jerome L. Thompson).

Fig. 4.4. a: a typical upland-site locality; b: a typical lowland-site locality (photographs by Jerome L. Thompson).

of the reservoir in 1939 (fig. 4.5a) shows plants at the edge of the water that may be bullrushes (*Scirpus* sp.). The saplings in the photograph are Siberian elms planted by the fire department in 1938. The same location (fig. 4.5b) is considerably different today. The reservoir is dry, bullrushes are absent, and Siberian elms have proliferated.

Holden (1962b) stated that in 1541 Coronado reported tall grasses near lakes and streams on the Southern High Plains that reached the stirrups of saddled horses. He concluded that Coronado was referring to switch grass (*Panicum virgatum*), sideoats grama, and big bluestem (*Andropogon gerardii*). Other accounts of the flora are contained in reports to Congress by military explorers who traversed the area in the middle 1800s.

All the early explorations followed the same route. On the way to Santa Fe the Southern High Plains was traversed on the north along the Canadian River. The return trip was made along the southern and eastern edges of the area. As late as 1859 maps of the Southwest label the Southern High Plains as unexplored (Emory, 1857–59). Because only peripheral areas were explored, the flora of the unexplored areas must be inferred.

Sketchy information on the flora is contained in some explorers' personal journals. Marcy (1850:42) recorded the lack of trees and shrubs on the "high table land" and reported that "the only herbage upon these barren plains is a very short buffalo grass." Later in his explorations Marcy (1850:62) described a lake in the southern region of the Southern High Plains that was about three feet deep, covered several acres, and had "rushes" growing in it. Pope (1885:28) reported that "more than one half the surface of the plains . . . furnishes grama grass in abundance and mesquite root entirely sufficient to supply fuel for all parties crossing it, in whatever numbers."

Fig. 4.5. A portion of the reservoir in 1939 (Pit A area) showing (a) bullrushes (*Scirpus* sp.) at the water's edge and (b) Siberian elm (*Ulmus pumila*) saplings (photographs from files at The Museum, Texas Tech University).

Botanical specimens were collected on the Southern High Plains by the Pope expedition and identified and reported by Torrey and Gray (1855). Several species listed by Torrey and Gray (1855) are found in the modern flora at Lubbock Lake. Gordon's bladderpod (*Lesquerella gordonii*), copper mallow (*Sphaeralcea augustifolia*), white milkwort, woolly locoweed, James's rush pea (*Hoffmanseggia jamesii*), Tahoka daisy (*Macheranthera tanacetifolia*), and wavy-leaf thistle are included. Two species, bullrush (*Scirpus lacustris*) and spikerush (*Eleocharis obstusa*), reported by Torrey and Gray (in Pope, 1855) may have been in the vicinity of the reservoir area as recently as 1939.

## FOSSIL FLORA

Bryant and Schoenwetter (chap. 5) present a discussion of the palynological work conducted at Lubbock Lake. Green (1962) recovered a few plant macrofossils. Most plant remains discussed in this chapter were recovered during four summers (1973–76) of LLP excavations at the site. The standard use of matrix washing techniques greatly increased the quantity of plant macrofossils recovered from the various stratigraphic units.

This type of recovery technique may be constricting the size of the returned sample. It is possible that plant remains, particularly seeds, smaller than 1.5 mm were lost through the screens during washing. However, plant remains have not been recovered in matrix· concentrates from the 0.55-mm–mesh screen used in processing snail-column samples. Although the recovered sample is relatively small, it has provided some interesting supportive evidence for the zooarchaeological and geological interpretations of former environments at the site.

### Stratum 1

Bullrush (*Scirpus* sp.), spikerush (*Eleocharis* sp.), netleaf hackberry (*Celtis reticulata*), seepweed (*Suaeda* sp.), and gromwell (*Lithospermum* sp.) seeds were found in stratum 1. Spikerush is unique to substratum 1B in Area 6. Seepweed and gromwell are found only in substratum 1B in Area 2. Bullrush and netleaf hackberry occurred in stratum 1, but only in Area 2 (table 4.2).

Pollen remains from stratum 1 show evidence of grasslands in the area (Oldfield and Schoenwetter, 1975). Johnson (chap. 8) proposes on the basis of the paleontological evidence that the area away from the stream was a parkland habitat. Although no grass seeds were recovered in this study, Pierce (chap. 6) reports that unidentified grass seeds were recovered from stratum 1 in gastropod samples. Evidence of netleaf hackberry and gromwell does not conflict with a parkland interpretation.

The occurrence of seepweed in substratum 1B poses some questions related to the association with the other plants. Seepweed species are currently restricted to saline and alkaline soils (Correll and Johnston, 1970). Geologic evidence for the presence of a saline or alkaline habitat is lacking from stratum 1. Perhaps certain seepweed species had different habitat requirements in the past and were part of the proposed parkland habitat. Another consideration is that localized saline or alkaline habitats could have existed upstream and the seed remains washed in.

### Stratum 2

Substratum 2e in Area 4 yielded seeds of bullrush and gaura (*Gaura* sp.). Although bullrush is a hydrophyte, geologic evidence indicates that the seed remains were blown in, rather than growing in the immediate area.

Table 4.2. Plant Macrofossils Recovered from Lubbock Lake

| Genus and Species | 5ℓ | 5B | 5A | 4B | 4A | 3ℓ | 2e | 2s | A Horizon (Firstview) Soil | Mid-2B | Lower 2B | 2A | 1B | 1A |
|---|---|---|---|---|---|---|---|---|---|---|---|---|---|---|
| *Argemone sp.* | × | | | | | | | | | | | | | |
| *Celtus reticulata* | × | | | | | | | × | × | | | | × | × |
| *Chara sp.* | | | | | | | | | | | | × | | |
| *Chenopodium sp.* | | | | | | | | | | × | | | | |
| *Eleocharis sp.* | | | | | | | | | | | | × | × | |
| *Equisetum sp.* | | | | | | | | | | | | × | | |
| *Gaura sp.* | | | | | | | × | × | | | | | | |
| Leguminosae (unidentified genera) | | | | | | × | | | | | | | | |
| *Lithospermum sp.* | | | | | | | | | | | | | | × |
| *Nymphaea* sp. | | | | | × | × | | | | | | | | |
| *Proboscidea sp.* | × | | | | | | | × | | | | | | |
| *Prosopis sp.* | | | × | | | | | | | | | | | |
| *Scirpus sp.* | × | × | × | × | | × | × | × | × | × | × | × | × | × |
| *Solanum sp.* | | × | | | | | | | | | | | | |
| *Solanum rostratum* | | × | | | | | | × | | | | | | |
| *Suaeda sp.* | | | | | | | | | | | | | | × |

Bullrush and netleaf hackberry seeds were recovered from the A horizon of the Firstview Soil in Areas 5 and 6. This soil represents a spring-fed marsh; and Johnson (chaps.7, 8) reports evidence of marsh-dwelling animals, such as ducks, mud turtles, red-bellied water snakes, and bullfrogs. The evidence of bullrush is supportive of these interpretations. Although netleaf hackberry is not a marsh plant, it may have been present away from the watercourse.

Bullrush seeds were found in substantial numbers in substratum 2s in Area 9. Remains of buffalo bur (*Solanum rostratum*), gaura, devil's-claw (*Proboscidea* sp.), and netleaf hackberry occasionally occurred. Substratum 2s is thought to be a shore facies of a pond deposit (Holliday and Allen, chap. 2; Holliday, 1985d). Again, bullrush seeds support that conclusion. The other genera recovered from substratum 2s are not hydrophytes. However, buffalo bur, netleaf hackberry, and some species of devil's-claw are found at relatively moist lowland localities. Species of guara are normally found in dry, sandy soil (Correll and Johnston, 1970). The gaura specimen found probably indicates transportation from an upland locality in the area.

Bullrush, goosefoot (*Chenopodium* sp.), and spikerush seeds were found in substrata 2A and 2B from Areas 5 and 6. Positive molds of *Chara* sp. (fig. 4.6a) and horsetail (cf. *Equisetum*) (fig. 4.6b) were recovered from 2A.

Strong evidence indicates that freshwater ponds were present during the deposition of substrata 2A and 2B (Holliday and Allen, chap. 2; Holliday, 1985b, c; Stafford, 1981; Compton, 1975). Johnson (chaps. 7, 8) reports pond-dwelling animals (such as bullfrogs; snapping, mud, and pond turtles; ducks; and muskrats) from these substrata. The fossil flora remains give credence to the existence of a pond ecosystem at this time. Bullrush, spikerush, horsetail, and *Chara* are found in hydric habitats.

Pollen evidence (Oldfield, 1975; Schoenwetter, 1975)

from substrata 2A and 2B indicate pine spruce, cattail (*Typha*), and sedges and rushes (Cyperaceae). The fossil seeds recovered support the pollen evidence of rushes. However, the seed evidence does not support the occurrence of pine and spruce pollen. Bryant and Schoenwetter (chap. 5) discuss the discrepancies in the pollen record at the site.

## Stratum 3

Bullrush and water lily (*Nymphaea* sp.) seeds were recovered from substratum 3ℓ in Area 6 together with one unidentified Leguminosae (pea family) seed. This material is in agreement with the geologic evidence that 3ℓ is a marsh deposit.

## Stratum 4

Two bullrush seeds were recovered in a sample from substratum 4B, and one water-lily seed was recovered from a sample in substratum 4A. The number of seeds was too small to be considered significant.

## Stratum 5

Stratum 5 yielded the largest number of plant macrofossils (over 5,000 seeds). Most of the seeds came from substratum 5ℓ and were collected from excavation Areas 1, 5, 6, and 9. Bullrush dominates the inventory of seeds. Devil's-claw, netleaf hackberry, and prickly poppy (*Argemone* sp.) are present, but only in small numbers.

Substratum 5ℓ is considered a marsh deposit. The fossil-seed evidence of bullrush supports this interpretation. The

Fig. 4.6. Fossil plant impressions from substratum 2A. a: *Chara* sp.; b: *Equisetum* sp. (horsetail) (photographs by Jerome L. Thompson).

evidence of bullrush further supports the historic report (Holden, 1962a) of a lake and marsh at the site. Johnson (chaps. 7, 8) notes the occurrence of yellow mud turtle, pond slider, and leopard frog from substratum 5ℓ. The fossil-seed evidence, historic records, geology, and paleontology reflect the hydric ecosystem at the site during this time. The occurrence of devil's claw, netleaf hackberry, and prickly poppy is indicative of the modern flora. Although prickly poppy is the only one of these plants present at the site, devil's-claw and netleaf hackberry are found farther downstream in Yellowhouse Draw.

Fossil seeds from substrata 5A and 5B were recovered in small amounts from Area 8. Bullrush, nightshade (*Solanum* sp.), and mesquite (*Prosopis* sp.) were represented. The number of seeds was too small to be considered significant.

## POTENTIAL PLANT RESOURCE UTILIZATION

The recovery of plant macrofossils from archaeological fea-tures at the site, such as hearths or cache pits, has not occurred, and no human-modified plant materials, such as baskets, cordage, sandals, or quids, have been recovered. However, since some of the genera found in the modern, historic, and fossil floral records have demonstrated economic value, speculations can be made on the potential for utilization.

Bullrush, or tule, is by far the most common type of plant macrofossil recovered from Lubbock Lake. It is found in nearly all the stratigraphic units and was present at the site until recently. Bullrushes can be used as a food and fiber source during all seasons. During the spring young shoots can be gathered and eaten raw. Later the base of the stalk can be eaten, but it is somewhat tougher (Harrington, 1972:24). When in flower, bullrush pollen can be gathered to be mixed with meal. After seeds develop, they can be collected and ground into meal. The rhizomatous rootstocks can be dried and ground into meal. The rootstocks can be collected in any season. Rootstock of the species *Scirpus validus* was found to contain up to 8% sugar and 5.5% starch and less than 1% protein (Harrington, 1972:24). The stems of bullrush species provide a narrow, pliable fiber source that can be used for weaving baskets, mats, or sandals.

Cattails, though not present among the macrofossils recovered from the site, were present in the pollen records of Oldfield (1975) and Schoenwetter (1975). Cattails can still be found downstream from the site in Yellowhouse Draw. Cattails, like bullrush species, can be a year-round source of food and fiber. The new shoots can be harvested in the spring and eaten raw or cooked. Later in the spring and early summer the young flower stalks can be roasted like corn. The pollen can also be collected and used as meal, as can the seeds.

The rootstocks can be utilized year round for food. They can be eaten raw or dried and pounded into flour (Niethammer, 1974:88). The flour from the rootstocks contains 80% carbohydrates and 6 to 8% protein (Harrington, 1972:13). Cattail pollen can be a rich source of carotene (vitamin A) (Bleything, 1972:22). Cattail leaves are a good source of weaving materials for mats and baskets. The "down" or "fluff" that appears on the cattail bloom spike at the end of the growing season may be used as insulation or as tinder for fire making (Harrington, 1972; Niethammer, 1974; Bleything, 1972).

Water lily is another hydrophyte of potential economic value. Seed evidence of this plant is limited at the site (substrata 3ℓ and 4A). Water lilies have thick, horizontal rhizomes, or rootstocks, which are anchored in the sediment at the bottom of shallow ponds and streams. These rootstocks, like those of cattails and bullrushes, can be gathered, dried, and pulverized into meal (Harrington, 1972:16). Harrington (1972:16) states that muskrats often stored the rootstocks in their dens and that the Indians raided the caches. The seed pods of water-lily species can be collected and roasted for food (Harrington, 1972:16; Medsger, 1966:116).

Evidence of netleaf hackberry is found in many stratigraphic units at the site (1, 2s, upper 2B, and 5ℓ) and is still present in localities downstream from the site in Yellow-house Draw. Netleaf hackberry, or sugarberry, can be a large shrub or a small tree. The fruit is a fleshy drupe about 8 to 9 mm in diameter, often beaked, and reddish or reddish-black. It has a sweet flesh that ripens in late summer. The fruit can be eaten when ripe or sun-dried for future use. Niethammer (1974:72) reports that the Papago and Apache ground or mashed the fruit into cakes and dried them for winter use. Wheat (1955) reported finding a cache of hack-berry seeds at a Protohistoric site in Yellowhouse Canyon (southeast Lubbock County).

Evidence of mesquite was found in substratum 5A at the site. Pope (1855:28) reported the occurrence of mesquite on the Llano Estacado in the 1850s, and this tree is common at the site today. It is a member of the pea family (Leguminosae), and seeds, or beans, are found in long pods on the tree. When ripe, these pods can be gathered, dried, stored, and ground as needed into a nutritious meal. The meal can be formed with water into cakes that can be dried and stored for future use (Niethammer, 1974:42). This meal provided high amounts of protein, carbohydrates, and calcium. Sixty grams of meal (approximately 4 tablespoons) contains 70 calories (Niethammer, 1974:42). Mesquite provides an excellent source of firewood since it makes a hot, long-burning fire.

Devil's-claw seeds occur in two stratigraphic units at the site (2s and 4–5ℓ). The fruit of this low-spreading annual is a curved, double-beaked capsule 10 to 15 cm long. When mature, it is black and very woody. The young fruit can be boiled while it is still green. The mature dry seeds are also edible. The seeds contain about 36% oil. The oil is very similar to sunflower and cottonseed oil (Niethammer, 1974: 94). Fiber can be obtained from the dry, mature seedpod and frequently occurs as the black design element in Pima and Papago basketry (Niethammer, 1974:95).

## SUMMARY

Evidence from the fossil-seed remains is generally compatible with the geologically and paleontologically based environmental interpretations for all stratigraphic units at the site. From the plant macrofossils it can be determined that a hydric ecosystem of one form of another existed at the site from the late Pleistocene until recently. The fossil-seed remains do not lend themselves to any definite statements concerning the flora outside this ecosystem.

From many sites throughout North America good evidence exists that the prehistoric inhabitants utilized the native flora in their economies. Whether or not these plants were utilized in these manners or utilized at all at Lubbock Lake is speculative. Until further research is conducted, the possibility of the utilization of resources will have to suffice, not as evidence of their use but as general information.

# 5. Pollen Records from Lubbock Lake

VAUGHN M. BRYANT, JR., AND JAMES SCHOENWETTER

The paleoenvironmental conditions that existed on the Southern High Plains are subjects of great interest in many disciplines. Paleontologists interpret the faunal record (Lundelius et al., 1983) to suggest that the region was an ideal breeding ground for a wide variety and fairly large number of Pleistocene animals for thousands of years. They ponder the sudden extinction of much of this fauna and search for environmental or other causes. Archaeologists (Sellards, 1952; Wormington, 1957; Johnson and Holliday, 1980, 1981, 1985) have long studied the elusive record of Paleoindian occupations on the Southern High Plains. They want to know what kinds of vegetation and climate existed during the Paleoindian era in hopes that the information will provide clues to Early Man's activities and possible dietary habits. Geologists (Haynes, 1975; Holliday, 1985b) note that the Southern High Plains contain a wide variety of late Quaternary sediments and the remains of large basins that once held considerable amounts of permanent water. They want to determine the factors that created those lakes and caused them to disappear. Ecologists such as Van Devender et al. (1977) found in wood-rat nests the remains of plants that no longer grow in areas bordering the Southern High Plains, and they wonder what ancient climatic and vegetational conditions may have existed during the late Pleistocene.

A number of individuals have tried to reconstruct the ancient vegetational and climatic sequences through the study and interpretation of fossil pollen recovered from sites in or near the Southern High Plains. One of the first to undertake such a study was Hafsten (1961), who examined samples from a number of deposits on the Southern High Plains, including Lubbock Lake. Wendorf (1961b) offered interpretations of certain late Pleistocene environmental conditions for the Southern High Plains based on a synthesis of palynological, faunal, and geological evidence. Oldfield and Schoenwetter's (1964, 1975) work reexamined some of the original sampling locations studied by Hafsten (1961) and expanded his study to include new sites. Wendorf (1970, 1975) used the information obtained by Oldfield and Schoenwetter (1975) to present new paleoenvironmental and vegetational interpretations for the Southern High Plains.

The paleoenvironmental record of the Southern High Plains and more specifically the Lubbock Lake area is still not fully resolved. Problems with original and subsequent interpretations of the geologic record and with sediment and fossil-pollen chronologies and suspicions about the accuracy of some of the radiocarbon dates add to the difficulty of producing a complete and reliable record for the Southern High Plains.

The most recent attempt to interpret the paleoenviron-mental record of the Southern High Plains was that by Bryant and Holloway (1983). They summarized all of the previous fossil-pollen studies from the Southern High Plains and offered their own interpretations of the paleovegetational conditions that existed during portions of the late Pleistocene and Holocene. However, new and intensive studies of the geology, paleontology, soils, fossil-pollen, and vegetation (similar to the studies conducted at Lubbock Lake) need to be completed for a number of other areas on the Southern High Plains. Only when such studies are completed can data that currently exist be better evaluated.

## LUBBOCK LAKE POLLEN RECORDS

### Earlier Studies

One of the most difficult problems for paleoenvironmental reconstruction of the Lubbock Lake area centers on the interpretation of the existing fossil-pollen records (Hafsten, 1961, Wendorf, 1961b, 1970, 1975; Oldfield, 1975; Schoenwetter, 1975; Oldfield and Schoenwetter, 1964, 1975). This problem is complicated by the difficulties in recovering fossil pollen from Lubbock Lake sediments. In the late 1950s, for example, Hafsten (1961) collected and examined 32 sediment samples from the Lubbock Lake reservoir area as part of a larger study focusing on the paleoenvironmental reconstruction of West Texas during the past 30,000+ years of history. However, he was unable to find any fossil pollen in the Lubbock Lake sediments.

Soon after Hafsten's (1961) initial study Oldfield and Schoenwetter (1964) analyzed additional sediment samples from the Lubbock Lake reservoir area for fossil pollen. Their analysis and detailed report were completed and submitted to the Museum of New Mexico in 1963, and a short note was published (Oldfield and Schoenwetter, 1964). Publication of the full report was delayed until the mid-1970s (Oldfield, 1975; Schoenwetter, 1975; Oldfield and Schoenwetter, 1975). In his study Schoenwetter (1975) analyzed two separate groups of samples that had been collected from the site by Hester and used those data to construct two pollen diagrams. He reported that extracting the fossil pollen required the processing of large volumes of sediment and that the analysis phase was made difficult by low fossil-pollen yield and the poor state of pollen preservation. Fossil-pollen counts from his 21 samples ranged from a low of 21 grains in one sample to a high of 338 grains in another.

Oldfield (1975) examined a third column of samples from Lubbock Lake sediments and encountered many problems during the extraction and analysis phase. He finally decided to use 13 of the Lubbock Lake sediment samples containing pollen counts ranging from 100 to 200 grains as a basis for constructing a third fossil-pollen diagram representing the paleovegetational change at Lubbock Lake. Thus by the mid-1970s the combined effort of three palynologists produced three different pollen records for the deposits at Lubbock Lake.

Although they believed that the pollen sequence from Lubbock Lake was incomplete, Oldfield and Schoenwetter (1975) used their data in conjunction with pollen records from other sites to suggest a paleovegetational sequence for the Southern High Plains. At Lubbock Lake the portion of the regional sequence that they thought was represented began with the latter part of the period that Wendorf (1961d) originally called the Scharbauer Interval (ca. 12,000–11,000 B.P.) but was renamed White Lake interval by Oldfield and Schoenwetter (1975). The Lubbock Lake sequence ended with the period Oldfield and Schoenwetter (1975) called the Yellowhouse Interval (ca. 10,000–9000 B.P.). The analysis of other West Texas sediments, combined with their data from Blackwater Draw, Lubbock Lake, and Anderson Basin led them to conclude that between ca. 14,000 and 9000 B.P. there were two periods during which the existing conifer tree cover expanded. Oldfield and Schoenwetter (1975) suggested that during these wetter episodes small stands of pine and spruce developed in habitats along streams, near draws, and in protected locales at higher elevations. High frequencies of Chenopodiaceae and composite pollen in some West Texas sediments and persistent percentages of *Ephedra* (Mormon tea) and grass pollen at other locales led them to conclude that fluctuations occurred in the total area of grasslands at the expense of pine parklands in West Texas during dry periods between ca. 14,000–13,000 and 12,000–11,000 B.P. In summary they concluded that 12,000–11,000 B.P. the Southern High Plains, including Lubbock Lake, could be characterized as supporting fewer trees than at an earlier time (Blackwater Subpluvial), when more pines may have been present in nearby areas, and at a later time (Lubbock Subpluvial), when the pines again returned in greater numbers.

Originally Wendorf (1961b, 1970) and others thought that the paleovegetational conditions during the Lubbock Subpluvial were a critical issue, since that period was thought to mark the end of the Pleistocene and the beginning of the Holocene. Lubbock Subpluvial horizon deposits were given added importance at Lubbock Lake because they were thought to date to the time period characterized by the activities of Folsom Paleoindians.

According to Wendorf (1970), the Lubbock Subpluvial episode dated to a time period between 10,300 and 10,600 B.P., which would place it at the very end of what Hafsten (1961) had termed the late-glacial interval. On the basis of the available pollen, diatom, and invertebrate faunal assemblages sampled in and around the Lubbock Lake reservoir area, Wendorf (1960) characterized the Lubbock Subpluvial as a period when cooler and moister climates prevailed on the Southern High Plains. Furthermore, he suggested, the return of cooler conditions with more available moisture resulted in the recolonization of Lubbock Lake by fairly dense conifer forests composed primarily of pines and spruce.

Wendorf's (1970) interpretation was based in part on Oldfield and Schoenwetter's (1975) yet unpublished report. In that report, however, they argued that climatic interpretation of the pollen data was not justified for the Southern High Plains as a whole, and especially not for specific portions such as those that included Lubbock Lake (Oldfield and Schoenwetter, 1975:169–70). They suggested that the most direct nonchronological inferences that could be made confidently about the pollen record were only those that identified the nature and the direction of regional ecological change. Paleovegetational reconstructions for the Southern High Plains should be viewed as secondary, derived inferences.

In the Lubbock Subpluvial-age sediments at Lubbock Lake, Oldfield (1975:138–40) found high percentages of fossil pine pollen (ranging from 30 to 70% with small traces of spruce pollen), while Schoenwetter (1975:112–13) found 60% fossil pine pollen in his sample. In addition, they noted that the Lubbock Subpluvial episode was evidenced by a relative increase in pine pollen in deposits of the San Jon, Crane Lake, and White Lake sites and in the diatomite deposits at Blackwater Draw, Plainview, and Anderson Basin. In their interpretation of the Lubbock Subpluvial interval Oldfield and Schoenwetter (1975) stated that the high percentages of pine pollen during that period at Lubbock Lake probably reflected a record influenced by better situations for tree growth along the edges of the draws of the Southern High Plains, where shelter and available moisture would have been at a maximum.

## Later Studies

Attempts to obtain additional fossil pollen data from Lubbock Lake did not stop after the completion of Oldfield and Schoenwetter's (1964, 1975) studies. In 1973, Bryant collected a total of 20 sediment samples from all principal strata and with the help of another palynologist (Dean) processed and examined all 20 samples. Their study revealed that some samples contained very minimal amounts of very poorly preserved fossil pollen and that none contained sufficient concentrations of fossil pollen to permit a statistically valid analysis. After trying other processing techniques on the same 20 samples, they concluded that pollen counts of 100 to 200 grains might be possible for a few of the samples. However, they estimated that to count sufficient numbers of fossil pollen grains from any one sample would require an estimated 10 to 40 hours of microscope work. They decided not to proceed further with the Lubbock Lake fossil pollen analysis for lack of funding and time. Furthermore, both felt that even if they invested the hundreds of hours needed to compile 100 to 200 grain counts for the samples the resulting data base probably would not be interpretable as an accurate reflection of paleovegetational conditions. The low density of pollen in the samples very strongly suggested the loss of certain pollen types through differential preservation.

In 1975, Bryant returned to Lubbock Lake to collect additional sediment samples to test the hypothesis that some of the newly exposed excavation areas might include strata containing preserved fossil pollen. On that trip Bryant and another palynologist, Weir, collected 50 samples from all principal strata of the site. Thirty-six of those sediment samples were subsequently processed by a variety of pollen-extraction procedures that had proved effective for recovering fossil pollen from similar arid southwestern environments. The results were essentially the same as those obtained from the 1973 study. Some of the new samples contained minimal amounts of fossil pollen, but they were poorly preserved and degraded and consisted mainly of durable types or types that were easy to identify because of their obvious morphological features. Mainly pollen from genera in the plant families Compositae, Chenopodiaceae, Poaceae, and Pinaceae were identifiable. Other pollen grains were so damaged that correct identification was impossible.

In 1977, Schoenwetter received two sediment samples from stratum 2 that had been collected by Holliday from deposits at Lubbock Lake. With the samples was a request that he process them using an extraction technique dissimilar from any other technique he had previously used and different from those used by Oldfield or Bryant. One of the two samples yielded sufficient pollen for a count, while the other did not.

In 1977 another effort to collect fossil pollen from the Lubbock Lake vicinity was attempted by McLaughlin (1978). She processed nine sediment samples from the stratum 2 equivalent in Yellowhouse Draw a few kilometers downstream from Lubbock Lake. Her attempt to recover fossil pollen was partly successful because she was able to derive analytical counts ranging from 100 to 294 grains for six of the nine samples. However, most of the pollen grains were very poorly preserved. One of the other three samples contained very few fossil pollen grains and thus was not countable. The remaining two samples were considered marginal in terms of fossil-pollen preservation and quantity. However, McLaughlin (1978) noted that these two samples could probably yield sufficient fossil-pollen counts if many hours of analysis time were spent examining the materials.

McLaughlin's (1978) fossil-pollen counts contained high percentages (60–90%) of chenopod and composite pollen with corresponding low percentages (5–20%) of grass and pine pollen. She interpreted her data to be similar to the fossil-pollen results obtained by Oldfield and Schoenwetter (1975) for the upper part of their White Lake interval. She made no mention of her low pine counts in relation to the higher pine counts encountered by Oldfield and Schoenwetter (1975) for portions of what they considered sediments of the Lubbock Subpluvial interval.

Several recent studies present insights that may help clarify the reasons why high percentages of pine pollen were found at Lubbock Lake and that question the validity of the concept of the Lubbock Subpluvial proposed by Wendorf

(1970). Hall (Holliday et al., 1985b) analyzed a series of soil samples collected from the buried A horizon of the Firstview Soil and found that pine and some spruce comprised almost all of the fossil pollen recovered from each of the examined sediment samples. He noted further that all of the fossil pollen in those samples was either highly corroded or degraded and that the total pollen concentration per gram of sediment was low. The poor preservation and almost total absence of fossil-pollen types other than pine and spruce led Hall (personal communication, 1985) to suspect that a wider variety of pollen types was probably deposited as part of the ancient pollen rain during the formation of the Firstview Soil. Perhaps suddenly or perhaps over a long period of time the more fragile pollen types become degraded and destroyed, and only the most durable types such as pine and spruce were left behind. From his analysis of fossil pollen from Lubbock Lake, Hall (Holliday et al., 1985b) concluded that the high percentages of conifer pollen in sediments assigned to the Lubbock Subpluvial were primarily a result of the overrepresentation of conifer pollen created by differential pollen preservation and/or initial overrepresentation in the pollen rain. Therefore, Hall (personal communication, 1985) suggested that those pollen spectra should not be used for vegetational or climatic reconstructions.

Schoenwetter responded negatively to Hall's assessment of the situation for two reasons. First, the pollen records from Southern High Plains sites assigned to the Lubbock Subpluvial period were not similar to those described by Hall from the Firstview Soil. The Lubbock Subpluvial samples contained more conifer pollen than samples believed to be older or younger, ranging from 30 to 75% in conifer-pollen frequency. In Hall's Firstview Soil samples conifer pollen comprised almost all of the pollen observed. Second, Oldfield and Schoenwetter (1975:167) recognized that the percentages of fossil-conifer pollen at Lubbock Lake and other nearby draw sites were more prominent than they were in Lubbock Subpluvial deposits at playa sites. They also acknowledged that the contrast in percentages could be due partly to overrepresentation resulting from differential preservation. However, that interpretation was presented only as a possibility. They preferred the interpretation that the protected slopes and margins of the draws offered better situations for tree growth than did the playa basins.

Recent chronological and stratigraphic studies (Holliday et al., 1983, 1985a) at the site indicate that the sediment samples on which Wendorf (1970) based his interpretations of the Lubbock Subpluvial, those containing high percentages of fossil pine with some spruce pollen present, may have come from a zone considerably younger than the stratum containing Folsom artifacts.

The diatomite containing the Folsom artifacts comprises the lower one-half of stratum 2 (substratum 2A) and dates from around 11,000–10,000 B.P. (Holliday, 1985b; Holliday et al., 1985b). Substratum 2B, above substratum 2A, consists of clayey, organic-rich marsh sediments dating from approximately 10,000–8500 B.P. From 8500 to 6300 B.P. little deposition occurred at Lubbock Lake, and the

Firstview Soil formed in the upper portion of substratum 2B (Holliday, 1985b; Holliday et al., 1985b).

The stratigraphic data accompanying the published diagrams of Oldfield (1975) and Schoenwetter (1975) suggested to Holliday (1985b) that the samples with the higher values for pine pollen may have come from the much younger Firstview Soil. Since the Firstview Soil represents a stable surface that existed for about 2,000 years, Holliday et al. (1985b) concluded that the soil could have acted as a long-term, natural trap for windblown pollen. Pine pollen is produced in great quantities and is known to travel long distances from its source area (Mack and Bryant, 1974). Thus Bryant (Holliday et al., 1985b) believed that pine-pollen concentration could develop in such a natural trap and could have been a primary factor contributing to the unusually high conifer-pollen counts Hall (Holliday et al., 1985b) found in Firstview Soil samples.

The authors of this chapter do not agree on the interpretation presented in Holliday et al. (1985b). Schoenwetter believes that it is highly unlikely that original Lubbock Lake samples containing high fossil pine-pollen counts came from the zone now assigned to the Firstview Soil. Oldfield's (1975:139) record of the Lubbock Lake III pollen profile stratigraphy documents that the samples definitely came from the lower part of the diatomite exposure at that Lubbock Lake location. Also, the conifer-dominant fossil-pollen record that Schoenwetter analyzed from Lubbock Lake came from the middle of the diatomite unit. Schoenwetter believes it unlikely that any of the Lubbock Lake pollen records attributed to the Lubbock Subpluvial could have dated to the time of Firstview Soil formation. Bryant believes that the complexity of the sedimentary record at Lubbock Lake makes it possible that both Oldfield's and Schoenwetter's samples might have come from younger, post-Folsom substrata. At this point, however, the issue is not resolvable. The locations of the original sediment columns sampled in the early 1960s are unknown and were probably destroyed by later excavations at the site.

In summary, the results of the past 25 years of pollen sampling and subsequent pollen analysis in the Lubbock Lake area have not solved the controversy surrounding the probable paleovegetational conditions of the Lubbock Lake area during the latest Pleistocene and earliest Holocene. Instead, the various fossil-pollen studies have added confusion to the issue.

Eight palynologists have collected, processed, and analyzed sediment samples from deposits in and around Lubbock Lake. Some of those researchers were unable to find any preserved pollen. Others found poorly preserved, marginal amounts of fossil pollen. Still others were able to find enough fossil pollen to produce counts in excess of the suggested minimum of 200 grains per sample (Barkley, 1934; Martin, 1963). Perhaps the basic reasons for these different results are two: (1) the problems of fossil pollen preservation and (2) differences of opinion among palynologists about the types of information that represent a sufficient basis for reasonable interpretation of pollen analytical data. In addition, palynological problems at Lubbock Lake have been compounded by the varying depositional environments through space and time and the long gaps between some of the fossil pollen studies conducted at that site.

## POLLEN PRESERVATION IN LUBBOCK LAKE SEDIMENTS

Palynologists are not sure exactly why pollen is well preserved in one type of sediment and yet is often destroyed in another sediment type. Since many variables (e.g., pH, Eh, bacteria, fungi, soil chemicals, mechanical agents, soil moisture, temperature) are suspected of being agents of pollen destruction (Bryant and Holloway, 1983), it is difficult to isolate, or blame, any single factor or specific set of factors when fossil pollen is not recoverable. Deposits at Lubbock Lake are an excellent case in point. All the various sediment samples examined from the Lubbock Lake area over a 25-year period from 1958 to 1983 were collected from deposits that were at least 1,000 years old, and some were more than 10,000 years old. Geological evidence suggests that pollen was deposited under a variety of depositional environments, such as lacustrine, marsh, alluvial, colluvial, and cultural sedimentation. All the originally deposited pollen grains were subjected to a variety of potentially destructive agents for long periods of time.

Both Oldfield and Schoenwetter (1975) and Hall (Holliday et al., 1985b) suspected that differential preservation might be one of the factors that created the high pine and spruce fossil-pollen counts from some of the deposits associated with Lubbock Lake. Hall's position is supported by geomorphological data indicating that the Lubbock Lake sediments presented a harsh environment of deposition for pollen during the formation of the Firstview Soil. Another indication of that situation is the low percentage of recoverable organic matter, which averaged generally less than 1% in the Lubbock Lake sediment samples that Bryant tested. Low percentage of organic matter is often an indication that preserved pollen is absent or rare (Bryant, 1978). However, Schoenwetter does not believe that these arguments are relevant to an assessment of the samples that Oldfield and Schoenwetter (1964, 1975) assigned to the Lubbock Subpluvial episode.

Finally, Holloway (1981) showed in laboratory experiments that repeated cycles of wetting and drying of sediments create surface tension pressures that tend to warp, collapse, tear, and break the fragile walls of pollen grains. Pollen types with thin outer walls and/or elaborate surface ornamentations tended to become broken or destroyed more rapidly than pollen grains with thicker walls and less surface ornamentation. Because the sediments associated with Lubbock Lake are known to have been subjected to cycles of repeated wetting and drying both during the geologic past and during excavation of the site (Holliday and Allen, chap. 2), those cycles could have caused differential fossil-pollen preservation in some strata and the total destruction of fossil pollen in other strata. Schoenwetter, however, pointed out that he, Oldfield, and McLaughlin were able to recover pollen from Lubbock Lake more regularly than were Hall, Hafsten, Bryant, Weir, and Dean. Furthermore, he commented that differential pollen preservation is not necessarily any more important as a rational explanation for pollen presence or absence than are other criteria, such as differences in pollen sample processing procedures or differences in standards for recognition of "acceptable" analyses.

## SUMMARY

The Lubbock Lake pollen analyses illustrate one of the controversies that still plague the field of palynology: What constitutes a valid fossil pollen data base? Three of the palynologists who worked with sediments from the Lubbock Lake area recovered sufficient pollen to conduct an analysis. On the other hand, five other palynologists reported finding insufficient pollen for analytical purposes.

Although their final conclusions differ, all eight palynologists agree on several aspects concerning the sediments recovered from the Lubbock Lake area. First, pollen preservation was not ideal, and much of the recovered pollen showed evidence of surface degradation. Second, although the point was not tested statistically, most of the researchers note that fossil-pollen density (pollen per gram of dried sediment) was sparse. Finally, they agree that the extraction techniques needed to recover fossil pollen from Lubbock Lake sediments were costly and time-consuming. The authors of this chapter agree on one further point: none of the fossil-pollen data collected to date from Lubbock Lake should be used as a basis for interpretation of the site-specific local paleoenvironment. Schoenwetter believes this to be as true today as it was when he and Oldfield first suggested it in their report to Wendorf in 1963. Bryant agrees but adds that his reasons focus mainly on the lack of reliability of using fossil-pollen records from sediments such as those associated with Lubbock Lake, which indicate that they were very harsh environments for organic preservation.

# 6. The Gastropods, with Notes on Other Invertebrates

## HAROLD G. PIERCE

Gastropods were relatively to extremely abundant in all but one of the strata at Lubbock Lake. During this study 29 terrestrial and 17 aquatic taxa were encountered. The purposes of this chapter are to present the individual gastropod faunas by stratum and assess their paleoenvironmental implications. The climatic interpretations were derived from the present climate of the modern area of sympatry of the various faunas. Since representative samples of all strata except stratum 5 were collected and processed by the author, a quantitative approach to faunal analysis with elementary statistical analysis of similarity coefficients was possible. Individual taxa are presented as a proportion (%) of a given fauna.

Other invertebrate fossils were also collected and studied. They are not a primary subject of this chapter; however, notes on their occurrence are included. Bivalves were found to be relatively abundant in all strata deposited in a suitable environment. Two families were observed, Unionidae and Sphaeriidae. The presence of unionid clams was most useful in determining the through-flowing nature of the streams at certain times. Ostracodes of the family Cyprididae were also common to abundant in strata deposited in suitable environments, with *Candona* spp. observed most frequently. A possible new species of the genus *Chlamydotheca* made a brief late Pleistocene to very early Holocene appearance on the Southern High Plains.

## PREVIOUS WORK

Leonard (1950), Leonard and Frye (1962), and Frye and Leonard (1957, 1963) conducted several valuable investigations of the molluscan faunas and associated sediments of Quaternary age on the Southern High Plains, some of which involved nearby localities of similar age. Leonard identified mollusks of several faunas subsequently described by Wendorf (1961c), which included material collected at Lubbock Lake. Environmental interpretations based on these faunas were of limited value because of an oversimplistic approach to the true tolerance and distribution ranges of the taxa involved.

Taylor (1960) dealt primarily with pre-Wisconsinan faunas. Schultz and Cheatum (1970) described a latest Wisconsinan fauna from Randall County, Texas. Drake (1975) identified, by comparison with descriptions and illustrations in the literature, the mollusks collected by others from several localities on the Southern High Plains. Misidentifications limit the value of that report. Pierce (1975) reported the faunas at Lubbock Lake, as well as several adjacent Wisconsinan localities, in a quantitative manner. Johnson et al. (1982) reported on late Quaternary invertebrates from a locality on the Rolling Plains near the eastern escarpment of the Southern High Plains.

The modern fauna was reported first by Clarke (1938) from a drift collection made in Randall County, Texas, but he failed to discriminate between reworked fossil and modern specimens. Cheatum and Fullington (1971, 1973) and Fullington and Pratt (1974) collected living and subfossil specimens along the margins of the Southern High Plains. Pierce (1975) reported three modern faunas and other isolated occurrences on and adjacent to the Southern High Plains.

## METHODS OF STUDY

The current methodology varies substantially from the methodologies of previous investigators. After a detailed study of the stratigraphic position and sedimentologic character of the strata involved, collection localities within the strata were selected on the basis of local abundance of mollusks. Samples were collected from substrata 1A, 1B–1C (undivided), 3ℓ, 4B, and 5 (undivided). Small bulk samples approximating 6 L were removed from a cleaned outcrop, usually by channeling, and processed by a technique modified from Hibbard (1949). The bulk sample was disaggregated in warm water before being washed gently through a nest of screens, the finest being no. 60 (0.25 mm). All fossil material was picked under a binocular microscope, and the coarser sediment fractions were studied.

At the time of picking, initial sorting was to genus. Subsequent sorting to specific level, at times to subspecific level, was verified carefully by comparison with an extensive personal reference collection of fossil and modern specimens. After final sorting and identification the number of individuals in each taxa was determined, usually by counting under the microscope. If large numbers of specimens were involved, normally > 400, a representative number, usually 100, was counted and weighed on a sensitive balance. Total numbers were computed on the basis of the total weight of all shells of that species. The counts of all taxa were reduced to percentages of the total terrestrial or aquatic gastropod faunas and tabulated.

Other fossil materials, such as bivalves, ostracodes, oogonia of *Chara* sp., and seeds, were treated in a similar fashion. The controlled molluscan samples were supplemented by material picked by Lubbock Lake personnel from large bulk volumes washed and screened at the site. Small specimens escaped the 1.6-mm (1/16-in) mesh screen, and slug plates usually were not recognized by the sorters. This problem was rectified with the modification of one of the washing racks to accept a third, small fossil screen of 0.55-mm mesh. In general these large-volume samples were used to supplement the controlled samples and occasionally revealed the presence of rarer species missed by the sampling technique. These samples are not a part of the statistical data.

In most families recognized, the shell is the basis of specific identification. Among the terrestrial families the succineids are the most notable exception. Within this family the highly variable shell morphology requires identification at specific levels, even at generic level, on the basis of soft-part studies. Only the more or less distinctive genus *Oxyloma* can be separated from the other genera of this family with any degree of certainty by shell morphology alone. Accordingly, the remaining succineid shells are lumped as cf. *Succinea*. Among the other terrestrials encountered, only the family Zonitidae is difficult, but it can be discriminated easily at specific level by comparison to a good reference collection.

Among aquatic families the lymnaeids are in a state of confusion. Hubendick (1951) was followed in dealing with members of this family. He recognized only 12 species of a single genus, *Lymnaea,* as sole representatives of this family in North America (genus *Lanx* excepted). Taxonomy of terrestrial taxa followed that of Pilsbry (1939–48) as modified by Burch (1962). Taxonomy of aquatic taxa generally followed that of Clarke (1973), except for the lymnaeids.

In some instances partial shells of gastropods were identifiable to specific level. Apertures of most pupillids were treated as complete shells in tabulation of results. For the valloniids, however, the reverse is true. Complete shells are necessary for positive specific identification, and the apertures of shells of this family are frequently missing. To solve this problem, a different technique was devised to record numbers and percentages. All shells identifiable to generic level were counted and recorded as *Vallonia* sp. Those with complete apertures that could be identified to specific level were counted and recorded separately. In general, experience with the valloniids indicated that the ratio between species established in this manner can be expanded to include the total population of the genus with little error. However, that assumption was not made in this study.

Elementary statistical analyses were used in the correlation of the Lubbock Lake gastropod faunas with other fossiliferous localities of similar age on the Southern High Plains. The simple coefficient used is that of Dice (Sneath and Sokal, 1973:131), which is based on a 2 × 2 matrix. This coefficient was found to be most sensitive to similarities while placing less weight on adventitious components and ignoring entirely species absent from both faunas. Species absent is a figure that can be manipulated to create artificial similarities. The coefficient of Dice is calculated as follows:

$$Cd = \frac{2a}{2a + b + c}$$

where *Cd* is the coefficient of Dice, *a* is the number of species in common, *b* is the number of species peculiar to stratum 1, and *c* is the number of species peculiar to stratum 2.

## PROBLEMS OF PALEOECOLOGIC INTERPRETATIONS

The basic assumption of paleoecologic interpretations from fossil assemblages was the uniformitarianism assumption. Fossil shells similar to those of living specimens were assumed to be of the same taxa and to have had the same habitat preferences as the living members. With conservative groups such as the terrestrial and freshwater gastropods, and during such a short time period as that encompassed by this study, this assumption was especially valid.

Among the problems normally encountered in a study such as this was the introduction of exotic species. Dead and empty snail shells are notoriously good floaters and often were transported hundreds of kilometers from their original habitats by floodwaters. When working with drift collections (all fossil fluviatile assemblages are drift collections), the investigator must be alert for the introduction of foreign species in this fashion. This study was unusually simple from that standpoint owing to the relatively small drainage basin involved and the general similarity of habitat within the basin. A second problem often encountered was introduction of specimens reworked from older deposits. Since the older sediments were remarkably unfossiliferous, reworking was insignificant.

The existence of relict or disjunct elements within a fossil fauna may be difficult to discern but, when identified, can be very significant in interpreting climatologic trends. A disjunct colony is one in which a riparian or aquatic species is found to exist outside, and separated by hostile environments from, the normal range of distribution of the species without evidence of previous contiguity. This existence results in apparently haphazard and illogical patterns of distribution. Among terrestrial species the distribution of *Vertigo ovata* on the Great Plains and in the Rocky Mountains is an excellent example. Nearly all aquatic species have disjunct colonies, and dispersion to these isolated, favorable locations is usually by shorebirds or waterfowl. A relict colony, on the other hand, is an isolated colony of a formerly widespread species that has managed to survive an unfavorable climatic change in an isolated favorable microenvironment. The presence of *Pupilla blandi* in protected reentrants along the eastern scarp of the Southern High Plains is relictual rather than disjunct. Aquatic species are often able to survive a climatic change otherwise fatal while living in the constant-temperature environment of a spring.

Paleoecologic interpretations of the fauna of the various strata were based on a whole-fauna approach. Unfortunately, distribution and habitat data for many species of terrestrial gastropods are incomplete, or the data are often of a conflicting nature. This confusion may be due to misidentification of species or poor records kept by some collectors. More often, however, the confusion results from mapping or describing the distribution of a species with little or no attempt to identify disjunct or relictual colonies that may extend the overall range of a species much beyond its real tolerance-limited range. An example is *Pupilla muscorum,* whose distribution was reported by Pilsbry (1948:934) as "south in the Rocky Mountain region through Colorado to

Socorro County, New Mexico, and northern Arizona, north to Anuk, Alaska." This distribution seemingly implies continuous range but in fact is not. The isolated occurrences in New Mexico and Arizona are as mountaintop relict colonies in Canadian, Hudsonian, and Alpine life zones (Bequaert and Miller, 1973), with one dwarfed New Mexico colony treading the limits of tolerance of the species in what is probably an upper Transition life zone (Pilsbry, 1948). In considering contiguous range, *Pupilla muscorum* probably does not occur south of Montana and the Dakotas. The assembly of distribution data and habitat preferences into usable form has been a major problem.

The environmental interpretations are based preferentially on terrestrial gastropods that are most sensitive to real changes of the local climate. Aquatic gastropods tend to be insulated by their habitat and are slower to respond to change. Considerable weight is given to first and last appearances of certain taxa representing modern climatic and geographic regions, that is, northern or montane, eastern or humid, and southwestern dry faunas. Despite all of the above, environmental interpretations are based on the best judgment and experience of the investigator.

## FAUNAL ANALYSES AND INTERPRETATIONS

A best-fit area of sympatry was selected from data on range and habitat preferences of the species. Climatic interpretations were based on climatologic data typical of the area of sympatry (NOAA, 1974).

The terrestrial gastropod faunas of Lubbock Lake and the modern fauna are listed in table 6.1. Except for the genus *Vallonia*, the relative abundance of the various species of each fauna is given as a percentage of the total terrestrial population. The large number of valloniids that could not be identified to specific level required a modification of counting procedure. All spire fragments that could be identified positively to generic level were counted as *Vallonia* sp. and calculated as a percentage of the fauna. Those specimens that could be identified to specific level were also counted and calculated as a percentage of the fauna but were entered in parentheses and as such are a part of the *Vallonia* sp. percentage. As an example, in substratum 1A, 870 shells constituting 29% of the population, could be identified as *Vallonia* sp., while among these 870, 60 (2%) could be identified as *V. gracillicosta*, and 270 (9%) could be identified as *V. cyclophorella*. The remaining 540 (89%) shells could not be identified to specific level.

The aquatic faunas are presented in a similar manner in table 6.2 along with group data on bivalves and ostracodes. The relative frequency data are percentages of the total aquatic gastropod population.

The percentage figures are based only on the controlled volume and clean-picked collections. The presence of rare species in the material sorted by Lubbock Lake personnel is acknowledged by a × in tables 6.1 and 6.2. Frequency data could not be established for these species, other than their apparent rarity in the fauna. For the modern fauna the × represents species known to be living in the immediate area.

These species include cf. *Succinea* and other species that were collected or reliably reported to be living either nearby or slightly farther north, e.g., *Helisoma trivolvis* (personally collected nearby) and *Deroceras laeve,* reported by R. Fullington (personal communication).

## Substratum 1A

The gastropod assemblage of this substratum differs markedly from those of the superjacent strata and can be differentiated easily on the presence of four key northern or montane taxa: *Vallonia cyclophorella, Pupilla muscorum, P. m. sinistra,* and *Vertigo gouldi basidens.* Although these four taxa are relatively common in Wisconsinan sediments on the Southern High Plains (Pierce, 1975), this is their only appearance at Lubbock Lake. They constitute 19% of the terrestrial population of this fauna. A strong eastern or northeastern element is also present, constituting 30.5% of the total. These species require some woodland or a moister environment than currently exists. Four of these species persist as relict colonies in sheltered reentrants on the eastern margin of the Southern High Plains *(Carychium exiguum, Gastrocopta pentodon, Vertigo ovata,* and *Deroceras laeva).*

The southwestern warm or dry element is very minor, constituting only 1% of the total. Of particular interest is the relationship between *Gastrocopta cristata* (0.1%), a western pupillid well adapted to grasslands, and *Gastrocopta procera* (0.3%), a more eastern species with a similar tolerance range but preferring at least scrub brush or trees. The middle Wisconsinan trend of *G. procera* dominance over *G. cristata* (Pierce, 1975) still persisted in substratum 1A, but in all younger strata the relationship shifted to dominance by *G. cristata,* suggesting a change to a dominance of grasslands. *Gastrocopta procera* has survived to this day on the Southern High Plains but remains subordinate to *G. cristata.*

The aquatic gastropods, with their insulated microcosm, tend to be less responsive to broad environmental changes than do terrestrial forms. However, they followed a similar pattern. Five species, 27.6% of the aquatic gastropods, have decided northern affinities; and one species, *Helisoma anceps* (11%), prefers cooler water and demands permanent, preferably flowing, water. Aquatic gastropods did not experience local extinction within this substratum.

Sphaeriid clams are common to abundant, as are cypridid ostracodes. Among plant remains fossil grass seeds were common, and the oogonia of *Chara* sp. were recovered.

The paleoenvironment of this fauna is northern. Discounting relict or disjunct colonies, an area of sympatry would be in the northern tier of states, with the area of southeastern North Dakota, northeastern South Dakota, and western Minnesota most representative. A mean annual temperature of 7.5° C (10° C cooler than present) with July-August norms of 25° C and January-February norms of −8° C is suggested. The strong eastern or woodland element suggests rather abundant moisture. At the suggested temperatures annual precipitation of 60 to 65 cm/yr would be

Table 6.1. Terrestrial Gastropod Faunas (see text)
(Percentage of Total Terrestrial Population)

| Genus and Species | 1A | 1B–C | 2 | 3 | 4B | 5 | Modern |
|---|---|---|---|---|---|---|---|
| *Carychium exiguum* (Say) | 9 | 7 | | | | | 2 |
| *Vallonia* sp. | 29 | 2 | | | | | 2 |
| *V. gracilicosta* (Reinhardt) | (2) | (0.1) | | | | × | (1) |
| *V. parvula* Sterki | × | (2) | × | | | | (0.6) |
| *V. cyclophorella* Sterki | (9) | | | | | | |
| *Pupilla blandi* Morse | 1 | 1 | × | | | | 6 |
| *P. muscorum* (Linn.) | 6 | | | | | | |
| *P. m. sinistra* Franzen | 1 | | | | | | |
| *Pupoides albilabris* (Adams) | 0.4 | 2 | 11 | × | 5 | × | 3 |
| *Gastrocopta cristata* (Pilsbry and Vanatta) | 0.1 | 6 | 11 | 0.8 | × | × | 7 |
| *G. pellucida hordeacella* (Pilsbry) | | | | 1 | | | 43 |
| *G. procera* (Gould) | 0.3 | 2 | | 0.4 | 2 | × | 11 |
| *G. armifera* (Say) | | 0.2 | | | | | × |
| *G. ruidoensis* (Cockrell) | 1 | 0.4 | | | | | 1 |
| *G. pentodon* (Say) | 9 | 12 | 22 | 8 | | | 1 |
| *Vertigo ovata* (Say) | 7 | 37 | 22 | 4 | | | 1 |
| *V. gouldi basidens* Pilsbry and Vanatta | 3 | | | | | | |
| *V. milium* (Gould) | 7 | 2 | × | | | | 2 |
| cf. *Succinea* | 11 | 4 | × | 40 | 9 | × | × |
| *Oxyloma*, cf. *O. retusa* (Lea) | | 6 | 22 | 1 | | | |
| *Discus cronkhitei* (Newcomb) | 3 | 3 | | | | | |
| *Helicodiscus parallelus* (Say) | 0.2 | 0.8 | | | | | |
| *H. eigenmanni* Pilsbry | | | × | 2 | | × | 2 |
| *H. singleyanus* (Pilsbry) | | | | 3 | | × | 9 |
| *Punctum minutissimum* (Lea) | | 0.4 | | | | | |
| *Deroceras laeve* (Muller) | 0.6 | | × | 0.8 | 2 | | × |
| *Nesovitrea hammonis electrina* (Gould) | 1 | 0.1 | | | | | |
| *Hawaiia minuscula* (Binney) | 10 | 12 | 11 | 39 | 82 | × | 9 |
| *Euconulus fulvus* (Muller) | 0.7 | 2 | | | | | |
| *Zonitoides arboreus* (Say) | 0.5 | 0.1 | | | | | |
| Total population recovered | 3,000 | 900 | 9 | 257 | 66 | | 322 |

Table 6.2. Aquatic Gastropod Faunas (see text)
(Percentage of Total Aquatic Population)

| Genus and Species | 1A | 1B–C | 2 | 3 | 4B | 5 | Modern |
|---|---|---|---|---|---|---|---|
| *Valvata tricarinata* (Say) | 0.1 | 0.1 | | | | | |
| *Promenetus exacuous* (Say) | 0.4 | 3 | 17 | | | | |
| *P. umbilicatellus* (Cockerell) | 4 | 0.2 | | | | | |
| *Helisoma anceps* (Menke) | 11 | 0.1 | | | | | |
| *H. trivolvis* (Say) | | | × | | | | × |
| *Gyraulus parvus* (Say) | 21 | 58 | 39 | × | × | × | 77 |
| *G. circumstriatus* (Tryon) | 8 | 5 | 1 | 15 | × | | |
| *G. deflectus* (Say) | 0.1 | 0.6 | | | | | |
| *Armiger crista* (Linn.) | 15 | 0.1 | 2 | | | | |
| *Ferrissia rivularis* (Say) | | 0.1 | 0.1 | | | | |
| *Laevapex fuscus* (Adams) | | 0.1 | 0.2 | | | | |
| *Physa anatina* (Lea) | 8 | 11 | 27 | × | | × | 4 |
| *P. gyrina* (Say) | × | 0.6 | × | 31 | × | | |
| *Aplexa hypnorum* (Linn.) | 1 | × | | 1 | | | 19 |
| *Lymnaea palustris* (Muller) | 8 | 0.1 | 11 | | × | | |
| *L. bulimoides* (Lea) | 0.2 | × | × | | | | |
| *L. humilis* (Say) | 22 | 21 | 2 | 53 | 100 | × | × |
| Total population recovered | 1,600 | 7,000 | 1,654 | 1,112 | 1 | | 26 |
| Sphaeriid clams | Common | Common | Common | Few | None | Few | Few |
| Unionid clams | | × | ? | | | | |
| Ostracodes | Abundant | Abundant | Abundant | Common | Rare | ? | Few |
| *Chlamydotheca* n.s.? | | × | × | | | | |

adequate. A woodland existed, probably more than just streamside, and the montane species suggest the presence of some conifers in the area.

This fauna correlates well with other late Wisconsinan faunas of the Southern High Plains with coefficients of *Cd* = 0.76–0.81 (Pierce, 1975). The aggrading nature of the clastic sediments of this substratum and the weathered nature of the snails from the upper part of this unit suggest deposition during an interstade. The local extinction of four terrestrial species between this unit and 1B–1C (undivided) suggested that a significant climatic change occurred during the hiatus. On the basis of fauna substratum 1A probably correlates to the Vigo Park member of the Tahoka Formation (Reeves, 1976). This member was radiocarbon-dated at about 18,000 B.P. (Reeves and Parry, 1965). Radiocarbon ages of about 11,100 B.P. from substratum 1B provide an upper age limit for substratum 1A.

## Substrata 1B–1C (Undivided)

The terrestrial gastropod assemblage of these substrata differs from that of the subjacent substratum in the absence of the markedly northern or montane species, and from those of the superjacent substrata in retaining a markedly northeastern woodlands or moist component in this fauna. By the end of deposition of these substrata five woodland or eastern species, *Discus cronkhitei, Helicodiscus parallelus, Nesovitrea hammonis electrina, Euconulus fulvus,* and

*Zonitoides arboreus,* constituting 6.4% of the terrestrial community of this fauna, experienced local extinction. *Punctum minutissimum* made a brief Wisconsinan appearance in this fauna. *Strobilops labyrinthica,* occurring in other Southern High Plains faunas of this approximate age, disappeared. *Gastrocopta pentodon* and *Vertigo ovata,* preferring but not bound to moist environments, constituted 49% of the terrestrial fauna. *Gastrocopta cristata* achieved dominance over *G. procera.*

The aquatic gastropods were slower to respond to changes of climate. The cooler or more northern group declined from 38.1% of the substratum 1A aquatic population to only 9% of the substrata 1B–1C aquatic population. Three species of northern affinities, *Valvata tricarinata, Promenetus umbilicatellus,* and *Gyraulus deflectus,* and another that demands permanent and prefers cool, flowing water, *Helisoma anceps,* experienced local extinction. *Armiger crista* and *Gyraulus circumstriatus* declined to minor importance in the fauna. Two freshwater limpets, *Ferrissia rivularis,* a fluviatile species, and *Laevapex fuscus,* which prefer quiet, weedy, lacustrine environments, appeared as minor elements.

Sphaeriid clams were common to abundant. A fragment of a unionid clam was recovered, emphasizing the existence of a permanent, through-flowing stream at this time. Cyprinid ostracods were common, and a probable new species of the genus *Chlamydotheca* first appeared at Lubbock Lake. This ostracod, found at five localities on the Southern High Plains, has proved to be an index fossil for correlation of late Wisconsinan (post–Vigo Park) to earliest Holocene faunas. Among plant remains only weed and grass seeds are common. Oogonia of *Chara* sp. were not encountered above substratum 1A, although fossilized *Chara* sp. molds were recovered from substratum 2A (Thompson, chap. 4).

The paleoenvironment of this fauna is somewhat cooler and moister than that of the present but markedly warmer than that of substratum 1A. Once again, disregarding relic populations in areas such as the Ozarks, and considering differences in climatic zonation owing to elevation that affect distribution in the western states, an area of sympatry for the aquatic fauna should be northeastern Kansas. A more northern area of sympatry for the aquatic snails, approximately equal to that of substratum 1A, is rejected for reasons previously cited. A mean annual temperature of 12.5° C (5° C cooler than present), with July-August norms of 28° C, January-February norms of −2.5° C, and annual precipitation of about 80 cm (almost twice the present precipitation of the Lubbock area) is suggested. The woodland was of lesser importance and was probably restricted to the banks of a small, permanent stream that had a relatively open body of water with probably marshy sides. The absence of montane species suggests the absence of conifers.

This fauna correlates well with four other latest Wisconsinan faunas on the Southern High Plains (one from stratum 2, another from Blackwater Draw Locality No. 1). The presence of *Chlamydotheca* n.s.? is significant in confirming this correlation. The overall cool, humid climate inferred suggests a minor Wisconsinan stade. Correlation with other faunas of similar age that are known to occur stratigraphically above the Vigo Park member of the Tahoka Formation results in correlation to the Brownfield Lake member of the Tahoka Formation (Reeves, 1976) or to a subsequent soil-forming interval.

## Stratum 2 (Undivided)

The sediments of stratum 2 are almost exclusively lacustrine to marsh and are not, therefore, rich in terrestrial gastropods. The original collections at this level resulted in an aquatic-to-terrestrial ratio of 99.9:0.1. Examination of material processed by Lubbock Lake personnel added 6 more species. Although all species except one are current residents of canyon reentrants on the eastern scarp of the Southern High Plains, these 12 species do not fully represent the modern fauna. They probably did not fully represent the terrestrial fauna living at the time of deposition of these sediments.

The one species not represented in the modern fauna is the amphibious *Oxyloma,* cf. *O. retusa,* which first appeared in substrata 1B–1C. *Helicodiscus eigenmanni,* a western species well adapted to drought, is tentatively identified from fragments. It is a new element that abruptly replaced *H. parallelus,* a more eastern species that prefers more humid conditions and some trees. *Helicodiscus parallelus* does not reappear on the Southern High Plains after latest Wisconsinan time. *Helicodiscus eigenmanni* becomes established in the substratum 3ℓ fauna and is the current resident.

Although overwhelmingly aquatic, this fauna is somewhat ambiguous, probably owing to the shelter provided by the aquatic environment. A decrease occurred in the number of permanent water species, with some northern elements (*Promenetus exacuous, Armiger crista, Ferrissia rivularis,* and *Lymnaea palustris* which total 30% of the aquatic fauna) disappearing by the end of deposition of stratum 2. *Gyraulus circumstriatus,* also northern but less decidedly so than the above species, is characteristic of temporary ponds. It persisted to become one of the dominant aquatic species of substratum 3ℓ. *Helisoma trivolvis,* a tolerant species, decreased and disappeared as the ponds filled and permanent water conditions disappeared. The local absence of *Lymnaea bulimoides* is unexplained because this snail is well adapted to temporary ponds.

Sphaeriid clams were common in this stratum. A single unionid fragment was recovered; however, this fragment may be an artifact. Cypridid ostracods were abundant and included many values of the possible new species of *Chlamydotheca.* Fossil grass seeds were relatively common. The paleoenvironment of this fauna is essentially that of the present; or perhaps, on the basis of the continued presence of *Oxyloma,* cf. *O. retusa,* which is not known south of northeastern Kansas at this time (Leonard, 1959), it was slightly cooler. However, *O. decampi gouldi,* a chronologically similar species, was reported for northwestern Oklahoma by Wallen and Dunlap (1953), but whether alive or as a drift specimen was not specified.

By the end of stratum 2 deposition the mean annual temperature had probably changed to conditions close to that of the present, about 17.5° C, with July-August norms of 29° C and January-February norms of 5° C. Annual precipitation had decreased probably to approximately that of today (45 cm). The fauna and sediments are typical of a permanent, shallow, well-vegetated, spring-fed pond or oxbow. The rarity of terrestrial specimens suggests that the marsh was rarely, if ever, flooded. The inferred springs of this pond may have marked the upper limit of water along Yellowhouse Draw. This cool, spring-fed pond would have provided a microcosm for relict cool-water species until the springs ceased. The occurrence of *Vallonia parvula* suggests the presence of cottonwood. Scattered trees probably were limited to the margin of the pond.

Owing to the paucity of terrestrial species, this fauna does not have high correlation coefficients with any other Southern High Plains fauna. However, this fauna is clearly transitional in nature between the faunas of substrata 1B–1C and substratum 3ℓ.

## Substratum 3ℓ

The fauna of this substratum is markedly different from the more mesic, even humid faunas of strata 1 and 2. The terrestrial fauna is essentially modern, possibly even more xeric than the modern fauna. The only exception is *Oxyloma,* cf. *O. retusa,* which was encountered only at the very bottom of this substratum. The fauna is depauperate, with a total of only 12 terrestrial species. About 86% of the total are from 6 very tolerant and drought-resistant species: *Gastrocopta cristata, Helicodiscus eigenmanni, Hawaiia minuscula,* cf. *Succinea, Gastrocopta pellucida hordeacella,* and *Helicodiscus singleyanus.* The last two, well adapted to a grass-root existence and tolerant of heat and drought, make their first appearance at Lubbock Lake in this substratum.

The aquatic fauna also changed, an indication of a severely altered environment. Only six species were recovered, and of the six only *Gyraulus parvus* and *Physa anatina* require other than temporary water. These two species are represented by only a few immature shells and could be due to adventitious dispersal from some location with permanent water, which may have been at some distance. The lymnaeid, which is of the form *parva* (Lea), is an inhabitant of marshy places and is just as likely to be found out of water as in it. All specimens are small and appear to represent individuals with a single season of growth. Sphaeriid clams were rare, although cypridid ostracodes were relatively common. *Chlamydotheca* n.s.? was not encountered.

The paleoenvironment of this fauna appeared to be rather severe, probably even more severe than that of the present. Temperatures may have been higher, and the effective moisture less. This pattern could have resulted from either decreased rainfall or increased evaporation. The sediments of this substratum appeared to be remarkably similar to those now being deposited in some Southern High Plains playas. The suggested climatology would be similar to that

of southeastern New Mexico, with a mean annual temperature of about 20° C, July-August norms of 30° C, and January-February norms of 10° C. Average annual precipitation probably did not significantly exceed 40 cm/yr.

## Substratum 4B

The fauna of this substratum resulted from a logical extension of the climatic trends that had developed thus far. This extremely depauperate fauna has six terrestrial species. Two aquatic species are present questionably. Of the terrestrial species it is probable that *Gastrocopta procera* and *Deroceras laeve,* represented by a single shell each, are reworked from subjacent units. The two aquatic species, again one shell each and both immature, may have been reworked, or may represent adventitious dispersal to a local but very temporary pothole. Considering numbers of individuals present, the total local fauna may have consisted of only four species, *Pupoides albilabris, Gastrocopta cristata, Hawaiia minuscula,* and cf. *Succinea.* However, in all probability, *Helicodiscus eigenmanni, H. singleyanus,* and *Gastrocopta pellucida hordeacella* also were present but, owing to an accident of collection, were not recovered in the samples. Sphaeriid clams were not recovered, and what little ostracod material was observed was fragmentary and probably reworked by deflation of subjacent deposits.

The paleoenvironment of this fauna was severe. Only the hardiest species were able to survive, and these in thin populations. The sediment is largely eolian. Considering the trend that persisted from substratum 1A to this substratum, the substratum 3ℓ climate if continued for a moderate period of time would result in the extreme conditions observed in this substratum.

## Stratum 5 (Undivided)

Eight species of terrestrial gastropods were recovered, all currently living on or in sheltered enclaves adjacent to the Southern High Plains. The eight species represent 50% of the modern snail fauna from a nearby fork of the upper Brazos River. Of the eight species of the modern fauna not found in stratum 5, four are small enough to have passed through the screens used. The remaining four species either were missed by accident or had not dispersed from their canyon refuges by this time.

The aquatic fauna is represented by six species. Two of the modern species, *Aplexa hypnorum* and *Helisoma trivolvis,* were not encountered. Three species not currently known had become temporarily reestablished in this fauna. *Physa gyrina* probably lives now on the Southern High Plains but has not yet been collected. Certainly the habitats are available. The other two, *Gyraulus circumstriatus* and *Lymnaea palustris,* are species whose present tolerance ranges seem to restrict them to more northerly climates (the Panhandle of Oklahoma and southern Kansas). Sphaeriid clams were observed, but ostracodes were not, probably owing to screen size.

The paleoenvironment of this fauna suggests a return to more moderate climatic conditions. Certainly the molluscan fauna had made an impressive recovery from that of substratum 4B. Considering the severity of the substrata 3ℓ and 4B climates postulated, it is apparent that moisture availability must have increased significantly. This change could have come about either from a reduction in evaporation or from an increase in precipitation. Considering historic knowledge of climatic cycles, it is probable that the amelioration of the climate was due to both increased precipitation and a reduction in mean annual temperature. A small drop in mean annual temperature to about 15° C, 2.5° C less than present, and an increase in annual precipitation to about 60–65 cm/yr probably would partly reverse the xeric conditions that obtained during the late Altithermal and restore groundwater and vegetation to the level observed by the first Euro-American colonists.

### Modern Fauna

Considering the rigorous climate of the Holocene, the diversity of the modern fauna is surprising, though encountered mostly in sheltered reentrants along the eastern scarp of the Southern High Plains. Eighteen species of terrestrial gastropods are found nearby, 16 of which are found in the modern fauna nearest Lubbock Lake. Of the 18 some are relicts, some may be relatively recent returnees (disjunct species), and some (almost half) are hardy species that apparently survived the worst of the Holocene on the Southern High Plains. More than 75% of individuals of the comparable modern colony are from these 8 hardy species, *Pupoides albilabris, Gastrocopta cristata, G. pellucida hordeacella, Helicodiscus singleyanus, H. eigenmanni, Hawaiia minuscula, Vallonia parvula,* and cf. *Succinea.*

Among the aquatic group some diversity persists, but less than during the recent, more optimum climate of stratum 5. All five species encountered are probably the result of adventitious dispersal and restocking by water birds from areas in which permanent water had persisted. All could have survived in the scattered subcaprock springs that were once common along the eastern scarp of the Southern High Plains. The low diversity of the aquatic fauna is largely a result of recent decreases in the amount of suitable habitat available. *Lymnaea palustris* and *Gyraulus circumstriatus,* who were able to reestablish residence temporarily at Lubbock Lake during stratum 5 times, again have retreated north, currently to the Oklahoma Panhandle and southern Kansas. In the modern faunas sphaeriid clams and cypridid ostracodes are relatively common. Unionid clams are absent.

The present Lubbock area mean annual temperature is 17.5° C, with July-August norms of 29.5° C and January-February norms of 5.5° C and an average annual precipitation of 45 cm. Slightly farther north, near Amarillo, where *Gastrocopta armifera* and *Deroceras laeve* are found, the mean annual temperature is 16.5° C with an annual precipitation of 50 cm.

## DISCUSSION AND CONCLUSIONS

Because terrestrial and aquatic gastropods are conservative but very sensitive to local environments, analysis of the faunas of the successive, well-dated strata at Lubbock Lake has proved to be most interesting and useful. Correlation with other localities on the Southern High Plains can be made with a high degree of confidence, especially if stratigraphy and sedimentology are also considered. An example is the correlation of a fauna collected and identified from Blackwater Draw Locality No. 1 (Pierce, 1975). The fauna is not that identified by Drake (1975). Without considering sedimentology or stratigraphy, this fauna correlates only relatively well with substrata 1B–1C at Lubbock Lake. However, this fauna correlates more closely to the fauna associated with a mammoth locality on the UU Ranch, southeast of Lubbock, Texas (Pierce, 1975). The UU Ranch fauna has a high correlation coefficient with the substrata 1B–1C fauna. Coefficients are as follows:

Blackwater Draw to substrata 1B–1C: $Cd = 0.65$
Blackwater Draw—UU Ranch: $Cd = 0.74$
UU Ranch—substrata 1B–1C: $Cd = 0.80$

The interrelated correlation level indicates a high degree of faunal similarity among the three sites. This correlation level implies very similar paleoenvironments at the time of deposition, which in turn can be used to determine essential time synchroneity for the three faunas. This synchroneity is confirmed by radiocarbon dates from substratum 1B–1C (Holliday et al., 1983) and Blackwater Draw (Hester, 1972) and by the presence of *Chlamydotheca* n.s.? at all three sites. Sedimentology and stratigraphy reinforce this conclusion.

Paleoenvironmental interpretations based on determination of areas of sympatry for faunal assemblages of a more or less continuous stratigraphic sequence such as that at Lubbock Lake can be used to develop a picture of overall climatic trends (fig. 6.1). On the Southern High Plains, the trend was one of warming and increasing aridity from late Wisconsinan to early Holocene, which resulted in an apparently general rise in the mean annual temperature from a late Wisconsinan low of 7.5° C to an Altithermal high of 20° C. This trend was temporarily reversed within the recent past (> 500 B.P.), followed by a slight modern rise to the present 17.5° C. In late Wisconsinan times moisture significantly was more abundant than at present. Through-flowing streams existed, and, at least initially, annual precipitation rate increased with the increasing mean annual temperature to maintain a humid to mesic climate. Near the end of the Pleistocene the climate began a rapid deterioration to the arid conditions of the Altithermal. Increased precipitation, along with the decrease in the mean annual temperature during the late Holocene, temporarily reestablished more mesic conditions, which subsequently

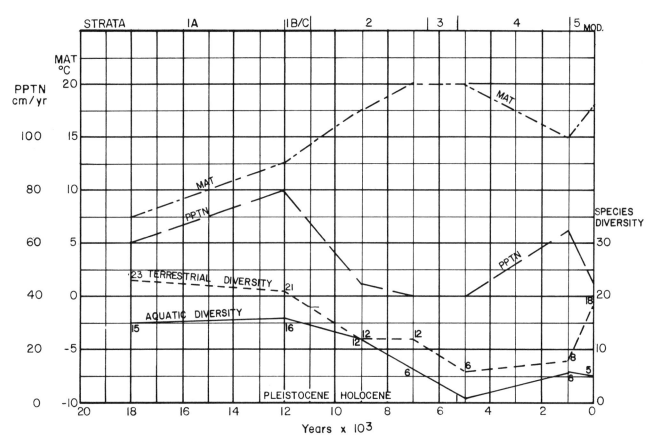

Fig. 6.1. Climatic trends and species diversity of the invertebrate fauna. MAT = mean annual temperature; PPTN = precipitation (drafting by Harold G. Pierce).

have deteriorated somewhat to the present semiarid low-latitude steppe climate (Koppen system) of the Southern High Plains.

Species diversity of the various faunas shows a close relationship to the climatic trends. The diversity of the terrestrial fauna decreased from a maximum of 23 species during the climatic optimum of substratum 1A to 6 species in the rigorous climate during which substratum 4B was deposited, followed by a rapid increase to the 18 species of the nearest modern fauna. This change displays a close but inverse relationship to the temperature curve (fig. 6.1). The aquatic fauna followed a similar trend, from a high of 16 species in substrata 1B–1C to 1 species in substratum 4B, 6 in stratum 5, and declining to 5 in the nearest modern fauna. In this curve the aquatic fauna shows a close correlation to the average annual precipitation curve. The previously derived conclusion (Pierce, 1975) that, insofar as terrestrial and freshwater gastropods are concerned, species diversity is a function of climate is reinforced.

Although not separately discussed, and not nearly as sen-

sitive as climatic indicators as the gastropods, the bivalves parallel these interpretations and conclusions. The presence of unionid fragments in substrata 1B–1C indicate that the stream that flowed through Lubbock Lake connected to a major river and was through-flowing. The unionids could have been dispersed to this area only in their parasitic glochidial stage by their host fish. The unionid fragment in stratum 2 is questioned as a possible artifact.

With the exception of *Chlamydotheca* n.s.? the ostracod faunas were not studied. The possible new species of *Chlamydotheca* made an abrupt appearance in the invertebrate faunas of the Southern High Plains in latest Wisconsinan sediments. This ostracod is found only in sediments that are stratigraphically above the Vigo Park dolomite member of the Tahoka Formation and persisted until very early Holocene. *Chlamydotheca* n.s.? was last observed in uppermost substratum 2B (about 8600 B.P.) With this short range *Chlamydotheca* n.s.? makes a nearly perfect index fossil for correlation of Paleoindian sites on the Southern High Plains.

# 7. Vertebrate Remains

## EILEEN JOHNSON

An extensive and varied vertebrate fauna is being recovered from Lubbock Lake deposits. The Lubbock Lake faunal assemblages represent the most extensive collections known for the Southern Plains, made even more significant by stratigraphic context and extensive geochronological control (Holliday et al., 1983, 1985a). A composite faunal list (table 7.1) charts the vertebrates by feature, cultural period, and stratigraphic occurrence. The table includes all identified faunal material recovered from both the LLP and previous investigations. An annotated account of the herpetofauna and mammalian fauna follows. Annotated accounts of the ichthyofauna (Hill, 1982) and the avifauna (Rea et al., n.d.) are treated elsewhere.

Most of the animals, particularly nonmammals, were recovered from matrix concentrates. This phenomenon demonstrates the importance and significance of using a fine-screen recovery technique as a standard archaeological field procedure. Environmental reconstruction relies heavily on this microfaunal composition, and without this assemblage little could be said about the changing ecosystem. The environmental frame of reference for interpretation of the archaeological assemblages would be lacking.

While most of the fauna is modern, some genera and species are extinct, and others have been extirpated. Some range changes are considerable. From a modern perspective the northern and southeastern faunal elements on the Southern Plains during the late Pleistocene are represented in a variety of forms. Their present-day ranges reflect changing environmental conditions over the last 12,000 to 15,000 years. Several of the larger mammals that occur throughout the record have disappeared from the draw or occur only rarely. These animals, such as bison, would still range in the area today if it were not for intensive European settlement and extermination programs.

Material was recovered from all cultural time periods. Many of the various assemblages reflect the local riparian community with an intermixture of adjacent and more distant, drier grasslands communities. Diversity and abundance vary through time, with a trend toward a post-Paleoindian depauperate fauna. This trend is corroborated by the trend seen with the snail fauna (Pierce, chap. 6).

Several Paleoindian sites have been excavated on the Southern High Plains, but few have detailed faunal accounts. The one exception is Blackwater Draw Locality No. 1 (J. Hester, 1972). Faunal studies are available from the pre-Clovis gray-sands stratum (Lundelius, 1972a), dating from 16,000 to 12,000 years ago (Haynes, 1975), and from the Clovis to Folsom age brown-sand wedge (Slaughter, 1975), dating from about 12,000 to 10,000 years ago (Haynes, 1975). A few late Pleistocene (Wisconsin) paleontological or archaeological localities with abbreviated faunal lists are known for the area (Evans and Meade, 1945; Wendorf et al., 1955).

An earlier fauna is known from the Slaton Quarry, a middle Pleistocene locality in Yellowhouse Canyon about 32.2 km (20 miles) below Lubbock Lake (Dalquest, 1967; Holman, 1969a; Womochel, 1977). The comparable forms between Slaton Quarry and Lubbock Lake demonstrate a long-term durability and flexibility to changing conditions on the Southern High Plains. Fauna from various levels at Lubbock Lake are compared to these Pleistocene and early Holocene localities in the Texas and New Mexico region.

Thousands of vertebrate remains were recovered and identified; the most numerous by far are those of mammals. Because of the large quantity it was impractical to list all catalog numbers and detailed specimen inventories associated with each animal. Therefore, an abbreviated specimen inventory was listed for the various forms in the annotated accounts. Several of the microvertebrates, particularly from the Paleoindian levels, were represented by only a few specimens. This phenomenon apparently reflected low species density, for other microvertebrates within the same feature were more common. Furthermore, several of these animals are characterized today by low population density. Such a situation points to the necessity of processing all excavated sediment instead of a representative sample, in which specimens of low-density animals would be missed.

Habitat information and range maps were taken from a number of sources (Burt and Grossenheider, 1964; Conant, 1975; Davis, 1974; Findley et al., 1975; Hall and Kelson, 1959; Hall, 1982; Raun and Gehlbach, 1972; Schmidly, 1977, 1983; Smith, 1956; Stebbins, 1966; Webb, 1970). Herptile taxonomy follows that of Conant (1975), and mammalian taxonomy generally follows that of Jones et al. (1986) unless otherwise noted. All snake material was identified by Thomas Van Devender (Arizona–Sonora Desert Museum). Identification of various other herptile material was also graciously provided by him. Identification of the bat, desert shrew, and fawn was provided by Russell Graham (Illinois State Museum), and of mammoth species by Jeffery Saunders (Illinois State Museum). All other identifications, as well as the interpretation of the material, are the author's.

## AMPHIBIANS

### Order Urodela
### Family Ambystomidae

*Ambystoma tigrinum* (Green), tiger salamander
   9 vertebrae (TTU-A13868, 13891, 11266, 14607, 14635,

Table 7.1. Composite Faunal List by Cultural Period and Stratigraphy

| Genus and Species (Common Name) | PALEOINDIAN | | | | | | | | | | | | | | | |
| --- | --- | --- | --- | --- | --- | --- | --- | --- | --- | --- | --- | --- | --- | --- | --- | --- |
| | Clovis | | | | Folsom | | | Unknown | Plainview | | | | | Firstview | | |
| | 1B | | 1C | | 2ALB1 | 2ALB2/2ALB3 | | 2ALB4 | 2ALB5 | 2B cienega /2B base | | 2s | 2B | A horizon Firstview Soil | | |
| | FA2-1 | non-f | FA6-9 | non-f | non-f | FA6-8 | non-f | FA6-15 | non-f | FA6-11 | non-f | FA9-1 | non-f | FA5-8 | FA5-10 | FA6-3 |
| **Fish** | | | | | | | | | | | | | | | | |
| *Lepisosteus* sp. (garfish) | a | | | | | | | | | | | | | | | |
| *Carpiodes cyprinus* (quillback)[b] | a | | | | | | | | | | | | | | | |
| *Ictalurus* sp., cf. *Ameiurus* (bullhead) | a | | | | | a | | | | a | | a | | | | |
| *Ictalurus melas* (black bullhead) | a | | | | | | | | | | | | | | | |
| *Ictalurus punctatus* (channel catfish) | a | | | | | | | | | | | | | | | |
| *Morone chrysops* (white bass)[b] | | | | | a | | | | | | | | | | | |
| *Lepomis* sp. (sunfish) | | | | | a | | | | | | | | | | | |
| *Lepomis cyanellus* (green sunfish) | a | | | | | | | | | | | | | | | |
| *Lepomis gulosus* (warmouth)[b] | | | | | a | | | | | | | | | | | |
| *Percina* sp. (logperch and blackside darter) | | | | | a | | | | | | | | | | | |
| **Amphibians** | | | | | | | | | | | | | | | | |
| *Ambystoma tigrinum* (tiger salamander) | a | | | | | | | | | a | | a | | | | |
| *Scaphiopus couchi* (Couch's spadefoot toad) | | | | | | | | | | | | | | | | |
| *Scaphiopus bombifrons* (plains spadefoot toad) or *S. hammondi* (western spadefoot toad) | a | | | | | | | | | | | | | | | |
| *Acris crepitans* (cricket frog) | a | | | | | | | | | | | | | | | |
| *Bufo cognatus* (plains toad) | a | | | | | | | | | | | | | | | |
| ‡*Bufo woodhousei bexarensis* (Friesenhahn Cave toad) | a | | | | | | | | | | | | | | | |
| *Bufo* sp. (toad) | a | | | | | | | | | | | a | | | | |

Non-f = non-feature
[a]In matrix (LLP).
[b]No longer occurs in area.
[c]*In situ* (LLP).
[d]Green's excavation.
[e]Evans and Meade's excavation.

| Early Archaic | Middle Archaic | | | | | | Late Archaic/Early Ceramic | Late Ceramic | | | Protohistoric | | | | | | | | | | | | Historic | | | | | | | | | |
|---|---|---|---|---|---|---|---|---|---|---|---|---|---|---|---|---|---|---|---|---|---|---|---|---|---|---|---|---|---|---|---|---|
| | ely | mid | | late | | | A horizon LL Soil | | | | | | | | | | | | | | | | | | | | | | | | | |
| 2e | 3ℓ | 4A | | 4B | | | | 4ℓ | 5ℓ | 5A1 | 5A1 | | | | | | | | | 5A2 | | 5ℓ | 5ℓ | | | | | | | | 5B1 | 5B2 | |
| FA4-1 | non-f | FA6-21 | FA5-4 | FA16-1 | non-f | FA8-14 | FA1-3 | FA1-2 | FA8-5 | FA8-2 | FA8-3 | FA8-4 | FA8-6 | FA8-13 | FA14-1 | FA15-1 | FA19-1 | FA19-2 | FA8-7 | FA8-12 | FA5-6 | FA1-1 | FA5-2 | FA6-1 | FA6-10 | FA6-14 | FA6-19 | non-f | FA8-9 | FA8-1 | FA8-11 |
| | | | | | | | | | | | | | | | | | | | | | | | | | | | | | | | |
| | | | | | | | | | | | | | | | | | | | | | | | | | | | | | | | |
| | | | | | | | | | | | | | | | | | | | | | | | | | | | | | | | |
| | | | | | | | | | | | | | | | | | | | | | | | | | | | | | | | |
| | | | | | | | | | | | | | | | | | | | | | | | | | | | | | | | |
| | | | | | | | | | | | | | | | | | | | | | | | | | | | | | | | |
| | | | | | | | | | | | | | | | | | | | | | | | | | | | | | | | |
| | | | | | | | | | | | | | | | | | | | | | | | | | | | | | | | |
| | | | | | | | | | | | | | | | | | | | | | | | | | | | | | | | |
| | | | | | | | | | | | | | | | | | | | | | | | | | | | | | | | |
| | | | | | | | | | | | | | | | | | | | | | | | | | | | | | | | |
| a | | | | | | | | | | | | | | | | | | | | | | | | | | | | | | | |
| | a | | | | | | | | | | | | | | | | | | | | | | | | | | | | | | |
| | | | | | | | | | | | | | | | | | | | | | | | | | | | | | | | |
| | | | | | | | | | | | | | | | | | | | | | a | | | | | | | | | | |
| | | | | | | | | a | | | | | | | | | | | | | | | | | | | | | | | |
| | | | | | | | | | | | | | | | | | | | | | | | | | | | | | | | |
| | | | | | | | | | | | | | | | | | | | | | | | | | | | | | | | |

Table 7.1. *Continued*

| Genus and Species (Common Name) | PALEOINDIAN | | | | | | | | | | | | | | | |
|---|---|---|---|---|---|---|---|---|---|---|---|---|---|---|---|---|
| | Clovis | | | | Folsom | | | Unknown | Plainview | | | | Firstview | | | |
| | 1B | | 1C | | 2ALB1 | 2ALB2/ 2ALB3 | | 2ALB4 | 2ALB5 | 2B cienega /2B base | | 2s | 2B | A horizon Firstview Soil | | |
| | FA2-1 | non-f | FA6-9 | non-f | non-f | FA6-8 | non-f | FA6-15 | non-f | FA6-11 | non-f | FA9-1 | non-f | FA5-8 | FA5-10 | FA6-3 |
| *Rana catesbeiana* (bullfrog) | a | | | | | a,c | | c | | a | | | a | | | a |
| *Rana palustris* (pickerel frog)[b] | a | | | | | | | | | | | | | | | |
| *Rana pipiens* (leopard frog) | a | | | | | a | | c | | a,c | | a | a | | | a,c |
| **Reptiles** | | | | | | | | | | | | | | | | |
| *Chelydra serpentina* (snapping turtle) | a,c | a | | a | | | | | c | c | | | | | | c |
| *Kinosternon flavescens* (yellow mud turtle) | a,c | | | | | a | | c | a | a,c | | a | c | | | a,c |
| ‡*Geochelone wilsoni* (extinct Wilson's tortoise) | | a | | | | | | | | | | | | | | |
| ‡*Geochelone* sp. (extinct tortoise) | | a,c | | | | | | | | | | | | | | |
| *Chrysemys scripta* (pond slider) | a,c | a,d | | d | | a,c | c | | | c | | | c | | | c |
| ‡*Terrapene carolina putnami* (extinct Carolina box turtle)[c] | a,c | | | | | | | | | | | | | | | |
| *Terrapene ornata* (ornate box turtle) | | | | | | | | | | | | | | | | c |
| *Trionyx* sp. (softshell turtle)[b] | a | | | | | | | | | | | | | | | |
| *Phrynosoma cornutum* (Texas horned lizard) | | | | | | | | | | | | | | | | a |
| *Eumeces obsoletus* (Great Plains skink) | | | | | | | | | | | | a | | | | a |
| *Coluber constrictor* (racer)[b] | | | | | | | | | | | | a,c | | | | |
| *Carphophis amoenus* (worm snake)[b] | a | | | | | | | | | | | | | | | |
| *Elaphe guttata* (corn snake)[b] | a | | | | | | | | | | | | | | | |
| *Gyalopion canum* (western hook-nosed snake)[b] | a | | | | | | | | | | | | | | | |
| *Heterodon nasicus* (western hog-nosed snake) | a | | | | | | | | | | | | | | | |
| *Lampropeltis getulus* (common king snake) | | | | | | | | | | | | | a | | | |
| *Lampropeltis triangulum* (milk snake) | a | | | | | | | | | | | | | | | |
| *Masticophis* sp. (coach- or whipsnake) | | | | | | | | | | | | | | | | |

| ARCHAIC | | | | | | CERAMIC | | | | PROTOHISTORIC | | | | | | | | | | | | HISTORIC | | | | | | | | | |
|---|---|---|---|---|---|---|---|---|---|---|---|---|---|---|---|---|---|---|---|---|---|---|---|---|---|---|---|---|---|---|---|
| Early Archaic | Middle Archaic ely | Middle Archaic mid | | Middle Archaic late | | Late Archaic/ Early Ceramic | Late Ceramic | | | | | | | | | | | | | | | | | | | | | | | | |
| 2e | 3ℓ | 4A | | 4B | | A horizon LL Soil | 4ℓ | 5ℓ | 5A1 | 5A1 | | | | | | | | | 5A2 | | 5ℓ | 5ℓ | | | | | | | 5B1 | 5B2 | |
| FA 4-1 | non-f | FA6-21 | FA5-4 | FA16-1 | non-f | FA8-14 | FA1-3 | FA1-2 | FA8-5 | FA8-2 | FA8-3 | FA8-4 | FA8-6 | FA8-13 | FA14-1 | FA15-1 | FA19-1 | FA19-2 | FA8-7 | FA8-12 | FA5-6 | FA1-1 | FA5-2 | FA6-1 | FA6-10 | FA6-14 | FA6-19 | non-f | FA8-9 | FA8-1 | FA8-11 |
| a | | | | | | | | | | | | | | | | | | | | | | | | | | | | | | | |
| | | | | | | | | | | | | | | | | | | | | | | | | | | | | | | | |
| a | a | | | | | | | | | | | | | | | | | | | | a | | a | | | | | | | | |
| | | | | | | | | | | | | | | | | | | | | | | | | | | | | | | | |
| | d | | | | | | | a | | | | | | | | | | | | d | a,c | | a | | | | | | | | |
| | | | | | | | | | | | | | | | | | | | | | | | | | | | | | | | |
| | | | | | | | | a | | a | | | | | | | | | | | a,c | a | | a,c | | | | | | | |
| | | | | | | | | | | | | | | | | | | | | | | | | | | | | | | | |
| | a | | | | | | | a | | | | d | | | a | | a | | c | | | a | a,c | a | | a | a | | c | | |
| | | | | | | | | | | | | | | | | | | | | | | | | | | | | | | | |
| | a | | | | | | | | | | | | | | | | | | | | a | | a | a | | | | | | | |
| | | | | | | | | | | | | | | | | | | | | | | | | | | | | | | | |
| | | | | | | | | | | | | | | | | | | | | | | | | | | | | | | | |
| | | | | | | | | | | | | | | | | | | | | | | | | | | | | | | | |
| | | | | | | | | | | | | | | | | | | | | | | | | | | | | | | | |
| | | | | | | | | | | | | | | | | | | | | | | | | | | | | | | | |
| a | | | | | | | | | | | | | | | | | | | | | | | | | | | | | | | |
| | | | c | | | | | | | | | | | | | | | | | | | | | | | | | | | | |
| | | | | | | | | | | | | | | | | | | | | | | | | | | | | | | | |
| a | | | | | | | | | | | | | | | | | | | | | | | | | | | | | | | |

Table 7.1. *Continued*

| Genus and Species (Common Name) | PALEOINDIAN | | | | | | | | | | | | | | | |
|---|---|---|---|---|---|---|---|---|---|---|---|---|---|---|---|---|
| | Clovis | | | | Folsom | | | Unknown | Plainview | | | | Firstview | | | |
| | 1B | | 1C | | 2ALB1 | 2ALB2/2ALB3 | | 2ALB4 | 2ALB5 | 2B cienega /2B base | | 2s | 2B | A horizon Firstview Soil | | |
| | FA2-1 | non-f | FA6-9 | non-f | non-f | FA6-8 | non-f | FA6-15 | non-f | FA6-11 | non-f | FA9-1 | non-f | FA5-8 | FA5-10 | FA6-3 |
| *Nerodia* cf. *cyclopion* (green water snake)[b] or *N.* cf. *rhombifera* (diamondback water snake)[b] | | | | | | | | | | | | a | | | | |
| *Nerodia erythrogaster* (red-bellied water snake) | | | | | | | | | | | | | a | | | |
| *Nerodia* sp. (water snake) | a | | | | | | | | | | | | | | | |
| *Pituophis melanoleucus* (bullsnake) | | | | | | | | | | | | | | | | |
| *Elaphe* or *Pituophis* sp. (rat, worm or bull snake) | | | | | | a | | | | | | | | | | |
| *Rhinocheilus lecontei* (long-nosed snake) | | | | | | | | | | | | | | | | |
| *Salvadora* sp. (patch-nosed snake)[b] | a | | | | | | | | | | | | | | | |
| *Sonora semiannulata* (ground snake)[b] | a | | | | | | | | | | | a | | | | |
| *Thamnophis* cf. *marcianus* (checkered garter snake) | | | | | | | | | | | | a | | | | |
| *Thamnophis proximus* (ribbon snake) | | | | | | | | | | | | a | | | | |
| *Thamnophis* cf. *sirtalis* (common garter snake)[b] | a | | | | | a | | | | a | | a | | | | a |
| *Tropidoclonion lineatum* (lined snake)[b] | a | | | | | | | | | | | a | | | | |
| *Virginia* cf. *striatula* (rough earth snake)[b] | a | | | | | | | | | | | | | | | |
| *Agkistrodon contortrix* (copperhead snake)[b] | | | | | | | | | | | | a | | | | |
| *Crotalus atrox* (western diamondback rattlesnake) | a | | | | | | | | | | | | | | | |
| Birds | | | | | | | | | | | | | | | | |
| *Podiceps* cf. *nigricollis* (eared grebe) | | | | | | | | | | a | | | | | | |
| *Podilymbus* cf. *podiceps* (pied-billed grebe) | | | | | | | | | | c | | | | | | |
| *Branta canadensis* (Canada goose) | c | | | | | | | | | | | | | | | |
| *Anser "Chen" caerulescens* (snow goose) | c | | | | | | | c | | | | | | | | |
| *Anas platyrhynchos* (mallard duck) | | a | | | | | | | | c | | | | a | | a |
| *Anas strepera* or *A. acuta* (gadwall or pintail duck) | a | | | | | | | c | | a | | | | | | c |

| ARCHAIC | | | | | | CERAMIC | | | | PROTOHISTORIC | | | | | | | | | | | | | HISTORIC | | | | | | | | | | |
|---|---|---|---|---|---|---|---|---|---|---|---|---|---|---|---|---|---|---|---|---|---|---|---|---|---|---|---|---|---|---|---|---|---|
| Early Archaic | Middle Archaic | | | | | Late Archaic/ Early Ceramic | Late Ceramic | | | | | | | | | | | | | | | | | | | | | | | | | | |
| | ely | mid | | late | | | | | | | | | | | | | | | | | | | | | | | | | | | | | |
| 2e | 3ℓ | 4A | | 4B | | A horizon LL Soil | 4ℓ | 5ℓ | 5A1 | 5A1 | | | | | | | | | 5A2 | | 5ℓ | 5ℓ | | | | | | | | | 5B1 | 5B2 |
| FA4-1 | non-f | FA6-21 | FA5-4 | FA16-1 | non-f | FA8-14 | FA1-3 | FA1-2 | FA8-5 | FA8-2 | FA8-3 | FA8-4 | FA8-6 | FA8-13 | FA14-1 | FA15-1 | FA19-1 | FA19-2 | FA8-7 | FA8-12 | FA5-6 | FA1-1 | FA5-2 | FA6-1 | FA6-10 | FA6-14 | FA6-19 | non-f | FA8-9 | FA8-1 | FA8-11 | | |
| | | | | | | | | | | | | | | | | | | | | | | | | | | | | | | | | | |
| | | | | | | | | | | | | | | | | | | | | | | | | | | | | | | | | | |
| | | | | | | | | | | | | | | | | | | | | | | | | | | | | | | | | | |
| | a | | | | | | | | | | | | | | | | | | | | | | | | | | | | | | | | |
| | | | | | | | | | | | | | | | | | | | | | | | | | | | | | | | | | |
| | | | | | c | | | | | | | | | | | | | | | | | | | | | | | | | | | | |
| | | | | | | | | | | | | | | | | | | | | | | | | | | | | | | | | | |
| | a | | | | | | | | | | | | | | | | | | | | a | | a | | | | | | | | | | |
| | | | | | | | | | | | | | | | | | | | | | | | a | | | | | | | | | | |
| | | | | | | | | | | | | | | | | | | | | | | | a | | | | | | | | | | |
| | | | | | | | | | | | | | | | | | | | | | | | | | | | | | | | | | |
| | | | | | | | | | | | | | | | | | | | | d | | | | | | | | | | | | | |

Table 7.1. *Continued*

| Genus and Species (Common Name) | PALEOINDIAN | | | | | | | | | | | | | | | |
|---|---|---|---|---|---|---|---|---|---|---|---|---|---|---|---|---|
| | Clovis | | | | Folsom | | | Unknown | | Plainview | | | Firstview | | | |
| | 1B | | 1C | | 2ALB1 | 2ALB2/ 2ALB3 | | 2ALB4 | 2ALB5 | 2B cienega /2B base | | 2s | 2B | A horizon Firstview Soil | | |
| | FA2-1 | non-f | FA6-9 | non-f | non-f | FA6-8 | non-f | FA6-15 | non-f | FA6-11 | non-f | FA9-1 | non-f | FA5-8 | FA5-10 | FA6-3 |
| *Anas acuta* (pintail duck) | a,c | a | | | | | | | | | | | | | | c |
| *Anas strepera* (gadwall duck) | | | | | | | | | | | | | | | | |
| *Anas* cf. *clypeata* (northern shoveler) | c | | | | | | | | a | | | | | | | |
| *Anas crecca carolinensis* (American green-winged teal) | | a | | | c | | | | | a,c | | a | | | | a,c |
| *Anas cyanoptera* or *A. discors* (cinnamon or blue-winged teal) | | | | | | | | | | | | | | | | c |
| *Anas* cf. *cyanoptera* (cinnamon teal) | | | | | | | | | | | | | | | | d |
| *Anas* sp. (duck) | a | | | | | | | | | | | | | | | a |
| *Anas* sp. (teal) | a,c | | | | | | | c | | | | a | | | | c |
| *Oxyura jamaicensis* (ruddy duck) | | | | | | | | | | | | | | | | |
| Cf. *Oxyura jamaicensis* (ruddy duck) | a | | | | | | | | | | | | | | | |
| *Circus cyaneus* (American marsh harrier or hawk) | | | | | | | | c | | | | | | | | |
| *Buteo* sp. (hawk) | | | | | | | | | | | | | | | | |
| *Tympanuchus cupido* (prairie chicken)[b] or | | | | | | | | | | | | | | | | |
| *"Pedioecetes" phasianellus* (sharp-tailed grouse)[b] | | | | | | | | | | | | | | | | a |
| *Meleagris* sp. (turkey)[b] | | a,c | | | | | | | | | | | | | | |
| *Rallus limicola* (Virginia rail)[b] | a | | | | | a | | | | | | | | | | |
| *Rallus* cf. *longirostris* (clapper rail)[b] | | | | | | | | | | | | | | d | | c |
| *Porzana carolina* (sora rail) | | | | | | | | | | | | | | | | a |
| Cf. *Laterallus exilis* (gray-breasted crake)[b] | | | | | | | | | | | | | | | | a |
| *Gallinula chloropus* (common gallinule) | | | | | | | | | | c | | | | | | |
| *Fulica americana* (American coot) | | | | | | | | | | c | | | | | | |
| *Charadrius* ("*Eupoda*") *montanus* (mountain plover)[b] | | | | | | | | | | c | | | | | | |

| ARCHAIC | | | | | | | CERAMIC | | | PROTOHISTORIC | | | | | | | | | | | | HISTORIC | | | | | | | | | |
|---|---|---|---|---|---|---|---|---|---|---|---|---|---|---|---|---|---|---|---|---|---|---|---|---|---|---|---|---|---|---|---|
| Early Archaic | Middle Archaic | | | | | Late Archaic/ Early Ceramic | Late Ceramic | | | | | | | | | | | | | | | | | | | | | | | | |
| | ely | mid | | late | | A horizon LL Soil | | | | | | | | | | | | | | | | | | | | | | | | | |
| 2e | 3ℓ | 4A | | 4B | | | 4ℓ | 5ℓ | 5A1 | 5A1 | | | | | | | | | 5A2 | | 5ℓ | 5ℓ | | | | | | | 5B1 | 5B2 | |
| FA4-1 | non-f | FA6-21 | FA5-4 | FA16-1 | non-f | FA8-14 | FA1-3 | FA1-2 | FA8-5 | FA8-2 | FA8-3 | FA8-4 | FA8-6 | FA8-13 | FA14-1 | FA15-1 | FA19-1 | FA19-2 | FA8-7 | FA8-12 | FA5-6 | FA1-1 | FA5-2 | FA6-1 | FA6-10 | FA6-14 | FA6-19 | non-f | FA8-9 | FA8-1 | FA8-11 |
| | | | | | | | | | | | | | | | | | | | | | | | | | c | | | | | | |
| | | | | | | | | | | | | | | | | | | | | | | | | | | | c | | | | |
| | | | | | | | | | | | | | | | | | | | | | | | | | | | | | | | |
| | | | | | | | | | | | | | | | | | | | | | | | | | | | | | | | |
| | | | | | | | | | | | | | | | | | | | | | | | | | | | | | | | |
| | | | | | | | | | | | | | | | | | | | | | | | | | | | c | | | | |
| | | | | | | | | | | | | | | | | | | | | | | | | | | | a | | | | |
| | | | | | | | | | | | | | | | | | | | | | | | | | | | c | | | | |
| | | | | | | | | | | | | | | | | | | | | | | | | | | | | | | | |
| | | | | | | | | | | | | | | | | | | | | | | | | | c | | | | | | |
| | | | | | | | | | | | | | | | | | | | | | | | | | | | | | | | |
| | | | | | | | | | | | | | | | | | | | | | | | | | | | | | | | |
| | | | | | | | | | | | | | | | | | | | | | | | | | | | | | | | |
| | | | | | | | | | | | | | | | | | | | | | | | | | | | | | | | |
| | | | | | | | | | | | | | | | | | | | | | | | | | | | a | | | | |
| | | | | | | | | | | | | | | | | | | | | | | | | | | | | | | | |

Table 7.1. *Continued*

| Genus and Species (Common Name) | PALEOINDIAN | | | | | | | | | | | | | | | |
| --- | --- | --- | --- | --- | --- | --- | --- | --- | --- | --- | --- | --- | --- | --- | --- | --- |
| | Clovis | | | | Folsom | | | | Unknown | Plainview | | | Firstview | | | |
| | 1B | | 1C | | 2ALB1 | 2ALB2/2ALB3 | | 2ALB4 | 2ALB5 | 2B cienega/2B base | | 2s | 2B | A horizon Firstview Soil | | |
| | FA2-1 | non-f | FA6-9 | non-f | non-f | FA6-8 | non-f | FA6-15 | non-f | FA6-11 | non-f | FA9-1 | non-f | FA5-8 | FA5-10 | FA6-3 |
| *Athene* cf. *cunicularia* (burrowing owl) | a | | | | | | | | | | | | | | | |
| *Chordeiles* cf. *minor* (common nighthawk) | | | | | | | a | | | | | | | | | |
| *Colaptes auratus* (northern flicker) | | | | | | a | | | | | | | | | | |
| Cf. *Sayornis saya* (Say's phoebe) | | | | | | | | | | | | | | | | |
| Cf. *Eremophila alpestris* (horned lark) | | | | | | c | | | | | | | | | | |
| *Corvus corax* (common raven)[b] | c | | | | | | | | | | | | | | | |
| *Mimus polyglottis* (northern [common] mockingbird) | | | | | | a | | | | | | | | | | |
| *Agelaius phoeniceus* (red-winged blackbird) | | | | | | | | | | | | | | | | c |
| Cf. *Agelaius phoeniceus* (red-winged blackbird) | | | a | | | | | | | | | | | | | |
| *Molothrus* cf. *ater* (brown-headed cowbird) | | | | | | | | | | | | | | | | c |
| Cf. *Pooecetes gramineus* (vesper sparrow) | a | | | | | | | | | | | | | | | |
| Mammals | | | | | | | | | | | | | | | | |
| *Blarina* sp. (shrew)[b] | | a | | | | | | | | | | | | | | |
| *Notiosorex crawfordi* (desert shrew) | | | | | | a | | | | a | | | | | | |
| *Tadarida brasiliensis* (Mexican freetail bat) | | | | | | | | | | | | | | | | |
| ‡*Holmesina septentrionalis* (extinct giant armadillo) | c | | | | | | | | | | | | | | | |
| *Sylvilagus* cf. *audubonii* (Audubon cottontail) | | | | | | | | | | | | | | | | d |
| *Sylvilagus* sp. (cottontail) | | | | | | | | | | a,c | | c | d | | | a |
| *Lepus californicus* (blacktail jackrabbit) | a,c | a | | | | a | | | | a,c | | a | d | | | a,c |
| *Spermophilus richardsonii* (Richardson's ground squirrel)[b] | a | a | | | | | | | | | | | | | | |
| *Spermophilus tridecemlineatus* (thirteen-lined ground squirrel) | a | | | | | a | | | | | | a | | | | a |
| *Spermophilus mexicanus* (Mexican ground squirrel) | a | | | | | | | | | a | | a | a | | | a |
| *Cynomys ludovicianus* (blacktail prairie dog) | a,c | | | | | a | | | a | a,c | | a,c | | | | a,c |

Site chronology / feature distribution table. Column group headers (left to right):

- **ARCHAIC** — Early Archaic: 2e (FA4-1); Middle Archaic — ely: 3ℓ (non-f), mid: 4A (FA6-21, FA5-4), late: 4B (FA16-1, non-f); Late Archaic/Early Ceramic: A horizon LL Soil (FA8-14)
- **CERAMIC** — Late Ceramic: 4ℓ (FA1-3), 5ℓ (FA1-2), 5AI (FA8-5)
- **PROTOHISTORIC** — 5AI (FA8-2, FA8-3, FA8-4, FA8-6, FA8-13, FA14-1, FA15-1, FA19-1, FA19-2); 5A2 (FA8-7, FA8-12); 5ℓ (FA5-6)
- **HISTORIC** — 5ℓ (FA1-1, FA5-2, FA6-1, FA6-10, FA6-14, FA6-19, non-f); 5B1 (FA8-9); 5B2 (FA8-1, FA8-11)

| FA4-1 | non-f | FA6-21 | FA5-4 | FA16-1 | non-f | FA8-14 | FA1-3 | FA1-2 | FA8-5 | FA8-2 | FA8-3 | FA8-4 | FA8-6 | FA8-13 | FA14-1 | FA15-1 | FA19-1 | FA19-2 | FA8-7 | FA8-12 | FA5-6 | FA1-1 | FA5-2 | FA6-1 | FA6-10 | FA6-14 | FA6-19 | non-f | FA8-9 | FA8-1 | FA8-11 |
|---|---|---|---|---|---|---|---|---|---|---|---|---|---|---|---|---|---|---|---|---|---|---|---|---|---|---|---|---|---|---|---|
|  |  |  |  |  |  |  |  |  |  |  |  |  |  |  |  |  |  |  |  |  |  |  | c |  |  |  |  |  |  |  |  |
|  |  |  |  |  |  |  |  |  |  |  |  |  |  |  |  |  |  |  |  |  |  | a |  |  |  |  |  |  |  |  |  |
|  |  |  |  |  |  |  |  |  |  |  |  |  |  |  |  |  |  |  |  |  |  | a |  |  |  |  |  |  |  |  |  |
|  |  |  |  |  |  |  |  |  |  |  |  |  |  |  |  |  |  |  |  |  |  |  |  |  |  |  |  |  | d |  |  |
|  |  |  |  |  |  |  |  |  |  |  | d |  |  |  |  |  |  |  | a | a | c |  |  |  |  |  |  |  | d |  |  |
|  | d |  |  |  |  |  |  |  |  |  | d |  |  |  |  |  |  |  |  |  |  |  |  |  |  | c |  |  |  |  |  |
|  |  |  |  |  |  | a |  |  |  |  |  |  |  |  |  |  |  |  |  |  |  |  |  |  |  |  |  |  |  |  |  |
|  | a |  |  |  |  | a,c |  |  | a,c |  |  | a |  |  |  |  |  |  | a,c | a | a | a | a,c | a,c | a,c |  | a,c |  | a |  | a |

Table 7.1. *Continued*

| Genus and Species (Common Name) | PALEOINDIAN | | | | | | | | | | | | | | | |
|---|---|---|---|---|---|---|---|---|---|---|---|---|---|---|---|---|
| | Clovis | | | | Folsom | | | | Unknown | Plainview | | | Firstview | | | |
| | 1B | | 1C | | 2ALB1 | 2ALB2/ 2ALB3 | | 2ALB4 | 2ALB5 | 2B cienega /2B base | | 2s | 2B | A horizon Firstview Soil | | |
| | FA2-1 | non-f | FA6-9 | non-f | non-f | FA6-8 | non-f | FA6-15 | non-f | FA6-11 | non-f | FA9-1 | non-f | FA5-8 | FA5-10 | FA6-3 |
| *Thomomys bottae* (valley pocket gopher)[b] | a | | | | | | | | | | | | | | | |
| *Geomys bursarius* (plains pocket gopher) | a,c | | | | | a | | | | a,c | | a | d | | | a,c |
| *Cratogeomys castanops* (Mexican pocket gopher) | | | | | | | | | | | | | | | | |
| *Perognathus* cf. *hispidus* (hispid pocket mouse) | | | | | | a | | | | | | | | | | |
| *Perognathus* sp. (pocket mouse) | a | | | | | | | | | | | | | | | |
| *Dipodomys ordii* (Ord's kangaroo rat) | | | | | | | | | | | | a | a | | | a,c |
| *Reithrodontomys montanus* (plains harvest mouse) | a | | | | | | | | | a | | | | | | |
| *Peromyscus* cf. *eremicus* (cactus mouse)[b] | a | | | | | | | | | | | | | | | |
| *Peromyscus* sp. (white-footed and pygmy mice) | | | | | | | | | | a | | | | | | |
| *Onychomys leucogaster* (northern grasshopper mouse) | a | | | | | | | | | | | a | | | | a |
| *Sigmodon hispidus* (hispid cotton rat) | | | | | | a,c | | | | a,c | | a | a,c | | | a |
| *Neotoma* cf. *micropus* (southern plains wood rat) | | a | | | | | | | | | a | | | | | a |
| *Neotoma* cf. *albigula* (white-throated wood rat) | | | | | | | | | | | | | | | | a |
| *Microtus pennsylvanicus* (meadow vole)[b] | a | a | | | | a,c | a | a | | a | | a | | | | |
| *Microtus ochrogaster* (prairie vole)[b] | a | a | | | | a | | | | a,c | | a | a | | | a |
| *Ondatra zibethicus* (muskrat)[b] | a,c | a,c | | | | a,c | | c | c | a,c | | a,c | | | a | a,c |
| *Synaptomys cooperi* (southern bog lemming)[b] | | | | | | | | | | a | | a | | | | |
| *Canis latrans* (coyote) | a,c | | | | | c | | | | | | | d | | | d |
| *Canis lupus* (gray wolf) | c | | | | | d | c | | | a | | a | c | | | |
| *Vulpes macrotis* (kit fox)[b] | e | | | | | | | | | | | | | | | |
| ‡*Arctodus simus* (short-faced bear) | c | | | | | | | | | | | | | | | |
| *Taxidea taxus* (badger) | | | | | | | | | | | | | | | | d |
| *Mephitis mephitis* (common striped skunk) | | | | | | | | | | | | | | | | |

| ARCHAIC | | | | | | CERAMIC | | | PROTOHISTORIC | | | | | | | | | | | | | HISTORIC | | | | | | | | | |
|---|---|---|---|---|---|---|---|---|---|---|---|---|---|---|---|---|---|---|---|---|---|---|---|---|---|---|---|---|---|---|---|
| Early Archaic | Middle Archaic | | | | | Late Archaic/Early Ceramic | Late Ceramic | | | | | | | | | | | | | | | | | | | | | | | | |
| | ely | mid | | late | | A horizon LL Soil | | | | | | | | | | | | | | | | | | | | | | | | | |
| 2e | 3ℓ | 4A | | 4B | | | 4ℓ | 5ℓ | 5A1 | 5A1 | | | | | | | | | 5A2 | | 5ℓ | 5ℓ | | | | | | | 5B1 | 5B2 | |
| FA4-1 | non-f | FA6-21 | FA5-4 | FA16-1 | non-f | FA8-14 | FA1-3 | FA1-2 | FA8-5 | FA8-2 | FA8-3 | FA8-4 | FA8-6 | FA8-13 | FA14-1 | FA15-1 | FA19-1 | FA19-2 | FA8-7 | FA8-12 | FA5-6 | FA1-1 | FA5-2 | FA6-1 | FA6-10 | FA6-14 | FA6-19 | non-f | FA8-9 | FA8-1 | FA8-11 |
| | | | | | | | | | | | | | | | | | | | | | | | | | | | | | | | |
| | a | | | | | | | | | | | | | | | | | | | | a | | | | | | | | | | |
| | d | a | | | | | | | | | | | | | | | | | | | | | | | | | | | | | |
| | | | | | | | | | | | | | | | | | | | | | | | | | | | c | | | | |
| | | | | | | | | | | | | | | | | | | | | | | | | c | | | a | | | | |
| | | | a | | c | | | | | | | | | | | | | | | | | | | | | | | | | | |
| | | | | | | | | | | | | | | | | | | | | | | | | | | | | | | | |
| | | | | | | | | | | | | | | | | | | | | | | | | | | | | | | | |
| | a | a | | | | | | | | | | | | | | | | | | | | | | | | | a | | | | |
| | | | | | | | | | | | | | | | | | | | | | | | | | | | | | | | |
| | | a | | | | | | | | | | | | | | | | | | | | | | | | | | | | | |
| | | | | | | | | | | | | | | | | | | | | | | | | | | | | | | | |
| | | | | | | | | | | | | | | | | | | | | | | | | | | | | | | | |
| | | | | | | | | | | | | | | | | | | | | | | | | | | | | | | | |
| | | | | | | | | | | | | | | | | | | | | | | | | | | | | | | | |
| | d | a,c | | | | | | | c | | | c | | | | | | | | | c | c | c | a,c | a,c | c | | | d | d | |
| | | | | | | | | | | c | | c | | a | | | | | | | c | a,c | | c | c | | c | | | | |
| | | | | | | | | | | | | | | | | | | | | | | | | | | | | | | | |
| | | | | | | | | | | | | | | | | | | | | | | | | | | | | | | | |
| | | | | | | | | | | | | d | | | | | | | | | | | | | | | | | | | |
| | | | | | | | | | | | | | | | | | | | | | | c | | | | | | | | | |

Table 7.1. *Continued*

| Genus and Species (Common Name) | PALEOINDIAN | | | | | | | | | | | | | | | |
|---|---|---|---|---|---|---|---|---|---|---|---|---|---|---|---|---|
| | Clovis | | | | Folsom | | | Unknown | | Plainview | | | Firstview | | | |
| | 1B | | 1C | | 2ALB1 | 2ALB2/ 2ALB3 | | 2ALB4 | 2ALB5 | 2B cienega /2B base | | 2s | 2B | A horizon Firstview Soil | | |
| | FA2-1 | non-f | FA6-9 | non-f | non-f | FA6-8 | non-f | FA6-15 | non-f | FA6-11 | non-f | FA9-1 | non-f | FA5-8 | FA5-10 | FA6-3 |
| *Felis* cf. *rufus* (bobcat) | | | | | | | | | | | | | | | d | |
| ‡*Mammuthus columbi* (Columbian mammoth) | a,c | c | c | | | | | | | | | | | | | |
| ‡*Equus mexicanus* (extinct stout-legged horse) | c | c | | | | | | | | | | | | | | |
| ‡*Equus francisci* (extinct small stilt-legged horse) | c | c | | | | | | | | | | | | | | |
| *Equus caballus* (modern horse) | | | | | | | | | | | | | | | | |
| ‡*Platygonus compressus* (extinct peccary) | a | | | | | | | | | | | | | | | |
| ‡*Camelops hesternus* (extinct camel) | c | c | | | | | | | | | | | | | | |
| ‡*Hemiaucheina* (extinct llama) | | d | | | | | | | | | | | | | | |
| *Odocoileus* sp. (deer) | | | | | | | | | | a | | | | | | c |
| ‡*Capromeryx* sp. (extinct antelope) | | c | | | | e | | | | | | | | | | |
| *Antilocapra americana* (pronghorn antelope) | | | | | | | | | | a,c | | | d | | | a,c |
| ‡*Bison antiquus* (extinct bison) | a,c | | a,c | | | a,c | | a,c | | a,c | | a,c | a,c | a,c | a,c | a,c |
| *Bison bison* (modern bison) | | | | | | | | | | | | | | | | |

16518, 14172, 24134); left femur (TTU-A21129); right humerus (TTU-A21130)

The vertebrae represent both large and small individuals. This salamander is the only one that inhabits the Southern High Plains today, and it has both an aquatic larval and a terrestrial stage. It is often neotenic, reproducing in its larval stage. The tiger salamander frequents temporary pools, ponds, and playas in the area.

Remains of *A. tigrinum* were found in late Kansan to late Pleistocene and early Holocene deposits throughout Texas (Holman, 1969b), including the Slaton Quarry (Holman, 1969a). Neotenic remains of *A. tigrinum* were recovered from late Pleistocene deposits at Illusion Lake, in Lamb County (erroneously reported as Bailey County; Holman, 1975). In New Mexico, *A. tigrinum* was reported from late Pleistocene and early Holocene deposits in Eddy (Holman, 1970; Harris, 1977a), Grant (Van Devender and Worthington, 1977), and Hidalgo (Harris, 1985a) counties.

## Order Anura
## Family Pelobatidae

*Scaphiopus couchi* Baird, Couch's spadefoot toad
  Urostyle fused with last vertebra (TTU-A7644)
The angle between the shaft and the wing is greater in *S. hammondi* and *S. bombifrons* than in the Lubbock Lake specimen. The upper surface of the vertebral portion is reduced in the former species but not on this specimen, and the cotyle is a flat oval as in modern specimens of *S. couchi*. These characteristics are the basis for identification (Van Devender, personal communication).

Couch's spadefoot toad ranges throughout most of the western two-thirds of Texas into Mexico and the Southwest. The Texas portion of the Southern High Plains is the northeastern limit of its modern range. Found in semiarid to arid regions, it is a species of shortgrass plains and mesquite savanna.

| ARCHAIC | | | | | CERAMIC | | | PROTOHISTORIC | | | | | | | | | | | | | | HISTORIC | | | | | | | | | |
|---|---|---|---|---|---|---|---|---|---|---|---|---|---|---|---|---|---|---|---|---|---|---|---|---|---|---|---|---|---|---|---|
| Early Archaic | Middle Archaic | | | Late Archaic/ Early Ceramic | Late Ceramic | | | | | | | | | | | | | | | | | | | | | | | | | | |
| | ely | mid | | late | | | | | | | | | | | | | | | | | | | | | | | | | | | |
| 2e | 3ℓ | 4A | | 4B | A horizon LL Soil | 4ℓ | 5ℓ | 5A1 | 5A1 | | | | | | | | | | 5A2 | | 5ℓ | 5ℓ | | | | | | | 5B1 | 5B2 | |
| FA4-1 | non-f | FA6-21 | FA5-4 | FA16-1 / non-f | FA8-14 | FA1-3 | FA1-2 | FA8-5 | FA8-2 | FA8-3 | FA8-4 | FA8-6 | FA8-13 | FA14-1 | FA15-1 | FA19-1 | FA19-2 | FA8-7 | FA8-12 | FA5-6 | FA1-1 | FA5-2 | FA6-1 | FA6-10 | FA6-14 | FA6-19 | non-f | FA8-9 | FA8-1 | FA8-11 | |
| | | | | | | | | | | | | | | | | | | | | | | | | | | | | | | | |
| | | | | | | | | | | | | | | | | | | | | | | | | | | | | | | | |
| | | | | | | | | | | | | | | | | | | | | | c | a,c | c | | c | | | d | | | |
| | | | | | | | | | | | | | | | | | | | | | | | | | | | | | | | |
| | | | | | | | | | | | | | | | | | | | | | | | | | | | | | | | |
| | c,d | | | | a | | c | | | | d | | | | | | | | | | c | a,c | c | a,c | | c | | | | c | |
| a,c | | | | | | | | | | | | | | | | | | | | | | | | | | | | | | | |
| | d | c | c | c | a,c | a,c | a,c | a,c | c | c | c | c | c | a,c | c | c | c | a,c | d | a,c | a,c | a,c | a,c | a,c | a,c | a,c | c | c | c | c | |

Although it is unknown from the fossil record in Texas, on the basis of size Mecham (1959) considered the *Scaphiopus* sp. material from Friesenhahn Cave (Edwards Plateau) to represent either *S. couchi* or *S. holbrooki hurteri*. Late Pleistocene and early Holocene records for *S. couchi* are reported from Grant (Van Devender and Worthington, 1977), Dona Ana (Brattstrom, 1964), and Eddy (Applegarth, 1979) counties, in southern New Mexico.

*Scaphiopus bombifrons* Cope or *S. hammondi* Baird, plains or western spadefoot toad
  Vertebra (TTU-A16485)
The vertebra is amphicoelus with subrounded cotyles, and the neural spine is reduced on the dorsal surface of the neural arch but developed into a posteriorly pointing spine. These features are characteristic of these spadefoot toads. Furthermore, the condyle is more fused in *S. couchi* than in these toads (Van Devender, personal communication).

The ranges of these two spadefoot toads overlap in western Texas, New Mexico, the Panhandle of Oklahoma, and Colorado. Both are found near permanent and temporary water, and they prefer sandy or gravelly soil for burrowing. Both are open-grasslands forms, although *S. hammondi* is known from desert scrub to mountain pine-oak woodlands.

These spadefoot toads are unknown from the fossil record of Texas but are reported from late Pleistocene and early Holocene deposits from Howell's Ridge (Van Devender and Worthington, 1977), Dry (Holman, 1970; Applegarth, 1979), and Dark Canyon (Applegarth, 1979) caves, in southern New Mexico.

**Family Hylidae**

*Acris* cf. *crepitans* Baird, cricket frog
  Ilium (TTU-A16119); 3 vertebrae (TTU-A9621, 16746, 11464)

In both the Lubbock Lake material and modern *Acris* specimens the dorsal prominence (crest) of the ilium is a distinct, round knob facing dorsolaterally. The anterior edge of the ventral acetabular expansion is nearly vertical. The ilia of *Hyla* and *Pseudacris* have thinner dorsal prominences that are not knobs. The anterior edge of the ventral acetabular expansion is broader and arched in these genera. *Gastrophryne* ilia have a thin dorsal prominence and an extremely expanded anterior edge of the ventral acetabular expansion. Holman (1964) further discusses these characteristics of the pelvic girdle. With the vertebrae *Gastrophryne* have a broad (anterior-posterior) centrum with distinctly rounded cotyle and condyle. The last vertebra and urostyle are fused and winged as in *Scaphiopus*. Vertebrae of *Hyla* and *Pseudacris* have a somewhat more distinct cotyle and condyle and a longer (anterior-posterior) neural arch. The Lubbock Lake specimens do not share these characteristics and are too small to be *Rana*. They, therefore, have been referred to this species (Van Devender, personal communication).

The cricket frog ranges throughout the Southern and Central Plains and much of the eastern half of the United States. It reaches part of its western limit on the Southern High Plains in the Lubbock area. Found in or near semipermanent to permanent waters, the cricket frog inhabits low vegetation along banks in areas receiving maximum sun. They are also found along small or intermittent streams with sandy, gravelly, or muddy bars.

Fossil remains of *A. crepitans* were reported from various late Kansan to late Pleistocene localities in Texas (Holman, 1969b), including Slaton Quarry (Holman, 1969a). It appears to be unknown in the fossil record of New Mexico.

## Family Bufonidae

*Bufo woodhousei bexarensis* Mecham, Friesenhahn Cave toad

Frontoparietal (TTU-A11098); right ilium (TTU-A9563)

An extinct subspecies, *B. w. bexarensis* is known from only two other late Pleistocene and early Holocene Texas localities, both on the Edwards Plateau. The type locality is Friesenhahn Cave (Mecham, 1959). This toad was also found at Schulze Cave (Holman, 1969c). Size is the major factor separating the larger extinct subspecies from the smaller modern *B. w. woodhousei* (Mecham, 1959; Holman, 1969c). Applegarth (1979) discounted size as a valid character to separate the larger late Pleistocene form from the modern subspecies and suggested that the two were the same subspecies. Although probably valid, without a taxonomic review as the basis the two forms are treated as separate subspecies.

The Lubbock Lake ilium displays *woodhousei* characteristics. The dorsal prominence is too well developed to be *Scaphiopus,* and the dorsal keel is not developed enough to be *Rana*. The dorsal prominence is about as high as it is long and is roughened at the angle to the shaft. It has a rugose knob perpendicular to the shaft. *Bufo cognatus* has a higher, thinner dorsal prominence. The shaft is more arched and thinner just anterior to the dorsal prominence in *B. cog-*

*natus* and is flatter and taller in *B. woodhousei*. Ilia of *B. speciosus* have the dorsal prominence slightly higher than *B. woodhousei* and with a posterior knob. The dorsal prominence in *B. valliceps* is lower and broader than in *B. woodhousei* (Van Devender, personal communication). Ilia of this subspecies are compared in table 7.2.

*Bufo woodhousei woodhousei* (Woodhouse's toad) now ranges throughout the plains area, including the Edwards Plateau and the Southern High Plains. The two subspecies probably occurred in similar habitats. Woodhouse's toad inhabits a variety of moist environments including marshes, floodplains, grasslands, and wooded areas.

Vertebrae (TTU-A9963, 14684, 16075), humerus (TTU-A9696), urostyles (TTU-A16215, 16714), and tibiofibula (TTU-A16872) were identified as *Bufo* sp. (medium-sized). Two other species of medium-sized toads besides *B. woodhousei,* (*B. cognatus* [Great Plains toad] and *B. speciosus* [Texas toad]) occur on the Southern High Plains.

## Family Ranidae

*Rana catesbeiana* Shaw, bullfrog

4 humeri (TTU-A11170, 9376, 13325, 14623); 3 radio-ulnae (TTU-A13033, 12781, 12780); 2 scapulae (TTU-A15532, 15533); 2 right ilia (TTU-A11173, 10665); 6 left ilia (TTU-A9882, 13079, 12790, 10668, 13121, 13195); other postcranial elements

The various species of *Rana* were distinguished on the shape of the articular surfaces and size of the specimens. Holman (1963, 1964, 1970) discussed various osteological aspects separating the species. The *R. catesbeiana* specimens are small, but the shape of the articular surfaces compares well with modern specimens, and these may represent young individuals. Holman (1966a) noted that the *R. catesbeiana* specimens from the Miller's Cave fauna, Edwards Plateau, represent small bullfrogs.

The bullfrog has a wide distribution throughout much of the United States. An aquatic frog, it inhabits ponds, marshes, and quiet waters of streams.

Remains of *R. catesbeiana* were found in late Pleistocene deposits in northeastern Texas (Holman, 1963) and deposits from late Pleistocene to early Holocene on the Edwards Plateau (Holman, 1966a). Mecham (1959) commented that the *Rana* sp. material from Friesenhahn Cave is probably *R. catesbeiana*.

Table 7.2. Measurements of Ilia of *Bufo woodhousei bexarensis* (Friesenhahn Cave Toad) from Texas Localities

| Locality and Catalog No. | Height of Acetabular Cup, mm |
|---|---|
| Lubbock Lake | |
| TTU-A9563 | 3.90 |
| Friesenhahn Cave | |
| 933-3650a | 4.75 |
| 933-3650b | 5.20 |
| Schulze Cave* | |
| C₂ | 3.70–7.70 (median, 5.68) |

*After Holman 1969b.

*Rana palustris* Le Conte, pickerel frog
2 humeri (TTU-A9869, 9880)

An eastern species, the pickerel frog ranges into eastern Texas. The nearest occurrence is in Brazos County, along the Brazos River system. The Yellowhouse system forms the western portion of this system. This frog inhabits permanent waters of springs, marshes, meadow streams, and the surrounding grasslands. *Rana palustris* is currently unknown elsewhere from the fossil records of Texas.

*Rana pipiens* Schreber, leopard frog
Skeleton (TTU-A7257); partial skeleton (TTU-A3022); 14 radio-ulnae (TTU-A9438, 9971, 10661, 10664, 10687, 11108, 13129, 13187, 13482, 13493, 15009, 21132); 25 humeri (TTU-A3022, 9574, 9742, 9748, 9756, 9760, 9834, 9846, 9918, 9986, 10645, 10685, 10802, 11170, 11909, 12782, 13934, 13972, 15009, 21131, 21775, 21881, 22593, 22596); 36 ilia, (TTU-A9882, 9920, 9921, 10689, 10702, 10733, 10736, 10737, 10738, 11016, 11393, 11491, 12788, 13080, 13132, 13934, 15009, 15552, 15778, 15796, 16561, 21867, 21874, 21956, 22969, 23141, 23184, 23190); 4 urostyles (TTU-A10783, 13194, 15552); 10 maxillae sections (TTU-A12743, 12791, 12798, 16141, 16378, 17224, 21778); 2 mandibles (TTU-A10681, 11096); 1 premaxilla (TTU-A16346); numerous other postcranial elements.

This frog occurs throughout most of the United States. The *R. pipiens* complex was separated into various species (Littlejohn and Oldham, 1968; Mecham, 1969; Mecham et al., 1973), but not on osteological characters. The different species of the complex were not distinguished in the Lubbock Lake specimens. Leopard frogs frequent permanent waters with areas of aquatic vegetation growth. They are commonly found in and around marshes, ponds, creeks, and other sources of water.

On the Southern High Plains remains of *R. pipiens* were recovered from the Slaton Quarry (Holman, 1969a) and the brown-sand wedge unit at Blackwater Draw Locality No. 1 (Slaughter, 1975). They were recorded from Sangamonian and early Wisconsinan deposits in Texas from Denton (Holman, 1963), Foard (Holman, 1962), and Harris (Holman, 1965a) counties. Late Pleistocene and early Holocene localities in Texas and New Mexico include Friesenhahn (Mecham, 1959), Miller's (Holman, 1966a), Dry (Holman, 1970; Applegarth, 1979), Dark Canyon (Applegarth, 1979), Shelter (Brattstrom, 1964), and Howell's Ridge (Van Devender and Worthington, 1977) caves. Numerous postcranial elements from Lubbock Lake were identified to *Rana* sp. and most probably are *R. pipiens*.

## REPTILES

### Order Chelonia
### Family Chelydridae

*Chelydra serpentina* (Linnaeus), snapping turtle
Proximal end of left humerus, fragments of other long bones, and carapace sections from one individual (TTU-A1918); right femur (TTU-A20845); left and right humeri (TTU-

A19750, 19712); left and right tibiae (TTU-A19713, 23649); right innominate (TTU-A20853); carapace sections (TTU-A2552, 2553, 2570, 4019, 4028)

This turtle is very common throughout the eastern half of the United States, including most of Texas. A large, aquatic turtle, the snapper favors permanent waters of marshes, ponds, and slow streams with abundant vegetation growth. In shallow water it prefers muddy areas where it can bury itself. The snapper is a bottom-dweller and feeds mainly on vegetation, although animal matter is also consumed. The snapper hibernates in the winter, emerging sometime between March and May.

*Chelydra serpentina* is known from late Pleistocene deposits in Hardeman County, Texas (Holman, 1964).

## Family Kinosternidae

*Kinosternon flavescens* (Agassiz), yellow mud turtle
Right and left humeri (TTU-A13393, 18019); right ilium and pubis (TTU-A8690); left pubis (TTU-A13317); numerous carapace and plastron sections

Shell sections of the mud turtle are distinctive by their shape and thinness. Postcranial bones are scarce but are identical to those of *K. flavescens* in the comparative collection.

Apparently not known from any late Pleistocene deposits in Texas (Holman, 1969b), the yellow mud turtle ranges today throughout the Central and Southern Plains into Mexico. It inhabits bodies of water in semiarid grasslands and woodlands, preferring muddy bottoms of either temporary or permanent waters. Mud turtles come out on land to feed and can be seen on land migrating from a drying pool or during rains.

## Family Testudinidae

*Geochelone wilsoni* (Milstead), extinct Wilson's tortoise
Pleural sections (TTU-A2562, 3034)

*Geochelone* carapace sections are distinctive in structure, having in cross section very dense bone. Various species of *Geochelone* occur throughout the Pleistocene of Texas (Holman, 1969b). These are large animals with very thick shells. *Geochelone wilsoni* is a small form of this genus and appears restricted to the late Pleistocene of the Southern Plains and Edwards Plateau. The small size and distinctive ridging are the basis of identification. The pleurals are thicker than those of *Gopherus berlandieri* and *G. agassizi* at a similar size (Moodie and Van Devender, 1979). One pleural is from a juvenile. The element has prominent growth ridges on both the dorsal and the ventral edges of the scute. In the young of *Chrysemys* and *Terrapene* they are mainly on the ventral edge.

*Geochelone wilsoni* was reported from several late Pleistocene and early Holocene localities in Texas and New Mexico. The type locality is Friesenhahn Cave (Milstead, 1956), on the Edwards Plateau. Other localities include Blackwater Draw Locality No. 1 (Slaughter, 1975); Dry

Cave (Moodie and Van Devender, 1979), in eastern New Mexico; the Domebo site (Slaughter, 1966a), in southern Oklahoma; and the Buckner Ranch site (Moodie and Van Devender, 1979), in south Texas.

*Geochelone* sp., extinct tortoise
    Carapace sections (TTU-A3919, 4084, 11261, 3919)
From a large species in the *G. crassiscutata* group, the material is characterized by very distinctive ridging on the carapace and its large size. A fossiliferous Blancan age deposit occurs at the site, and the possibility exists of reworking of material into the Clovis-age stream. However, *G. crassiscutata* was a food source for man in Florida (Clausen et al., 1979).

*Geochelone* cf. *crassiscutata* is known from Sangamonian deposits in Dallas County (Slaughter, 1966b) and the Wisconsinan Ingleside fauna in San Patricio County (Lundelius, 1972b).

## Family Emydidae

*Chrysemys scripta* (Schoepff), pond slider
    Complete shell (TTU-A24614); skull and mandible (TTU-A24963); left humerus (TTU-A24616); right scapula (TTU-A24616); left ilium (TTU-A21589); numerous carapace and plastron sections
Besides size, shape, and thickness, pond-slider carapace sections are distinctive in their strong ridging and very rugose nature (fig. 7.1). The synonymy of Weaver and Rose (1967) for the genera *Pseudemys* and *Chrysemys* is followed.

*Chrysemys scripta* occurs throughout most of Texas into the central plains and prairie region and through the Southeast. An aquatic turtle, the pond slider seldom comes ashore. It favors areas of dense vegetation in quiet waters with muddy bottoms.

An extinct subspecies of *C. scripta* is known from the late Kansan deposits in Knox County, Texas (Preston, 1966). Except for shell thickness, the extinct subspecies (*C. s. bisornata*) is identical to the modern subspecies *C. s. elegans*. The only difference between the complete Lubbock Lake shell (fig. 7.1) and modern *C. s. elegans* is the thicker shell of the Lubbock Lake specimen. Because shell thickness alone was not considered a valid taxonomic character, the Lubbock Lake specimen was considered to represent a thick-shelled individual of *C. s. elegans*. The Knox County specimen may well represent the same.

*Chrysemys scripta* is known from Sangamonian deposits in Denton County (Holman, 1963) and Wisconsinan deposits in Harris (Holman, 1965a) and San Patricio (Lundelius, 1972b) counties. *Chrysemys* sp. is recorded from late Pleistocene deposits in Hardeman County (Holman, 1964).

*Terrapene carolina putnami* (Hay), extinct Carolina box turtle .
    Partial shell (TTU-A3030); anterior plastral lobe (TTU-A3051); 2 hypoplastrons (TTU-A5411, 17662); 2 xiphiplastrons (TTU-A24657); left tibia (TTU-A24657); left scapula (TTU-A24657); carapace and other plastral pieces
Remains of the extinct Carolina box turtle are distinguished

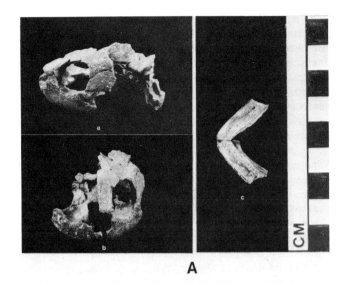

**A**

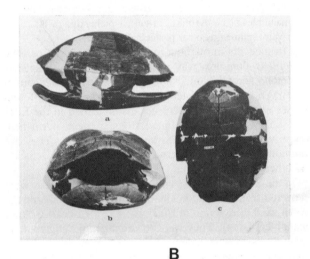

**B**

Fig. 7.1. Skull (TTU-A24963, substratum 1C) and shell (TTU-A24614, substrata 2A/2B) of *Chrysemys scripta* (pond slider). A: lateral (a) and anterior (b) views of skull and dorsal (c) view of mandible; B: lateral (a), anterior (b), and ventral (c) views of shell (photographs by Jerome L. Thompson).

by size, shape, and shell thickness. On the basis of size, the Lubbock Lake specimens are a large form. But because size is variable, particularly during this time period, whether they represent Milstead's (1967, 1969) extinct subspecies or an intermediate form is a moot point. Measurements (table 7.3) on the partial shell and anterior lobe (fig. 7.2) are comparable with the *putnami* form of the Friesenhahn Cave population (Milstead, 1956, 1969), the intermediate form from the Ingleside fauna (Lundelius, 1972b; Milstead, 1967, 1969), and the specimen (= *T. canaliculata*) from Blackwater Draw Locality No. 1 (Lundelius, 1972a). The anterior lobe is not as large as that from the intermediate form at the Lewisville locality (Holman, 1966b; Milstead, 1967) but is much larger than the small *triunguis* identified in the late Pleistocene deposits at Cave-Without-A-Name (Holman, 1968).

The Carolina box turtle is an eastern animal that no longer occurs in the area. The closest occurrence today of the modern form (*T. carolina triunguis*) is in eastern Texas and Oklahoma. This terrestrial box turtle favors relatively flat terrain in open woodlands, thickets, and fields. It hibernates in the winter, becoming active again in the spring. Holman (1969b) summarized the Sangamonian and Wisconsinan occurrences in Texas. *Terrapene carolina* ssp. indet. was reported from Sangamonian and early Wisconsinan deposits in Dallas (Slaughter, 1966) and Denton (Holman, 1963) counties.

The Southern High Plains are the northwesternmost extension of the range of *T. carolina* (whatever the subspecies). A record at Burnet Cave (Gehlbach and Holman, 1974), Guadalupe Mountains, New Mexico, extends its late Pleistocene range even farther west. *Terrapene carolina putnami* is also reported from the Slaton Quarry (Dalquest, 1967; Milstead, 1967), Blackwater Draw Locality No. 1 (Lundelius, 1972a, Slaughter, 1975; E. Hughes, 1984), and Anderson Basin No. 1 (Lundelius, 1972a). Milstead (1967) identified the Anderson Basin No. 1 material as *T. c. triunguis*.

*Terrapene ornata* (Agassiz), ornate box turtle
    Right humerus (TTU-A134); left humeri (TTU-A871, 13276); left femur (TTU-A228); right coracoid (TTU-A87); left tibia (TTU-A21133); numerous carapace and plastron sections

The ornate box turtle can be distinguished from the Carolina box turtle by the comparative flatness of the carapace, lack of a keel, and the larger and longer plastron. The ornate box turtle is a common terrestrial turtle throughout the Central and Southern Plains into Louisiana and the Southwest. Preferring sandy soil, it inhabits prairie grasslands and treeless areas. It hibernates during the winter and is active from March to November. It tolerates arid conditions by burrowing to escape the excessive heat. Many carapace fragments were identified to *Terrapene* sp. and probably are from *T. ornata*.

Fossil *T. ornata* remains were reported from Sangamonian deposits in Denton County (Holman, 1963; Milstead, 1969). Other late Pleistocene records in Texas are currently unknown (Holman, 1969b).

## Family Trionychidae

*Trionyx* sp., softshell turtle
    Carapace sections (TTU-A5000, 5494, 9712, 16098, 16757, 24651)

The carapace sections have the characteristic pitting of the genus, but the material is too fragmentary for species identification. Two species occur in Texas, *T. muticus* (smooth softshell) and *T. spiniferus* (spiny softshell).

Although spiny softshells have a wider distribution and occur in western Texas, both forms are found along the Ca-

nadian River in the Texas Panhandle. These aquatic turtles are essentially river turtles but occur in other quiet bodies of water and are often found buried in the mud or sand of shallow waters. They hibernate by November and become active again in April or May.

Remains of *Trionyx* occur in several Pleistocene localities in Texas (Holman, 1969b), including the Ingleside fauna (Lundelius, 1972b) on the Gulf Coast and Quitaque local fauna (Dalquest, 1964) near the eastern escarpment of the Southern High Plains.

Table 7.3. Maximum Shell and Anterior Lobe Measurements of *Terrapene carolina putnami* (Extinct Carolina Box Turtle)

| Locality and Catalog No. | Shell | Anterior Lobe | |
|---|---|---|---|
| | Length, mm | Length, mm | Width, mm |
| Lubbock Lake | | | |
|   TTU-A3030 | 221 | | |
|   TTU-A3051 | | 85 | 116.4 |
| Blackwater Draw | | | |
|   937-899 | | 81.1 | — |
| Friesenhahn | | | |
|   933-3586 | 235 | | |
|   933-3239 | 213 | | |
|   933-2104 | | 98.9 | 124.2 |
|   933-3586 | | 86.7 | 115.0 |
|   933-2512 | | 83.3 | 104.4* |
| Ingleside | | | |
|   30967-617 | 208 | | |
|   30967-363 | 192 | | |
|   30967-682 | 188 | | |
|   30967-270 | | 85.1 | 119.4 |
|   30967-1983 | | 82.3 | 110.5 |
|   30967-260 | | 77.5 | 99.6 |
| Lewisville† | | 100.0 | 141.0 |
| Slaton Quarry | | | |
|   882-515 | | 84.4 | 116.0* |

*Estimate, owing to damage to edge.
†From Holman 1966b.

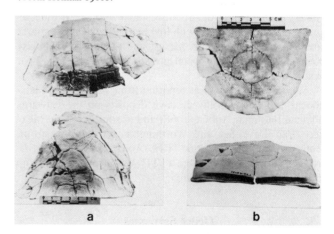

Fig. 7.2. Partial carapace (TTU-A3030) and anterior plastral lobe (TTU-A3051) of *Terrapene carolina putnami* (extinct Carolina box turtle) from stratum 1. a: lateral and anterior views of carapace; b: dorsal and posterior views of plastral lobe (note deep hinge joint characteristic of *Terrapene*) (photographs by Jerome L. Thompson).

## Order Squamata
## Suborder Lacertilia
## Family Iguanidae

*Phrynosoma cornutum* (Harlan), Texas horned lizard
  Dentaries (TTU-A9361, 15553); horned parietal (TTU-A7911, 15264); frontal (TTU-A1774)
This lizard occurs throughout most of Texas and from the Central Plains to Mexico. The three species can be differentiated by the horns on the posterior of the parietal as well as from other skull elements. The Texas horned lizard has two long horns. The dentary of this species has an angular ventrolateral edge, and the teeth are reduced to small pegs. Holman (1968, 1970) and Robinson and Van Devender (1973) further discuss mandibular and dental differences between the species.

The favored habitats of the horned lizard are the arid and semiarid areas of open terrain with sparse vegetation. They prefer sandy, rocky, or loamy soil.

*Phrynosoma cornutum* was reported from the Slaton Quarry (Holman, 1969a) and from late Pleistocene and early Holocene cave deposits in Kendall County, Texas (Holman, 1968), and Eddy (Holman, 1970; Applegarth, 1979), Grant (Van Devender and Worthington, 1977), and Dona Ana (Brattstrom, 1964) counties, New Mexico.

### Family Scincidae

*Eumeces obsoletus* (Baird and Girard), Great Plains skink
  Left maxilla (TTU-A18169); left mandible (TTU-A18635); 2 vertebrae (TTU-A12747, 15531)
Teeth of this skink are transversely expanded with simple crowns that are curved inward lingually and have striae on the lingual surface. Meckel's canal is open ventrolaterally (Van Devender, personal communication). Holman (1966a) noted additional characteristics.

The Great Plains skink ranges throughout the Central and Southern Plains into the Southwest and Mexico. It inhabits grasslands in open areas with low plant growth. In semiarid areas it inhabits canyons, mesas, and mountains in grassy areas and areas of low plant growth in rock outcrops near water.

*Eumeces obsoletus* was reported from various late Pleistocene and early Holocene cave deposits on the Edwards Plateau (Holman, 1966a, 1968) and in southern New Mexico (Van Devender and Worthington, 1977; Brattstrom, 1964). A maxillary section (TTU-A9917) may be from *E. obsoletus,* while a vertebra (TTU-A15326) may be from this skink or a horned lizard.

### Order Serpentes
### Family Colubridae

*Coluber constrictor* Linnaeus, racer
  123 vertebrae (TTU-A13842, 13871, 13971)
The vertebrae cataloged as TTU-A13842 were found *in situ,* representing the coiled, partial skeleton of an individual. Racers occur throughout a large part of the United States, including the northern Texas Panhandle area and the Rolling Plains east of the Southern High Plains. They inhabit meadows, prairies, and open woodlands and are often found in grassy areas along water sources.

Fossil remains of *C. constrictor* were recovered from Sangamonian deposits in Dallas County (Slaughter, 1966). Late Pleistocene and early Holocene records are known from the Edwards Plateau (Hill, 1971) and southern New Mexico (Brattstrom, 1964).

*Carphophis amoenus* (Say), worm snake
  3 vertebrae (TTU-A11162, 11365, 16111)
Worm snakes are an eastern species, the closest occurrence to the site being in central Oklahoma. This snake favors moist habitats in wooded areas. The western form follows stream valleys in the prairie area. The Lubbock Lake specimens represent both the first Texas late Pleistocene fossil record and the westernmost range extension for this snake.

*Elaphe guttata* Linnaeus, Great Plains rat snake
  3 vertebrae (TTU-A9999, 11164)
The Great Plains rat snake (*E. g. emoryi*) ranges throughout Texas, extending into the Southeast, the Central Plains, and New Mexico. Favoring canyon or hillside areas, this snake is often found near water.

*Elaphe guttata* is known from late Pleistocene deposits on the Edwards Plateau (Hill, 1971) and in southeastern New Mexico (Holman, 1970).

*Gyalopion canum* Cope, western hook-nosed snake
  Vertebra (TTU-A11080)
The western hook-nosed snake ranges south of the Southern High Plains into Mexico. Although not occurring in the region today, specimens were taken less than 161 km (100 miles) east of Lubbock, off the escarpment, in King and Dickens counties (Chrapliwy and Ward, 1963). *Gyalopion canum* is a burrowing snake that inhabits semiarid grasslands and desert shrub habitats.

*Gyalopion canum* was reported from the late Pleistocene and early Holocene deposits at Howell's Ridge Cave, in southern New Mexico (Van Devender and Worthington, 1977).

*Heterodon nasicus* Baird and Girard, western hognose snake
  5 vertebrae (TTU-A9775, 9793, 11215, 16120, 16286)
Occurring throughout the plains area, the western hognose snake favors prairie grasslands and floodplain areas with sandy soils. This snake has a long temporal fossil distribution in Texas from late Kansan to early Holocene (Holman, 1969b). On the Southern High Plains it was reported from the brown-sand wedge at Blackwater Draw Locality No. 1 (Slaughter, 1975). *Heterodon nasicus* also is known from a late Pleistocene and early Holocene cave deposit in southern New Mexico (Van Devender and Worthington, 1977).

*Lampropeltis getulus* Linnaeus, common kingsnake
  55 vertebrae (TTU-A8481, 9380, 13884, 13959, 15029)

The kingsnake ranges throughout most of the southern half of the United States. A nocturnal and terrestrial snake, it occurs in a variety of habitats. It is often found along stream banks or in marshlands, where it feeds on turtle eggs, small lizards, birds, rodents, and other snakes.

Fossil remains of *L. getulus* were recovered from late Pleistocene and early Holocene deposits in Texas (Holman, 1964; Hill, 1971) and New Mexico (Brattstrom, 1964; Van Devender and Worthington, 1977). Holman (1969a) reported it from the Slaton Quarry.

*Lampropeltis triangulum* (Lacepede), milk snake
Vertebra (TTU-A11263)
Occurring on the Southern High Plains today, the milk snake ranges throughout Texas, south into Mexico, and north to the Northern Plains and eastward. It lives in a wide variety of habitats, from woodlands to rocky canyons to open prairie. Late Pleistocene and early Holocene Texas records of *L. triangulum* are from the Edwards Plateau and Hardeman County (Holman, 1969b).

*Nerodia* cf. *cyclopion* (Dumeril and Bibron) or *N.* cf. *rhombifera* (Hallowell), green water snake or diamondback water snake
48 vertebrae (TTU-A13980)
The material recovered represents a single individual. The Gulf Coast of Texas is the nearest occurrence of the green water snake. An aquatic snake, it inhabits ponds, marshes, and other waterways, preferring quiet waters along banks and edges. The diamondback water snake does not range onto the Southern High Plains today. However, it reaches the eastern fringe area in its modern distribution and is known from the Brazos River system. It inhabits permanent waters, basks on grassy banks, and occasionally can be found in adjacent grassland areas along a waterway.

Both species are currently unknown from other late Pleistocene and early Holocene deposits in Texas and New Mexico.

*Nerodia erythrogaster* (Forster), red-bellied water snake
Vertebra (TTU-A7817)
This water snake ranges throughout the Southeast, the Central Plains, and most of Texas. It inhabits permanent to semipermanent waters from rivers to ditches and occasionally comes ashore.

Records of this snake from other late Pleistocene deposits in Texas are tentative since the material reported represents either *N. erythrogaster/N. fasciata?* (banded water snake) or *N. erythrogaster/N. sipedon?* (common water snake) (Holman, 1963, 1969b). *Nerodia* (= *Natrix*) *erythrogaster* is reported from the Slaton Quarry (Holman, 1969a). One vertebra (TTU-A9774) was identified to *Nerodia* sp. and could represent either *N. erythrogaster* or *N. rhombifera*.

*Pituophis melanoleucus* (Daudin), bull snake
Vertebra (TTU-A7724)
Bull snakes range throughout much of the Southeast, the plains, and the western United States. Although occurring in a wide variety of habitats, in the West they favor grass-

lands and open brushlands.

*Pituophis melanoleucus* remains were reported from the late Pleistocene deposit of Friesenhahn Cave (Mecham, 1959) and Cave-Without-A-Name (Hill, 1971), on the Edwards Plateau, and late Pleistocene and early Holocene records at Howell's Ridge Cave (Van Devender and Worthington, 1977), Shelter Cave, and Conkling Cavern (Brattstrom, 1964), in southern New Mexico. A broken vertebra (TTU-A2519) was identified as either *Pituophis* sp. or *Elaphe* sp.

*Rhinocheilus lecontei* Baird and Girard, long-nosed snake
Vertebra (TTU-A9379)
A burrowing, nocturnal animal, this snake occurs throughout the Southern Plains into Mexico and west into California and the Great Basin area. Throughout much of its range the long-nosed snake is found in dry prairies, brushlands, and deserts.

*Rhinocheilus lecontei* is known from late Pleistocene and early Holocene deposits on the Edwards Plateau (Hill, 1971) and from Grant County, New Mexico (Van Devender and Worthington, 1977), and the Guadalupe Mountains (Logan, 1977). Holman (1969a) reported it from the Slaton Quarry.

*Salvadora* sp., patch-nosed snake
Vertebra (TTU-A16466)
Both Holman (1970) and Van Devender and Worthington (1977) noted the difficulty of separating the two species of this genus on vertebrae. This genus has a southern distribution from Central Texas, the Trans-Pecos, and the Southwest into Mexico. In its western range *S. grahamiae* generally inhabits open woodlands in mountainous areas. In its more humid eastern range (central to south Texas), it ranges into prairies. *Salvadora hexalepis* inhabits semiarid grasslands.

Not known from the fossil record in Texas, *Salvadora* sp. was reported from late Pleistocene and early Holocene deposits in southern New Mexico (Holman, 1970; Van Devender and Worthington, 1977; Harris 1985a).

*Sonora semiannulata* Baird and Girard, ground snake
9 vertebrae (TTU-A7746, 9430, 9803, 11048, 11429, 13994, 15046, 15258, 17229)
This small, secretive snake occurs throughout the Southern Plains and into the Southwest and California. It frequents a variety of habitats in prairies and open woodlands, preferring sandy soils along creek bottoms, rocky hillsides, or open areas.

This ground snake is unknown from late Pleistocene and early Holocene deposits elsewhere in Texas. Van Devender and Worthington (1977) reported remains of *S. semiannulata* from late Pleistocene and early Holocene deposits in southern New Mexico.

*Thamnophis* cf. *marcianus* Baird and Girard, checkered garter snake
2 vertebrae (TTU-A13965, 15050)
The checkered garter snake ranges throughout the Southern Plains into Mexico and the Southwest. Primarily inhabiting

lowland grassland areas, this snake occurs in and around ponds, streams, and other areas of water. *Thamnophis marcianus* or *T. radix* (plains garter snake) was reported from both late Kansan and late Pleistocene deposits in Knox and Hardeman counties, just east of the Southern High Plains (Holman, 1964, 1965b), and in late Pleistocene deposits in Eddy County, New Mexico (Holman, 1970).

*Thamnophis proximus* Say, ribbon snake
   11 vertebrae (TTU-A9415, 13867, 13874, 13876, 13883, 13960, 13993)
The ribbon snake occurs throughout most of Texas and into the Central Plains and eastward. A semiaquatic snake, it inhabits the grassland edges of ponds, streams, marshes, and other areas of permanent water.

   *Thamnophis proximus* was reported from several localities in Texas ranging in time from Illinoian (Holman, 1969a) to late Pleistocene and early Holocene deposits (Holman, 1969b). Holman (1970) recorded it from late Pleistocene deposits in Eddy County, New Mexico, and it was present in the brown-sand wedge (= *T. sauritus*) at Blackwater Draw Locality No. 1 (Slaughter, 1975).

*Thamnophis* cf. *sirtalis* Linnaeus, common garter snake
   15 vertebrae (TTU-A9867, 9952, 9982, 9983, 11131, 7982, 12741, 12787, 13877)
The common garter snake ranges throughout the northwestern to eastern United States, including eastern Texas. Disjunct populations in New Mexico, Kansas, and the northern Panhandle of Texas attest to the greater northern extent of its former range. This garter snake inhabits situations similar to those of the last two snakes above.

   Remains of *T. sirtalis* were reported from the brown-sand wedge at Blackwater Draw Locality No. 1 (Slaughter, 1975) and from late Pleistocene deposits at Cave-Without-A-Name, Kendall County, Texas (Hill, 1971). Fourteen vertebrae (TTU-A9744, 9745, 9794, 9950, 11041, 11049, 11167, 11183, 9728, 9950, 11041, 11049, 11167, 11183, 9728, 9729, 9415, 13992, 10536, 10683) were identified as *Thamnophis* sp.

*Tropidoclonion lineatum* Hallowell, lined snake
   3 vertebrae (TTU-A11184, 13990, 16599)
Occurring in the Central Plains and eastern Texas, the lined snake has a disjunct distribution. The nearest isolated population is in the northwest corner of the Panhandle extending into New Mexico and Colorado. This snake inhabits prairies, sparsely wooded areas, and floodplains. In the Texas and New Mexico areas *T. lineatum* is known elsewhere only from late Kansan deposits in Knox County (Holman, 1965b).

*Virginia* cf. *striatula,* rough earth snake
   9 vertebrae (TTU-A9727, 9862, 11040, 11081, 11185, 11186, 11191, 9812, 15515)
An eastern genus, *V. striatula* ranges into eastern Texas. Specimens were taken in Throckmorton County, less than 322 km (200 miles) east of Lubbock (Raun and Gehlbach, 1972). It is a small, secretive, nocturnal, terrestrial snake.

Although inhabiting wooded areas, *V. striatula* also occurs in grassy slopes and moist areas around streams and other bodies of water.

   *Virginia striatula* was reported from late Pleistocene deposits in Denton County, Texas (Holman, 1963).

### Family Viperidae

*Agkistrodon contortrix* Linnaeus, copperhead
   6 vertebrae (TTU-A13869, 13880, 13987)
A poisonous snake, the copperhead does not occur on the Southern High Plains today but ranges through the Trans-Pecos, Central Texas, the Central Plains area, and farther east. Two subspecies have ranges that are closest to the Southern High Plains, *A. c. laticinctus* (broad-banded copperhead) and *A. c. pictigaster* (Trans-Pecos copperhead). Although favoring wooded areas, the former also occurs in brushy areas of grasslands, and the latter in oases and canyons with permanent water.

   Remains of *A. contortrix* were found in late Pleistocene deposits in Kendall (Hill, 1971) and Hardeman (Holman, 1965b) counties, Texas. One vertebra (TTU-A13878) was identified as either *Agkistrodon* sp. or *Crotalus* sp.

*Crotalus atrox* Baird and Girard, western diamondback rattlesnake
   2 vertebrae (TTU-A9648, 24703)
Another poisonous snake, this rattlesnake ranges throughout much of the Southern Plains into the Southwest and Mexico. A semiarid species, it occurs in a variety of habitats from grasslands to brushlands and rocky canyons to floodplains. On the Southern High Plains it frequents the mixed-grass prairie and outcrops of the draws and canyons.

   Fossil remains of *C. atrox* were recovered from late Pleistocene and early Holocene deposits on the Edwards Plateau (Mecham, 1959; Holman, 1966a), in the Guadalupe Mountains (Logan, 1977), and from Eddy (Holman, 1970) and Dona Ana (Brattstrom, 1964) counties, New Mexico. Holman (1969a) reported it from the Slaton Quarry. One vertebra (TTU-A13989) was identified as *Crotalus* sp.

## MAMMALS

### Order Insectivora
### Family Soricidae

*Blarina* sp., shrew
   Upper-left incisor (TTU-A10566)
No species identification is possible owing to the broken nature of the specimen. Although in general only one species of *Blarina* has been recognized in North America (*B. brevicauda*), the taxonomy of this species is now in question (Genoways and Choate, 1972). Three species appear to be extant on the basis of size differences and probably have been separated since the Pleistocene (Graham and Semken, 1976).

The *Blarina* at Lubbock Lake is currently the western-most known occurrence of the genus (fig. 7.3). All three species occurred in Texas during the late Pleistocene (Graham and Semken, 1976:437). *Blarina* sp. was reported from the Ben Franklin local fauna in northeastern Texas (Slaughter and Hoover, 1963) and is probably *B. brevicauda* (Graham and Semken, 1976:437).

*Notiosorex crawfordi* (Coves), desert shrew
    Right and left mandible pair (TTU-A19797, edentulous; TTU-A18418); left mandible (TTU-A28066)
The desert shrew ranges throughout southern and western Texas into the southwestern states. Although considered a desert species, it is found in a variety of habitats in Texas, including cattail marshes (Davis, 1974).

Late Pleistocene and early Holocene records of this shrew are known from the Edwards Plateau (Lundelius, 1967) and from southern Texas into New Mexico (Lundelius, 1967, 1984; Findley et al., 1975; Logan, 1977; Logan and Black, 1979; Dalquest and Stangl, 1984; Harris, 1977a, 1985a). A possible record was reported for Denton County, Texas (Slaughter and Ritchie, 1963).

## Order Chiroptera
## Family Molossidae

*Tadarida brasiliensis* (I. Geoffroy), Mexican freetail bat
    Right mandible (TTU-A15218)
Ranging throughout a major portion of the United States into Mexico, this bat usually occurs in large colonies. It is the most abundant bat in the southwestern United States. Caves are the general roosting area, but hollow trees are also used, and in historic times buildings supplied suitable habitat for roosting. A migratory animal, by late December this bat has moved south into Mexico for the winter months (December–February) (Davis et al., 1962). However, wintering over was documented in eastern Texas. Spenrath and LaVal (1974:11) suggested that temperature and availability of food are limiting factors for such events.

The Mexican freetail bat was reported from Laubach Cave (Graham, 1974), on the Edwards Plateau, and Dry (Findley et al., 1975) and U-Bar (Harris, 1985a) caves, in southern New Mexico. A late Holocene record is known for the Edwards Plateau (Frank, 1964).

## Order Edentata
## Family Pampatheriidae

*Holmesina septentrionalis* (Leidy), extinct giant armadillo
    Distal end of humerus (TTU-A25011); scute (TTU-A25270)
James (1957) described the skeletal material of the extinct giant armadillo, while Edmund (1985) detailed the differences in scutes in the various genera. The humerus of this extinct giant armadillo differs from that of modern armadillo (*Dasypus novemcinctus*) in size and proportion. The extinct form was much larger and had a prominent fossa on the lateral surface above the condyles. The Lubbock Lake material was also compared with appropriate *H. septentrio-*

*nalis* material from San Patricio (TMM 30967-1079; Lundelius, 1972b) and Harris (H.C.T.4; James, 1957) counties, Texas (table 7.4).

Fossil distribution (James, 1957) indicates that the extinct giant armadillo was primarily a southeastern form with much the same distribution as that of the modern armadillo. Lundelius (1972b:36) suggested that this distribution relationship indicated that the extinct giant armadillo was limited by winter temperatures in the North and aridity in the West. Its presence in a fauna indicates moisture and mild winter temperatures.

*Holmesina septentrionalis* was recorded in Sangamonian deposits in Dallas County (Slaughter, 1966) and in late Pleistocene localities on the Gulf Coast (James, 1957; Slaughter and McClure, 1965; Lundelius, 1972b). James (1957) summarized other localities along the Gulf Coast and in eastern Texas.

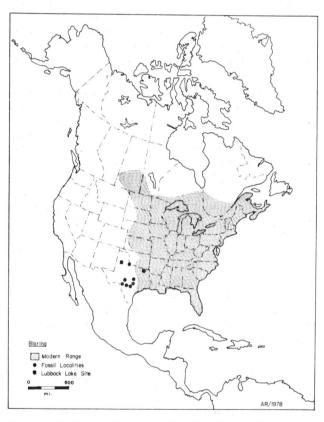

Fig. 7.3. Modern distribution and fossil localities in Texas of *Blarina* (shrew) in relation to Lubbock Lake (drafting by Anne Rust).

Table 7.4. Measurements of Adult *Holmesina septentrionalis* (Extinct Giant Armadillo) Material

(In Millimeters)

| Location of Measurement | Humerus, Left (TTU-A25011) |
|---|---|
| Width, distal extremity | 81 |
| Width, distal articulating surface | 55 |
| Anterior-posterior width, distal extremity | 32 |

## Order Lagomorpha
## Family Leporidae

*Sylvilagus* cf. *audubonii* (Baird), Audubon cottontail
    Right mandibles (TTU-A842, 843); left mandible (TTU-A956); right tibia (TTU-A22250)
The Audubon cottontail favors short grasslands, desert scrub, and areas of scattered piñon and juniper. The ranges of the Audubon and the eastern cottontail (*S. floridanus*) overlap considerably in western Texas, where they occur in different habitats. Osteologically the Audubon cottontail is somewhat stockier and longer-limbed than the eastern cottontail, but the greatest differences are seen in the skull and the mandibles. The Audubon cottontail has a shorter skull and tooth row and larger bullae than those of the eastern cottontail. The mandibles are slightly smaller with a shorter tooth row than those of the eastern cottontail.

Findley et al. (1975:84–86) demonstrated that two mandibular measurements, depth of dentary and alveolar length of tooth row ($P_3 - M_3$), separate *S. audubonii* from *S. floridanus*. Also, the posterior reentrant angle of the $P_3$ is more strongly crinkled in *S. audubonii* than in *S. floridanus*. The $P_3$ in the Lubbock Lake specimens is extremely crinkled. One mandible (TTU-A956) was complete enough for measurements and measures 11.4 mm deep and 13.3 mm long. When plotted with the material from Findley et al. (1975:85), this specimen falls within the *S. audubonii* range. Further differences between the two species are noted by Pettus (1956), Dalquest et al. (1969), and Lundelius (1972b).

*Sylvilagus audubonii* was reported from the Slaton Quarry (Dalquest, 1967; Womochel, 1977) and late Pleistocene and early Holocene deposits at Burnet (Schultz and Howard, 1935), U-Bar (Harris, 1985a), and Isleta (Harris and Findley, 1964) caves, in southern New Mexico, and Fowlkes Cave (Dalquest and Stangl, 1984), in Trans-Pecos, Texas. Pettus (1956) reported both species from Friesenhahn Cave. However, Graham (1976) identified only *S. floridanus* and relegated most of the material to *Sylvilagus* sp. Dalquest et al. (1969:226) did likewise for cottontail remains from Schulze Cave, although they noted that *S. audubonii* was probably represented.

*Sylvilagus* sp., cottontail
    Proximal end of right and left ulnae (TTU-A967, 21937); distal end of left humerus (TTU-A971); left scapula (TTU-A968); right innominates (TTU-A848, 970, 24702); left innominate (TTU-A970); distal end of right and left femora (TTU-A969); proximal end of right and left tibiae (TTU-A24739, 881); distal end of right tibia (TTU-A24702); right calcanei (TTU-A840, 971); metatarsals (TTU-A848); foot elements (TTU-A847, 876, 4718, 13848, 15092)
Cottontail species can be distinguished with whole or nearly whole long bones. However, identification is difficult with only ends of long bones. *Sylvilagus floridanus* is probably represented.

*Lepus californicus* (Gray), blacktail jackrabbit
    Fragmentary right mandible (TTU-A15849); right ulnae (TTU-A861, 869, 892, 963); distal end of right radius (TTU-A24701); distal end of right and left humeri (TTU-A844, 880, 859, 954, 3917, 13374); right scapulae (TTU-A957, 29680); left scapulae (TTU-A859, 955); right innominate (TTU-A859); left innominates (TTU-A859, 880); proximal end of femur (TTU-A892); distal end of right femur (TTU-A905); right calcanei (TTU-A892, 955); left calcanei (TTU-A844, 874, 880, 892); right astragali (TTU-A892, 13082); right cuboid (TTU-A13082); numerous molars.
Blacktail and whitetail (*L. townsendi*) jackrabbits can be distinguished skeletally on the basis of size differences, the long bones of the whitetail being stockier and longer (Dalquest et al., 1969). The blacktail jackrabbit ranges throughout a large part of the western United States, including most of Texas. It inhabits open prairies and areas of desert vegetation but is also found in areas of piñon and juniper.

Remains of blacktail jackrabbit were reported from Slaton Quarry (Dalquest, 1967) and late Pleistocene and early Holocene deposits of the Edwards Plateau (Friesenhahn Cave, Pettus, 1956; Graham, 1976; Miller's Cave, Patton, 1963; Schulze Cave, Dalquest et al., 1969), Val Verde County (Lundelius, 1984), and Trans-Pecos (Dalquest and Stangl, 1984; Ayer, 1936). Harris (1977a) recorded it from late Pleistocene deposits in Dry Cave, southeastern New Mexico.

## Order Rodentia
## Family Sciuridae

*Spermophilus richardsonii* (Sabine), Richardson's ground squirrel
    Left $P^3$ (TTU-A26003); left $P^4$ (TTU-A16005); left $M^1$ (TTU-A16429); right $M^2$ (TTU-A18711); left $M^2$ (TTU-A10607); right $M^3$ (TTU-A24067, 36011); left $M_1$ (TTU-A14883); left $M_2$ (TTU-A14759); right $M_3$ (TTU-A9796)
Several individuals are represented since teeth are very worn, moderately worn, or unworn. The specimens are within the subgenus *Spermophilus*. The lower molars exhibit the shared dental trait of an almost closed pit in the trigonid basin (Bryant, 1945), and the upper teeth exhibit a connected metaloph and protocone. They compare favorably with this species and are the same size as modern specimens. The closest modern occurrence of Richardson's ground squirrel is in central Colorado. It inhabits sagebrush or grasslands, usually near water. Aestivating by late summer, this ground squirrel becomes active again by midwinter.

During the Pleistocene the range of Richardson's ground squirrel extended into the Central and Southern Plains (fig. 7.4). This ground squirrel is known from localities in Kansas (Hibbard and Taylor, 1960; Schultz, 1967), Oklahoma (Stephens, 1960), New Mexico (Harris, 1970), and possibly Hardeman County, Texas (Dalquest, 1965). Holocene records outside its modern range are currently unreported.

*Spermophilus tridecemlineatus* (Mitchell), thirteen-lined ground squirrel
    Left $M^1$ (TTU-A13487, 16429, 10678); left $M^2$ (TTU-A12202); right $P_4$ (TTU-A14808); left $P_4$ (TTU-A4302); right $M_1$ (TTU-A27214); left $M_1$ (TTU-A13932); right $M_2$ (TTU-A13487); right $M_3$ (TTU-A1625)

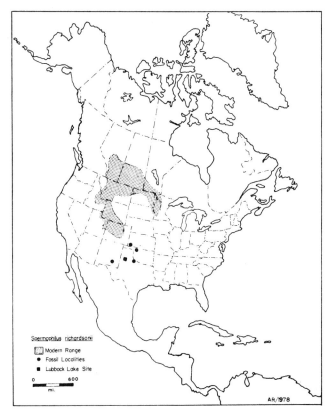

Fig. 7.4. Modern and extralimital fossil distribution of *Spermophilus richardsonii* (Richardson's ground squirrel) in relation to Lubbock Lake (drafting by Anne Rust).

The thirteen-lined ground squirrel ranges throughout the plains, inhabiting shortgrass prairies. The teeth of this ground squirrel are much smaller than those of the preceding form and exhibit a different specific crown pattern. Among other features the metaloph and protocone are separate. Other dental traits are discussed by Bryant (1945) and Hall and Kelson (1959).

The thirteen-lined ground squirrel is part of the prairie-dog-town community, living commensally with most members and providing prey for a few. Colonies in the Texas Panhandle were in hibernation by late October and had a consistent emergence time from mid-March to April.

The thirteen-lined ground squirrel was reported from late Pleistocene and early Holocene localities in Hardeman and Motley counties, Texas (Dalquest, 1964, 1965), and southern New Mexico (Harris, 1970; Findley et al., 1975).

*Spermophilus mexicanus* (Erxleben), Mexican ground squirrel
  Left P$^4$ (TTU-A2501, 4396, 23130); right M$^1$ (TTU-A22604); right M$^2$ (TTU-A20685); right M$^3$ (TTU-A23342); left M$_1$ (TTU-A13905)
Another grasslands animal, the Mexican ground squirrel has a more limited range than that of the thirteen-lined ground squirrel (above). It prefers sandy and gravelly soils and has a southern distribution of southwestern Texas and

southeastern New Mexico into Mexico. Lubbock County is at its northern limits.

*Spermophilus mexicanus* and *S. tridecemlineatus* are in the same subgenus (*Ictidomys*) and share the dental traits characteristic of that group (Bryant, 1945; Hall and Kelson, 1959). The distinction is based on size, *S. mexicanus* being the larger of the two.

Dalquest (1965; Dalquest et al., 1969) noted difficulty in separating the teeth of *S. mexicanus* and *S. richardsonii* because of their approximately equal size. However, in this study it was found that the dental traits for these two species are distinct and separated on the basis of an almost closed pit in the trigonid basin in *S. richardsonii*.

*Spermophilus mexicanus* is rare in the fossil record. A possible occurrence was noted from the late Pleistocene Hardeman County locality (Dalquest, 1965). It was reported from early Holocene deposits at Schulze Cave (Dalquest et al., 1969). Lundelius (1967) recorded its occurrence in late Holocene deposits in two caves in West Texas.

*Cynomys ludovicianus* (Ord), black-tailed prairie dog
  12 right mandibles, (892-273; TTU-A865, 917, 928, 1901, 5062, 5423, 8704, 9681, 12396, 17381, 28669); 8 left mandibles (TTU-A928, 3083, 5532, 7462, 9428, 11822, 25628, 26731); right maxilla (TTU-A16172); 3 left maxillae (TTU-A8711, 24663, 36581); numerous isolated teeth and postcranial material.
Ranging throughout the plains, the black-tailed prairie dog inhabits most of western Texas. This animal typically favors shortgrass prairies.

On the Southern High Plains remains of black-tailed prairie dog were reported from the brown-sand wedge at Blackwater Draw Locality No. 1 (Slaughter, 1975) and white-sand unit at Scharbauer (Gazin, 1955). Several late Pleistocene and early Holocene localities are known throughout Texas (Slaughter and Ritchie, 1963; Slaughter and McClure, 1965; Lundelius, 1972b; Dalquest et al., 1969; Dalquest, 1965; Dalquest and Stangl, 1984; Graham, 1976) and New Mexico (Schultz and Howard, 1935; Harris, 1977a).

### Family Geomyidae

*Thomomys bottae* (Eydoux and Gervais), valley pocket gopher
  Left P$^4$ (TTU-A4341); left P$_4$ (TTU-A16721)
The modern range of this gopher in Texas and New Mexico is generally west of the Pecos River (Schmidly, 1977; Findley et al., 1975). The teeth of this gopher are much smaller than those of other gophers in the fauna, and their premolars are distinctive. Valley pocket gophers occur in a variety of soil types and habitats, from deserts to grasslands and mountain meadows. Most of their existence is spent within the burrow system, the depth of which depends on the quality of the soil.

Although Hall (1981; Hall and Kelson, 1959) synonymized *T. bottae* with *T. umbrinus* (southern pocket gopher), various studies (Patton and Dingman, 1968; Hoffmeister, 1969; Patton, 1973; Findley et al., 1975; Thaeler, 1980) separated them. On the basis of Jones et al. (1986), the taxonomic status of *T. bottae* is retained as a separate species. In areas of sympatry Patton and Dingman (1968) found an ecological separation between the two in soil types and elevations.

Findley et al. (1975:343) listed both species from the late Pleistocene and early Holocene deposits of Burnet Cave, in southeastern New Mexico. However, Harris (1977a) questioned the validity of the *T. umbrinus* identifications because of the fragmentary remains. *Thomomys bottae* was reported from several late Pleistocene and early Holocene cave deposits throughout New Mexico (Findley et al., 1975; Harris, 1977a), and cave deposits in the Guadalupe Mountains (Logan, 1977; Logan and Black, 1979), the Trans-Pecos (Dalquest and Stangl, 1984), and Val Verde County, Texas (Lundelius, 1984).

*Geomys bursarius* (Shaw), plains pocket gopher
    2 complete skeletons (TTU-A13320, 13395); 3 skulls (892-2M, 892-99, TTU-A985); 5 right mandibles (892-425, TTU-A1535, 20247, 23939); 2 left mandibles (TTU-A860, 962); isolated teeth and limb bones

The plains pocket gopher ranges throughout much of the plains and most of Texas. A burrowing animal, it prefers grasslands with sandy soils.

*Geomys bursarius* was reported from Slaton Quarry (Dalquest, 1967), late Pleistocene and early Holocene localities on or near the Southern High Plains (Dalquest, 1964; Slaughter, 1975), and elsewhere in Texas (Slaughter and Hoover, 1963; Dalquest, 1965; Dalquest et al., 1969; Lundelius, 1967).

*Cratogeomys castenops* (Baird), yellow-faced pocket gopher
    Partial skull (TTU-A985); upper left I (TTU-A28866); lower left and right I (TTU-A28902, 28903); right $P_4$ (TTU-A28900); right $M^3$ (TTU-A28901)

Although synonymized with *Pappogeomys* by Russell (1968), *Cratogeomys* was recently reelevated to generic status because of marked karyotypic differences between the two subgenera of this group of pocket gophers (Jones et al., 1986). Size and incisor grooving separate the three groups of pocket gophers. Upper incisors of *Cratogeomys* have a single groove, while those of *Thomomys* have none, and those of *Geomys* have two (Schmidly, 1977). In *Cratogeomys* the enamel plates on the lower molars are only on the posterior side (Lundelius, 1979).

This pocket gopher ranges throughout the Southern High Plains and Trans-Pecos into Mexico and eastern New Mexico. Another burrowing animal, it prefers deep, rock-free, sandy soils with some moisture. *Cratogeomys castenops* inhabits both deserts and grassy plains.

Late Pleistocene and early Holocene records of *C. castenops* occur in the Trans-Pecos (Ayer, 1936; Lundelius, 1984; Lundelius et al., 1983; Dalquest and Stangl, 1984), the Guadalupe Mountains (Logan and Black, 1979), and southern New Mexico (Schultz and Howard, 1935; Harris, 1980, 1985a, b).

## Family Heteromyidae

*Perognathus* cf. *hispidus* Baird, hispid pocket mouse
    Right mandible (TTU-A25604); right $M^2$ (TTU-A10578)

Four species of *Perognathus* occur in the area today. Three of these species are difficult to distinguish from isolated teeth owing to their identical small size and very similar tooth structure (*P. merriami, P. flavescens,* and *P. flavus*). However, the hispid pocket mouse is much larger, three to five times the size of these forms. On the basis of the size of the mandible and teeth, the specimens are referred to this species.

*Perognathus hispidus* ranges throughout the Central and Southern Plains and all of Texas, favoring sandy soils and shortgrass prairie. They are limited to areas of moist, soft soil and avoid brushy and dense grass areas.

The hispid pocket mouse was reported from Slaton Quarry (Dalquest, 1967) and late Pleistocene and early Holocene deposits in New Mexico (Harris, 1970) and Texas (Dalquest, 1965; Dalquest et al., 1969; Dalquest and Stangl, 1984; Lundelius, 1967; Slaughter and Ritchie, 1963).

*Dipodomys ordii* (Woodhouse), Ord kangaroo rat
    2 partial skeletons (TTU-A9006, 13028); 2 right $P^4$ (TTU-A12757, 15511); 2 left $P^4$ (TTU-A18898, 19874); 3 right $P_4$ (TTU-A9394, 12758, 13127); 3 left $P_4$ (TTU-A10671, 10693, 18345); isolated molars

The Ord kangaroo rat is sympatric with two other species over much of its range. *Dipodomys spectabilis* (bannertail kangaroo rat) and *D. merriami* (Merriam kangaroo rat) occur in the Trans-Pecos and El Paso areas and farther west. The bannertail kangaroo rat is much larger, and the Merriam form is smaller than the Ord kangaroo rat. The Texas kangaroo rat (*D. elator*) has a very restricted range of north-central Texas into Oklahoma, but the western edge of its range overlaps that of *D. ordii*. However, this form also is larger than Ord's kangaroo rat.

The $P_4$ of the Ord kangaroo rat is distinctive, and there are no indications that other *Dipodomys* species are present in the collections. Isolated molars can be differentiated on the basis of size, and all appear to be *D. ordii*. The two partial skeletons are from very young individuals that still retain their deciduous premolars (Wood, 1935). Both juveniles probably died in their burrows, one being found at the bottom of a burrow.

The Ord kangaroo rat inhabits areas of sandy soil. They are burrowing, nocturnal animals. As with the other fossorial forms, the microenvironment of their burrows protects them from climatic extremes and seasonal fluctuations.

*Dipodomys ordii* is known from the Slaton Quarry local fauna (Dalquest, 1967) and a few late Pleistocene and early Holocene localities in Texas (Dalquest, 1965; Dalquest et al., 1969; Dalquest and Stangl, 1984) and New Mexico (Harris and Findley, 1964; Schultz and Howard, 1935).

## Family Cricetidae

*Reithrodontomys montanus* (Baird), plains harvest mouse
    Right $M_1$ (TTU-A16754)

This mouse ranges throughout the Central and Southern Plains into Mexico. It is another shortgrass prairie species, favoring areas of well-drained soils. It makes its nest either at the surface or in a shallow burrow. A low-density population exists throughout its range, aridity and the lack of continuous grass cover being factors in population control (Findley et al., 1975).

The ranges of the three common harvest mice in the Southern Plains (*Reithrodontomys montanus, R. megalotis,* and *R. fulvescens*) overlap in the Trans-Pecos area and the Southern High Plains. The dental patterns of these three mice are similar except for the third molar (Hooper, 1952). However, *R. montanus* is the smallest of the three, and this size difference is reflected in the teeth. The small size forms the basis of this identification. A left edentulous mandible (TTU-A11135) from the same feature as the tooth was referred to the genus.

*Reithrodontomys montanus* was reported from Friesenhahn (Graham, 1976) and Schulze (Dalquest et al., 1969) caves, on the Edwards Plateau, and Fowlkes Cave (Dalquest and Stangl, 1984), in Trans-Pecos, Texas. Harris (1985a) reported *R. megalotis/R. montanus* from U-Bar Cave, in southwestern New Mexico.

*Peromyscus* cf. *eremicus* (Baird), cactus mouse
Left $M_2$ (TTU-A11221)

This mouse has a modern range of West Texas (Trans-Pecos) into Mexico and the Southwest. Isolated teeth of *Peromyscus,* particularly worn specimens, are often difficult to determine to species. However, the Lubbock Lake specimen is from a young individual with the tooth in beginning wear. The cusps are still high, and the pattern is distinct. The tooth structure is simple, without accessory lophs or styles.

The $M_2$ in *Peromyscus eremicus* is usually the least variable (Hooper, 1957:17, 41). The typical pattern is the simple structure without accessory characters. Dalquest et al. (1969) noted that the simple pattern is characteristic of *P. eremicus* and the subgenus to which it belongs. The ranges of other mice of this subgenus occur even farther west than those of *P. eremicus.* Hooper's (1957) criteria and discussion and comparison with the modern form constitute the basis for this identification. The tooth size and structure conform to those seen in modern specimens.

Although restricted today to desert habitat, these animals aestivate to escape the hottest part of the summer. They are generally found in rocky outcrops and along cliffs, although Findley et al. (1975) reported them as occasionally occurring on plains with sandy soil among mesquite trees. They are seedeaters, feeding on mesquite beans and hackberry seeds.

*Peromyscus eremicus* was reported from cave deposits in Trans-Pecos, Texas (Dalquest and Stangl, 1984), and southwestern New Mexico (Harris, 1985a). Graham (1976:77) relegated the identified specimen, originally reported from Friesenhahn Cave (R. Martin, 1968a), to *Peromyscus* sp.

*Onychomys leucogaster* (Wied), northern grasshopper mouse

Right $M^2$ (TTU-A3293); right $M_1$ (TTU-A14899); 2 right $M_2$ (TTU-A10690, 16710)

The teeth of this species can be distinguished from those of the southern grasshopper mouse (*Onychomys torridus*) by size, the northern form being the larger of the two species. This insectivorous and carnivorous mouse occurs throughout the plains and most of the western United States. It favors sandy soils of grassland areas and open brushlands.

Womochel (1977) reported *O. leucogaster* from the Slaton Quarry. Remains of this mouse were recovered from late Pleistocene and early Holocene localities in Hardeman (Dalquest, 1965), Denton (Slaughter and Ritchie, 1963), and Val Verde (Lundelius, 1984) counties, the Edwards Plateau (Lundelius, 1967; Dalquest et al., 1969; Graham, 1976), the Trans-Pecos (Dalquest and Stangl, 1984), and the Guadalupe Mountains (Logan, 1977) of Texas. In New Mexico it was reported from cave deposits in Eddy (Harris, 1970), Hidalgo (Harris, 1985a), and Bernalillo (Harris and Findley, 1964) counties.

*Sigmodon hispidus* (Say and Ord), hispid cotton rat
6 right mandibles (892-98; TTU-A7556, 7606, 7669, 18238, 23442); 9 right $M^1$ (TTU-A13199, 13477, 14819, 17257, 18158, 18355, 18385, 23398, 28854); 3 left $M^1$ (TTU-A10659, 13065, 15547); right $M_1$ (TTU-A23391); 2 left $M_1$ (TTU-A18376, 23391); 6 right $M^2$ (TTU-A10659, 18137, 18150, 18355, 18376, 18385); 7 left $M^2$ (TTU-A10659, 13096, 13117, 15548, 18098, 18137, 19118); 2 left $M_2$ (TTU-A13923, 21632); 4 right $M^3$ (TTU-A10659, 18150, 18376, 18385); 3 left $M^3$ (TTU-A13114, 18137, 18449)

The hispid cotton rat occurs widely throughout most of the southern United States, preferring moist areas of tall grasses and sedges. Throughout its range temperature and moisture are the controlling factors. Population declines are correlated with long periods of below-freezing temperatures, snow cover, and frozen ground (Goertz, 1964), as well as drought and loss of grass cover (Davis, 1974). One unerupted $M^1$ (TTU-A1370), identified as *Sigmodon* sp., in all likelihood is *S. hispidus.*

Slaughter (1975) reported the hispid cotton rat from Blackwater Draw Locality No. 1, and it is known from other late Pleistocene and early Holocene localities throughout Texas (Dalquest, 1965; Dalquest et al., 1969; Dalquest and Stangl, 1984; Graham, 1974; Lundelius, 1967; Slaughter et al., 1962; Slaughter and Hoover, 1963; Slaughter and McClure, 1965; Slaughter and Ritchie, 1963).

*Neotoma* cf. *micropus* Baird, Southern Plains wood rat
Right $M^1$ (TTU-A17692); right $M^2$ (TTU-A23392); right $M^3$ (TTU-A17693); right $M_1$ (TTU-A23397); left $M_1$ (TTU-A23397); right $M_2$ (TTU-A10700); 2 left $M_2$ (TTU-A23397); left $M_3$ (TTU-A23397)

Harris (1984) discussed the dental similarities and differences in *N. micropus, N. albigula* (white-throated wood rat), and *N. floridana* (eastern wood rat). Size and dental characters can separate *N. micropus* and *N. floridana.* The white-throated wood rat is smaller than the Southern Plains wood rat, but the teeth are very similar to those of that wood rat. The $M_1$ is the most distinctive, but the third, or posterior, loph of the $M_2$ appears to be more elongated in *N. micropus* than in *N. albigula*. The larger size of the specimens is the basis for the referred identification.

The Southern Plains wood rat inhabits semiarid brushlands to grassland areas and is rarely found in rocky areas. In the Trans-Pecos area it is common in the brushy thickets along the Rio Grande (Schmidly, 1977).

*Neotoma micropus* was reported from a few late Pleistocene and early Holocene localities in Texas (Slaughter and McClure, 1965; Dalquest, 1965; Dalquest et al., 1969; Dalquest and Stangl, 1984) and New Mexico (Logan, 1977; Logan and Black, 1979; Harris, 1984).

*Neotoma* cf. *albigula* Hartley, white-throated wood rat
Right $M^3$ (TTU-A23125); left $M_2$ (TTU-A18318)
On the basis of the small size of the teeth and shape of the third (posterior) loph, the specimens are referred to this species. *Neotoma albigula* appears to have a constricted third loph, while that in *N. micropus* is open. A broken, isolated $M^2$ (TTU-A10646) and limb elements were identified as *Neotoma* sp.

These two wood rats are sympatric in the Lubbock area and over a large part of their ranges. In areas where these animals occur together, *N. albigula* inhabits the rocky areas, whereas *N. micropus* is found in the open grassland.

*Neotoma albigula* was recovered from the Slaton Quarry (Dalquest, 1967). Late Pleistocene and early Holocene records for this wood rat in Texas come from Hardeman County (Dalquest, 1965), Edwards Plateau (Dalquest et al., 1969), the Trans-Pecos (Ayer, 1936; Dalquest and Stangl, 1984); and the Guadalupe Mountains (Logan, 1977; Logan and Black, 1979). It was recovered from numerous cave localities in southern New Mexico (Harris, 1984, 1985a) and Isleta Caves (Harris and Findley, 1964), in north-central New Mexico.

*Microtus pennsylvanicus* (Ord), meadow vole
Partial skeleton (TTU-A19828); right edentulous mandible (TTU-A18854); 3 left mandibles (892-326; TTU-A9624, 18467); 10 right $M^1$ (TTU-A4343, 9751, 13077, 14750, 14752, 16178, 27118, 27517, 37129); 7 left $M^1$ (TTU-A11179, 13494, 13904, 15761, 16233, 18422, 27107); 13 right $M^2$ (TTU-A9590, 11443, 13077, 14779, 15761, 16013, 16124, 16248, 16428, 16903, 16918, 18421); 11 left $M^2$ (TTU-A9953, 10615, 11252, 14950, 16305, 16443, 16681, 16775, 16850, 18421, 27009); 8 right $M^3$ (TTU-A9595, 13928, 14874, 16233, 16577, 16819, 18421, 27133); 10 left $M^3$ (TTU-A11230, 13077, 13928, 13944, 14241, 14752, 16475, 16832, 18899, 26016); 23 right $M_1$ (TTU-A9965, 10589, 11335, 13077, 13916, 14726, 14887, 15761, 16038, 16100, 16104, 16919, 17214, 17721, 18421, 18429, 18442, 18513, 18631, 18718, 36042, 37522); 33 left $M_1$ (TTU-A9672, 9703, 10591, 11438, 13031, 13077, 13916, 14517, 14715, 14718, 14721, 14723, 14756, 15782, 16053, 16067, 16100, 16412, 17162, 17842, 18095, 18412, 18421, 18442, 18535, 18691, 18854, 23347, 23435, 36043, 37522, 37538); 7 right $M_2$ (TTU-A13944, 14775, 16044, 18421, 18442, 27021); 10 left $M_2$ (TTU-A13077, 13944, 14474, 14772, 14880, 18429, 18442, 23347, 37522, 37538); 4 right $M_3$ (TTU-A13077, 14735, 16843, 18442); 2 left $M_3$ (TTU-A14756, 18095)

Isolated teeth of *Microtus* are at times difficult to distinguish as to species. The $M_1$ is the most distinctive, and species identification is based on the number and shape of the triangles and the shape of the trefoil. Furthermore, $M^2$ of *M. pennsylvanicus* is unique in having a fifth posterior loop; no other major species of *Microtus* has this character. The presence of two species was determined by examining all $M_1$ and $M^2$ specimens in the collection and considering the possible candidates from modern ranges. After species were established, other molars were examined for placement in one or the other of the two species. This placement was not always possible; and many teeth are identified to genus only.

The meadow vole is a northern animal in distribution, and its closest occurrence to the area today is northern New Mexico (fig. 7.5). Findley et al. (1975:255) noted that the disjunct distribution in New Mexico represents relict populations. Distributional factors include competition, temperature maxima, and humidity (moisture). Another grasslands species, the meadow vole inhabits grass-sedge communities near permanent waters, including marshes, streams, ponds, and lakes. Although it is found in tall-grass areas, it is not optimal habitat, and the vole prefers vegetation growing along waterways (Findley et al., 1975; Thompson, 1965).

*Microtus pennsylvanicus* was known from Wisconsinan deposits at Howard Ranch (Dalquest, 1965) and late Pleistocene and early Holocene deposits in northeastern (Slaughter and Hoover, 1963), north-central (Dalquest, 1964), and Central (Lundelius, 1967; Dalquest et al., 1969) Texas. On the Southern High Plains, *M. pennsylvanicus* was reported from late Pleistocene and early Holocene deposits at Blackwater Draw Locality No. 1 (Slaughter, 1975) and the Rex Rodgers site (Schultz, 1978). This vole was recovered at U-Bar Cave (Harris, 1985a), in southwestern New Mexico. Smartt (1972) and Findley et al. (1975) summarized other occurrences of fossil *M. pennsylvanicus* throughout New Mexico (fig. 7.5).

*Microtus ochrogaster* (Wagner), prairie vole
2 left mandibles (TTU-A13937, 13941); 7 left $M^1$ (TTU-A14683, 14746, 14799, 20458, 20707, 23077, 37132); 5 right $M^2$ (TTU-A9640, 14760, 14767, 16891, 20801); 7 left $M^2$ (TTU-A13074, 13941, 14888, 16262, 17124, 20707); right $M^3$ (TTU-A15839); left $M^3$ (TTU-A13074); 7 right $M_1$ (TTU-A4364, 11378, 13074, 14755, 14841, 27129, 27768); 8 left $M_1$ (TTU-A2500, 11149, 13074, 13133, 14738, 14771, 17119); 2 right $M_2$ (TTU-A13074); 3 left $M_2$ (TTU-A7674, 13074, 13133); right $M_3$ (TTU-A13074); left $M_3$ (TTU-A13074)

The prairie vole ranges over most of the Central and Northern Plains and prairie region (fig. 7.6). It is absent from the Southern Plains today, although a relict population exists in northeastern New Mexico (Findley et al., 1975). This vole favors dry, open prairies. The distributional factors include humidity (moisture), temperature maxima, habitat availability, and competition (Dice, 1922; Findley, 1954).

Within its current range the prairie vole comes into habitat competition with the meadow vole wherever the two spe-

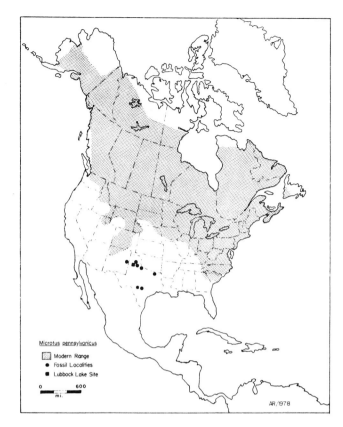

Fig. 7.5. Modern distribution and fossil localities in Texas and the Southern High Plains (Llano Estacado) of *Microtus pennsylvanicus* (meadow vole) in relation to Lubbock Lake (drafting by Anne Rust).

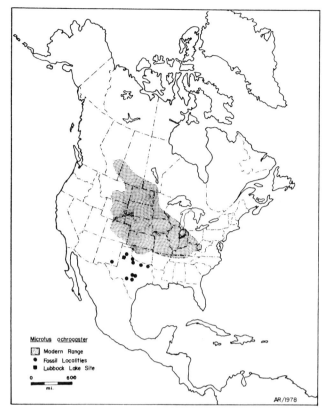

Fig. 7.6. Modern distribution and fossil localities in Texas and the Southern Plains of *Microtus ochrogaster* (prairie vole) in relation to Lubbock Lake (drafting by Anne Rust).

cies are sympatric. In the area of sympatry the prairie vole is restricted to the dry grasslands, and the meadow vole to marshy areas near water. When only one of these species occurs in an area, the particular vole is found in both habitats (Findley, 1954).

*Microtus ochrogaster* was encountered in several late Pleistocene and early Holocene localities on or near the Southern High Plains (Slaughter, 1975; Dalquest, 1964), in New Mexico (Smartt, 1972; Findley et al., 1975), and in Central Texas (Graham, 1974; Patton, 1963). Several localities in or near eastern Texas list the *M. ochrogaster/ pinetorum* complex (Dalquest, 1965; Dalquest et al., 1969; Slaughter and Hoover, 1963; Slaughter and Ritchie, 1963; Graham, 1976).

*Ondatra zibethicus* (Linnaeus), muskrat
  Juvenile skeleton (TTU-A15933); 12 skulls (892-101; 892-249; 892-275; 892-432; TTU-A15902, 19055, 19439, 19826, 20005); 28 right mandibles (892-2E; 892-100; 892-297; 892-326; 892-426; TTU-A927, 11982, 11991, 15691, 15841, 16838, 18136, 18239, 19075, 19650, 19708, 19825, 20843, 21786, 21926, 23029, 23031, 23704, 23705, 23723, 23966, 28801, 36673); 24 left mandibles (892-2E; 892-320; 892-326; 892-426; 892-429; TTU-A927, 931, 9375, 11982, 11991, 15692, 15707, 15848, 18291, 19229, 19824, 21786, 23648, 23740, 23632, 23641, 28391, 28813, 28831);

9 right maxillae (TTU-A927, 9378, 9686, 13556, 19459, 20209, 25365, 28828, 37548); 10 left maxillae (TTU-A1618, 18068, 18373, 19459, 19818, 20544, 23429, 28832, 37526, 37548); numerous isolated teeth and postcranial material
Although no longer occurring in the Yellowhouse system, muskrats occur today along the Canadian River at the northern edge of the Southern High Plains. Favoring open waters, they inhabit marshes, ponds, and streams and live among the cattails and rushes.

*Ondatra zibethicus* was reported from various late Pleistocene and early Holocene localities (fig. 7.6) in Texas (Slaughter and Ritchie, 1963; Slaughter and Hoover, 1963; Dalquest, 1965; Lundelius, 1967) and New Mexico (Harris, 1970).

*Synaptomys cooperi* Baird, southern bog lemming
  3 right $M^1$ (TTU-A23367, 23377); left $M^1$ (TTU-A23370); right $M^2$ (TTU-A14760); left $M_1$ (TTU-A18403); right $M^2$ (TTU-A14760); left $M_1$ (TTU-A18403); right $M_2$ (TTU-A18733); 2 left $M_2$ (TTU-A18124, 23377); right $M_3$ (TTU-A18848)
This lemming has a modern northeastern distribution with relict populations in southwestern Kansas and northwestern Arkansas. Found in a variety of grasslands habitats near water, the southern bog lemming inhabits marshes, dry and moist meadows with dense vegetation, and sphagnum bogs

(Doutt et al., 1973). The relict population in southwestern Kansas inhabit the marshy areas around spring-fed ponds (Hibbard and Rinker, 1942).

This small rodent exhibits a negative Bergmann's response. It is largest in the southern and western sections of its range and decreases in size going north (Guilday et al., 1964). Patton (1963) demonstrated that the *S. cooperi* at Miller's Cave, in Central Texas, represents the subspecies *S. c. paludis*. This subspecies, the largest form, is the relict population in Kansas (Hibbard and Rinker, 1942). Lubbock Lake specimens are large and may well represent this subspecies. However, another large subspecies, *S. c. gossii,* is possible. Fossil remains of this subspecies were recovered at Schulze Cave (Dalquest et al., 1969), another Central Texas locality. These two subspecies are closely related and may be descendants of the same ancestral stock (Wetzel, 1955).

*Synaptomys cooperi* was recorded from numerous Texas localities (fig. 7.7). Specimens from several localities were originally identified as *S. australis,* an extinct form, but reevaluation (Dalquest et al., 1969) placed them in *S. cooperi.* Fossil localities (Sangamonian to early Holocene) in Central Texas were summarized by Graham (1976). Other localities occur in southeastern (Slaughter and Mc-Clure, 1965), northeastern (Slaughter and Hoover, 1963; Slaughter and Ritchie, 1963; Slaughter et al., 1962), and north-central (Dalquest, 1962b, 1964, 1965) Texas.

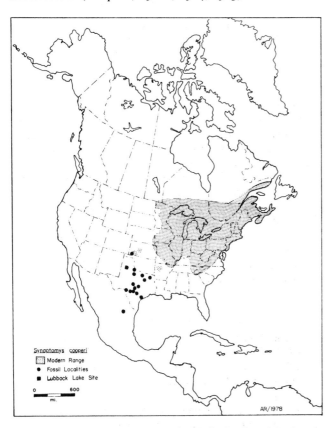

Fig. 7.7. Modern and extralimital fossil distribution of *Synaptomys cooperi* (southern bog lemming) in relation to Lubbock Lake (drafting by Anne Rust).

## Order Carnivora
## Family Canidae

*Canis latrans* (Say), coyote
    2 partial skeletons (TTU-A845, 22182); 2 skulls (892-291; TTU-A10948); 5 right mandibles (892-2E, 892-3A, TTU-A3070, 22406, 27804); 5 left mandibles (892-254, TTU-A1688, 4983/4987, 22200, 27932); left maxilla (TTU-A858); numerous isolated teeth and postcranial material

Coyotes live in a wide variety of habitats, from prairies and grasslands to open woodland and brushy areas. Young are born in late spring to early summer (April–June). Remains of domestic dog (*C. familiaris*) and coyote can be difficult to distinguish. The cranial material was checked for characteristics of dog. Olsen (personal communication) examined the suspicious specimens and found all of them to be coyote.

Coyotes have a long ecological record on the Southern High Plains, extending from the middle Pleistocene (Slaton Quarry; Womochel, 1977) to today. *Canis latrans* is reported from the Motley County locality (Dalquest, 1964), just off the Southern High Plains, and the gray-sand stratum at Blackwater Draw Locality No. 1 (Lundelius, 1972a). Late Pleistocene and early Holocene localities are known throughout Texas (Dalquest, 1965; Dalquest et al., 1969; Lundelius, 1967, 1972b; Slaughter, 1961; Slaughter and Hoover, 1963; Slaughter and Ritchie, 1963) and New Mexico (Findley et al., 1975; Harris, 1985a).

*Canis lupus* Linnaeus, gray wolf
    Right mandible (TTU-A1825); 2 left mandibles (892-255; TTU-A568); 2 right maxillae (892-256; 892-273); postcranial material

Once ranging throughout North America, wolves were extirpated from most of the United States. The wolves commonly followed the bison herds, and the double extermination program aimed at the wolf and bison historically combined to reduce drastically the range of both animals. The wolf tolerates a wide variety of habitats, from forests to open grasslands. Broken, open country providing good denning localities is favored. Wolf cubs are born once a year, primarily in March and April.

All material recovered consistently is smaller than the comparative skeletons from the Northern Plains, but much too large to be coyote. Dalquest et al. (1969) found that the *C. lupus* remains from Schulze Cave, on the Edwards Plateau, were smaller than those of the northern form. Lundelius (1972a) noted a slightly smaller size for the *C. lupus* material from the gray sand at Blackwater Draw Locality No. 1. However, Slaughter (1975) observed a slightly larger size in the teeth from the brown-sand wedge of that locality. In Texas and New Mexico fossil records of *C. lupus* are limited to these localities.

*Vulpes macrotis* (Merriam), kit fox
    Skull and mandibles (892-291)

The differences in tooth structure and length of tooth row separate the kit fox from the swift fox (*V. velox*). The kit fox is a western form, occurring in part today in the Trans-

Pecos area of Texas south into Mexico, west into New Mexico, and north to the southern and western borders of the Southern High Plains (Davis, 1974; Packard and Bowers, 1970).

While commonly inhabiting desert areas of low vegetation, the kit fox also occurs in grasslands and areas of juniper. Kit foxes prefer open, sandy ground. They live in burrows in open areas, and young are born in March and April. Kit foxes are nocturnal animals, and the relative abundance of nocturnal rodents acts as a population control.

The only fossil record for the region is from Conkling Cavern, New Mexico (Conkling, 1932).

## Family Ursidae

*Arctodus simus* (Cope), extinct short-faced bear
   Upper left canine (TTU-A20111); right first metacarpal (TTU-A17598); right second metacarpal (TTU-A20220); left third metacarpal (TTU-A17909); right scapholunar (TTU-A5264); radius (TTU-A25024)
In Kurtén's (1967) revision of the genus *Arctodus* he synonymized several genera and species designations and recognized two species of *Arctodus*, *A. pristinus* and *A. simus*. The dental and osteological features of the two bears are discussed in detail by Kurtén (1967). Numerous partial skeletons of *A. simus* are known, and the osteology is well described (Merriam and Stock, 1925; Kurtén, 1967).

The short-faced bear had a wide distribution from Alaska to Mexico and California to Pennsylvania (fig. 7.8). It ranged in time from middle Pleistocene (Irvingtonian fauna) to the latest Pleistocene (Rancholabrean fauna).

*Arctodus simus* had a short, broad face more similar to the faces of the large cats than to those of bears in general. A highly carnivorous form, the carnassial pair retains its shearing function, but the posterior molars are large and broad for crushing. The mandible was structured for strength, with a double masseteric fossa and the condyle (and pivot of the mandible) on the same plane as the cheek teeth. The body was built for both power and speed. The neck was short, and the appendicular skeleton was characterized by its great length and the slender proportions of the long bones. *Arctodus simus* was a long-legged bear, the hind limbs being longer than the forelimbs, but the metatarsals shorter than the metacarpals (Merriam and Stock, 1925; Kurtén, 1967). Because of these features Kurtén (1967:49) suggested that *A. simus* was adapted to "relatively fast terrestrial movement, but little in the way of climbing or digging." This adaptive mode of existence is different from that of most other bears.

An allometric growth study (Kurtén, 1967) showed that the fossil populations easily divide into male (larger) and female (smaller) groups. On the basis of body length Kurtén (1967:51) estimated the weight ranges of males (350–75 kg) and females (150–270 kg). The Lubbock Lake material is from one individual. Comparison of measurements on the Lubbock Lake specimens (table 7.5) indicates that the Lubbock Lake short-faced bear was a male, and the largest specimen (postcranially) yet reported.

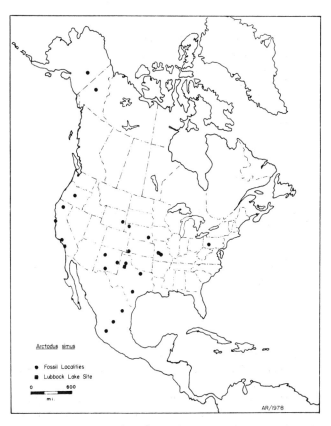

Fig. 7.8. Fossil distribution of *Arctodus simus* (short-faced bear) in relation to Lubbock Lake (drafting by Anne Rust).

Little is known of the ecological requirements of *A. simus*. Remains were found in both cave and open sites. Although *Arctodus* is closely related to the genus *Tremarctos* (spectacled bears) of South America, it probably occupied a variety of habitats more similar to those of the black bear (*Ursus americanus*). More exclusively carnivorous than modern black bears, the short-faced bear was probably capable of bursts of speed. Kurtén (1967:50) considered this bear the most powerful, predaceous carnivore of the North American Pleistocene. When remains of *Arctodus* and *Ursus* were found in the same deposit, *Arctodus* was more abundant (Merriam and Stock, 1925:9–10). Pleistocene *Tremarctos* ranged along the Gulf Coast area sympatrically with *Ursus* where *Arctodus* was absent. Kurtén (1963:14) suggested competition between the two groups and the dependence of *Arctodus* on the large extinct herbivores as factors in the extinction of *Arctodus* at the end of the Pleistocene.

Several *Arctodus* localities are known throughout Texas and New Mexico. Ranging in time from Sangamonian to the end of the Pleistocene, this record indicates some frequency of this bear in the faunal assemblage. *Arctodus simus* was reported at Cueva Quebrada (Lundelius, 1984) and Moore Pit (Slaughter, 1966b), and Kurtén (1967) summarized other Texas localities. Haynes (1975) noted the existence of an *Arctodus* locality near Blackwater Draw Locality No. 1, and Harris (1985a) found it at U-Bar Cave, in southwestern

Table 7.5. Measurements of *Arctodus simus* (Extinct Short-faced Bear) Material
(In Millimeters)

| Location of Measurement* | Canine (TTU-A20111) | Scapho-lunar (TTU-A5264) | Metacarpal I (TTU-A17598) | Metacarpal II (TTU-A20220) | Metacarpal III (TTU-A17909) |
|---|---|---|---|---|---|
| Anterior–posterior diameter at base of enamel | 34.1 | | | | |
| Greatest anterior–posterior diameter | | 85.0 | | | |
| Greatest transverse diameter | | 84.0 | | | |
| Anterior–posterior diameter of radial facet | | 50.6 | | | |
| Depth at transverse midline | | 43.7 | | | |
| Width of head | | 31.9 | | | |
| Greatest length | | | 100.0 | 135.0 | 142.0 |
| Proximal width | | | 32.3 | 32.0 | 50.0 |
| Proximal anterior–posterior diameter | | | 28.1 | 44.0 | 31.0 |
| Least transverse width of shaft | | | 16.8 | 29.4 | 22.3 |
| Greatest distal width over epicondyles | | | 27.2 | 33.7 | 32.3† |

*Measurement locations taken from Merriam and Stock 1925 and Kurtén 1967.
†Worn epicondyle.

New Mexico. Other New Mexico localities were summarized by Findley et al. (1975).

## Family Mustelidae

*Taxidea taxus* (Schreber), badger
  Tibia (TTU-A893); 2 humeri (TTU-A882, 24704); proximal end of femur (TTU-A882).

Badgers occur throughout most of the western and plains areas. They generally inhabit open grasslands to desert areas but are more abundant in grassland areas. Throughout the plains the badger's range closely parallels that of ground squirrels and prairie dogs, its major food sources.

*Taxidea taxus* was reported from Slaton Quarry (Dalquest, 1967; Womochel, 1977). Late Pleistocene and Holocene records are known from Central Texas (Lundelius, 1967; Dalquest et al., 1969) and throughout New Mexico (Findley et al., 1975; Harris, 1977a, 1985a).

*Mephitis mephitis* (Schreber), striped skunk
  Left mandible (TTU-A4683)

Very common throughout most of North America, striped skunks can be found in a variety of habitats. They occur in woodlands, brushy areas, and open prairie. In the Texas–New Mexico area they are most common in the grassland areas. The hog-nosed skunk (*Conepatus mesoleucus*) is similar in size to the striped skunk, and the dental characters separating the two were discussed by Graham (1976). Striped skunks are nocturnal animals and have a wide range in food habits, from carrion to insects and grains.

Remains of striped skunk were found at other late Pleistocene and early Holocene localities in Texas (Dalquest, 1965; Dalquest et al., 1969; Lundelius, 1967, 1984) and New Mexico (Conkling, 1932; Harris and Findley, 1964; Harris, 1977a, 1985a).

## Family Felidae

*Felis* cf. *rufus* (Schreber), bobcat
  Broken M₁ (TTU-A833)

The molar compares most favorably with that of the bobcat. Bobcats occur in a wide variety of habitats but favor rocky canyons and brushy areas. The bobcat is mainly a nocturnal animal, and its diet is made up of birds, rabbits, and small rodents.

Late Pleistocene and early Holocene remains of bobcat were reported from Central Texas (Lundelius, 1967; Dalquest et al., 1969; Graham, 1974), the Gulf Coast area (Lundelius, 1972b), Trans-Pecos (Ayer, 1936; Dalquest and Stangl, 1984), and throughout New Mexico (Findley et al., 1975; Harris, 1977a, 1985a).

## Order Proboscidea
## Family Elephantidae

*Mammuthus columbi* Falconer, Columbian mammoth
  Right and left M² (TTU-A17813, 17814); 4 broken M (TTU-A5242, 5399, 9036, 11998); 2 right mandibles with dP₃ (TTU-A5444, 17540); right maxilla with dP³ (TTU-A5325); left dP³ (TTU-A17658); 2 right dP₂ (TTU-A5444, 20115); 2 left dP³ (TTU-A5168, 5179); juvenile tusk (TTU-A17659); 25 adult tusk sections (TTU-A5259, 16941, 17504, 17505, 17510, 17554, 17555, 17564, 17565, 17570, 17637, 17742, 17743, 17751, 17752, 17753, 17757, 17762, 17764, 17766, 17937, 20164, 25184, 25188, 25189); 10 adult skull parts (TTU-A16913, 17767, 17768, 17778, 17786, 17795, 17801, 17806, 17809, 17811); tooth fragments and postcranial material

Two complete molars were recovered, and measurements of the teeth (table 7.6) fall within those recorded for this species (Saunders, 1970). Graham (1976) studied the juvenile dentition of *M. columbi* in detail. Laws (1966) created an eruption and wear aging schedule for the modern African elephant. The Lubbock Lake juvenile dentition was identified to tooth (and aged when possible) with the use of these two studies. Three individuals (an adult and two youths) are represented in the material, and the young represent an African age equivalent of a 1-year-old and a 2-year-old (Laws, 1966).

Little can be said about the specific habitat of this extinct elephant. It was a browser and probably inhabited

Table 7.6. Tooth Measurements of *Mammuthus columbi* (Columbian Mammoth)

(In Millimeters)

| Catalog No. | No. Plates[a] | Position | Length[b] | Height[c] | Breadth[d] | Enamel[e] |
|---|---|---|---|---|---|---|
| TTU-A17813 | 8 | M² (R) | 150.5 | 213.0 | 94.0 | 1.0 |
| TTU-A17814 | 9 | M² (L) | 138.0 | 251.0 | 95.0 | 2.0 |
| TTU-A5242 | 5 | M— | — | 85.0 | 62.8 | 1.9 |
| TTU-A17658 | 7 | M³ (L) | — | — | 78.0 | 2.0 |
| TTU-A5325 | 6 | dP³ (R) | — | 29.8 | 27.9 | 0.8 |
| TTU-A5444 | 3 | dP₃ (R) | — | 27.8 | 19.0 | 1.5 |

[a]Number of lamellae, or plates, preserved.

[b]Length measured at right angle to the general axis of the lamellae (posterior and anterior cementum are not included).

[c]Height of deepest plate, excluding roots, measured from the enamel-root boundary on the side of the molar.

[d]Greatest breadth of widest lamella, excluding marginal cementum.

[e]Thickness of enamel exposed by wear on the grinding surface.

grassland-savanna areas. It is generally assumed that, since this elephant is a southern species, it probably occurred in a habitat and ecological niche similar to those of the modern African elephant. The optimum habitat for modern African elephants involves suitable amounts of browse, woody growth, and grasslands with available water supply and shade. However, the range of variation is great, from forest edge to open grasslands. Laws et al. (1975:177) found that woody or fibrous material is a nutritional requirement. When the elephants are in a grassland area, grasses are the major dietary item, with limited browsing depending on availability (Laws et al., 1975).

The Columbian mammoth is known throughout the Southwest and Texas from late Pleistocene localities and archaeological sites (Saunders, 1970; Mawby, 1967; Harris, 1977a; Lundelius, 1972a; Slaughter, 1975; Sellards, 1955a; Graham, 1976; Dalquest et al., 1969; Slaughter and Mc-Clure, 1965) and into the Northern Plains (Figgins, 1933; Anderson, 1975, 1984).

## Order Perissodactyla
## Family Equidae

*Equus mexicanus* (Hibbard) group, extinct large, stout-legged horse

   Left maxilla with M²-M³ (TTU-A20214); M₃ (892-299); right scapula (TTU-A20155); right radius (TTU-A13806); distal metapodials (TTU-A3298, 22463); 3 first phalanges (892-275; TTU-A7689, 939)

Pleistocene horse taxonomy is complex and fluid, compounded by the frequent lack of associated dentition and postcranial material and the denoting of new species on the basis of isolated teeth or partial tooth rows. The true range of variation within a species is unknown, as is how the various species may have divided up the grasslands habitat and which niche may have gone with which species.

The Lubbock Lake material was previously identified as *E. scotti* (Johnson, 1976, 1983; Johnson and Holliday, 1985). Lundelius (1972a:160), in his study of horse mate-

rial from Blackwater Draw Locality No. 1, synonymized *E. scotti* and *E. midlandensis* and reassigned previous identifications (*E. caballos caballos* and *E.* cf. *excelus*) of large horse material to *E. scotti*. Harris and Porter (1980:60) later synonymized *E. midlandensis* with *E. niobrarensis* and separated *E. scotti* from *E. midlandensis*. They reassigned the Blackwater Draw Locality No. 1 and Lubbock Lake material and other Southern Plains *E. scotti* remains to *E. niobrarensis*.

Winans (1985) recently revised the fossil species of the genus *Equus* and reduced the multitude of species to five morphological groups. These groups are based on dental characters and metapodial measurements and can be divided on zebrine versus nonzebrine dental traits, large versus small forms, and stout versus stilt-legged shapes. Winans (1985:171) recognized only two species groups that characterized the Rancholabrean land-mammal age (late Pleistocene): a large, nonzebrine, stout-legged horse, *E. mexicanus;* and a small, nonzebrine, stilt-legged horse, *E. francisci.* Because of sample size, spatial distribution, and temporal problems, these groups may or may not be composed of more than one valid species. Nevertheless, the scheme brings order to previous chaos and is workable in terms of type of horse identified and possible ecological considerations.

Winans (1985:171) recognized *E. scotti* as a valid morphological group limited to the Irvingtonian (middle Pleistocene) and characterized as a large, zebrine, stout-legged horse. *Equus niobrarensis* was synonymized with *E. scotti* and therefore limited to the Irvingtonian. *Equus midlandensis* was synonymized with *E. mexicanus.* Remains identified as *E. scotti* or *E. niobrarensis* from various late Pleistocene localities on the Southern Plains and New Mexico more appropriately are part of the *E. mexicanus* group (Winans, 1985:162).

A grazing animal, this horse inhabited grassland areas. *E. mexicanus* was about the size of the modern horse (table 7.7). The maxilla is from a young horse, the M² in beginning wear and the tip of the paracone of the M³ at the alveolar line. On the basis of an eruption and wear schedule for modern horse (*E. caballus*), the equivalent age of this juvenile would be about two years (Sisson and Grossman, 1953).

Several late Pleistocene localities of *E. mexicanus* (= *E. midlandensis, E. scotti, E. niobrarensis*) occur on or near the Southern High Plains (Lundelius, 1972a; Slaughter, 1975; Gazin, 1955; Dalquest, 1964, 1965), throughout the Southern Plains (Lundelius, 1984), and into New Mexico (Harris and Porter, 1980; Harris, 1985a).

*Equus francisci* (Hay) group, extinct small, stilt-legged horse

   Occipital region of skull (TTU-A5272); left P⁴ (TTU-A5183); left M³ (TTU-A5265); left P₄ (TTU-A13676); broken metatarsal (TTU-A5018); right forelimb: humerus (TTU-A2742), radius (TTU-A2744, 2745), ulna (TTU-A2743), metacarpal (TTU-A2741), 3 splint bones (TTU-A2751, 2752, 17866), 3 carpals (TTU-A2748, 2749, 2750), first and second phalanges (TTU-A2740, 2747)

Table 7.7. Measurements of Adult *Equus mexicanus* (Extinct Stout-Legged Horse) Material
(In Millimeters)

| Location of Measurement | Radio-ulna, Right Side (TTU-A13806) | Metapodial (TTU-A22463) | 1st Phalange, Right Side (TTU-A7689) | 1st Phalange, Right Side (TTU-A939) | 1st Phalange, Left Side (892-285) |
|---|---|---|---|---|---|
| Length of radius | 300* | | | | |
| Length between centers of articulating surfaces | | | 79 | 98 | 74 |
| Width of shaft (narrowest point)† | 44 | 39* | | | |
| Anterior–posterior width (same point)† | 29 | 27 | | | |
| Width, proximal articulating surface | | | 52 | 56 | 60 |
| Anterior–posterior width, proximal articulating surface | 44* | | 34 | 29 | 42 |
| Width, distal articulating surface | 80 | 51 | 46 | 49 | 42 |
| Anterior–posterior width, distal articulating surface† | 48 | | 22 | 21 | 26 |

*Estimate.

†For radio-ulna, measurement applies to radius only.

*Equus francisci* ranged from middle to late Pleistocene and was sympatric with *E. scotti* during the middle (Irvingtonian) and *E. mexicanus* in the late (Rancholabrean) Pleistocene (Winans, 1985). Distinctly different in size and structure from *E. mexicanus* (tables 7.7, 7.8), *E. francisci* was much smaller, with more slender limbs. On the basis of size and proportion of limbs, the small horse was a fast-running form. The Lubbock Lake material previously was unidentified to species (Johnson, 1976, 1983; Johnson and Holliday, 1985), but Winans (1985) in her revision of *Equus* taxonomy, recognized only one small, stilt-legged horse from the late Pleistocene. *Equus quinni* was synonymized with *E. francisci*. This species group (Winans, 1985:159) exhibits a considerable range of variation. The Lubbock Lake metacarpal was compared with a number of middle to late Pleistocene "species" in the Texas–New Mexico region. The metacarpal is longer than those identified as *E. francisci* or *E. conversidens* (cf. Lundelius, 1972a, 1984; Lundelius and Stevens, 1970; Harris and Porter, 1980; table 7.8).

Another grassland grazer, the niche that *E. francisci* occupied in relation to that of *E. mexicanus* is unknown. On the Southern Plains a small horse is invariably associated with a large horse.

Most small-horse material from the Southern High Plains (Lundelius, 1972a; Gazin, 1955; Dalquest, 1964, 1965), Southern Plains (Lundelius, 1984), and southern New Mexico (Harris and Porter, 1980; Harris, 1985a) was identified as *E. conversidens*, *E. francisci*, or *E. quinni*. These horses form the *E. francisci* group (Winans, 1985:159).

*Equus caballus* Linneaus, modern horse

2 partial skulls (TTU-A9492, 10942); right maxilla (TTU-A12503); left maxilla (TTU-A12504); anterior mandible section (TTU-A2821); right mandible (TTU-A26837); 4 left mandibles (892-296, TTU-A1980, 10941, 13537); numerous isolated teeth and postcranial material.

The two partial skulls recovered show a pronounced difference in the external occipital protuberance (attachment area of the ligamentum nuchae) and the nuchal crest. In one skull (TTU-A10942) the protuberance is very shallow and broad, while in the other (TTU-A9492) it is narrow, prominent, and very rugose. The latter specimen also has a more rugose nuchal crest. The shallow, broad protuberance is common or normal in horses, and this latter skull may be from a mule.

## Order Artiodactyla
## Family Tayassuidae

*Platygonus compressus* Le Conte, extinct peccary
Right P$_2$ (TTU-A3155)

The tooth is from a young animal, and the cusps of this hypsodont tooth are worn only slightly. The premolar measures 10.4 mm in length, 5.1 mm anterior width, and 6.7 mm posterior width. These measurements fall within the range of variation for a Texas population (Slaughter, 1966:491), which is a larger form than the eastern population (Guilday et al., 1971). Common during the late Pleistocene, this animal was widespread geographically from Pennsylvania (Ray et al., 1970) to California (Merriam and Stock, 1921).

*Platygonus compressus* was an open-country browsing animal. Guilday et al. (1971:311) suggested that factors of competition, predation, and low reproductive capacity combined with the stress of environmental change and habitat destruction brought about this peccary's extinction at the end of the Pleistocene.

The extinct peccary is known from several late Pleistocene localities in Central and north-central Texas (Graham, 1976; Lundelius, 1967; Slaughter, 1966c; Slaughter and Ritchie, 1963), the Gulf Coast area (Lundelius, 1972b), and New Mexico (Lundelius, 1972a).

Table 7.8. Measurements of Adult *Equus francisci* (Extinct Small Stilt-Legged Horse) Material
(In Millimeters)

| Location of Measurement | 1st Phalange, Left Side (TTU-A16354) | 2nd Phalange, Right Side (TTU-A2747) | 2nd Phalange, (TTU-A20167, TTU-A20168) | Humerus, Right Side (TTU-A2742) | Humerus, Left Side (TTU-A3021) | Radio-ulna, Right Side (TTU-A2745) | Metacarpal, Right Side (TTU-A2741) | Scapula, Left Side (TTU-A20245) |
|---|---|---|---|---|---|---|---|---|
| Overall length | | | | | | 254 | | |
| Length between centers of articulating surfaces | | 33 | 41 | | | | | |
| Width, proximal extremity* | | | | | | 77 | 48 | |
| Anterior–posterior width, proximal extremity | | | | | | | 31 | |
| Width, proximal articulating surface* | 50 | 40 | 47 | | | 68 | | 49 |
| Anterior–posterior width, proximal articulating surface | 37 | 28 | 29 | | | 34 | | |
| Anterior–posterior width of articulating surface of capitate-trapezium | | | | | | | 28 | |
| Width, shaft (at narrowest point)* | | | | 32 | 41 | 41 | 31 | |
| Anterior–posterior width of shaft at same point* | | | | 42 | 48 | 30 | 25 | |
| Width at distal extremity | | | | 70 | 76 | 67 | 43 | |
| Anterior–posterior width, distal extremity* | | | | 79 | 52 | 44 | 34 | |
| Width, distal articulating surface | | 40 | 43 | | | | | |
| Anterior–posterior width, distal articulating surface | | 24 | 24 | | | | | |

*Radius only.

## Family Camelidae

*Camelops hesternus* (Leidy), extinct camel
  Partial radio-ulna (892-273); distal end of right humerus (TTU-A16963); distal ends of 2 right tibiae (TTU-A20039, 24636); proximal end of left metatarsal (892-275); tarsal (TTU-A20057); 6 first phalanges (892-297, TTU-A941, 4014, 5432, 13793, 16626)

Measurements on the material (table 7.9) compare well with those listed for *Camelops hesternus* by Webb (1965). This camel was widespread throughout southern California and the southwest to the Northern Plains (Miller, 1971; Mawby, 1967; Anderson, 1974, 1984; Frison et al., 1978). Hibbard and Taylor (1960) thought this animal to be a browser, but Webb (1965) considered it a grazer capable of some browsing.

*Camelops* sp. is reported from several late Pleistocene archaeological sites, including Lehner (Haynes et al., 1975), Blackwater Draw Locality No. 1 (Lundelius, 1972a), Scharbauer (Gazin, 1955), and Bonfire Shelter (Dibble and Lorrain, 1968). Other Northern Plains and western localities were summarized by Frison et al. (1978). Since *C. hesternus* is the common late Pleistocene camel, most of these occurrences are probably of that animal. Several late Pleistocene paleontological records of *Camelops* sp. or *C. hesternus* are reported throughout Texas (Dalquest, 1964, 1965; Lundelius, 1967, 1972b, 1984; Slaughter and Ritchie, 1963) and New Mexico (Conkling, 1932; Findley et al., 1975; Harris, 1977a).

*Hemiaucheina* sp., extinct llama
  Right M$^1$ (TTU-A24621); right M$_1$ (TTU-A24625)
Species identification on isolated teeth is difficult, and no attempt was made here. The extinct llama was a browsing animal probably favoring a habitat similar to that of the extinct camel, one of open shrub country and grasslands. Smaller than *Camelops hesternus*, *Hemiaucheina* presumably would have occupied a different niche in that habitat.

*Tanupolama* was revised and split into two genera, *Hemiaucheina* representing the Great Plains form (Webb, 1974). Widespread throughout the Southwest and Texas during the late Pleistocene, various species of *Hemiaucheina* (= *Tanupolama*) were recovered from Rancho La Brea (Stock, 1928). *Hemiaucheina* (= *Tanupolama*) *macrocephala* was reported from both Slaton Quarry (Dalquest, 1967) and the gray-sand stratum at Blackwater Draw Locality No. 1 (Lundelius, 1972a). The Lubbock Lake material may well represent this species. Records of *Hemiaucheina* (= *Tanupolama*) sp. were reported from late Pleistocene deposits east of the Southern High Plains (Dalquest, 1965), in Central Texas (Lundelius, 1967), and throughout New Mexico (Findley et al., 1975).

## Family Cervidae

*Odocoileus* sp., deer
  Deciduous dentition (TTU-A18099, 19432, 19434, 19435, 19594, 19599, 19600, 19602, 19603, 19610, 19612, 19615)

Table 7.9. Measurements of Adult *Camelops hesternus* (Extinct Camel) Material
(In Millimeters)

| Location of Measurement | 1st Phalange, (892-297) | 1st Phalange, Right Side (TTU-A941) | 1st Phalange, Left Side (TTU-A3028) | 1st Phalange, (TTU-A4014) | 1st Phalange, Left Side (TTU-A13793) | 1st Phalange, Right Side (TTU-A16626) | Humerus, Left Side (TTU-A16963) | Tibia, Right Side (TTU-A20039) | Tibia, Left Side (TTU-A24636) | Metatarsal (892-275) | Metatarsal, Left Side (TTU-A3059) |
|---|---|---|---|---|---|---|---|---|---|---|---|
| Length between centers of articulating surfaces | 111 | 110* | 105 | 129 | 124 | | | | | | |
| Width, proximal extremity | | | | | | | | | | 79 | 70 |
| Anterior–posterior width, proximal extremity | | | | | | | | | | 56 | 54 |
| Width, proximal articulating surface | 43* | 47 | | 40 | 48 | 47 | | | | | |
| Anterior–posterior width, proximal articulating surface | 38 | | | 32 | 38 | 39 | | | | | |
| Anterior–posterior width, T articulating surface | | | | | | | | | | 37 | 34 |
| Width, distal extremity | | | | | | | 112 | 102 | 91 | | |
| Anterior–posterior width, distal extremity | | | | | | | 104 | 58 | 53 | | |
| Width, distal articulating surface | 35 | 34 | 40 | 25 | 36 | | | | | | |
| Anterior–posterior width, distal articulating surface | 28 | | 34 | 21 | 28 | | | | | | |

*Estimate.

Because of the nature of the material species designation was not attempted. Both whitetail deer (*Odocoileus virginianus*) and mule deer (*O. hemionus*) range over the western half of Texas into New Mexico. These species are widespread throughout North America, although mule deer are restricted to the plains and western areas. Deer are primarily grazers in a grasslands environment but occasionally browse on shrubs and consume fruit. Whitetail deer generally prefer brushy to wooded areas, whereas mule deer favor more open areas. Both, however, are found in a variety of habitats from the plains to the mountains. Deer are crepuscular feeders and rest during the day in secluded places. They occur in small groups but may come together in larger groups in the winter. Fawning season is in the summer, and the young have been weaned by late fall. Home ranges are small, and deer remain in favored areas for long periods of time.

Late Pleistocene and early Holocene records of *O. virginianus* are numerous throughout most of Texas to the Gulf Coast (Ayer, 1936; Dalquest, 1965; Dalquest et al., 1969; Slaughter and Hoover, 1963; Slaughter and Ritchie, 1963; Lundelius, 1967, 1972b). This deer is known from Slaton Quarry (Dalquest, 1967) and late Pleistocene deposits near the Southern High Plains (Dalquest, 1964; Schultz and Howard, 1935). Late Pleistocene and early Holocene rec-

ords of *O. hemionus* are rare. Slaughter (1975) reported it in the brown-sand wedge at Blackwater Draw Locality No. 1. It is known from cave deposits of the Guadalupe Mountains in southeastern New Mexico (Findley et al., 1975), in southwestern New Mexico (Harris, 1985a), and in Trans-Pecos, Texas (Ayer, 1936).

## Family Antilocapridae

*Capromeryx* sp., extinct antelope
Astragalus (892-2E); distal end of left tibia (TTU-A15538)
Since species descriptions are based on dentition and horn cores, no species identification was attempted with the material recovered. A browsing animal, this small antelope probably inhabited a grasslands environment similar to that of the modern pronghorn antelope. During the Pleistocene, *Capromeryx* (= *Breameryx*) was widespread from southern California to the plains. Slaton Quarry (Meade, 1942) is the type locality for *C. minimus*, and measurements of the Lubbock Lake remains were compared with this material (table 7.10).

*Capromeryx* sp. is recorded at localities on the Southern High Plains (Slaughter, 1975; Gazin, 1955) and throughout Texas (Lundelius, 1967, 1972b; Slaughter and McClure,

Table 7.10. Measurements of Tibiae and Astragali of *Capromeryx* (Extinct Antelope)
(In Millimeters)

| Site and Catalog No. | Tibia | Astragalus | Site and Catalog No. | Tibia | Astragalus |
|---|---|---|---|---|---|
| Lubbock Lake Site (*Capromeryx* sp.) | | | Slaton Quarry (*Capromeryx minimus*) | | |
| TTU-A15538 (left) | $13.0^a$ $6.0^b$ | | 882-153 | | $16.9^c$ $12.7^d$ $13.3^{e,j}$ $12.2^f$ $20.2^g$ |
| 892-2E (left) | | $17.0^c$ $14.0^d$ $11.0^e$ $11.7^f$ $22.2^g$ | No. 26 (left) | $13.5^a$ $5.0^b$ | |
| Sims Bayou (*Capromeryx* sp.)$^h$ | | | No. 26 (right) | $12.9^a$ $4.5^b$ | |
| — | | — — — $12.5^f$ $19.1^g$ | 4730 (left) | | $15.1^c$ $11.5^d$ $11.6^e$ $10.7^f$ $19.6^g$ |
| Ingleside Fauna (*Capromeryx minor*)$^i$ | | | 4762 (left) | | $16.9^c$ $13.1^d$ $12.5^e$ $11.5^f$ $21.6^g$ |
| 30967-2137 | | $16.1^c$ $12.5^d$ $11.9^e$ $12.5^f$ $20.8^g$ | 6368 (right) | | $14.9^c$ $11.3^d$ $10.5^e$ $10.1^f$ $19.5^g$ |
| 30967-743 | | $16.3^c$ $11.6^{d,j}$ $12.2^e$ $11.6^f$ $19.7^g$ | 4761 (right) | | $15.5^c$ $12.2^d$ $12.3^e$ $10.0^f$ $20.7^g$ |

$^a$Distal anteroposterior width.
$^b$Medial maleolus length.
$^c$Length between articulated surfaces.
$^d$Width of distal trochlea.
$^e$Width of proximal trochlea.
$^f$Anteroposterior (medial) thickness.
$^g$Overall length.
$^h$After Slaughter and McClure (1965).
$^i$Access courtesy of Texas Memorial Museum, University of Texas at Austin.
$^j$Edges damaged.

1965; Slaughter and Ritchie, 1963) and in cave deposits of southern New Mexico (Conkling, 1932; Findley et al., 1975; Harris, 1977a).

*Antilocapra americana* Ord, pronghorn antelope
   Complete skeleton (TTU-A903); left maxilla (TTU-A4931); right mandible (TTU-A799); 2 left mandibles (TTU-A24705, 2964); numerous isolated teeth and postcranial material
Primarily a browser, the pronghorn antelope favors sagebrush but eats some grasses. It inhabits sagebrush areas, plains, and prairies. Pronghorn antelope historically had a wide distribution, covering nearly the entire plains and the western United States.

The pronghorn antelope is a diurnal herd animal, although it feeds into the night. More browse is taken in the fall than in the summer, and forbs constitute a major part of the diet. Mating is seasonal, and generally two fawns are born in late spring. Nursery herds form and may stay to-

gether into the winter. Winter distribution is affected by food supply, south-facing slopes, amounts of sunshine, and protection from cold north winds (Davis, 1974; Schmidly, 1977).

Late Pleistocene localities for *A. americana* are unknown on the Southern High Plains. Only a few late Pleistocene and early Holocene localities are known in Central Texas (Lundelius, 1967), northeast Texas (Slaughter and Hoover, 1963), and Trans-Pecos (Ayer, 1936), Texas, and from throughout New Mexico (Findley et al., 1975).

*Bison antiquus* (Leidy), extinct bison
   10 skulls (892-2E; TTU-A1596, 2299, 2300, 2678, 11099, 19362-65, 19379, 23018, 27949); 19 right mandibles (892-449; TTU-A949, 2407, 2766, 9029, 13048, 13790, 13851, 17030, 18305, 18760, 19064, 19350, 19379, 19392, 23598, 24721, 27901, 37116); 22 left mandibles (892-2E, 892-294, 892-449; TTU-A949, 1552, 2302, 2380, 2765, 3326, 13449, 17333,

18304, 18666, 19170, 19351, 19378, 19862, 23599, 23631, 24716, 36122, 36123); 5 right maxillae (TTU-A998, 1554, 9383, 14155, 19872); left maxilla (TTU-A14160); numerous isolated teeth and postcranial material

Primarily a grassland animal, this bison was widespread during the late Pleistocene, ranging from California to Kentucky and Alaska to the Valley of Mexico (Skinner and Kaisen, 1947). It occurred throughout the Wisconsinan and was one of the forms that characterized that period.

*Bison antiquus* is one of the few large Rancholabrean animals that did not become extinct at the end of the Pleistocene. Instead, it continued to appear in the faunal record well into the Holocene, gradually evolving into modern bison (*B. bison*). The animal is essentially the same bison, the difference being a size diminution through time. This change appears to be a response to environmental stress (Guthrie, 1970). Although approaches differ, most modern researchers now agree that *B. antiquus* and *B. occidentalis* were the same species (Hillerud, 1966; Johnson, 1974; Wilson, 1974a, b) and that the two forms represent interbreeding subspecies.

*Bison antiquus* (= *B. taylori, B. occidentalis, B. bison antiquus, B. b. occidentalis*) is known from numerous late Pleistocene and early Holocene archaeological sites throughout the plains and western North America in addition to paleontological localities. Remains of this bison were recovered from most Paleoindian sites on or near the Southern High Plains (Barbour and Schultz, 1941; Harrison and Smith, 1975; Lundelius, 1972a; Roberts, 1942; Sellards, 1955b; Sellards et al., 1947; Slaughter, 1975; Speer, 1975; Wendorf et al., 1955). Localities are widespread throughout Texas and New Mexico (e.g., Dalquest, 1965; Dibble and Lorrain, 1968; Lundelius, 1967, 1972b; Findley et al., 1975; Schultz, 1943).

*Bison bison* (Linnaeus), modern bison

18 skulls (892-3E; 892-4E; 892-6A; 892-6CK; 892-6K; TTU-A595, 596, 597, 598, 599, 1917, 3743, 7401, 7440, 9310, 9311, 13212, 24543); 20 horn cores (892-6K; 892-259; TTU-A368, 496, 572, 593, 1554, 1732, 3000, 3023, 3993, 6994, 8609, 8613, 12601, 12705, 13737, 15066, 24525, 24560); 13 right mandibles (892-4E; TTU-A703, 5893, 7252, 8921, 9034, 12997, 13737, 17412, 17472, 24525, 24712, 24754); 17 left mandibles (TTU-A1720, 1731, 6554, 8919, 9004, 9019, 10042, 10961, 11652, 13201, 22439, 24781, 24842, 24956, 26939, 36122, 36123); 3 right maxillae (TTU-A9283, 24525, 24678); 5 left maxillae (TTU-A590, 8152, 13737, 22230, 24525); numerous isolated teeth and postcranial material

Historically numbering into the millions, modern bison had a widespread distribution throughout the plains-prairie region and from the Northwest to the eastern United States. The current spotty and disjunct distribution of bison reflects the near extinction of these animals as a result of commercial hunting during the late 1880s.

Bison are diurnal herd animals. They are grazers in a grasslands environment but occasionally browse on tree bark. Herd composition consists of bull and cow groups. Bull groups contain males of 4 years or older, while cow groups are nursery herds, containing females, calves, yearlings, and 2-year-olds of both sexes. Bulls 3 years old can be found in either group (McHugh, 1958:14). Cows become sexually mature at 2 years and calve in the third year. Spring is the general calving season, although out-of-season births occur. Cow groups are the larger segment of the herd and demonstrate greater cohesiveness as a group, in group response, and in daily activity pattern (McHugh, 1958).

Most localities of modern bison in Texas and New Mexico are archaeological sites. Records are most numerous in the plains area of the western half of Texas and eastern half of New Mexico (e.g., Tunnell and Hughes, 1955; Dibble and Lorrain, 1968; Dalquest, 1962a; J. Holden, 1952).

## DISCUSSION

The herpetofauna is mainly Paleoindian, representing late Pleistocene and early Holocene assemblages. The mammalian fauna spans the entire time range, although concentrated at opposite ends of that range. Much of the fauna reflects a watercourse and riparian habitat with a more distal drier-grasslands component. Many of the species are significant because they are good climatic or environmental indicators, occur outside their modern ranges, constitute fossil temporal or spatial records, or are a combination of the foregoing.

The recognition of *Geochelone wilsoni* and *Bufo woodhousei bexarensis* in the late Pleistocene assemblage is significant because of their limited fossil record. In addition, *Geochelone* is considered a good climatic marker, indicating warmer winters than the modern regime (Hibbard, 1960; Holman, 1969b). Although *G. wilsoni* was small enough to have been a burrowing form, living relatives (Testudinidae) are mainly restricted to subtropical and tropical habitats. These circumstances imply that the presence of *G. wilsoni* would also indicate mild winters (Slaughter, 1966b, 1975; Moodie and Van Devender, 1979).

The above-freezing winters allowed several species that today have retreated to eastern Texas to range westward onto the Southern High Plains. The extent of a gallery forest into the Southern High Plains is debatable. Most of the extralimital eastern forms can occur in a variety of habitats, the major requirements being amount of moisture and availability of permanent water.

*Terrapene carolina* is perhaps the best indicator of trees in the area. It had retreated from the area by the end of the Pleistocene and did not persist into the early Holocene. Although sympatric today in eastern Texas, the temporal distribution of *T. ornata* and *T. carolina* did not overlap at Lubbock Lake. *Terrapene carolina* was limited to stratum 1, and *T. ornata* entered the record post-11,000 years. Milstead (1967) identified a carapace section (ANSP 13780) as *T. o. ornata* from Anderson Basin No. 1, listing it as coming from the Wisconsin period. However, Stock and Bode (1936) noted that this specimen came from the "blue sands," which is the diatomite unit at Anderson Basin No. 1 (Haynes, 1975:59). The record is an early Holocene one. A second specimen (937-201) identified by Milstead (1967) as

*T. o. ornata* from Blackwater Draw Locality No. 1 came from the bottom of well M at Station E, an aboriginal well dug during the Archaic period (Hester, 1972:33, 37). The temporal pattern for *T. ornata* at Blackwater Draw appears to follow that at Lubbock Lake and was also noted for two cave localities in the Guadalupe Mountains (Gehlbach and Holman, 1974).

This replacement pattern indicates that a number of changes were occurring, including a decrease in available moisture, greater annual temperature fluctuation, more marked seasonal differentiation, decline in the amount and distribution of trees, and a concomitant increase in amount and distribution of grasses.

Other factors affected range distribution. The northern distribution of *Sigmodon hispidus* is limited by mean annual temperature and length of the growing season. Mohlhenrich (1961) found in New Mexico that these parameters are greater than 55° F and 180 or more days, respectively.

Competition occurs between *Sigmodon hispidus* and *Microtus pennsylvanicus*. Although suitable habitat is available throughout the southeastern area, only *S. hispidus* is present. During the late Pleistocene these animals were sympatric in this region westward across Texas into New Mexico. *Sigmodon hispidus* still occupies this range. An area of sympatry exists today along the northeastern and southeastern borders of these two cricetids, respectively. *Sigmodon hispidus* can tolerate (and even requires) higher average summer temperatures than *M. pennsylvanicus*. Their area of sympatry today appears to be at the limits of tolerance for the meadow vole (R. Martin, 1968b).

The cotton rat and meadow vole were sympatric at Lubbock Lake only in the early Holocene substratum 2A and lower 2B deposits. Remains of the meadow vole were relatively abundant, while those of the cotton rat were few. Meadow vole was scarce in the A horizon of the Firstview Soil, while cotton rat remains increased. This situation reflects (1) the stress of both the warming and the drying conditions occurring at the beginning of the Holocene and (2) habitat competition (replacement) by cotton rats. It forms the backdrop for the pattern of microtine retreat seen on the Southern High Plains at this time.

*Microtus pennsylvanicus* vacated Lubbock Lake before the end of the Paleoindian period, for remains of this animal are absent from the top of substratum 2B and above. The base of substratum 2B dates at approximately 10,000 B.P. and the development of the overlying Firstview Soil at ca. 8600 B.P. The meadow vole is known from two other late Pleistocene localities on the Southern High Plains. Deposits at Blackwater Draw Locality No. 1/brown-sand wedge local fauna (Slaughter, 1975) and Rex Rodgers (Schultz, 1978), date before 9000 B.P. Thus by about 9,000 years ago this animal had retreated from the Southern High Plains.

Associated radiocarbon dates (11,135 ± 450 B.P. and 9550 ± 375 B.P.) with the Ben Franklin local fauna (Slaughter and Hoover, 1963) indicate that northeastern Texas may have followed the same retreat pattern as that on the Southern High Plains, with *M. pennsylvanicus* gone from the area by 9,000 years ago.

*Microtus pennsylvanicus* retreated from Central Texas (the southernmost known range extension) around 10,000 years ago (Lundelius, 1974). The retreat of this animal from Central Texas, followed by the retreat from the Southern High Plains and northeastern Texas by 9,000 years ago, reflects the time differential south to north of changing environmental conditions at the end of the Pleistocene and early Holocene.

During the late Pleistocene and early Holocene, *Microtus pennsylvanicus* and *M. ochrogaster* were sympatric across Texas and New Mexico. Retreat of the prairie vole from the region progressed at a much slower pace than that of the meadow vole, which reflects the prairie vole's greater tolerance to humidity and temperature changes. *Microtus ochrogaster* was last recorded for Central Texas at Miller's Cave, with an associated radiocarbon date of 3008 ± 410 B.P. (Patton, 1963; Lundelius, 1967). Late Holocene localities at the northern edge of the Southern High Plains include Foard (Dalquest, 1962a), Randall (Lundelius, 1974), and Wheeler (Frank, 1964) counties. These late Holocene occurrences represent either relict populations in a restricted, favorable habitat (Dalquest, 1962a) or reentrance onto the northern portion of the Southern High Plains owing to the return of more mesic conditions at that time (Holliday, 1985d; Hall, 1982).

At Lubbock Lake the latest occurrence of *M. ochrogaster* is in the A horizon of the Firstview Soil. The one specimen recovered (left $M^1$, TTU-A23077) indicates a very low density compared with that of earlier deposits. This situation reflects both the less-than-optimal climatic conditions and perhaps competition from cotton rats.

After 8500 B.P., *M. ochrogaster* retreated from the southern part of the Southern High Plains, reflecting a progressive trend south to north of warmer and drier conditions. Lundelius (1967:311) noted a similar pattern for *Blarina brevicauda* on the Edwards Plateau, though west to east across the area, also attributed to a progressive warming and drying climate across the plateau.

*Ondatra zibethicus*, previously abundant, became rare in the A horizon of the Firstview Soil and was absent from later deposits. Muskrat remains from Blackwater Draw Locality No. 1 (Lundelius, 1972a; Slaughter, 1975) dated at or before 10,000 B.P. (Haynes, 1975). By 8500 B.P. muskrat had retreated from Lubbock Lake and from at least the southern part of the Southern High Plains.

The southern bog lemming was widespread throughout the Southern Plains into Mexico during Sangamonian, Wisconsinan, and early Holocene periods (fig. 7.7). The record at San Josecito Cave, in Nuevo León (Cushing, 1945), represents the most southern border of this lemming's range, while that at Lubbock Lake is the westernmost known occurrence. The retreat of *Synaptomys cooperi* from across Texas appears to have followed a pattern similar to that of *Microtus pennsylvanicus,* but with a time differential of up to 1,000 years.

Lundelius (1974) suggested that *S. cooperi* retreated from Central Texas about 10,000 years ago, along with *M. pennsylvanicus,* but radiocarbon dates associated with Schulze Cave (Dalquest et al., 1969) indicated retreat by 9000 B.P. Data from northeastern Texas (Slaughter and Hoover, 1963), indicate retreat by 9,000 years ago. The occurrence at Lubbock Lake dates approximately 10,000 B.P. *Synaptomys cooperi* appears to have retreated from the Southern High Plains 1,000 years before vacating Central and northeastern Texas.

The Lubbock Lake record of *Holmesina septentrionalis* is the westernmost known and the latest geologic occurrence (11,100 ± 100 B.P.; Holliday et al., 1983) of this extinct giant armadillo. Its presence in the Clovis-age megafaunal processing station is the first known association with man.

Although modern armadillos burrow and hibernate to escape short-term cold periods, they cannot tolerate extensive cold temperatures. The extinct giant armadillo was too large (ca. 0.9 m [3 ft] tall and 1.8 m [6 ft] long) to be a burrowing form. All other fossil and modern forms are tropical to subtropical animals. This armadillo appears to be another sensitive indicator for mild winters lacking prolonged freezing temperatures.

Prairie-dog towns were a focal point of the short-grasslands faunal community. At various times of the year animals such as Audubon cottontails, burrowing owls, grasshopper mice, deer mice, kangaroo rats, thirteen-lined ground squirrels, jackrabbits, box turtles, tiger salamanders, and snakes took advantage of small mammals and insects, plant growth, and abandoned holes for nesting, hibernating, and security. Bison and pronghorn antelope favored town areas because of the increased growth of forbs.

Like prairie-dog towns, the burrow system of pocket gophers had a community of vertebrates associated with it (Vaughn, 1961). These various animals sought shelter in the burrows, used them as foraging routes, or occupied them (with or without the presence of the gophers). Community members from Lubbock Lake include ornate box turtles, bull snakes, desert cottontails, ground squirrels, Ord's kangaroo rats, northern grasshopper mice, prairie voles, striped skunks, and tiger salamanders.

Of the pocket gophers in general, *Cratogeomys castenops* is the most adapted to xeric conditions caused by decreasing rainfall. Factors favoring distributional expansion (and replacement of *Thomomys* in areas of sympatry) are increased aridity leading to decreasing soil moisture and increasing xerophytic plants (Schmidly, 1977; Reichman and Baker, 1972). The Lubbock Lake specimens are the only known fossil records of *C. castenops* for the Southern High Plains. They occurred during the first drought period of the Altithermal and subsequent interval before the second drought period (Holliday, 1985b; Holliday and Allen, chap. 2; Johnson and Holliday, 1986).

The presence of *Arctodus simus* in the Clovis-age megafaunal processing station is the latest known occurrence of this bear in the geological record (11,100 ± 100 B.P.; Holliday et al., 1983) and the first demonstrable association with man. Two questionable records of the association of the short-faced bear and man were reported in the early literature from cave localities in southern New Mexico that were quarried by paleontologists. At Burnet Cave (Schultz and Howard, 1935) a Clovis point was found with a hearth in association with extinct bison and muskox. Four vertebrae

of *Arctodus* were recovered in the cave deposits, but their associations were not noted. At Conkling Cavern (Conkling, 1932), the various vertebrate assemblages encountered are late Pleistocene. Conkling (1932:12) reported the partial remains of two human skeletons, one "in close proximity" to remains of *Arctodus* and ground sloth. Neither the human remains nor the large veterbrate fauna were studied in detail, and stratigraphic relationships are unknown.

The astragalus of a *Capromeryx* recovered by Evans and Meade (Sellards, 1952) marks the latest known occurrence of this antelope in the geologic record. It came from substratum 2A, which ranges from ca. 10,800 to 10,000 B.P. (Holliday et al., 1983). *Capromeryx* sp. was reported from all three strata at Scharbauer (Gazin, 1955) and the brown sand wedge at Blackwater Draw Locality No. 1 (Slaughter, 1975). These occurrences strengthen the argument of an early Holocene presence of this animal on the Southern High Plains.

## SUMMARY

A retreat pattern occurred in several directions at various times. This general sequential reduction reflects two periods of major change in the shift toward a modernized climate, one at around 11,000 B.P. and another at 8500 B.P. Faunal fluctuations within the intervening deposits of that time span hint at readjustments to the changing conditions.

The assemblages at Lubbock Lake reflect the animal communities existing in the local environs at a particular time. They represent a living community and not simply an assemblage associated only after death. Such community associations are particularly noticeable with prairie-dog and pocket-gopher burrow systems. Although burrowing animals are common in the assemblages, few burrow disturbances were noted in excavation. These remains record deaths in the vicinity of but not within the burrow system.

The presence of man is a factor in the assemblages. While man exploited the resources, he neither depleted them nor altered the local environment to any great extent. At Lubbock Lake man, as both a predator and a competitor, is a community member interacting in a noncatastrophic manner with the rest of the community. At other localities such as large-scale kills, interaction is catastrophic, and the assemblage represents a disjunct segment of a community.

The concept of the Lubbock Lake assemblages representing living communities is an important one for paleoenvironmental reconstruction. While proximal and distal communities are represented (Shotwell, 1955, 1958), these communities are immediately adjacent in the restricted area of the draw. Although the larger animals could traverse a greater area than the site's environs in their seasonal activities, their behavioral patterns and low densities suggest that Lubbock Lake was part of their home range.

Numerous assemblages are recognized temporally, reflecting an evolving community responding to changing environmental conditions. Competitive factors may be reflected with high and low densities of certain species. Although grassland forms are dominant throughout, subsidiary dependence on wooded or brushy areas, humidity and available surface moisture, and temperature fluctuations change the faunal makeup.

The assemblages reflect the conditions of Yellowhouse Draw and not necessarily the uplands of the Southern High Plains. These uplands did have an influence on species distribution, for grassland forms are recorded in upland deposits (e.g., Evans and Meade, 1945), and the range of northern animals changed with temperature and moisture regimes.

# 8. Paleoenvironmental Overview

## EILEEN JOHNSON

The local environment, the ecosystem of which it was a part, and the climate form the framework for understanding the cultural adaptations and processes occurring in a region. At Lubbock Lake this framework is based on the faunal record (Hill, 1982; Rea et al., n.d.; Johnson, chap. 7; Pierce, chap. 6), hydrologic and geomorphic data (Holliday, 1982, 1985d; Holliday and Allen, chap. 2), and vegetation data (Thompson, chap. 4; Murry, 1982; Robinson, 1982). Given the extensive faunal record, the emphasis is on faunal communities and ecology of the draw area.

Microvertebrates are particularly important in delineating the various habitat groupings, but the entire faunal assemblage from each period was considered. Some animals because of their specific requirements offered limitations to a range of conditions. Furthermore, the disharmonious faunas (Semken, 1974, 1983; Lundelius et al., 1983) during the late Pleistocene and early Holocene indicate superimposed, compressed ecological zones with altered community structures and vegetation patterns and probable increased competition. These altered vegetation patterns probably had a greater diversity and mosaic distribution, as reflected by the disharmonious faunas, and were themselves disharmonious floras.

The draw is narrow, and its greatest expanse in the site area is approximately 500 m. The diachronic vertebrate fauna constitutes six major habitat groupings. These groupings grade into each other, and many of the species recovered can occur in a variety of habitats. For those species not ranging into the area today, habitat preferences from the nearest area of occurrence were considered. For extinct forms the paleontological custom of using analogous forms and habitat preferences of the nearest related species was followed. In determining geographic faunal or floral elements, the region closest to Lubbock Lake and the Southern High Plains or the region of greatest sympatric overlap was considered. In that manner, although an animal or plant may have had a widespread distribution, it was viewed as part of a suite of animals or plants that characterized a particular region.

Bryant (1969; Bryant and Shafer, 1977) defined various combinations and states of vegetation applicable to the Texas region during the late Pleistocene and Holocene. A woodland was an open-canopy forest with a grass-and-herb understory. Parkland was a grasslands interrupted occasionally with small groves and isolated trees. Savanna was an uninterrupted grasslands with a few scattered trees. A scrub grasslands was a prairie with bushy areas and rare trees (Bryant and Shafer, 1977:6).

The general term "savanna grasslands" previously used to describe the environs of Yellowhouse Draw (Johnson, 1974, 1976) indicated small, scattered groves of trees (both parkland and savanna situations) as opposed to woodland or gallery forest. The two latter terms imply a much greater extent of wooded area.

The three major grass subfamilies were identified (Robinson, 1982), and their modern distribution (Gould and Shaw, 1983) reflects in general a disharmonious pattern similar to that seen for the vertebrates. Pooid (= festucoid) grasses are primarily a northern floral element that generally prefers cool to cold climates with a good moisture regime during the growing season. Limiting factors are temperature and available moisture. These grasses are $C_3$ plants that are short-day grasses (limited available sunshine for growing and flowering). Panicoid grasses are primarily a southeastern floral element that prefers moist, humid tropic or subtropical habitats. Temperature and available moisture are limiting factors. These grasses have both $C_3$ and $C_4$ plants and are long-day grasses (maximum available sunshine). Chloridoid grasses are primarily a southwestern floral element that prefers warm, dry climates. These grasses are $C_4$ plants that are long-day grasses.

In general, summer rains and periodic summer droughts characterize and promote grasslands. Various types of modern grass associations (Gould and Shaw, 1983) occur, but because specifics beyond subfamilies are lacking, it is difficult to identify the paleograss associations beyond generalities.

## RECONSTRUCTIONS

### Clovis Period

At the end of the Pleistocene a low-gradient, sometimes muddy stream meandered through the draw inhabited by gars, minnows, quillbacks, catfish, sunfish, migratory geese, muskrats, surface-feeding and ruddy ducks, rails, water snakes, western ribbon snakes, snapper and softshell turtles, and bullfrogs. These animals indicate an abundant growth of emergent vegetation that included sedges. Extensive areas of bottom sand provided suitable places for turtles to bury themselves.

Bullfrogs, geese, surface-feeding ducks, and various turtles were found in and around the stream. The riparian wet meadows and sedge beds were inhabited by meadow voles, rails, tiger salamanders, pickerel and leopard frogs, and the common garter snake.

Scattered small groves of netleaf hackberry along with gromwell were inhabited by shrews, turkeys, Carolina box turtles, and worm snakes. The open prairie (pooid and panicoid grasses) was inhabited by prairie voles, giant armadillos, and large browsing-grazing animals (mammoths, camels, llamas, bison, peccaries, extinct antelopes, and horses). Richardson's ground squirrels and various toads occupied the ecotonal area of prairie to wet meadows. Bears, wolves, and coyotes traversed the area, as did ravens, red-winged blackbirds, vesper sparrows, and patch-nosed snakes. A prairie-dog-town community existed in short-grass areas, inhabited by prairie dogs, ground squirrels, grasshopper mice, burrowing owls, and western hognose

and ground snakes. Cactus mice, kit foxes, and Wilson's tortoises could be found in drier, sandier parts of the grass-lands (table 8.1) or scrub areas along the draw's slopes where seepweed would grow.

The draw environs are reconstructed as a parkland of

Table 8.1. Lubbock Lake Paleoindian Vertebrate Local Faunas

| Clovis Local Fauna (11,100 B.P.) | Folsom Local Fauna (10,800–10,300 B.P.) | Plainview Local Fauna (10,000 B.P.) | Firstview Local Fauna (8600 B.P.) |
|---|---|---|---|
| *Lepisosteus* sp.* | *Ictalurus* (cf. *Ameiurus*) sp. | *Ictalurus* sp. | *Ictalurus* sp. |
| *Carpiodes cyprinus** | *Morone chrysops** | *Ictalurus* (cf. *Ameiurus*) sp. | *Ambystoma tigrinum* |
| *Ictalurus* (cf. *Ameiurus*) sp. | *Lepomis gulosus** | *Ambystoma tigrinum* | *Rana catesbeiana* |
| *Ictalurus melas* | *Percina* sp. | *Bufo* sp. | *Rana pipiens* |
| *Ictalurus punctatus* | *Rana catesbeiana* | *Rana catesbeiana* | *Chelydra serpentina* |
| *Lepomis cyanellus* | *Rana pipiens* | *Rana pipiens* | *Kinosternon flavescens* |
| *Ambystoma tigrinum* | *Kinosternon flavescens* | *Chelydra serpentina* | *Chrysemys scripta* |
| *Scaphiopus bombifrons* or S. *hammondi* | *Chrysemys scripta* | *Kinosternon flavescens* | *Terrapene ornata* |
| *Acris crepitans* | *Elaphe* or *Pituophis* sp. | *Chrysemys scripta* | *Phrynosoma cornutum* |
| *Bufo cognatus* | *Thamnophis* cf. *sirtalis** | *Terrapene ornata* | *Eumeces obsoletus* |
| ‡*Bufo woodhousei bexarensis* | *Anas crecca carolinensis* | *Eumeces obsoletus* | *Thamnophis* cf. *sirtalis** |
| *Rana catesbeiana* | *Rallus limicola* | *Coluber constrictor** | *Anas platyrhynchos* |
| *Rana palustris** | *Fulica americana* | *Lampropeltis getulus* | *Anas acuta* |
| *Rana pipiens* | *Chordeiles* cf. *minor* | *Nerodia* cf. *cyclopion** or N. cf. *rhombifera** | *Anas crecca carolinensis* |
| *Chelydra serpentina* | *Colaptes auratus* | *Sonora semiannulata** | *Anas cyanoptera* |
| *Kinosternon flavescens* | Cf. *Eremophila alpestris* | *Thamnophis marcianus* | *Tympanuchus cupido* or *Centrocercus urophasianus* |
| ‡*Geochelone wilsoni* | *Mimus polyglottis* | *Thamnophis proximus* | *Tympanuchus cupido* or "*Pedioecetes*" *phasianellus* |
| ‡*Geochelone* sp. | *Notiosorex crawfordi* | *Thamnophis* cf. *sirtalis** | |
| *Chrysemys scripta* | *Lepus californicus* | *Tropidoclonion lineatum** | *Rallus* cf. *longirostris** |
| ‡*Terrapene carolina putnami* | *Spermophilus tridecemlineatus* | *Agkistrodon contortrix** | *Porzana carolina* |
| *Trionyx* sp.* | *Cynomys ludovicianus* | *Podiceps* cf. *nigricollis* | Cf. *Laterallus exilis** |
| *Carphophis amoenus** | *Geomys bursarius* | *Podilymbus* cf. *podiceps* | *Agelaius phoeniceus* |
| *Elaphe guttata* | *Perognathus* cf. *hispidus* | *Anas platyrhynchos* | *Molothrus* cf. *ater* |
| *Gyalopion canum** | *Sigmodon hispidus* | *Anas strepera* or A. *acuta* | *Sylvilagus* cf. *audubonii* |
| *Heterodon nasicus* | *Microtus pennsylvanicus** | *Anas clypeata* | *Lepus californicus* |
| *Lampropeltis triangulum* | *Microtus ochrogaster** | *Anas crecca carolinensis* | *Spermophilus tridecemlineatus* |
| *Nerodia* sp. | *Ondatra zibethicus** | *Gallinula chloropus** | *Spermophilus mexicanus* |
| *Salvadora* sp.* | *Canis latrans* | *Fulica americana* | *Cynomys ludovicianus* |
| *Sonora semiannulata** | *Canis lupus* | *Charadrius montanus** | *Geomys bursarius* |
| *Thamnophis* cf. *sirtalis** | ‡*Capromeryx* sp. | *Notiosorex crawfordi* | *Dipodomys ordii* |
| *Tropidoclonion lineatum** | ‡*Bison antiquus* | *Sylvilagus* sp. | *Onychomys leucogaster* |
| *Virginia* cf. *striatula** | | *Lepus californicus* | *Sigmodon hispidus* |
| *Crotalus atrox* | | *Spermophilus tridecemlineatus* | *Neotoma* cf. *micropus* |
| *Branta canadensis* | | *Spermophilus mexicanus* | *Neotoma* cf. *albigula* |
| *Anser caerulescens* | | *Cynomys ludovicianus* | *Microtus pennsylvanicus** |
| *Anas platyrhynchos* | | *Geomys bursarius* | *Microtus ochrogaster** |
| *Anas acuta* | | *Dipodomys ordii* | *Ondatra zibethicus** |
| *Anas* cf. *clypeata* | | *Reithrodontomys montanus* | *Canis latrans* |
| *Anas crecca carolinensis* cf. *Oxyura jamaicensis* | | *Onychomys leucogaster* | *Canis lupus* |
| *Meleagris* sp. | | *Sigmodon hispidus* | *Taxidea taxus* |
| *Rallus limicola* | | *Neotoma* cf. *micropus* | *Felis* cf. *rufus* |
| *Fulica americana* | | *Microtus pennsylvanicus** | *Odocoileus* sp. |
| *Athene* cf. *cunicularia* | | *Microtus ochrogaster** | *Antilocapra americana* |
| *Corvus corax** | | *Ondatra zibethicus** | ‡*Bison antiquus* |
| Cf. *Agelaius phoeniceus* | | *Synaptomys cooperi** | |
| Cf. *Pooecetes gramineus* | | *Canis lupus* | |
| *Blarina* sp.* | | *Odocoileus* sp. | |
| ‡*Holmesina septentrionalis* | | *Antilocapra americana* | |
| | | ‡*Bison antiquus* | |

*No longer occurs in the area.
‡Extinct.

Table 8.1. *(Continued)*

| Clovis Local Fauna (11,100 B.P.) | Folsom Local Fauna (10,800–10,300 B.P.) | Plainview Local Fauna (10,000 B.P.) | Firstview Local Fauna (8600 B.P.) |
|---|---|---|---|
| *Lepus californicus* | | | |
| *Spermophilus richardsonii** | | | |
| *Spermophilus tridecemlineatus* | | | |
| *Spermophilus mexicanus* | | | |
| *Cynomys ludovicianus* | | | |
| *Thomomys bottae** | | | |
| *Geomys bursarius* | | | |
| *Reithrodontomys montanus* | | | |
| *Peromyscus* cf. *eremicus** | | | |
| *Onychomys leucogaster* | | | |
| *Neotoma* cf. *micropus* | | | |
| *Microtus pennsylvanicus** | | | |
| *Microtus ochrogaster** | | | |
| *Ondatra zibethicus** | | | |
| *Canis latrans* | | | |
| *Canis lupus* | | | |
| *Vulpes macrotis** | | | |
| ‡*Arctodus simus* | | | |
| ‡*Mammuthus columbi* | | | |
| ‡*Equus mexicanus* | | | |
| ‡*Equus francisci* | | | |
| ‡*Platygonus compressus* | | | |
| ‡*Camelops hesternus* | | | |
| ‡*Hemiauchenia* sp. | | | |
| ‡*Capromeryx* sp. | | | |
| ‡Bison antiquus | | | |

small patches of hackberry trees and shrubs along the stream and valley floor with adjacent wet meadows grading into large expanses of grasslands (fig. 8.1). Wide areas of the grasslands probably grew in sandy soil. Mild, frost-free winters are indicated by the presence of extinct tortoise, extict giant armadillo, Carolina box turtle, earth snake, and panicoid grasses. Cooler summers are indicated by the northern faunal elements (Richardson's ground squirrel, microtines) and pooid grasses. More available moisture is indicated by both the grasses and the northern and southeastern faunal elements.

**Folsom and Plainview Periods**

The vertebrate faunal assemblages for the Folsom and Plainview periods are distinct and defined as such (table 8.1). These assemblages indicate similar environmental settings in the draw during the two cultural periods. They represent the continued presence of a savanna from Folsom through Plainview times. The hydrologic system was also similar. Because of these factors, this 1,000-year span was treated as a single period for purposes of paleoenvironmental reconstruction.

During Folsom and Plainview times a series of clear ponds with weedy growth (chara) were interconnected by a low-volume stream that kept fresh water flowing through the valley floor. Dependent woodland forms, such as the Carolina box turtle, are absent from the record. Lined and earth snakes lingered. The amount of wooded areas decreased from a parkland to a savanna. Catfish, white bass, sunfish, and log perch inhabited the ponds. The surround-ing banks and sedge beds (rushes, horsetail) were inhabited by bullfrogs, water snakes, surface-feeding and diving ducks, rails, gallinules, coots, muskrats, cotton rats, bog lemmings, meadow voles, desert shrews, garter snakes, leopard frogs, and snapping, mud, and pond turtles.

The extent of the open grasslands increased at the expense of the parkland. Bison and extinct and pronghorn antelope inhabited the prairie (pooid and panicoid grasses), prey to wolves and coyotes. Smaller animals inhabiting this area included jackrabbits, pocket gophers, prairie voles, nighthawks, mockingbirds, flickers, horned larks, and ornate box turtles. The prairie-dog-town community continued in shortgrass areas, represented by prairie dogs, ground squirrels, hispid pocket mice, mountain plovers, and western ground snakes. Copperheads and rattlesnakes occupied rocky hillsides of the draw among scattered hackberry trees or shrubs. Sandy slopewash areas supported gaura, devil's-claw, goosefoot, and buffalo bur. Sandy-soiled grasslands continued, favored by Mexican ground squirrels, kangaroo rats, pocket gophers, ornate box turtles, and western ground snakes.

The prairie habitat became dominant in the draw environs, with scattered hackberry trees or shrubs on the slopes and around the ponds (fig. 8.2). Mild winters persisted (southeastern animals still occurred in the assemblage), but the absence (and extinction) of the tortoise and giant armadillo indicates the onset of at least occasional periods of freezing temperatures. Summers were warming as some of the northern forms retreated from the area, yet summers were still cool enough for meadow voles and bog lemmings to inhabit the site area.

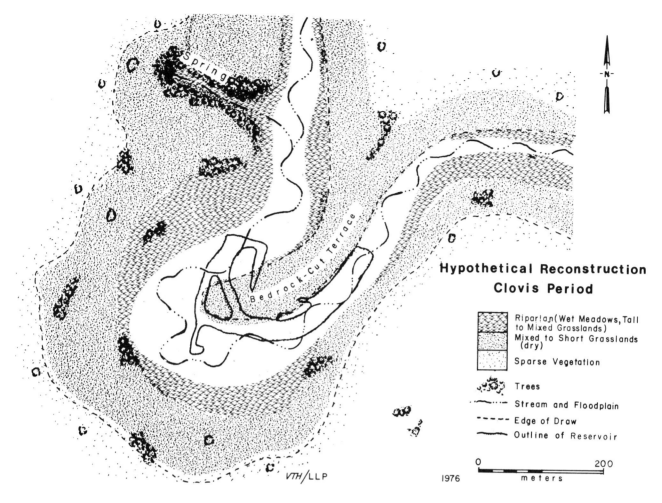

Fig. 8.1. Hypothetical reconstruction of the Lubbock Lake local environs in Yellowhouse Draw during the Clovis period (11,500 to 11,000 B.P.).

## Firstview Period

The valley floor by Firstview times was a wet meadow-marshlands area that graded into an open prairie (pooid, panicoid, and chloridoid grasses). The marshland was a boggy area with a water table close to or occasionally at the surface but without expanses of water of any appreciable depth. Muskrats were rare, and small catfish lingered. The marsh was habitable for surface-feeding ducks, crakes, mud and pond turtles, water snakes, and bullfrogs. Garter snakes, leopard frogs, rails, and red-winged blackbirds were part of the riparian community. Cotton rats, increasing in abundance, inhabited the moist, tall grass cover and sedge beds in the meadows; meadow and prairie voles were rare.

Woodland animals are lacking. Probable areas of brushland are indicated by the bobcat. The sandy-soil open grasslands continued to be inhabited by bison, pronghorn antelopes, coyotes, pocket gophers, Mexican ground squirrels, Southern Plains wood rats, jackrabbits, grouse, ornate box

turtles, Great Plains skinks, and king snakes. Prairie dogs, thirteen-lined ground squirrels, kangaroo rats, grasshopper mice, and Audubon cottontails inhabited the local prairie-dog town and were prey for badgers and coyotes. Remains of horned lizards indicate some areas of sparse vegetation in the sandy-soil grasslands.

The local environs (fig. 8.3) during this period continued to be dominated by a prairie habitat surrounding the marsh. Rare trees (hardwoods) and some brushland indicate a scrub-grasslands situation. The grasslands appear to be transitional from a mixed-prairie to a desert-plains grasslands. The association of the three grass subfamilies indicates a continued disharmonious flora but reflects the increasing early Holocene warming and drying trend with the introduction of the southwestern floral element. Yearly precipitation or effective moisture pattern was decreasing with a probable concomitant shift in rainfall pattern away from spring-summer toward summer-winter rains. Periodic summer droughts continued. Shallow surface-water resources were present. The known fauna is close to a modern one (table 8.1).

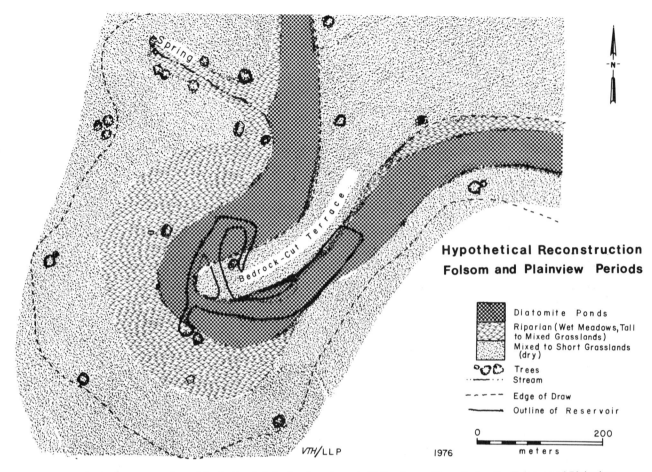

Fig. 8.2. Hypothetical reconstruction of the Lubbock Lake local environs in Yellowhouse Draw during the Folsom and Plainview periods (10,800 to 10,000 B.P.).

## Archaic Period

The vertebrate faunal record for the Archaic (table 8.2) is basically a modern one adapted to a prairie with some brushland. During the Early Archaic (table 8.2), a freshwater marsh where bullrushes grew continued in the valley axis and was inhabited by frogs and tiger salamanders. Bison roamed the extensive, treeless prairie. Gaura grew in dry, sandy slopewash areas.

The local environs reflect warming and drying conditions. Northern and southeastern faunal elements are absent, indicating a decrease in available moisture and humidity levels. Eolian sedimentation began to accumulate, indicating the beginning of a reduction in vegetation cover.

At the beginning of the Middle Archaic (table 8.2) a brackish marsh in the valley axis supported bullrushes and water lilies and was inhabited by water snakes, mud turtles, and leopard frogs. Yellow-faced pocket gophers, cotton rats, and bull and ground snakes could be found in the riparian habitat around the restricted marsh. Areas of sandy-soil grassland were inhabited by plains pocket gophers. Remains of pronghorn antelope indicate the presence of forbs and other herbaceous vegetation in the grasslands. Other open-prairie inhabitants were bison, box turtles, spadefoot toads, and jackrabbits, while coyotes traversed the area.

The presence of yellow-faced gophers denotes semiarid to arid conditions. Dental abnormalities in the bison indicate poor range conditions owing to excess grit on the vegetation. Massive eolian sedimentation occurred, and the grit may have been due to the large amounts of dust in the air at that time. The sedimentation also indicates increased reduction in vegetation cover probably owing to decreasing effective moisture.

A brief period of landscape stability and respite occurred during the middle of the Middle Archaic (table 8.2). A small freshwater stream flowed in the valley axis and supported water lilies. Yellow-faced pocket gophers continued in the bottomland, while the prairie was inhabited by bison, coyotes, and kangaroo rats. Brushy areas were home to wood rats.

The localized reactivation of spring discharge appears to be due to a rise in water table resulting from an increase in precipitation. The formation of the Yellowhouse Soil indicates a cessation of blowing dust and vegetation denuding and return to a stable vegetation cover. The respite interval was not as xeric as the preceding period but still was dry

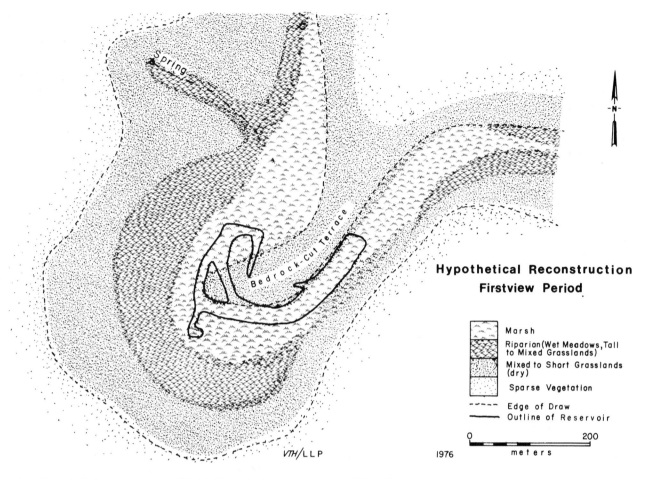

Hypothetical Reconstruction
Firstview Period

Marsh

Riparian(Wet Meadows,Tall to Mixed Grasslands)

Mixed to Short Grasslands (dry)

Sparse Vegetation

----- Edge of Draw

——— Outline of Reservoir

0                    200
meters

Fig. 8.3. Hypothetical reconstruction of the Lubbock Lake local environs in Yellowhouse Draw during the Firstview period (8600 B.P.).

Table 8.2. Lubbock Lake Archaic Vertebrate Local Faunas

| Early Archaic | Middle Archaic | | | Late Archaic |
|---|---|---|---|---|
| | Beginning | Middle | End | |
| (8500–6400 B.P.) | (6400–5500 B.P.) | (5500–5000 B.P.) | (5000–4500 B.P.) | (4500–2000 B.P.) |
| *Ambystoma tigrinum* | *Scaphiopus couchi* | *Cratogeomys castanops* | *Lampropeltis getulus* | *Spermophilus tridecemlineatus* |
| *Rana catesbeiana* | *Rana pipiens* | *Dipodomys ordii* | *Rhinocheilus lecontei* | *Cynomys ludovicianus* |
| *Rana pipiens* | *Kinosternon flavescens* | *Sigmodon hispidus* | *Dipodomys ordii* | *Antilocapra americana* |
| *Heterodon nasicus* | *Terrapene ornata* | *Neotoma albigula* | *Bison bison* | *Bison bison* |
| *Masticophis* sp. | *Nerodia erythrogaster* | *Canis latrans* | | |
| ‡*Bison antiquus* | *Pituophis melanoleucus* | *Bison bison* | | |
| | *Lepus californicus* | | | |
| | *Geomys bursarius* | | | |
| | *Cratogeomys castanops* | | | |
| | *Sigmodon hispidus* | | | |
| | *Canis latrans* | | | |
| | *Antilocapra americana* | | | |
| | *Bison bison* | | | |

and warm (semiarid), as indicated by the continued presence of the yellow-faced pocket gopher.

Available surface water decreased greatly again during the end of the Middle Archaic (table 8.2). The recovered local fauna reflects only the open prairie. The presence of the long-nosed snake suggests dry-prairie-to-desert conditions. Dental abnormalities in bison reappeared. Massive eolian sedimentation recurred, indicating a second period of blowing dust, reduction in vegetation cover, and decreasing effective moisture.

During the Late Archaic the marshland returned in the valley axis. Only the open prairie is reflected in the local fauna (table 8.2). Prairie dog and thirteen-lined ground squirrel reappear. Blowing dust and sedimentation ceased, indicating a return to a stable vegetation cover. All these occurrences point to an ameliorated climate with more available moisture.

Although no hard data are available, some speculations can be made on the character of the open grassland during the Archaic period, based primarily on climatic conditions derived from the geologic evidence and its relationship to modern grass associations and secondarily on the local faunas. The prairie probably changed in character during the xeric-less xeric-xeric-mesic sequence. It is proposed that during the first drought desert-plains grassland (in which chloridoid grasses dominate) replaced the transitional, disharmonious mixed prairie of the preceding period. During the respite interval a mixed prairie (pooid and chloridoid grasses dominate) or combination mixed prairie-desert-plains grasslands occurred (another disharmonious flora?). The second drought saw a return of the desert-plains grasslands, to be replaced by a harmonious mixed prairie during the long mesic period of the Late Archaic.

## Ceramic into Historic Periods

A spring-fed stream and wet meadow-marshland complex increased in size in the valley axis during the Ceramic period. Bullrushes grew along the banks. Few faunal data (table 8.3) are available for this period, but the fauna reflects the grassland habitat (bison, prairie dog, thirteen-lined ground squirrel).

By the Protohistoric period the marshland complex was widespread in the valley axis. Bullrushes grew along the banks, and the marsh was inhabited by mud and pond turtles and leopard frogs (table 8.3). Hackberry trees or shrubs had returned, and walnut trees grew along the valley axis. Mesquite shrubs or trees grew in the bottomland and alluvial slopes of the draw, along with devil's-claw, nightshade, and prickly poppy. The brushland was home to cottontails, badgers, and rattlesnakes. Horned lizards, ornate box turtles, plains pocket gophers, prairie dogs, and jackrabbits inhabited the open sandy plains. Coyotes and wolves traversed the area, and bison and pronghorn antelope roamed the grasslands.

The local environs of the draw were those of a mesquite savanna surrounding a riparian marshland complex. The grassland fauna indicates a shortgrass regime with forbs and other herbaceous plants. Tall-grass prairie animals are lacking.

General conditions remained the same during the Historic period. The sedge beds and marsh were inhabited by pintails, gadwalls, teals, ruddy ducks, coots, mud and pond turtles, garter snakes, tiger salamanders, and leopard frogs. Hackberry, walnut, and cottonwood or willow grew along the valley axis, providing refuge for freetail bats, phoebes, mockingbirds, meadowlarks, and hawks. Mesquite continued, as did devil's-claw, nightshade, and prickly poppy.

Skunks and coyotes traversed the brush to open prairie. Horned lizards, box turtles, prairie dogs, and cottontails inhabited the open prairie along with bison and pronghorn antelope.

The local environs continued as a mesquite savanna surrounding the extensive marsh. The grassland fauna indicates a continued shortgrass regime with forbs and other herbaceous plants.

The recurrence and additions of hardwoods underscore the greater availability of moisture and less arid conditions than those of the Middle Archaic. However, the climate throughout this period was unstable, as indicated by proxy geologic and pedologic environmental data. A basically modern climate, as reflected by the faunas, has existed for the past 4,500 years, but with minor departures toward some aridity through increased temperatures and decreased effective moisture. A cyclical drought pattern began in the late Ceramic, extended into the Historic, and continues today. As the pattern persisted, drought intervals may have been more frequent and of less duration although not necessarily of less intensity. The droughts appear not to have been severe enough to alter significantly the faunal community but did cause periodic vegetative denuding and surface erosion leading to deposition and altered landscapes.

## PALEOINDIAN LOCAL FAUNAS

Restricted temporal and spatial distribution are the two criteria on which to base the establishment of a local fauna (Taylor, 1960; Tedford, 1970). The faunal assemblages from the major periods at Lubbock Lake meet these criteria, there being a single locality and known time periods bracketed by radiocarbon dates. Several distinct stratigraphic, environmental, and cultural subdivisions exist within the major periods. The most extensive changes occurred during the Paleoindian period. Four sequential local faunas are proposed as typical for the area during the appropriate time period (table 8.1). These Paleoindian (late Pleistocene to early Holocene) local faunas were followed by Archaic (middle Holocene) and Ceramic to Historic (late Holocene) sequential local faunas (tables 8.2, 8.3).

The earliest of the Paleoindian local faunas is the Lubbock Lake Clovis local fauna, at about 11,100 B.P. (Holliday et al., 1983). The Lubbock Lake Folsom local fauna dates ca. 10,800 to 10,300 B.P. (Holliday et al., 1983, 1985). The Lubbock Lake Plainview local fauna dates to ca. 10,000 B.P. (Holliday et al., 1983). The Lubbock Lake Firstview local fauna dates ca. 8600 B.P. (Holliday et al., 1983).

Although several archaeological localities from the various Paleoindian cultural time periods are known from the Southern High Plains, most are kill sites of mammoth or bison, with few or no recordings of other animals. These scant assemblages represent catastrophic death assemblages of herd herbivores but not of the faunal communities associated with them. The one exception is Blackwater Draw Locality No. 1.

At Blackwater Draw Locality No. 1 (Lundelius, 1972a;

Table 8.3. Lubbock Lake Ceramic through Historic Vertebrate Local Faunas

| Early Ceramic (2000–1000 B.P.) | Late Ceramic (1000–500 B.P.) | Protohistoric (A.D. 1450–1650) | Historic (A.D. 1650–1930) |
|---|---|---|---|
| Spermophilus tridecemlineatus | Bufo cognatus | Acris crepitans | Rana pipiens |
| Cynomys ludovicianus | Kinosternon flavescens | Rana pipiens | Kinosternon flavescens |
| Antilocapra americana | Chrysemys scripta | Kinosternon flavescens | Chrysemys scripta |
| Bison bison | Terrapene ornata | Chrysemys scripta | Terrapene ornata |
| | Cynomys ludovicianus | Terrapene ornata | Phrynosoma cornutum |
| | Canis latrans | Phrynosoma cornutum | Sonora semiannulata* |
| | Antilocapra americana | Sonora semiannulata* | Thamnophis cf. marcianus |
| | Bison bison | Crotalus atrox | Thamnophis proximus |
| | | Sylvilagus spp. | Anas acuta |
| | | Lepus californicus | Anas sp. (duck) |
| | | Cynomys ludovicianus | Anas strepera |
| | | Geomys bursarius | Anas sp. (teal) |
| | | Canis latrans | Oxyura jamaicensis |
| | | Canis lupus | Buteo sp. |
| | | Taxidea taxus | Fulica americana |
| | | Antilocapra americana | Cf. Sayornis saya |
| | | Bison bison | Mimus polyglottis |
| | | | Tadarida brasiliensis |
| | | | Sylvilagus audobonii |
| | | | Lepus californicus |
| | | | Cynomys ludovicianus |
| | | | Perognathus cf. hispidus |
| | | | Sigmodon hispidus |
| | | | Canis latrans |
| | | | Canis lupus |
| | | | Mephitis mephitis |
| | | | Equus caballus |
| | | | Antilocapra americana |
| | | | Bison bison |

*No longer occurs in the area.

Slaughter, 1975), the gray sands and their associated fauna (Lundelius, 1972a) are considered to predate the Clovis period (Haynes, 1975). The brown sand-wedge local fauna (Slaughter, 1975) transgresses the Clovis and Folsom periods. The local fauna is a mixed one from these two periods and cannot be used for comparison with either the Clovis or the Folsom local fauna at Lubbock Lake. Harris (1977b, 1985b) discussed several incongruities in identification and interpretation in the brown sand-wedge local fauna (Slaughter, 1975). In general, however, the local faunas and general draw reconstructions are in reasonable agreement. These local faunas indicate a widespread occurrence of the animals across the eastern half of the Southern High Plains and probable similarities of habitats in Blackwater and Yellowhouse draws.

During the Paleoindian occupation at the site animals that are now extinct or no longer range onto the Southern High Plains inhabited the site's environs. The Clovis period was most affected by this phenomenon, in which 44% of the known fauna are exotics. Mammals are the most striking group of vertebrates in responding to change. Of the Clovis mammalian assemblage at least half do not occur at the site in post-Clovis times.

By the Folsom period the number of exotic faunal elements decreases to 30%. The same pattern (29%) holds for the Plainview period. By Firstview times the fauna is well

toward being a modern one, 16% of the fauna being exotics. The one extinct animal is Bison antiquus, and six species no longer inhabit the area today.

Within the Lubbock Lake Clovis local fauna, 19 extant animals no longer range into the area. A modern analog does not exist today. Instead, three distinct areas of sympatry exist, controlled to a great extent by climatic conditions and vegetation. Geographic faunal elements are from the northern, northeastern, southeastern, and Trans-Pecos regions. The northern element is composed of Spermophilus richardsonii, Microtus pennsylvanicus, M. ochrogaster, and Ondatra zibethicus; the northeastern element, of Carpiodes cyprinus and Carphophis amoenus. The general area of sympatry today for the northern element is central Colorado; for the northeastern element, eastern Kansas.

The southeastern faunal element includes Blarina sp., Terrapene carolina, Trionyx sp., Thamnophis cf. sirtalis, Tropidoclonion lineatum, Virginia cf. striatula, and Rana palustris. Today East Texas is the area of sympatry for these animals. The Trans-Pecos influence includes Vulpes macrotis, Peromycus cf. eremicus, Thomomys bottae, Salvadora sp., Sonora semiannulata, Gyalopion canum, and Corvus corax.

Several animals that were sympatric are allopatric today, indicating that the climatic and environmental conditions that existed at Lubbock Lake during Clovis times do not have a modern analog. The northern and southeastern assemblages indicate a more equitable climate than that of the present.

Today the average maximum temperature in central Colorado is about 32° C (90° F), while that of the Southern High Plains is 38° C (100° F) (Hunt, 1974:59). The average minimum temperature in eastern Texas is about −7° C (20° F), with nearly 300 frost-free days (Hunt, 1974:59). However, the presence of *Geochelone* and *Holmesina* in the fauna suggests frost-free winters, with an average minimum temperature greater than 0° C (32° F). Hunt (1974) bracketed the average minimum temperature on the Southern High Plains between the −18° and −7° C (0° and 20° F) isotherms, although average January temperatures are 3° C (38° F) (Haragan, 1983). Eastern Texas averages about 102 cm (40 in) of rain, more than twice the average precipitation on the Southern High Plains today.

The temperature range (with an adjustment to accommodate the presence of *Geochelone* and *Holmesina*) and precipitation estimates from the snail fauna (Pierce, chap. 6) of this time are in general agreement. Within the parameters of the invertebrate and vertebrate assemblages, the range of temperature fluctuation appears to have been less during the Clovis period, with 10°–14° C (50°–58° F) variation (28°–32° to 0° C [82°–90° to 32° F]) versus the 56°+ C (100°+ F) variation (38° to −18° C [100° to 0° F]) today (cf. Haragan, 1983:65). These assemblages indicate both much more precipitation and more effective moisture than those of the present. A lower evaporation rate existed with the more equitable climate. And the rainy season appears to have come at a different time than today.

The absence of *Sigmodon hispidus* at this time is of note. It first occurs during the suprajacent Folsom period (2A local bed 2) at post−11,000 years. Although Slaughter (1975) reported cotton rat from the brown sand-wedge local fauna, the fauna and time periods are mixed, and its exact occurrence in time is uncertain. Other late Pleistocene records are unknown for the region. *Sigmodon hispidus*, then, appears to be absent from the Southern High Plains during late Pleistocene times.

Mohlhenrich (1961) found that the northern distribution of this animal in New Mexico was governed by the requirements of a mean annual temperature of greater than 13° C (55° F) and a growing season of 180 or more days. Too great a cooling in the summer (lowering the mean annual temperature below 13° C [55° F]) could explain its absence. Panicoid grasses indicate a growing season of greater than 180 days. *Sigmodon hispidus* is present in late Pleistocene Central Texas localities (Lundelius, 1967), indicating conditions somewhat warmer (and an adequate growing season) than those on the Southern High Plains at that time.

Wendorf (1961a) estimated Clovis summers on the Southern High Plains to have been 5.5° (10°) cooler than present summers, an estimate in general agreement with the difference between the modern average maximum temperatures of central Colorado and the Southern High Plains. The faunal evidence at Lubbock Lake supports the hypothesis of cooler summers and warmer winters during Clovis times and coincides with the climatic conditions postulated by

Hibbard (1960), Dalquest (1965), and more recently by Lundelius et al. (1983), Harris (1985b), Van Devender and Spaulding (1979), and Spaulding et al. (1983) for the late Pleistocene. Independent evidence from D/H ratios of meteoric water also indicates cooler summers and warmer winters at this time (Yapp and Epstein, 1977). The Trans-Pecos faunal element in the Clovis assemblage may be involved more with effective moisture patterns and the time of the rainy season than with general aridity.

Six animals from the Lubbock Lake Folsom local fauna and 12 animals from the Lubbock Lake Plainview local fauna are no longer extant on the Southern High Plains. Two major sympatric areas show continued but decreasing northern and southeastern faunal elements in the assemblages. The northeastern faunal element is represented by *Synaptomys cooperi*. A single Trans-Pecos form, *Sonora semiannulata*, still lingers.

The area of sympatry for the northern forms moved southward, though continuing in Colorado. The northern segment of the Folsom assemblage is composed of *Microtus pennsylvanicus*, *M. ochrogaster*, and *Ondatra zibethicus*. The Plainview assemblage includes these three species, *Coluber constrictor*, and *Charadrius montanus*. Today the area of sympatry for these animals is generally the southeastern corner of Colorado. The range of *Synaptomys cooperi* retreated far to the northeast. The area of sympatry with this bog lemming included is extreme southeastern Nebraska. This situation underscores the branched northern faunal element in the Lubbock Lake assemblages that persisted into the early Holocene.

The Folsom southeastern segment consists of *Thamnophis* cf. *sirtalis*, *Morone chrysops*, and *Lepomis gulosus*; that of the Plainview assemblage includes *Tropidoclonian lineatum*, *T. sirtalis*, *Agkistrodon contortrix*, *Nerodia cyclopion/rhombifera*, and *Gallinula chloropus*. The area of sympatry, although still eastern Texas, has shifted westward.

As with the earlier period, the faunas indicate cooler summers and warmer winters, more equitable climatic conditions than those of the present. However, a marked difference between the Clovis versus Folsom and Plainview local faunas indicates a greater fluctuation of temperatures than previously (but not as great as that of modern times). The general northern area of sympatry shifted southward, where average maximum temperatures are greater than 32° C (90° F) and approach the 38° C (100° F) maximum for the Southern High Plains today. The disappearance of *Geochelone* from the faunal record and the westward shift of the southeastern sympatry indicate that winter temperatures were colder than previously with below-freezing periods. The average minimum temperature today in eastern Texas is −7° C (20° F) (Hunt, 1974:59). Minimum and maximum temperatures probably fluctuated more than in the Clovis period. Highs of greater than 32° C (90° F) and lows below 0° C (32° F) produced a fluctuating range of perhaps near 21° C (70° F). The occurrence of *Sigmodon hispidus* in Folsom, Plainview, and later deposits indicates higher mean annual temperatures and warmer summers than previously.

The fauna by Firstview times is well toward being a modern one and marks a sharp decrease in the extent of disharmony over the preceding period. Northern forms are represented by *Microtus pennsylvanicus, M. ochrogaster,* and *Ondatra zibethicus;* southeastern forms, by *Thamnophis* cf. *sirtalis* and *Rallus* cf. *longirostris.*

All three microtines are rare in the deposits for this time. This scarcity indicates rising maximum summer temperatures near modern conditions and less than optimal conditions (decreased rainfall and humidity). The southeastern faunal element appears minor. *Thamnophis* cf. *sirtalis* may be a relict form, a residual of the central Brazos River riparian biome seen much more strongly in the preceding faunas. *Rallus longirostris* is an anomaly in that this bird is a coastal saltwater marsh rail (Oberholser and Kincaid, 1974). The Lubbock Lake setting is a freshwater marsh (Holliday, 1985d; Holliday and Allen, chap. 2). The occurrence of the gray-breasted crake (*Lateralus* cf. *exilis*) at this time is another anomaly. Today its range is restricted to northern South America with scattered records into Central America. Little is known of this bird other than that it is a freshwater-marsh inhabitant (Rea et al., n.d.). The significance of these two birds is unknown.

## SUMMARY

Compressed and overlapped ecological and climatic zones, habitat creation and destruction, changing faunal and floral community assemblages, and relict populations are factors that influence environmental reconstruction. Allopatric species that were once sympatric and the various areas of sympatry extant today for the faunas underscore that environmental conditions at the end of the Pleistocene and early Holocene no longer exist today at any one locality, and no one area can be singled out as being most like that during the late Pleistocene and early Holocene.

The shifting of ecological and climatic zones southward and westward during the late Pleistocene was not a simple displacement or range extension. Not all zones shifted; rather, new ecological conditions were created as zones overlapped with new faunal and floral associations. Faunas were more varied, and the community structure was altered to accommodate the new interactions. Vegetation distribution must have been more discontinuous and patchy. This mosaic effect would accommodate new floral associations and create habitats that no longer exist. Modern conditions do not offer the full range of variation under which an animal or plant can live; thus the possibilities of detailed reconstructions are limited. This limiting factor can obscure the recognition of unknown habitats and ecotonal zones and the placement of animals or plants in their proper community.

Range changes and redistribution took place at differing rates depending on the tolerances of the various species and the continued existence of favorable areas. Relict populations created in the retreat attest to the former extent of an animal's range. The conditions under which a relict population exists today may not be the same as the conditions under which it lived in the area during the late Pleistocene but are those that can be tolerated by that species.

The late Pleistocene and early Holocene faunas reflected pluvial conditions over about a 3,000-year period. This pluvial period was one of milder winters, cooler summers, and more available moisture than modern conditions. Within this period, however, the equitable climate of the latest Pleistocene shifted to a warming trend and greater seasonality in the early Holocene marked by colder winters and warming summers. A major faunal changeover occurred at that time. This significant biotic and ecosystemic change marked a definite boundary between the latest Pleistocene and earliest Holocene that is well dated to 11,000 B.P. and also denoted by major geologic changes. A 1,000-year period of some stability ensued with gradual adjustments and realignments. The last pluvial-related fauna was nearly a modern one. This fauna denoted another major climatic shift around 8500 B.P., marking the end of pluvial conditions and an increased warming and drying trend. This trend persisted into the xeric conditions of the mid-Holocene. The early part of the mid-Holocene was a climatically transitional period in that conditions represented a point on a drying trend that led to the aridity of the Altithermal. It was a near-semiarid setting of much less available moisture, warmer and dustier than the pluvial conditions of the preceding period but more mesic and milder than the succeeding one.

The middle of the mid-Holocene was the time of the two-drought Altithermal characterized by dust-laden, hot, dry conditions. A 500-year period of respite occurred between the droughts. That period of respite brought relatively cooler, moister conditions and a cessation of blowing dust. By the end of the mid-Holocene the climate had ameliorated with a return to more mesic conditions and a stable landscape. This period marked the end of the warmer, drier trend and the beginning of a cooler, moister trend that peaked toward the end of the early Ceramic.

The late Holocene climate and environmental record appear to reflect a semiarid fluctuating setting of more moisture or less moisture within an overall drying trend. Basically, a modern climate has existed for the past 4,500 years with minor departures toward some aridity. A cyclical pattern of eolian deposition and then landscape stability developed. Progressively less areal extent and thickness of deposit were involved, indicating less duration or less severity of the droughts or both.

The Southern High Plains as reflected at Lubbock Lake has remained a grasslands throughout the last 11,100 years, although its character and associated faunal communities have changed. The pattern is one of fluctuations in available moisture and temperature that affected relative humidity, precipitation, and seasonality. These factors in turn effected both minor and major ecosystemic and biotic changes throughout the late Quaternary.

# 9. Lubbock Lake Artifact Assemblages

EILEEN JOHNSON AND VANCE T. HOLLIDAY

More than 40 cultural features have been excavated by the Lubbock Lake Project. The following descriptions are of the lithic and bone tool kits, manufacturing debris, and other nonlithic items recovered. In the discussion the material is grouped by the cultural chronology.

Three main cultural activities are represented by features at the site: camps, processing stations, and kill/butchering locales. Camps are habitation areas in which human beings lived for a period of time. Food debris and other types of discarded material are scattered across the occupation floor and in and around hearths. A kill/butchering locale is an area in which one to a few animals were slaughtered. This type of event is characterized by a distinctive pattern of bone disposal, focus on one kind of large game animal, and the remains of essentially complete carcasses. Processing stations are areas of secondary butchering and by-product retrieval. This type of event is characterized by random bone disposal, a high degree of bone breakage for marrow and grease extraction, lack of certain major skeletal elements, and the presence of several different kinds of game. These activity types represent various spatial and temporal phases of a subsistence subsystem and differ in the handling of the food resource and the patterns formed.

Lithic tools and manufacturing debris form the largest group of artifacts. At the end of the 1979 season more than 2,100 lithic items had been recovered. A relatively small portion (6%) of the inventory included projectile points and other tools. Most of the material recovered represented manufacturing debris. The paucity of lithic tools reflects the relative regional scarcity of outcrops of adequate material. This circumstance appears to have had an effect on the Lubbock Lake lithic tool assemblage, for tools were conserved and reused. Known outcrops on and near the Southern High Plains containing suitable knapping material are few (Holliday and Welty, 1981).

Most surficial deposits on the Southern High Plains consist of unconsolidated Pleistocene materials that bury suitable lithic resources. Generally suitable material is available only along the escarpment and in deeper reentrant drainages. Source areas are either outcrops of material formed *in situ* or gravel deposits. The principal geologic units with adequate material for tool manufacture include the Quartermaster Formation, the Dockum Group (including the Tecovas Formation), the Antlers Sand, the Edwards Limestone, and the Ogallala Formation (fig. 9.1). The basic terminology used for the various rock types was presented by Holliday and Welty (1981), with some modifications following Mattox and Yeats (1984).

A significant portion of the Lubbock Lake lithic inventory is made of fine-grained chert that varies in color from tan to light, medium, and dark gray and dark blue. Although the material is referred to as Edwards Formation chert, it is not possible to demonstrate that the material was imported from Central Texas, where outcrops of chert in the Cretaceous Edwards Formation are very common. Identical material occurs in gravel and cobble form in the Ogallala Formation, which crops out extensively along the eastern escarpment of the Southern High Plains. This material was probably derived from Cretaceous deposits that were being eroded as the Ogallala was being deposited.

Various other types of lithic material occur in the assemblages, including the multicolored Alibates agate and red to brown jasper from the Tecovas Formation. Other material includes light-colored medium to coarse-grained quartzite; dark gray to black medium-grained quartzite; medium-grained purple quartzite; and brown to yellow jasper, all probably from the Ogallala Formation. A dense, fine-grained, silica-cemented siltstone, commonly referred to as Potter chert, probably comes from the Potter Member of the Ogallala Formation. Silicified caliche and opal occur in various pedogenic calcretes ("caliches") in the region.

## THE ASSEMBLAGES

The following descriptions are of Lubbock Lake material recovered during the Texas Memorial Museum (TMM) work, West Texas Museum (WTM) explorations, and Lubbock Lake Project (LLP) excavations (1973–79). Materials recovered during the WPA work are described elsewhere

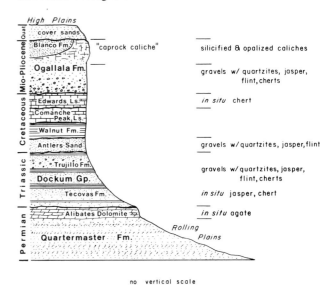

Fig. 9.1 Composite stratigraphic column of geologic units of the eastern side of the Southern High Plains (Llano Estacado) and respective rock types suitable for tool manufacture (from Holliday and Welty, 1981).

(Wheat, 1974; Johnson and Holliday, 1986).

Basic descriptive data include material, noticeable wear pattern, and dimensions (projectile points, table 9.1; other tools, table 9.2). An analysis of microwear polishes on Paleoindian lithic tools was presented by Bamforth (1985).

## Paleoindian Period

*Clovis* The principal Clovis-age feature (FA2-1) is a megafaunal processing station situated on a point bar of a meandering stream that subsequently was buried by sandy overbank sediments. The lithic tool kit is limited and consists of pounding stones and caliche boulders. The pounding stones are hand-sized. One implement (TTU-A16407) is a triangular-shaped, indurated caliche cobble with a battered pointed end. It was found adjacent to a mandible in a small cluster of baby mammoth skull and tusk fragments. A dolomite pounding stone (TTU-A36620) was recovered

with the battered, disarticulated skull of a 2-year-old (African age equivalent) mammoth. Other pounding stones (TTU-A17854, 36621, 36660) are of silicified caliche and were found in or near bone clusters.

A quartz pebble (TTU-A16960) exhibits edge crushing at both ends. The larger end was more heavily used and shows bifacial use damage flake scarring. A small quartzite pebble (TTU-A16999) found in a cluster of adult mammoth skull and tusk sections exhibits a very slight discoloration at both ends, but noticeable damage is lacking.

Two caliche boulders (TTU-A4433, 5150) were probably used as the anvil and large pounding stone necessary for breaking open massive mammoth-limb elements. The boulders represent manuports, for the low-velocity stream did not have the strength to carry these materials.

A bear radial diaphysis (TTU-A25024) was opened through controlled breakage with the high-velocity-impact technique (Bonnichsen, 1979; Morlan, 1980; Johnson, 1982, 1985). Initial and rebound fracture fronts are not pre-

Table 9.1. Projectile Point Measurements (In Millimeters)

Table 9.1. *Continued*

| Period, Age, and Catalog No. | Length | Width | Thickness |
|---|---|---|---|
| Paleoindian | | | |
| Clovis | | | |
| TMM892-74[a] | 47.75 | 24.92 | 5.58 |
| Folsom | | | |
| TTU-40-36-136[b] | 74.00 | 26.00 | 5.00 |
| TMM892-2[b] | 49.30 | 21.43 | — |
| TMM892-3[a] | 28.10 | 17.50 | 2.75 |
| TMM892-4[a,c] | 26.32 | 18.30 | 3.45 |
| TMM892-70[a,c] | 17.43 | 24.25 | 3.55 |
| TMM892-71[a] | 30.70 | 19.80 | 3.50 |
| TMM-892-76[b] | 37.40 | 20.60 | 4.20 |
| TMM892-77[a,c] | 22.42 | 19.50 | 3.23 |
| TTU-A1 | 31.30 | 19.00 | 3.22 |
| Plainview | | | |
| TTU-A18464[c] | 56.95 | 21.35 | 6.30 |
| TTU-A19941[c] | 39.20 | 20.52 | 5.22 |
| TTU-A23935 | 38.45 | 18.78 | 5.06 |
| TTU-61-3 | 65.75 | 25.42 | 6.68 |
| Firstview | | | |
| TMM892-69[a,b] | 72.80 | 21.40 | 7.00 |
| TTU-A863[c] | 44.90 | 18.80 | 5.60 |
| TTU-A7563[c] | 16.55 | 21.50 | 7.30 |
| TTU-A19285[c] | 35.67 | 24.92 | 7.90 |
| Ceramic | | | |
| TTU-A7205[c] | 9.54 | 9.62 | 2.86 |
| Protohistoric | | | |
| Garza | | | |
| TTU-A133[c] | 14.80 | 11.15 | 3.10 |
| TTU-A602[c] | 20.00 | 15.42 | 2.60 |
| TTU-A633/634 | 40.55 | 16.61 | 2.92 |
| TTU-A3283 | 15.70 | 15.72 | 3.70 |
| TTU-A3320 | 27.32 | 15.72 | 3.55 |
| TTU-A11563 | 20.92 | 13.35 | 2.70 |
| TTU-A12395[c] | 23.95 | 11.95 | 2.50 |

| Period, Age, and Catalog No. | Length | Width | Thickness |
|---|---|---|---|
| Harrell | | | |
| TTU-A515[c] | 9.18 | 7.01 | 2.95 |
| TTU-A8333[c] | 7.58 | 7.18 | 2.65 |
| TTU-A11558 | 9.23 | 7.76 | 2.26 |
| Lott | | | |
| TTU-A201[c] | 12.02 | 10.34 | 2.41 |
| TTU-A2122 | 27.40 | 12.20 | 2.47 |
| Unidentifiable | | | |
| TTU-A113[c] | 25.75 | 13.13 | 2.62 |
| TTU-A603 | 23.61 | 10.50 | 2.72 |
| TTU-A604 | 8.74 | 10.93 | 2.13 |
| TTU-A3273[c] | 17.33 | 9.63 | 1.92 |
| TTU-A15026[c] | 10.73 | 5.35 | 1.92 |
| Historic | | | |
| Washita | | | |
| TTU-A8332[c] | 8.55 | 9.80 | 2.58 |
| TTU-A12656 | 16.08 | 8.26 | 2.95 |
| Harrell | | | |
| TTU-A21792[c] | 13.75 | 14.75 | 2.50 |
| Fresno | | | |
| TTU-A13424[c] | 17.25 | 13.22 | 2.15 |
| Lott | | | |
| TTU-A6904[c] | 21.10 | 11.39 | 1.89 |
| Unidentifiable | | | |
| TTU-A6905[c] | 13.75 | 8.25 | 2.15 |
| TTU-A6906[c] | 10.86 | 8.90 | 3.51 |
| TTU-A9120[c] | 12.15 | 11.78 | 4.06 |
| TTU-A12344 | 21.65 | 11.03 | 2.21 |
| TTU-A15541[c] | 23.65 | 10.10 | 2.85 |
| TTU-A17035[c] | 21.78 | 13.40 | 2.15 |
| TTU-A28106[c] | 9.16 | 14.06 | 4.47 |
| TTU-A28398[c] | 16.14 | 11.00 | 3.87 |
| TTU-A29632[c] | 10.00 | 8.76 | 2.04 |

[a]Measurements taken from cast of point.

[b]Measurements taken from drawing.

[c]Point is broken.

served on the element. From the intersecting fracture fronts and the direction of surface features, it appears that the medial, middiaphysis cleavage blow was just distal to the working edge. A technological wedge flake was removed from the anterior shaft. The exposed compact bone and adjacent surfaces of the working edge exhibit localized polishing, cortical use damage flaking, and edge rounding (Johnson, 1985, fig. 5.16A).

A large mammal anteroproximal tibial section (TTU-A25059) exhibits helical fracture surfaces. The piece is the result of the intersection of several radiating fracture fronts from the cleavage blow, but the blow location was indeterminable. A series of use flakes had been removed from the exposed compact bone of the working edge. The inner-cancellous surface is smoothed. Edge rounding and use flake removal at the left distal corner occur on the cortical surface. Wear polish covers these areas and the flake scars.

Table 9.2. Lubbock Lake Lithic Tool Measurements
(In Millimeters)

| Period, Age, and Catalog No. | Type* | Length | Width | Thickness |
|---|---|---|---|---|
| Paleoindian | | | | |
| Clovis | | | | |
| TMM892-84 | UCT | 66.40 | 34.50 | 11.85 |
| TTU-A3024 | COR | 100.04 | 84.81 | 41.00 |
| TTU-A4433 | BLD | 500.00 | 314.00 | 294.00 |
| TTU-A5150 | BLD | 425.00 | 417.00 | 213.00 |
| TTU-A7906† | UNI KNF | 32.98 | 23.98 | 4.96 |
| TTU-A16407 | PWD | 95.14 | 76.50 | 52.42 |
| TTU-A16960 | UTZ PEB | 59.60 | 31.70 | 22.95 |
| TTU-A16999 | UTZ PEB | 46.30 | 36.72 | 32.15 |
| TTU-A17854 | PWD | 103.40 | 79.40 | 70.57 |
| TTU-A36620 | PWD | 109.58 | 77.95 | 55.86 |
| TTU-A36621 | PWD | 79.51 | 76.60 | 56.15 |
| TTU-A36660 | PWD | 135.23 | 77.10 | 49.82 |
| Folsom | | | | |
| TMM892-72 | RET FLA | 20.91 | 13.19 | 2.27 |
| TMM892-78 | RET FLA | 38.35 | 24.35 | 3.90 |
| TTU-A2655 | FLA TOL | 83.42 | 32.45 | 9.95 |
| TTU-A2754 | PWD | 92.31 | 76.15 | 67.48 |
| TTU-A18264 | PWD | 80.65 | 65.95 | 42.48 |
| TTU-A18465 | UTZ FLA | 28.52 | 29.84 | 13.42 |
| TTU-A19094 | PWD | 83.50 | 46.50 | 24.10 |
| TTU-A19811 | PWD | 136.32 | 77.12 | 61.30 |
| Unknown | | | | |
| TTU-A2506 | FLA TOL | 18.94 | 17.74 | 3.08 |
| TTU-A14069 | UTZ FLA | 32.05 | 30.10 | 8.48 |
| TTU-A19580 | UNI | 36.26 | 17.29 | 5.16 |
| TTU-A22812 | FLA TOL | 30.16 | 27.00 | 10.06 |
| Plainview | | | | |
| TMM892-79 | UCT | 36.49 | 34.61 | 8.08 |
| TMM892-80 | UCT | 42.18 | 34.20 | 4.18 |

*Abbreviations: ANV—anvil, BEV TOL—beveled tool, BIF—biface, BKD BLD—backed blade, BLD—blade, CHP—chopper, COR—core, DEB—debitage, DEN—denticulate, DRL—drill, END SCR—end scraper, FLA—flake, FLA TOL—flake tool, GST—groundstone, KNF—knife, MET—metate, PEP—pebble, PRE—preform, PWD—pounding stone, RET FLA—retouched flake, SCR—scraper, UCT—unifacial cutting tool, UNI—uniface/facial, UTZ—utilized.
†Broken.

Table 9.2. *Continued*

| Period, Age, and Catalog No. | Type* | Length | Width | Thickness |
|---|---|---|---|---|
| TMM892-83 | UCT | 31.18 | 23.64 | 3.51 |
| TTU-A1639 | BIF | 40.94 | 33.28 | 15.30 |
| TTU-A3049 | BIF | 83.37 | 41.79 | 11.17 |
| TTU-A15921 | UCT | 29.58 | 39.11 | 21.15 |
| TTU-A15983 | UCT | 29.62 | 25.33 | 7.16 |
| TTU-A15999 | UTZ FLA | 13.49 | 9.07 | 2.45 |
| TTU-A18075 | UTZ FLA | 20.55 | 14.18 | 3.52 |
| TTU-A18463 | UCT | 28.51 | 35.30 | 9.45 |
| TTU-A18759† | KNF | 46.45 | 31.68 | 5.78 |
| TTU-A19424 | UTZ FLA | 28.05 | 20.10 | 5.19 |
| TTU-A19568 | COR SCR | 27.00 | 21.70 | 10.78 |
| TTU-A19710 | UTZ FLA | 13.98 | 13.34 | 2.55 |
| TTU-A24961 | UNI KNF | 69.07 | 40.45 | 6.30 |
| TTU-A24962 | BIF | 90.89 | 49.80 | 8.50 |
| TTU-A27940† | GST | 12.90 | 11.23 | 9.85 |
| Firstview | | | | |
| TMM892-75 | BIF | 47.23 | 22.98 | 8.78 |
| TMM892-92† | END SCR | 24.55 | 23.35 | 7.33 |
| TTU-A1573 | UCT | 21.28 | 18.91 | 5.36 |
| TTU-A1577 | UCT | 72.98 | 41.27 | 16.46 |
| TTU-A1603 | UTZ FLA | 18.65 | 43.94 | 8.70 |
| TTU-A2980 | BIF DNT | 40.20 | 23.59 | 12.45 |
| TTU-A2981 | UTZ FLA | 25.06 | 41.50 | 6.40 |
| TTU-A2982 | UTZ FLA | 40.58 | 57.92 | 14.38 |
| TTU-A2987 | UTZ FLA | 42.34 | 35.96 | 14.11 |
| TTU-A2999 | UCT | 38.91 | 20.75 | 11.40 |
| TTU-A7515 | UTZ FLA | 71.42 | 40.12 | 23.91 |
| TTU-A7523 | UTZ FLA | 44.06 | 45.43 | 21.24 |
| TTU-A7529 | UCT | 62.20 | 54.44 | 26.53 |
| TTU-A7534 | UTZ FLA | 50.12 | 49.28 | 15.96 |
| TTU-A7535 | COR CHP | 49.00 | 35.44 | 26.22 |
| TTU-A7541 | UCT | 53.61 | 35.21 | 10.46 |
| TTU-A7542 | UCT | 20.75 | 28.85 | 7.00 |
| TTU-A7548 | UTZ DEB | 33.18 | 21.95 | 14.25 |
| TTU-A7555 | COR | 55.90 | 37.46 | 30.23 |
| TTU-A7561 | COR | 35.20 | 27.84 | 17.06 |
| TTU-A7571 | UTZ FLA | 23.26 | 32.40 | 10.79 |
| TTU-A7572 | UTZ FLA | 16.40 | 21.90 | 5.12 |
| TTU-A7616 | COR | 51.20 | 49.71 | 31.30 |
| TTU-A7618 | UCT | 36.36 | 21.25 | 6.36 |
| TTU-A7619 | UTZ FLA | 24.82 | 19.63 | 2.42 |
| TTU-A7621 | UTZ FLA | 28.66 | 20.50 | 6.28 |
| TTU-A7622 | BIF | 59.59 | 29.22 | 16.52 |
| TTU-A7623 | UCT | 35.24 | 32.16 | 11.35 |
| TTU-A7625 | COR CHP | 84.45 | 61.32 | 36.68 |
| TTU-A11823 | UCT | 54.56 | 45.32 | 15.88 |
| TTU-A11975 | UTZ FLA | 43.06 | 34.94 | 15.86 |
| TTU-A13046 | UTZ FLA | 42.69 | 40.26 | 15.85 |
| TTU-A13070 | COR | 36.05 | 26.66 | 14.76 |
| TTU-A13071 | UTZ FLA | 21.26 | 31.00 | 8.95 |
| TTU-A13128† | UTZ FLA | 7.25 | 3.32 | 1.46 |
| TTU-A13306† | BIF | 42.88 | 24.62 | 16.60 |
| TTU-A13307† | UTZ FLA | 39.32 | 28.09 | 11.46 |
| TTU-A13311† | UTZ FLA | 20.69 | 39.15 | 5.87 |
| TTU-A13312 | UTZ FLA | 27.98 | 37.92 | 17.70 |
| TTU-A13313 | UCT | 35.32 | 37.61 | 10.72 |
| TTU-A13321† | UNI | 18.72 | 16.70 | 5.64 |
| TTU-A13351 | UTZ FLA | 98.92 | 66.35 | 31.20 |
| TTU-A13352 | COR CHP | 93.80 | 66.40 | 45.18 |
| TTU-A13359 | UCT | 45.05 | 32.80 | 13.90 |

Table 9.2. *Continued*

| Period, Age, and Catalog No. | Type* | Length | Width | Thickness |
|---|---|---|---|---|
| TTU-A13360 | UTZ FLA | 76.22 | 68.14 | 27.42 |
| TTU-A13361 | UTZ FLA | 53.54 | 57.26 | 13.44 |
| TTU-A13363 | UTZ FLA | 26.92 | 19.89 | 5.85 |
| TTU-A13364† | COR | 34.24 | 26.34 | 12.25 |
| TTU-A13373 | UTZ FLA | 29.80 | 44.78 | 14.00 |
| TTU-A13380 | UTZ FLA | 32.20 | 46.05 | 8.50 |
| TTU-A13382 | UTZ FLA | 44.78 | 60.79 | 15.24 |
| TTU-A13400 | COR | 52.10 | 44.56 | 40.79 |
| TTU-A13401 | KNF | 50.04 | 28.88 | 12.82 |
| TTU-A13402 | UTZ FLA | 21.24 | 14.65 | 3.72 |
| TTU-A13451 | UTZ FLA | 42.99 | 50.18 | 9.63 |
| TTU-A13452 | UTZ FLA | 54.40 | 46.48 | 22.39 |
| TTU-A13458† | UTZ FLA | 11.32 | 5.24 | 3.22 |
| TTU-A15000 | UTZ FLA | 59.68 | 36.18 | 19.43 |
| TTU-A15200 | UTZ FLA | 43.50 | 33.12 | 8.06 |
| TTU-A15409† | BIF | 61.19 | 40.59 | 12.66 |
| TTU-A15582† | BIF | 16.23 | 11.46 | 6.51 |
| TTU-A15638 | UTZ FLA | 30.90 | 19.30 | 5.82 |
| TTU-A15645 | UCT | 42.48 | 38.52 | 17.06 |
| TTU-A15676 | UTZ FLA | 15.68 | 10.15 | 1.60 |
| TTU-A15901 | BKD BLD | 36.22 | 15.19 | 3.95 |
| TTU-A15935 | UCT | 27.40 | 22.10 | 5.21 |
| TTU-A15936 | UCT | 26.35 | 18.25 | 4.86 |
| TTU-A15939 | COR UNI | 65.05 | 43.45 | 28.05 |
| TTU-A15986 | UTZ FLA | 16.60 | 18.08 | 4.22 |
| TTU-A15998 | COR | 94.15 | 78.40 | 50.71 |
| TTU-A18192 | UTZ FLA | 38.17 | 35.54 | 6.85 |
| TTU-A18259 | UTZ FLA | 38.80 | 43.85 | 13.88 |
| TTU-A19012 | UTZ FLA | 53.10 | 31.08 | 20.05 |
| TTU-A19119 | UCT | 43.62 | 43.95 | 10.90 |
| TTU-A19152† | UTZ FLA | 14.00 | 16.48 | 5.95 |
| TTU-A19292† | UTZ FLA | 10.55 | 17.95 | 1.98 |
| TTU-A19293 | UCT | 29.49 | 19.56 | 4.63 |
| TTU-A19823 | UCT | 45.85 | 37.46 | 15.02 |
| TTU-A19960 | UTZ FLA | 30.69 | 15.62 | 4.21 |
| TTU-A21667 | UCT | 98.22 | 79.19 | 24.85 |
| TTU-A21814 | UCT | 46.30 | 42.55 | 14.93 |
| TTU-A21815 | UCT | 63.23 | 23.62 | 6.70 |
| TTU-A21975† | UCT | 32.19 | 18.65 | 7.98 |
| TTU-A21976 | UCT | 26.68 | 25.70 | 12.78 |
| TTU-A22743 | UCT | 79.18 | 55.48 | 24.42 |
| TTU-A22771 | UNI | 92.46 | 72.69 | 30.77 |
| TTU-A23146 | UTZ FLA | 30.45 | 24.92 | 8.91 |
| TTU-A26922 | UTZ FLA | 55.96 | 44.54 | 11.84 |
| TTU-A29553 | UCT | 39.53 | 53.10 | 13.94 |
| TTU-A29576 | UTZ FLA | 49.95 | 21.55 | 9.88 |
| TTU-A29695 | COR | 90.48 | 68.96 | 40.89 |
| TTU-A29700 | UTZ FLA | 60.35 | 44.29 | 20.26 |
| TTU-A37642 | UTZ FLA | 13.90 | 13.40 | 3.96 |
| Ceramic | | | | |
| TTU-A1173† | UTZ FLA | 21.41 | 21.55 | 4.54 |
| TTU-A1467 | UCT | 65.20 | 43.72 | 13.45 |
| TTU-A3516 | UTZ PEB | 31.85 | 39.92 | 16.00 |
| TTU-A3726 | UTZ FLA | 13.62 | 17.55 | 3.72 |
| TTU-A3847 | UTZ FLA | 15.46 | 17.99 | 3.42 |
| TTU-A3848 | UCT | 17.98 | 13.72 | 3.84 |
| TTU-A4927† | BIF | 17.00 | 8.42 | 4.79 |
| TTU-A5980† | UTZ FLA | 14.00 | 7.45 | 2.54 |
| TTU-A5996† | UTZ FLA | 10.72 | 10.40 | 1.18 |
| TTU-A6436 | UTZ FLA | 13.39 | 20.68 | 5.83 |

Table 9.2. *Continued*

| Period, Age, and Catalog No. | Type* | Length | Width | Thickness |
|---|---|---|---|---|
| TTU-A6437 | UTZ FLA | 8.42 | 10.47 | 2.05 |
| TTU-A6471† | UTZ FLA | 16.96 | 7.66 | 3.29 |
| TTU-A7125 | COR | 49.05 | 38.95 | 27.35 |
| TTU-A7129 | UTZ FLA | 12.20 | 11.60 | 5.30 |
| TTU-A7190 | COR | 70.48 | 51.55 | 45.96 |
| TTU-A7363 | COR | 78.62 | 71.23 | 62.30 |
| TTU-A7364 | UTZ PEB | 39.95 | 37.63 | 18.87 |
| TTU-A7410 | UCT | 14.65 | 13.55 | 2.01 |
| TTU-A7460 | UCT | 47.25 | 51.94 | 20.14 |
| TTU-A9255 | COR | 48.92 | 47.11 | 28.15 |
| TTU-A24822 | UTZ FLA | 25.60 | 19.08 | 5.72 |
| TTU-A24832 | UTZ FLA | 21.30 | 21.30 | 4.50 |
| TTU-A24843 | UTZ FLA | 33.55 | 37.73 | 7.50 |
| Protohistoric | | | | |
| TTU-A43 and 44 | UTZ FLA | 23.86 | 25.28 | 2.72 |
| TTU-A96 | UTZ FLA | 45.04 | 32.74 | 10.89 |
| TTU-A98 | UTZ FLA | 24.78 | 25.64 | 4.43 |
| TTU-A135† | UTZ FLA | 10.41 | 10.05 | 2.83 |
| TTU-A137 | UTZ BLD | 24.10 | 31.25 | 8.69 |
| TTU-A170 | UTZ FLA | 27.34 | 20.18 | 3.47 |
| TTU-A172 | UTZ FLA | 23.17 | 15.68 | 4.92 |
| TTU-A173 | UCT | 32.84 | 21.88 | 5.20 |
| TTU-A174† | UCT | 12.73 | 13.15 | 2.22 |
| TTU-A175† | UCT | 12.36 | 15.20 | 1.82 |
| TTU-A186 | UCT | 17.86 | 9.13 | 3.50 |
| TTU-A195 | UTZ DEB | 33.48 | 27.56 | 7.83 |
| TTU-A196 | UTZ FLA | 13.34 | 14.76 | 2.53 |
| TTU-A203 | UTZ DEB | 18.94 | 16.26 | 8.05 |
| TTU-A211 | UTZ FLA | 23.32 | 15.15 | 4.54 |
| TTU-A212 | UTZ FLA | 28.34 | 18.06 | 3.72 |
| TTU-A213 | UTZ FLA | 9.31 | 18.89 | 2.55 |
| TTU-A220 | BIF PRE | 47.46 | 39.95 | 13.32 |
| TTU-A230 | UTZ FLA | 29.13 | 20.32 | 6.83 |
| TTU-A237 | UTZ DEB | 29.70 | 24.38 | 8.44 |
| TTU-A244 | UTZ FLA | 46.04 | 31.33 | 9.66 |
| TTU-A312 | UTZ FLA | 33.32 | 19.55 | 8.28 |
| TTU-A314 | UTZ FLA | 6.50 | 5.82 | 1.85 |
| TTU-A317 | UTZ FLA | 12.05 | 10.50 | 3.59 |
| TTU-A338 | UTZ DEB | 18.55 | 18.43 | 10.53 |
| TTU-A346 | UCT | 21.72 | 17.00 | 5.95 |
| TTU-A399 | UCT | 48.66 | 37.35 | 11.20 |
| TTU-A430 | UCT | 53.48 | 15.18 | 7.87 |
| TTU-A431† | UTZ FLA | 14.00 | 24.00 | 2.51 |
| TTU-A440 | UTZ FLA | 22.92 | 17.60 | 4.52 |
| TTU-A514 | UTZ FLA | 16.71 | 12.92 | 2.13 |
| TTU-A517 | UTZ FLA | 19.78 | 16.25 | 5.00 |
| TTU-A557† | BIF KNF | 19.90 | 23.41 | 3.15 |
| TTU-A558 | UTZ FLA | 17.98 | 15.89 | 4.32 |
| TTU-A559 | UTZ FLA | 16.14 | 22.13 | 6.67 |
| TTU-A562 | FLA TOL | 20.28 | 20.21 | 5.17 |
| TTU-A604† | UTZ FLA | 26.60 | 37.04 | 7.51 |
| TTU-A606 | UTZ FLA | 33.32 | 20.83 | 8.00 |
| TTU-A607 | UCT | 32.45 | 18.40 | 7.17 |
| TTU-A629 | UTZ FLA | 23.96 | 16.88 | 4.00 |
| TTU-A653 | UTZ FLA | 20.81 | 21.24 | 3.55 |
| TTU-A654† | BIF | 12.27 | 7.92 | 2.15 |
| TTU-A665 and 666 | UCT | 48.50 | 26.31 | 7.69 |
| TTU-A667 | UCT | 15.28 | 11.49 | 1.96 |
| TTU-A1783 | UNI CHP | 140.48 | 112.78 | 58.13 |

Table 9.2. *Continued*

| Period, Age, and Catalog No. | Type* | Length | Width | Thickness |
|---|---|---|---|---|
| TTU-A2121† | BIF | 26.13 | 16.74 | 6.23 |
| TTU-A2127 | BIF | 23.68 | 15.10 | 9.00 |
| TTU-A3264† | BIF | 19.90 | 8.42 | 2.74 |
| TTU-A3272 | FLA TOL | 17.03 | 20.00 | 4.30 |
| TTU-A3274† | BIF | 23.30 | 15.50 | 4.22 |
| TTU-A3383 | SCR | 36.44 | 23.21 | 8.79 |
| TTU-A5666† | DRL | 22.98 | 12.28 | 2.96 |
| TTU-A5764 | UTZ FLA | 13.95 | 13.42 | 3.17 |
| TTU-A5812† | UTZ FLA | 12.02 | 15.70 | 4.29 |
| TTU-A5873† | UNI | 14.54 | 13.30 | 2.84 |
| TTU-A5894† | UTZ FLA | 13.20 | 8.00 | 1.80 |
| TTU-A5895† | UTZ FLA | 12.20 | 7.32 | 1.84 |
| TTU-A5897 | UTZ FLA | 13.78 | 12.15 | 3.58 |
| TTU-A6003 | UTZ FLA | 19.69 | 18.26 | 2.95 |
| TTU-A6325† | BIF | 18.06 | 17.00 | 3.69 |
| TTU-A6806 | PRE | 29.03 | 19.18 | 6.70 |
| TTU-A8274† | UTZ FLA | 18.36 | 21.00 | 4.92 |
| TTU-A8281 | BIF | 17.62 | 9.68 | 4.12 |
| TTU-A8317† | UTZ FLA | 16.62 | 25.52 | 4.76 |
| TTU-A8390† | UTZ FLA | 22.70 | 15.21 | 3.96 |
| TTU-A8394 | UTZ FLA | 13.05 | 11.45 | 3.54 |
| TTU-A8396† | UTZ FLA | 25.84 | 30.66 | 11.96 |
| TTU-A8444 | MET | 69.42 | 46.52 | 33.81 |
| TTU-A8465† | MET | 66.68 | 62.45 | 26.17 |
| TTU-A9082 | UTZ FLA | 22.55 | 16.88 | 4.22 |
| TTU-A9085† | UNI | 10.30 | 9.89 | 4.58 |
| TTU-A9301 | COR | 41.55 | 35.35 | 32.05 |
| TTU-A9448 | UCT | 28.50 | 18.40 | 7.68 |
| TTU-A11742 | END SCR | 41.44 | 34.11 | 15.15 |
| TTU-A11966† | BIF | 16.12 | 17.02 | 3.97 |
| TTU-A12403 | FLA TOL | 11.12 | 14.48 | 2.64 |
| TTU-A12425† | UTZ FLA | 20.45 | 14.11 | 3.58 |
| TTU-A12426 | UTZ FLA | 18.02 | 12.23 | 5.38 |
| TTU-A12439† | UTZ FLA | 21.00 | 9.89 | 2.28 |
| TTU-A12444 | UTZ FLA | 14.03 | 11.18 | 2.37 |
| TTU-A12483 | FLA TOL | 29.14 | 29.10 | 5.53 |
| TTU-A15118† | UTZ FLA | 16.25 | 20.65 | 2.82 |
| TTU-A15277 | UTZ FLA | 17.60 | 12.10 | 3.21 |
| TTU-A26050 | UTZ FLA | 31.14 | 23.77 | 4.42 |
| TTU-A26054 | UTZ FLA | 11.12 | 11.83 | 1.56 |
| Historic | | | | |
| TTU-A1997 | UTZ PEB | 135.10 | 25.15 | 11.28 |
| TTU-A4544† | UTZ FLA | 14.99 | 17.94 | 4.45 |
| TTU-A4928 | UTZ FLA | 20.90 | 14.68 | 5.53 |
| TTU-A4980 | UTZ PEB | 25.55 | 25.05 | 8.05 |
| TTU-A6491† | BEV TOL | 4.94 | 3.81 | 2.21 |
| TTU-A8058† | BIF | 11.03 | 4.52 | 4.35 |
| TTU-A8146 | UTZ FLA | 17.14 | 22.03 | 3.98 |
| TTU-A8712† | UTZ FLA | 15.43 | 12.22 | 3.01 |
| TTU-A10337† | BIF | 9.09 | 7.80 | 4.23 |
| TTU-A10926† | UTZ FLA | 20.50 | 20.00 | 5.31 |
| TTU-A12004 | UNI | 4.58 | 4.05 | 2.40 |
| TTU-A12343 | UTZ FLA | 8.55 | 7.42 | 2.78 |
| TTU-A12355† | UTZ FLA | 8.62 | 7.46 | 1.95 |
| TTU-A12375 | UTZ FLA | 9.76 | 9.21 | 1.95 |
| TTU-A12841 | UTZ FLA | 20.75 | 16.65 | 4.94 |
| TTU-A13421† | FLA TOL | 10.10 | 10.48 | 2.58 |
| TTU-A19501 | PWD/CHP | 105.95 | 93.20 | 74.50 |
| TTU-A19639 | FLA TOL | 51.55 | 37.80 | 14.18 |
| TTU-A23449† | BIF KNF | 29.01 | 26.25 | 9.08 |
| TTU-A25675 | ANV | 234.00 | 135.00 | 75.00 |
| TTU-A26517 | UTZ FLA | 15.36 | 8.50 | 5.17 |

Table 9.2. *Continued*

| Period, Age, and Catalog No. | Type* | Length | Width | Thickness |
|---|---|---|---|---|
| TTU-A26655† | MET | 91.06 | 77.85 | 30.28 |
| TTU-A26862† | BIF KNF | 30.73 | 32.19 | 7.14 |
| TTU-A28054 | FLA TOL | 105.62 | 70.00 | 28.01 |
| TTU-A28123† | UTZ FLA | 21.78 | 7.83 | 3.35 |
| TTU-A28190† | UTZ FLA | 10.84 | 8.76 | 2.45 |
| TTU-A28197 | UTZ FLA | 18.62 | 21.20 | 5.48 |
| TTU-A28200 | UTZ FLA | 10.65 | 7.86 | 2.80 |
| TTU-A28201† | UTZ FLA | 9.31 | 7.27 | 1.70 |
| TTU-A28204 | UTZ FLA | 7.94 | 9.05 | 2.04 |
| TTU-A28339 | UNI | 29.58 | 21.06 | 7.64 |
| TTU-A28340 | UTZ FLA | 24.94 | 12.15 | 2.53 |
| TTU-A28585 | UTZ PEB | 26.81 | 22.73 | 10.46 |
| TTU-A28703 | UTZ FLA | 15.88 | 12.38 | 3.77 |
| TTU-A28704 | PWD | 130.00 | 89.00 | 64.00 |
| TTU-A29602 | UTZ PEB | 42.42 | 39.45 | 15.00 |
| TTU-A29711 | UTZ PEB | 32.78 | 21.73 | 9.48 |

A refitted tool (TTU-A17619, 20054) was made from an ungulate diaphyseal section. The pieces were found in adjacent excavation units at the edge of the cluster of adult mammoth skull and tusk sections.

A Clovis point (TTM 892-74) found on the spoil bank above Area 2 fits the Clovis type 2 category (Hester, 1972: 97). The specimen (Edwards Formation chert) has a slightly expanding base and reaches its widest point about two-thirds the distance from base to tip (fig. 9.2a). The edges converge to form the tip, and the blade has straight sides. Fluting occurs on both faces, one flute extending along the face to about the widest point; lateral and basal grinding are present. Flaking on the well-fluted side is irregular, and on the other face the workmanship approaches oblique parallel flaking. Both the base and the blade are reworked. The reworking and edge damage suggest its reuse as a butchering tool.

A unifacial tool (TMM 892-84; tan chert) was recovered from substratum 1B on the west side of the reservoir cut (Sellards, 1952). This tool (fig. 9.2b, 9.2b') exhibits steep angle retouch along one side and has a graverlike point at one end.

A broken unifacial flake tool (TTU-A7906) recovered during stratigraphic trenching near Area 6 was made from medium-gray Edwards Formation chert (Fig. 9.2c). The dorsal side of the unbroken edge exhibits a series of very fine, long parallel flake scars and intense use-damage flaking. A large silicified caliche core (TTU-A3024) found in geologic trench 34 is bidirectional and exhibits several large flake-removal scars.

*Folsom* A Folsom bison kill/butchering locale (FA6-8) is situated on the marshy bank of a pond. The lithic tool kit consists of a unifacial tool, a utilized flake, and silicified caliche cobbles. The unifacial tool (TTU-A2655; Alibates agate) was found at the periphery of a bone-reduction area lying on top of a broken bone expediency tool (TTU-A2760). Unifacial retouch occurs along all sides with the bulbar area removed (fig. 9.3a). The left edge exhibits very steep angle retouch and intense use damage. Retouch along the right edge is shallow, and both retouch and use damage

Fig. 9.2. Clovis-age lithic tools from substratum 1B. a: Clovis projectile point (TMM 892-74); b: unifacial tool (TMM 892-84); b¹: line drawings of unifacial tool (TMM 892-84); c: unifacially retouched flake tool (TTU-A7906) (line drawings by Hal Story, courtesy of Texas Memorial Museum, University of Texas at Austin; TMM 892 artifact access courtesy of Texas Archaeological Research Laboratory, University of Texas at Austin; photographs by Jerome L. Thompson).

is not as extensive as on the other side. Use-damage flakes were removed bifacially from the apex.

A core rejuvenation flake (TTU-A18465; Alibates agate) has use-damage flake scarring along the right edge. Caliche cobbles (TTU-A2754, 18264, 19094, 19811) were found in contexts that indicate their use as pounding stones in the controlled breakage of bone, although use damage on the stones is lacking. The resharpening flakes found *in situ* or recovered from matrix concentrates are of Alibates agate and Edwards Formation chert. Proposed muscle separators include two metatarsals (TTU-A2658, 2702), a metacarpal (TTU-A2729), a tibia (TTU-A2775), and a humeral diaphyseal section. Proposed choppers were made from a metacarpal (TTU-A19804/21535), metatarsal (TTU-A2707), and a femur (TTU-A2771) (Johnson, 1982, fig. 7, 1985).

Lubbock Lake Folsom points (Edwards Formation chert) exhibit quite a range of morphology (table 9.1). Nine points were recovered. A tenth point, found in dredge material by a local collector, was unavailable for study. Specimens TTU 40-36-136, TTM 892-2, and TMM 892-76 are missing. Length and width were determined from existing photographs and drawings.

Five points were recovered *in situ*, associated with remains of extinct bison (*Bison antiquus*). Specimen TMM 892-71 (fig. 9.3b, c, c') was found along the southeast wall of the reservoir cut, 22.9 m (75 ft) southwest of Station I (fig. 1.7) and 20.3 cm (8 in) above the base of substratum 2A (TARL). This specimen is fluted on both sides, and channel flake scars extend almost the full blade length. The convex sides expand to a point about three-fourths the distance from base to tip and then quickly converge to form a relatively blunt tip. The base is strongly concave, and grinding is evident along the expanding sides.

Specimen TMM 892-76 (fig. 9.3d, d') may represent an incomplete point, similar to step 5 of Folsom point production at Adair-Steadman (Tunnell, 1977). This point was found along the south wall of the reservoir, west-southwest of Station D (fig. 1.7) and 17.8 to 20.3 cm (7 to 8 in) above the base of substratum 2A (TARL). Fluting extends about halfway along one face and three-fourths on the opposite face. The edges are convex and expand to about midpoint and then converge to form a blunt, almost rounded tip. The base is deeply concave.

Specimen TMM 892-70 is the base of a Folsom point (fig. 9.3g, h, h') found along the southeast wall of the reservoir, 35 m (115 ft) southwest of Station I (fig. 1.7) and 20.3 cm (8 in) above the base of substratum 2A (TARL). This measurement places it 12.2 m (40 ft) from specimen TMM 892-71. Fluting is evident on both faces, though somewhat obscure on one side. The obscurity is due to nipple retouch in preparation for fluting the other face. The base is deeply concave, and the sides were ground. The base size suggests that originally it may have been as large as specimen TTU 40-36-136. The basal portions of both these artifacts are very similar in size, shape, and workmanship. Each measure 20 mm between tips of the basal tangs. The basal concavities are 7 mm deep and exhibit slight basal nipples.

Specimen TMM 892-77 is a reworked Folsom midsection (fig. 9.3i) that apparently broke during manufacture and was subsequently resharpened and used as a butchering tool. This specimen was found along the south side of the reservoir, 16.8 m (55 ft) west-southeast of Station D (fig. 1.7) and 20.3 cm (8 in) above the base of substratum 2A (TARL). The measurements place it 3.7 m (12 ft) from specimen TMM 892-76. Flaking along the sides is crude. The rounded end exhibits retouch flaking on one face, superimposed over the flute. Retouch is evident along the break on the opposite end of the same face.

Specimen TTU-A1 is fluted on both faces (fig. 9.3e, f, f'). The sides are straight and expand very slightly to a point three-fourths the distance from base to tip. The basal concavity is deep, a slight nipple is present, and a basal corner is broken. Lateral grinding occurs on the expanding sides. The distal left lateral edge exhibits crushing and intense step fracturing from use. This point is very similar in size, shape, and workmanship to TMM 892-71.

Five Folsom points were recovered from the surface. Specimen TTU 40-36-136 is fluted on both sides with channel flake scars extending almost the full length of the artifact (fig. 9.4). The sides are convex and expand slightly to a point three-fourths the distance from base to tip and then converge to form the tip. The base is deeply concave and has a nipple.

Artifact TMM 892-2 is a large, complete point that presumably is fluted on both sides. The only existing drawing and photograph show the same face (figs. 9.3j, 9.5a). The observable flute extends most of the point length. The sides are convex and gradually expand to a point about half the length of the specimen and then converge to form the tip.

Specimen TMM 892-3 (fig. 9.3k) was accessioned as an unfluted Folsom (TARL). In outline the point is similar to specimen TMM 892-71, with straight sides expanding to a

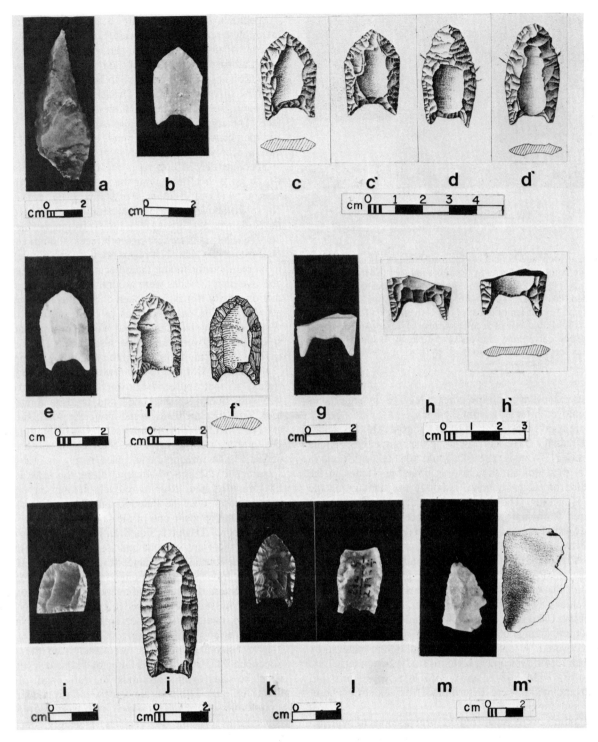

Fig. 9.3. Folsom period lithic tools from substratum 2A. a: unifacially retouched flake tool (TTU-A2655); b: obverse side of Folsom projectile point (TMM 892-71); c, c': line drawings of obverse and reverse sides of Folsom projectile point (TMM 892-71); d, d': line drawings of obverse and reverse sides of Folsom projectile point (TMM 892-76) (now missing); e: reverse side of Folsom projectile point (TTU-A1); f, f': line drawings of obverse and reverse sides of Folsom projectile point (TTU-A1); g: reverse side of base of Folsom projectile point (TMM 892-70); h, h': line drawings of obverse and reverse sides of Folsom projectile point (TMM 892-70); i: reworked midsection of Folsom projectile (TMM 892-77); j: line drawing of Folsom projectile point (TMM 892-2) (now missing); k: Folsom projectile point (TMM 892-3); l: broken Folsom projectile point (TMM 892-4); m, m': photograph of dorsal side and line drawing of ventral side of flake tool (TMM 892-78) (line drawings by Hal Story, courtesy of Texas Memorial Museum, University of Texas at Austin; TMM 892 artifact access courtesy of Texas Archaeological Research Laboratory, University of Texas at Austin; photographs by Jerome L. Thompson).

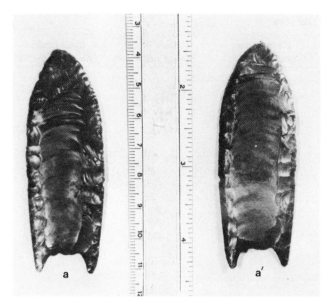

Fig. 9.4. Obverse (a) and reverse (a′) sides of Folsom projectile point (TTU 40-36-136) (nowing missing) (from files at The Museum, Texas Tech University).

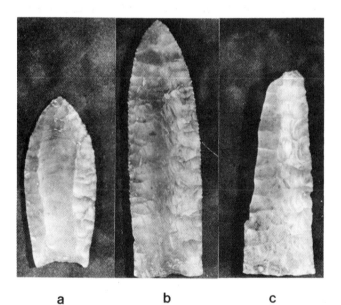

a    b    c

Fig. 9.5. Stratum 2 Paleoindian projectile points recovered by Texas Memorial Museum (now missing). a: Folsom projectile point (TMM 892-2); b: Firstview projectile point (TMM 892-69); c: reworked projectile point (TMM 892-1) (photograph courtesy of Texas Archaeological Research Laboratory, University of Texas at Austin).

point about two-thirds the distance from base to tip and then converging to form the tip. The expanding sides are ground, and the base is concave with a nipple. A very large channel flake scar is evident across the distal two-thirds of the artifact extending almost from side to side. Some retouch is visible around the nipple.

Artifact TMM 892-4 is a broken Folsom base that is fluted on one face (fig. 9.3ℓ). The sides constrict just above the base and then expand one-half to two-thirds the distance to the missing tip. Grinding is evident along the expanding sides. The base is concave and has a nipple, and a basal tang is broken. The fluted face exhibits retouch around the nipple. The unfluted face exhibits well-executed oblique flaking.

Two retouched flakes (Edwards Formation chert) were recovered during TMM excavations in the area of Folsom point TMM 892-70. Specimen TMM 892-72 was found 31.4 m (103 ft) southwest of Station I (fig. 1.7) and 20.3 cm (8 in) above the base of substratum 2A (TARL). The small, rectangular broken flake exhibits steep angle retouch and use-damage scarring along both sides parallel to the long axis. Ventral retouch along a third edge produced a concave side.

Specimen TMM 892-78 was found 36.6 m (120 ft) southwest of Station I (fig. 1.7) and 20.3 cm (8 in) above the base of substratum 2A (TARL). This unifacial tool is roughly triangular and has a snapped distal end (fig. 9.3m, m′). Steep angle retouch and use damage scarring occur along the right edge. Utilization of the irregular left edge resulted in use-damage flake removal along the side.

*Unknown Cultural Affiliation* Another bison kill/butchering locale (FA6-15), post-Folsom but pre-Plainview in stratigraphic sequence, yielded a few lithic tools (Edwards Formation chert). A broken unifacial tool (TTU-A19580) has steep retouch and use-damage flaking along one edge. Unifacial flake tool (TTU-A2506) exhibits steep retouch and use damage along the right ventral edge. Another flake tool (TTU-A22812) has intense use-damage flaking along the left ventral edge.

*Plainview* A Plainview bison kill/butchering locale (FA6-11; Johnson and Holliday, 1980) and a bison kill/butchering locale (FA9-1) of Plainview age were situated on the marshy shores of ponds. The combined lithic tool kit includes projectile points, knives, percussion flake tools, and utilized flakes. Plainview points were resharpened and used as butchering tools, in much the same manner as that demonstrated for Kersey points from Jurgens (Wheat, 1976, 1979; Greiser, 1977). Resharpening produced serrated or scalloped edges.

The blade of a point (TTU-A18464; Alibates agate) is parallel-sided with serrated edges (Johnson and Holliday, 1980; fig. 4). The serration points are crushed and worn, and use-damage flake scaring occurs along both edges. Lateral grinding is evident just above the basal break. The point is lenticular in cross section with a thickness index of 29 (table 9.3). Flaking is irregular, oblique parallel.

A second point (TTU-A19941; Alibates agate) is a basal section with a new tip (Johnson and Holliday, 1980, fig. 4). It was reworked and reused along alternate broken edges and the distal end. One edge was scalloped, and the other has a broad notch. The entire working edge is crushed and exhibits slight wear polish and use-damage flake scarring. The unmodified basal portion contracts slightly toward the proximal end, and one ear is broken. The original flaking appears to be irregular parallel, although reworking oblite-

Table 9.3. Indices of Late Paleoindian Projectile Points, Plainview and Lubbock Lake Sites

| Site and Catalog No. | Total Length/Blade Width (%) | Blade Length/Blade Width (%) | Blade Width/Stem Width (%) | Blade Width/Blade Thickness (%) | Blade Length/Stem Length (%) |
|---|---|---|---|---|---|
| Plainview Type* | | | | | |
| Collection | | | | | |
| Absolute range | 31–52 | | 88.5–100 | 17.5–32 | |
| Normal range | 35–38 | | 88.5–100 | 22.5–27 | |
| Lubbock Lake | | | | | |
| Firstview | | | | | |
| TMM892-69* | 30 | 41 | 95 | 32 | 35 |
| TTU-A863 | | | | 25 | |
| TTU-A7563 | | | | 33 | |
| TTU-A19285 | | | | 29 | |
| Plainview | | | | | |
| TTU-A18464 | | | | 29 | |
| TTU-A19941 | | | | 35 | |
| Surface finds | | | | | |
| TMM892-1* | | | | Ca. 40 | |
| TMM892-73* | | | | 34 | |
| TMM892-85* | Ca. 35 | | | 29 | |

*Access courtesy of Texas Archaelogical Research Laboratory, University of Texas at Austin.

rated much of it. Basal thinning flakes occur on both faces, and lateral and basal grinding is evident along the original edges. The artifact is lenticular in cross section with a thickness index of 25 (table 9.3).

Four unifacial cutting tools exhibit different retouch patterns, with use-damage flake scarring along the working edge. These tools include a percussion flake (Alibates agate) retouched along the distal end (TTU-A18463; Johnson and Holliday, 1980, fig. 5b); a percussion flake (silicified caliche) retouched on three edges (TTU-A15921; Johnson and Holliday, 1980, fig. 5c); a flake (chert of unknown source) retouched along a broken edge (TTU-A15983; Johnson and Holliday, 1980, fig. 5a); and core scraper (Edwards Formation chert) unifacially flaked around the edges (TTU-A19568; Johnson and Holliday, 1980, fig. 5d). A broken, alternately beveled knife (TTU-A18759; Edwards Formation chert) exhibits heavy use along both edges with use-damage flake scarring (fig. 9.6a).

Utilized flakes are smaller and thinner than the retouched tools, and the pattern varies. One flake (TTU-A18075; Edwards Formation chert) has wear at the right distal corner. Another (TTU-A19424; Edwards Formation chert) is a hinge flake with use-damage flake scarring restricted to the left laterodistal edge. A third (TTU-A15999; Edwards Formation chert) has use-damage flakes removed along both the right lateral and distal edges. The fourth utilized flake (TTU-A19710; chalcedony) demonstrates use-damage flake scarring along the left posterolateral and right anterolateral edges on the ventral side.

More than 300 resharpening flakes and debitage were recovered *in situ* and from matrix concentrates. One piece is a small wedge of quartzite (TTU-A27940) with one ground surface. Other materials are Edwards Formation chert, Alibates agate, Tecovas jasper, white chert of unknown source, chalcedony, and silicified caliche. Edwards Formation chert dominates (over 50%). This wider variety of material types than those seen in the recovered tools indicates that a greater number of tools were used than were recovered.

Twelve bone expediency tools were recovered from the locale. Several scapula knives (TTU-A15944, 13852, 13858) exhibit distinct working-edge preparation. Two detachment points were necessary to isolate the tool segment. A blow was delivered along the anterior border that resulted in a helical fracture, and the blade was pounded out (Johnson and Holliday, 1980, fig. 6a; Johnson, 1982, fig. 7e; Johnson, 1985, fig. 5.20, 5.21). These actions freed the tool segment and created the scalloped working edge. The discarded manufacturing debris was found in the locales.

Four rib tools (TTU-A15724, 15968, 19024, 13666) had the distal end broken through pounding, which was the only modification before use. The broken end became rounded and worn, and the exposed inner-cancellous material was smoothed from use (Johnson and Holliday, 1980, fig. 6b). A rib tool (TTU-A13666) may have cracked in use or through ground action, for the two pieces were found in articulation. The tip shows several small use-damage flake scars and wear polish along the ventral side with one large flake scar on the dorsal side.

Two proposed choppers were created from the proximal end of one metatarsal that was split diagonally. Both tools subsequently split into two pieces from heavy use. One (TTU-A13646/13648) is composed of the medial posteroproximal end. The broad, pointed working end exhibits edge rounding, wear polish, and battering. Large hinge fractures occur on one side of the working tip, and numerous small fractures on the other side (Johnson and Holliday, 1980, fig. 7a).

The other tool (TTU-A13647/13649) consists of the lateral and anteroproximal end. Two large thinning flakes were removed from the broad working edge before use. The tool exhibits a localized high-gloss wear polish from heavy use. The edges are very worn and rounded and exhibit damage flake scarring. The broken edges also show rounding and wear polish. When the pieces are fitted together, the working edge is discontinuous (Johnson 1982, fig. 7b; 1985, fig. 5.15c).

Another proposed chopper was made from a left calcaneum (TTU-A16455). The tool consists of part of the tuber calcis and dorsal ridge. The working end is the distal end of the dorsal ridge. This edge is rounded and worn and exhibits use polish and hinge fracturing. The inner-cancellous surface is smoothed and polished. The shaft edges are badly eroded.

Two items are broken pieces of probable expediency tools. One (TTU-A13598) appears to be part of a working edge and exhibits wear polish on the edge and use-damage flake scarring on the ventral side. The other (TTU-A13651) appears to be a shaft section of a tool, with wear polish along the edges.

A rib (TTU-A13832) had the proximal end ground and polished on both sides. It apparently cracked and was dis-

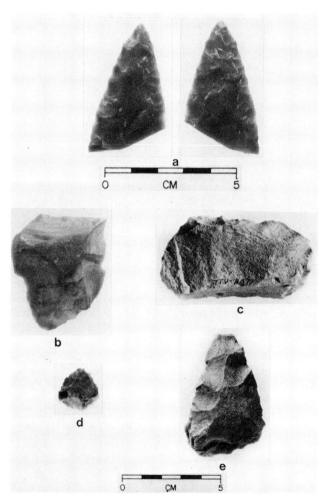

Fig. 9.6. Stratum 2 Paleoindian lithic tools. a: broken, alternately beveled knife (TTU-A18759), Plainview period; b: retouched flake tool (TTU-A11823), Firstview period; c: retouched flake tool (TTU-A1577), Firstview period; d: uniface (TTU-A1573), Firstview period; e: biface (TTU-A15409), Firstview period (photographs by Nicky L. Olson).

carded. The polishing does not extend beyond the broken edge, yet the pieces were found articulated.

*Firstview* Several activity areas (FA6-3, FA5-8/10) were situated along the edges of the marsh. One complex area, which included a bison kill/butchering locale (FA6-3), produced a large inventory of artifacts. Bamforth's (1985) results indicated that what was originally interpreted as camping debris in one area of the complex (Johnson and Holliday, 1981) may represent plant-harvesting activities. A projectile point midsection, 26 other tools, 7 cores, 35 utilized flakes, and 71 unmodified flakes and other manufacturing debitage were recovered in the camp or plant-harvesting area (Johnson and Holliday, 1981; Bamforth, 1985).

The combined lithic tool kit from the kill/butchering locales includes a projectile point, a knife, percussion flake unifacial tools, and utilized flakes. The projectile point (TTU-A19285; Tecovas quartzite) is a basal portion that exhibits parallel sides, a slightly concave base, and lateral and basal grinding (Johnson and Holliday, 1981, fig. 8c). The thickness index is 29. These characters conform to the Firstview type (Wheat, 1972).

An alternately beveled knife (TTU-A13401; Tecovas quartzite) is subtriangular in shape with a blunted proximal end (Johnson and Holliday, 1981, fig. 8d). Use-damage flake scarring occurs along both edges.

A unifacial tool (TTU-A15645; purple quartzite) is made on a percussion flake and exhibits retouch and use-damage flake scarring along three sides. Another implement (TTU-A19119; silicified caliche) has retouch and use-damage flake scarring along the right lateral edge and a worn and rounded, scalloped left lateral edge. One tool (TTU-A11823; Alibates agates) exhibits retouch and use-damage flake scarring along the distal end (fig. 9.6b).

A fourth implement (TTU-A1577; quartzite) has steep retouch and use wear along the right lateral edge (fig. 9.6c). Another unifacial cutting tool (TTU-A7542; Alibates agate) was made on a hinge flake (Johnson and Holliday, 1981, fig. 8b). It has steep retouch along the left lateral edge on the ventral side and use-damage flake scarring. A sixth tool (TTU-A2999; chert of unknown source) is a contracting flake that shows steep retouch along the right lateral edge, with use-damage flake scarring along the left and right lateroapex edges.

A core uniface (TTU-A15939; silicified caliche) has numerous hinge fractures along the laterodorsal surface of the unidirectional core (Johnson and Holliday, 1981, fig. 8a). A small uniface (TTU-A1573; Tecovas jasper) exhibits retouch and heavy wear on all four sides (fig. 9.6d). A broken biface (TTU-A15409; Tecovas quartzite) was retouched and used along the broken edge and alternately used along the lateral edges (fig. 9.6e). Use-damage flake scarring occurs along these edges.

Other tools are utilized percussion flakes, and material type and use-wear pattern vary. Five flakes (TTU-A13451, Potter chert; TTU-A1603, Tecovas jasper; TTU-A13433, Alibates agate; TTU-A13452, silicified caliche; TTU-A13373, Potter chert) exhibit wear along the distal end and right lateral edge. Two contracting flakes (TTU-A19152, Alibates agate; TTU-A15200, quartzite) have use-damage flake scarring along the left lateral edge on the ventral side. Another (TTU-A15000, Potter chert) combines the distal end and left lateral edge.

Unmodified percussion flakes are of quartzite (TTU-A11934) and Potter chert (TTU-A15001). Resharpening flakes and debris were recovered from the kill/butchering locales. Many material sources are represented, including Edwards Formation and Potter cherts, Alibates agate, chalcedony, Tecovas jasper, quartzites, and silicified caliche. Although Edwards Formation chert is the dominant material (38%), no tools made from this resource were recovered.

A bone expediency tool was made from an anterior border section of a left scapula (TTU-A21523). Retouch flaking occurs along the anterolateral edge, with use-damage flake scarring and wear polish (Johnson and Holliday, 1981:9; Johnson, 1985, fig. 5.15D).

A box turtle (*Terrapene ornata*) peripheral plate (marginal) has incised lines along the inside surface (TTU-A13405; fig. 9.7a). The distal inner surface of the peripheral was smoothed, and nine diagonally running parallel lines were incised along half the surface. The line position indicates that they had continued across the suture to the adjacent peripheral.

The first incised line (innermost) is 9 mm wide, and the others are 3 to 4 mm wide. The spacing is also variable; the ridge between lines 1 and 2 is 10 mm wide, and between others, 3.5 to 4.5 mm wide. The length of line also varies. Line 1 is 2.5 mm long before it terminates in a broken edge. Of lines 2 to 9, 4 is the longest at 7.24 mm, and 9 is the shortest at 1.25 mm. The fourth ridge has a shallow incised line diagonally across it where the incising tool slipped and scored the ridge. Two more incised lines (wedge-shaped) finish the decoration. The lines converge at the top of line 8, with one running perpendicular across the line tops and beyond and the other along the bend of the peripheral. The latter line runs the full distance (suture to suture) of the peripheral (11.35 mm). The perpendicular line extends 8 mm: 5.7 mm across the line tops and 2.3 mm beyond. The converging lines form a 20° angle.

TMM excavations associated with bison bone at Station M produced four unifacial tools (Edwards Formation chert): a broken hinge flake (TMM 892-79) with retouch along the left lateral edge (fig. 9.8a); broken flake (TMM 892-83) retouched ventrally on the distal end and lateral edges and dorsally at the left lateroproximal corner (fig. 9.8b); and a flake (TMM 892-80) with retouch along the right lateral edge and utilization wear along the left lateral edge and distal end (fig. 9.8c). Specimen TMM 892-81 (fig. 9.8d, d′), missing, was accessioned as a "small, enlongate flint spall with sharp projecting tip, one edge finely retouched, possible a broken side scraper" (TARL).

Only a worn tip of a plaster cast, a photograph (fig. 9.5b), and a set of drawings (fig. 9.8e, e′) remain of projectile point TMM 892-69. A set of indices was determined on the basis of the cast, photograph, and drawings. Stem measurements are approximations. A close photographic inspection reveals smoothing (interpreted as grinding) along the lower edges, as contrasted with serrated edges along the middle and distal sections. The zone where

both sides exhibit this smoothing is considered the base (Wheat, 1972:149). The indices (table 9.3) fall within the Firstview category (Wheat, 1972:149).

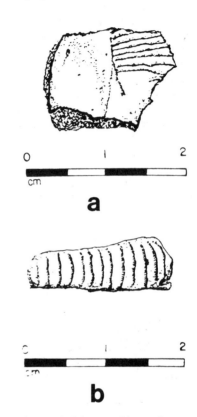

Fig. 9.7. Firstview period decorated bone pieces. a: turtle carapace section with incised lines (TTU-A13405); b: broken bird-bone bead with incised lines (TTU-A916)

Specimen TMM 892-75 is a broken, beveled biface (Edwards Formation chert) with a constricting base and now triangular blade (fig. 9.9a). Both the blade and the base are broken. The remaining side and broken section of the blade and adjacent beveled base exhibit bifacial flaking and use-damage scarring. The tool was recovered 22.9 m (75 ft) south-southeast of Station F (fig. 1.7).

Specimen TMM 892-92 (Edwards Formation chert) is the distal end of a steeply retouched end scraper (fig. 9.9b). The tool is now rectangular in outline and trapezoidal in cross section. The lateral edges and distal end exhibit use-damage flake scarring, in particular along the left lateral and distal end. This tool came from the southwest corner of the reservoir, near specimen TMM 892-75.

Missing specimens TMM 892-144 and TMM 892-145 are listed as "scrapers" from "Station N, Str. 3, dept 2 ft." (TARL) Assuming the depths to be from the top of stratum 3 rather than the surface, these artifacts may be from upper substratum 2B. A drawing of TMM 892-145 (fig. 9.8f, f′) illustrates a possible end scraper that is ovate in outline.

Projectile point TTU-A863 (Edwards Formation chert) was heavily reworked (fig. 9.9c). The remaining original width was projected. The index of relative thickness was de-

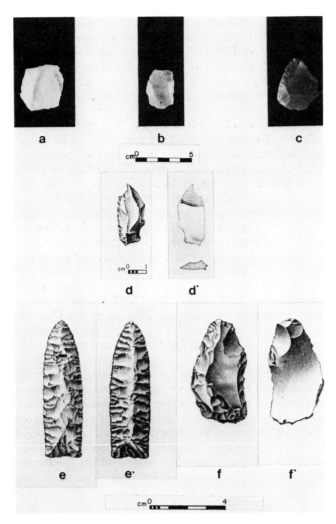

Fig. 9.9. Firstview period lithic tools. a: beveled knife (TMM 892-75); b: broken retouched uniface (TMM 892-92); c: reworked projectile point (TTU-A863) (TMM 892 artifact access courtesy of Texas Archaeological Research Laboratory, University of Texas Austin; photographs by Jerome L. Thompson).

Fig. 9.8. Firstview period lithic tools recovered by Texas Memorial Museum excavations. a: retouched hinge flake tool (TMM 892-79); b: bifacially retouched flake tool (TMM 892-83); c: retouched flake tool (TMM 892-80); d, d': drawings of dorsal and ventral views of retouched flake tool (TMM 892-81) (now missing); e, e': drawings of obverse and reverse sides of Firstview projectile point (TMM 892-69) (now missing); f, f': drawings of dorsal and ventral views of retouched flake tool (TMM 892-145) (now missing) (line drawings by Hal Story, courtesy of Texas Memorial Museum, University of Texas at Austin; TMM 892 artifact access courtesy of Texas Archaeological Research Laboratory, University of Texas at Austin; photographs by Jerome L. Thompson).

termined to be about 25. This figure is at the lower end of such indices for Firstview but within the range (Wheat, 1972:149). Because the original shape is unknown, some nonparallel-sided varieties, such as Milnesand, should be considered. A thickness index of 25 also falls well within the Milnesand range (Wheat, 1972:149).

A broken tubular bone bead (split lengthwise; TTU-A916) has 13 incised lines (fig. 9.7b). The bead is thin-walled (1.3 mm) and probably from bird. Both ends were rounded and smoothed. Subsequent depositional erosion

has pitted the ends and obscured one incised line. The tube is 17.1 mm long, and the lines ring the tube around its circumference. Line spacing is approximaely 1 mm, ranging from 0.9 to 1.15 mm, and the width of the incised lines is uniformly 0.15 mm.

## Archaic Period

Archaic period activity areas include a stratified series of camps and bison kill/butchering locales and an oven. Diagnostics are rare, and cultural assignment was based on stratigraphic position and radiocarbon ages (Holliday et al., 1983, 1985a; Johnson and Holliday, 1986). Data on Archaic assemblages from all excavations are in Johnson and Holliday (1986). Assemblages from two major LLP features are summarized.

*Early Archaic* A bison kill/butchering locale (FA4-1) lacked tools, but the use of lithic tools was indicated by the resharpening debris recovered and cut marks on the elements. Lithic sources included cherts from Edwards Formation, Potter, and an unknown source; Alibates agate; Tecovas jasper; chalcedony; quartzite; and silicified caliche.

*Middle Archaic* A caliche-capped ash-filled pit (FA16-1) was interpreted as an oven. A broken caliche-encrusted sandstone slab metate (TTU-A3458) was found in the rock covering. Used on both sides, the metate had a double concave cross section. Wheat (1974) recovered a Bulverde point (TTU-A60163; Edwards Formation chert), a Middle Archaic type, in the same deposits approximately 25 m to the north. The point was broken and reworked (Johnson and Holliday, 1986, fig. 14d). Other Middle Archaic projectile points recovered elsewhere in the site include Ellis and Trinity (Johnson and Holliday, 1986, fig. 16c; Wheat, 1974).

*Late Archaic* A Marcos point (TTU-A12325; Edwards Formation chert) was recovered from a Protohistoric feature. It was broken and subsequently reworked (Johnson and Holliday, 1986, fig. 16d).

## Ceramic Period

Ceramic period activity areas included a stratified series of camps (Area 8) and processing stations (Area 1). The Ceramic processing station lithic tool kit (FA1-2, FA1-3) consists of a projectile point, a biface, unifacial tools, and utilized flakes. The projectile point (TTU-A7205; Edwards Formation chert) is a midsection. The biface (TTU-A4927; Tecovas jasper) is a small wedge section. The edge exhibits wear damage in the form of edge crushing and rounding.

One unifacial tool (TTU-A7410; Edwards Formation chert) is a small, broken section that exhibits bifacial use-damage flake scarring. Another (TTU-A1467; burned silicified caliche) is triangular-shaped with retouch along the left lateral edge and use wear along both edges (fig. 9.10a). A small percussion flake (TTU-A3848; silicified caliche) exhibits ventral retouch along the left laterodistal edge and slight use-damage scarring. A discoidal percussion flake (TTU-A7460; purple quartzite) has steep angle retouch around the circumference with intense crushing and damage flake scarring along the right lateroproximal edge and distal end (fig. 9.10b). Two silicified caliche pebbles (TTU-A7364, 3516) were retouched or used along an edge.

One utilized percussion flake (TTU-A3847; Alibates agate) exhibits use-damage flake scarring along the lateral edges. Other utilized percussion flakes (TTU-A1173, TTU-A3726, TTU-A7129; Edwards Formation chert) have use-damage flake scarring along the left lateral edge. Cores consisted of a small, unidirectional conical core (TTU-A7125; Potter chert; fig. 9.10c); a unidirectional core (TTU-A7190; silicified caliche); and two multidirectional cores (TTU-A9255, 7363; silicified caliche).

Small, unmodified percussion flakes (Alibates agate, purple quartzite, silicified caliche) were scattered throughout one station (FA1-2). The resharpening debris indicates the use of unrecovered tools in the stations. Material sources include Edwards Formation chert, Alibates agate, a chert of unknown source, milky quartz, and silicified caliche.

Bone expediency tools were few. The distal end of a humerus (TTU-A7275) exhibited wear polish, edge rounding, and flake step fracturing from use. A scapula tool (TTU-A7136) was similar to scapula knives from the Plainview period, but with a broader scalloped effect. The broken blade edge was rounded and smoothed with noticeable wear polish, but use damage flake scarring was lacking.

A late Ceramic living surface (FA8-5) yielded three utilized flakes and three unmodified ones (Edwards Formation chert and silicified caliche). One utilized flake (TTU-A24822; Edwards Formation chert) exhibits intense use-damage flake scarring and edge rounding on the left ventral lateral edge. Another flake (TTU-A24832; chert of unknown source) has use-damage flaking on the right lateral edge. The third flake (TTU-A24843) has use-damage and edge rounding along the distal end and right posterolateral edge.

Two stratified camping features, lacking diagnostics, may be either Late Archaic or early Ceramic on the basis of stratigraphic position (A horizon of Lubbock Lake Soil). The lower living surface (FA8-14) yielded 4 small utilized flakes and 38 items of knapping debris. Two broken utilized flakes (TTU-A5996, Edwards Formation chert; TTU-A6471, white chert of unknown source) exhibit use-damage flake scarring along the working edge. The third flake

Fig. 9.10. Late Ceramic period lithic tools. a: unifacially retouched tool (TTU-A1467); b: unifacially retouched flake tool (TTU-A7460); c: unidirectional conical core (TTU-A7125) (photographs by Nicky L. Olson).

(TTU-A6437, chalcedony) has use wear along one side, and the Edwards Formation chert flake (TTU-A6437) exhibits wear along both sides. The upper living surface (FA8-8) yielded 14 flakes and broken sections of Edwards Formation chert.

## Protohistoric Period

Most Protohistoric features and associated assemblages were described in detail by Johnson et al. (1977). These features include sequential living surfaces (FA8-2, FA8-4), hearths (FA14-1, FA15-1, FA8-6), and a processing station (FA5-6).

Edwards Formation chert is the major lithic source. The tool assemblage represented on the living surfaces included projectile points, a knife, bifaces, unifacial tools, and utilized flakes. Projectile points include Garza (TTU-A602, Johnson et al., 1977, fig. 5a; TTU-A633/634, Johnson et al., 1977, fig. 5b; TTU-A133, Tecovas jasper, Johnson et al., 1977, fig. 4g; TTU-A3283, fig. 9.11a; TTU-A3320, fig. 9.11b), Harrell (TTU-A515), and Lott (TTU-A201).

Four additional sequential camping areas are known for Area 8. The adjacent living surface (FA8-3) to double hearth FA8-6 produced a small utilized percussion flake (TTU-A6003; Edwards Formation chert) that exhibits use damage along the left lateral edge. A T-shaped drill (TTU-A5666; Edwards Formation chert) has an alternately beveled tip (fig. 9.11c). The base is broken, and a heat potlid fracture is visible at midsection. A total of 88 retouch and resharpening flakes were recovered from the hearth fill, all but 2 of Edwards Formation chert.

Living surface FA8-7 produced a unifacially flaked Garza point (TTU-A12395; Edwards Formation chert; fig. 9.11d) with a broken corner tang. A broken flake tool (TTU-A12403; Edwards Formation chert) exhibited right posterolateral retouch and use-damage flaking on the ventral side.

Six unmodified flakes and broken sections were recovered along with knapping debris. Material represented in this debris includes Edwards Formation chert, chert of unknown source, chalcedony, and obsidian.

Living surface FA8-12 produced three utilized flakes, an unmodified one, and six knapping debris. One utilized flake (TTU-A12444; chalcedony) has use-damage flaking along the ventral right lateral edge. Another (TTU-A12439) is broken and exhibits damage flaking on the ventral right lateral edge. The third (TTU-A12426) has use-damage flaking on the left lateral edge. Knapping debris material includes Edwards Formation chert, Alibates agate, Tecovas jasper, chert of unknown source, and chalcedony.

A third living surface (FA8-13) yielded a percussion flake tool, two broken utilized flakes, an unmodified flake, and three knapping debris. The flake tool (TTU-A12483; Tecovas quartzite) has steep angle retouch and some edge crushing along the distal end.

Two sequential living surfaces in Area 4 yielded a projectile point, biface sections, and unmodified flakes. A Lott point (TTU-A2122; Edwards Formation chert; fig. 9.11e) is bifacially flaked, with a broken shoulder tang. One biface (TTU-A2121; Edwards Formation chert) is the blade section. The other biface (TTU-A2127; Edwards Formation chert) is a broken distal end that has steep angle retouch and intesive use wear dorsally and a few flat, horizontal flakes removed ventrally.

The exposed small section of a living surface associated with hearth FA4-3 yielded 10 unmodified flakes and broken sections from a variety of materials that included Edwards Formation chert, Alibates agate, Tecovas jasper, purple quartzite, and silicified calichie. Knapping debris material included Edwards Formation chert, Alibates agate, and purple quartzite.

A keeled, snub-nosed scraper was associated with hearth FA19-2. The tool (TTU-A3383; Tecovas jasper) is made on

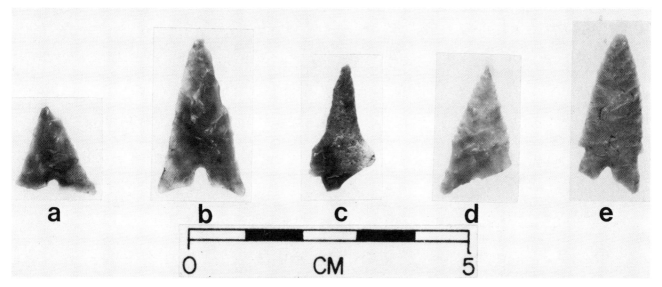

Fig. 9.11. Protohistoric period lithic tools. a: Garza projectile point (TTU-A3283); b: Garza projectile point (TTU-A3320); c: T-shaped drill (TTU-A5666) with broken base; d: Garza projectile point (TTU-A12395) with broken right basal corner; e: Lott projectile point (TTU-A2122) with broken left shoulder tang (photographs by Nicky L. Olson).

a percussion flake and is retouched along three edges. The distal-end retouch is steep, and intense use-damage flake scarring is centered along the distal end with some on adjacent anterolateral edges.

The processing-station lithic tool kit consisted of projectile points, bifaces, unifacial tools, a chopper, and utilized flakes. Projectile points included Garza (TTU-A11563, Tecovas jasper, Johnson et al., 1977, fig. 7a), and Harrell (TTU-A8333, chalcedony; TTU-A11558, Edwards Formation chert).

Nineteen bone expediency tools are from bison elements. A proximal end of a metacarpal (TTU-A11599) received a posteromedial blow to open the shaft. Numerous hinge fractures and heavy wear polish appear on the discontinuous working edge (fig. 9.12a). Another proximal end of a metacarpal (TTU-A11795) was split longitudinally after being opened, and the lateral half was used as the tool. The apex

of the triangular working edge exhibits wear polish, and large use-damage flake scars on three sides.

The longitudinally split medioproximal end of a radius (TTU-A11771) shows use-damage flake scarring, hinge fracturing, and heavy battering from wear. Use polish extends from the working edge to the ventral side. A pelvic acetabular section (TTU-A11746) exhibits a controlled break along the ilial shaft. Several large use-damage flake scars were removed on the dorsal and ventral sides. Wear polish covers the working surface (fig. 9.12b).

The diaphyseal section of a humerus (TTU-A8366) represents the working edge and part of the shaft of a tool. The tip is broad and rounded, with several hinge fractures blunting the end. A high-gloss wear polish occurs along the ventral side, and a series of thinning flakes was removed from one side of the shaft.

Other broken implements were made from proximal ends

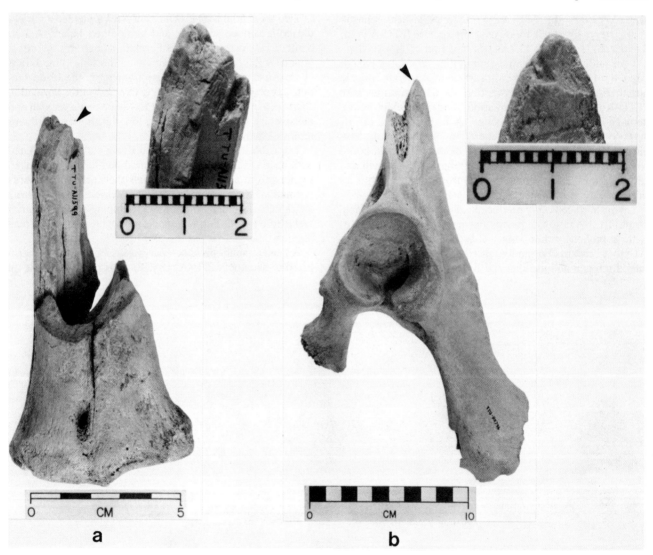

a          b

Fig. 9.12. Protohistoric period bone expediency tools (arrows point to location of closeups). a: proximal end of bison metacarpal (TTU-A11599) featuring a helical fracture surface and closeup of fractured edge exhibiting use-wear polish, use-damage flaking, and edge rounding; b: bison acetabular triangle (TTU-A11746) featuring a helical fracture surface on the ischial branch and closeup of a fractured edge exhibiting use-wear polish and edge rounding (photographs by Nicky L. Olson).

of tibiae. One (TTU-A9302) is the major portion of the medial diaphysis and working edge. The working edge is blunted by numerous hinge fractures. High-gloss wear polish occurs along the ventral sides and edges. Another tool (TTU-A9018) is represented by a lateral shaft and working edge. High-gloss wear polish extends along the dorsal surface and covers the flake scars (Johnson, 1985, fig. 5.11B).

Two large rib sections (TTU-A11702, 11747) had blunted ends from numerous hinge fractures, some rounding of edges, and wear polish.

Several broken sections of tools were from split rib sections (TTU-A9239, 9489, 11579, 11719). One (TTU-A11579) had a tapered tip with a rounded and highly worn ventral surface and high-gloss wear polish. A tibial shaft section (TTU-A11677) had a narrow, triangular tip that exhibited heavy wear polish, rounding, and removal of one large use-damage flake.

A bone awl (TTU-A561) was fashioned from a split section of mammal bone (fig. 9.13a). The proximal two-thirds were cut to shape, ground, and polished. Smoothing was limited to the dorsal surface of the midsection. The working end was tapered to a point, ground, and polished on the entire circumference. The awl tip was broken. The tool measured 73.25 mm in length and 12.4 mm at proximal width.

Parts of two tubular bone beads (TTU-A218; fig. 9.13b) were made from small-mammal long-bone elements whose ends were cut and ground smooth. The beads were ovoid in form and undecorated. Modification was limited to shaft grinding to produce a rounder configuration and polishing. Bead measurements were almost identical, which suggested both a standardization of form and paired elements from the same animal. Inner dimensions for one bead were 5.85 × 3.90 mm; outer dimensions, 8.75 × 6.10 mm; and length, 27.65 mm. The second bead measured 5.80 × 3.85 mm, 8.70 × 6.20 mm, and 26.25 mm in length. Bone wall thickness varied from 1 to 1.35 mm.

A shell bead (TTU-A5165), possibly *Olivella,* was a cupped ovoid in form and had a large central hole (fig. 9.13c). The item measured 7 × 5.8 × 2.1 mm, and hole diameter was 2 mm on both sides. The cut margin of the bead was ground smooth.

Sherds from two types of pottery were located on the living floor. One was a thin-walled, micaceous ware, locally known as Apache pottery. The pottery appeared to be undecorated, but only body sherds were found. The other type was unnamed and appears to be local (southern half of the Southern High Plains) in distribution. It was a thick-walled, coarse-tempered brushware that ranged in color from a buffy orange to black from the firing process.

## Historic Period

Testing in the Historic deposits produced a series of stratified camping events (Area 8) and processing stations (Areas 1, 5, 6) and a kill/butchering locale (Area 9). All are aboriginal features, but the uppermost level of the former activity types (FA8-1, FA1-1, FA5-2, FA6-19) additionally yielded European materials.

Sequential camping events (FA8-9, FA8-1, FA8-11) are represented by very thin flake scatters and few tools. European goods are absent from the earlier one (FA8-9). The main material source is Edwards Formation chert. Tools include the blade of an indeterminate projectile point (TTU-A12344) and tip (TTU-A6491) of an alternately beveled tool. A small section of a uniface (TTU-A12004, Tecovas jasper) has bifacial use-damage flake scarring. Utilized flakes (TTU-A12343, 12355, 12375) exhibit use-damage flake scarring along the edge. Knapping debris material includes Edwards Formation chert, Alibates agate, Tecovas jasper, white chert of unknown source, chalcedony, obsidian, and silicified caliche.

Sherds (TTU-A12358, 12360, 12379) of coarse-tempered brushed ware were located on living surface FA8-9. A tubular bone bead (TTU-A6225) was manufactured from a small-mammal long bone (fig. 9.13f). The bead is slightly bowed and exhibits the natural curve of the element. One end is unfinished and retains the incised cut lines (both 1.1 mm distant from the final break). The rough inner-cancellous material forms a discontinuous edge surface. The finished end is ground and polished, and some shaft smoothing and polishing are evident. Bead length is 56.5 mm. Outer diameter of the finished end is 8.15 mm with an inner diameter of 4.25 mm. Maximum wall thickness is 1.3 mm with an inner diameter of 3.9 mm. Maximum wall thickness at this end is 1.85 mm.

The processing-station lithic tool kit is dominated by the use of Edwards Formation chert. The kit includes projectile points, bifaces, unifacial flake tools, choppers, pounding stones and anvils, and utilized flakes. Most projectile points are damaged, with several midsections (TTU-A9120; TTU-A6906; TTU-A6905, obsidian) and tips (TTU-A15541; TTU-A28398; TTU-A29632) recovered. Points consisted of Washita (TTU-A8332, chalcedony, fig. 9.14a; TTU-A12656, chalcedony, fig. 9.14b), Harrell (TTU-A21792, fig. 9.14c), Fresno (TTU-A13424, fig. 9.14d), Lott (TTU-A6904, fig. 9.14e), and an indeterminate base (TTU-A28106, Alibates agate).

A bifacially flaked midsection (TTU-A23449, chert of unknown source) has both edges crushed and rounded, and these edges exhibit slight polish. A second midsection (TTU-A26862) is incompletely flaked across the surfaces. Although use-damage flake scarring occurs along both edges, edge crushing along one side indicates greater use of that edge. A broken biface tip (TTU-A10337, silicified caliche) lacks wear damage. A small, broken biface wedge (TTU-A8058) exhibits use-damage flake scarring.

A large percussion flake tool (TTU-A28054; silicified caliche) exhibits retouch and use-damage flaking along the broad, steep distal bit. A second flake tool (TTU-A19639) has ventral retouch along the left lateral edge with bifacial use damage. One unifacial cutting tool (TTU-A28339) exhibits retouch along the distal end with intense crushing and rounding of the right lateral edge. Although bifacial retouch occurs along the left lateral edge, it lacks wear damage.

Another small flake tool (TTU-A13421) is retouched along the proximal end and left lateral edge. Use-damage flake scarring occurs on the left ventral and right dorsal lat-

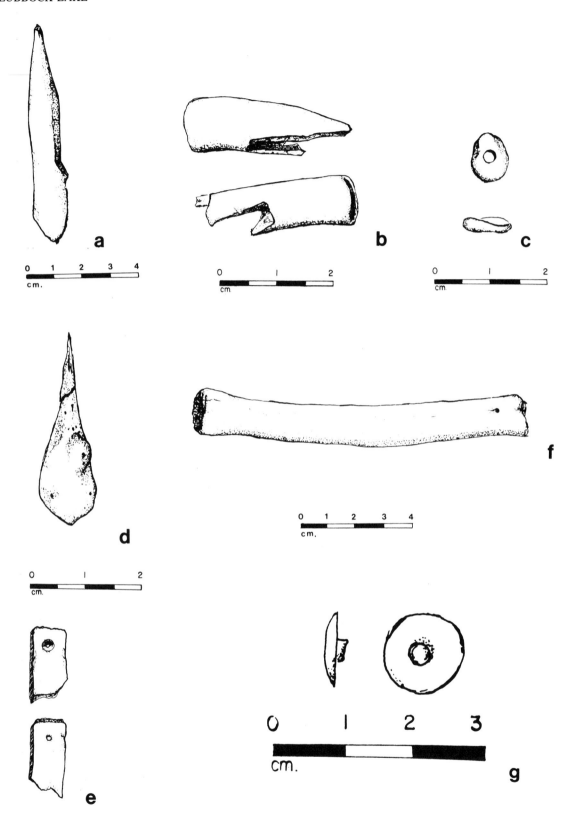

Fig. 9.13. Protohistoric and Historic period formal bone tools and bone and shell decorative items. a: split bone awl (TTU-A561), Protohistoric period; b: broken tubular bone beads (TTU-A218), Protohistoric period; c: shell cupped bead (TTU-A5165), Protohistoric period; d: split bone awl (TTU-A4593), Historic period; e: broken bone pendant (TTU-A14900), Historic period; f: tubular bone bead (TTU-A6225), Historic period; g: bone button (TTU-A12342), Historic period.

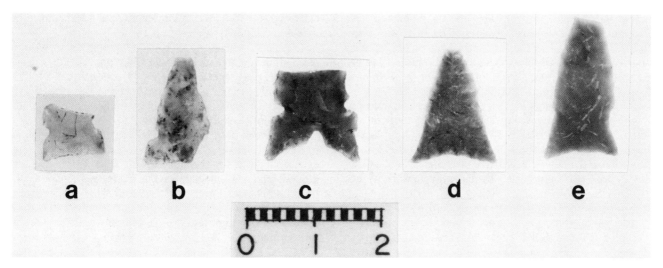

Fig. 9.14. Historic period projectile points. a: Washita point base (TTU-A8332); b: Washita point (TTU-A12656); c: Harrell point (TTU-A21792); d: Fresno point (TTU-A13424); e: Lott point (TTU-A6904) (photographs by Nicky L. Olson).

eral edges. Five small silicified caliche pebbles (TTU-A29602, 4980, 29711, 1997, 28585) were retouched or used along an edge.

A large cobble (TTU-A19501; Potter chert) had several flakes removed to form the face. Intense use damage in the form of flake scarring and crushing occurs along the edge. A sandstone metate fragment (TTU-A26655) has a battered edge.

A large, flat rock and a hand-sized, triangular-shaped cobble (both silicified caliche) were found in a context strongly suggesting their use as an anvil (TTU-A25675) and pounding stone (TTU-A28704). Although use wear is lacking, they were found near each other surrounded by broken bones and bone scrap.

Utilized flakes (14) have use-damage flake scarring along the distal (1; chert of unknown source); distal and right lateral (1); distal and both sides (2; one Tecovas jasper); left lateral (4; one chalcedony, two chert of unknown source); right lateral (3); and both sides (3; one chert of unknown source).

A large core rejuvenation flake (TTU-A7585) and a small chunk of obsidian (TTU-A10925) were recovered. Resharpening debris is dominated by Edwards Formation chert but includes Alibates agate, Potter chert, chert of unknown source, purple quartzite, milky quartz, and silicified caliche.

The bone expediency tool assemblage consists of 31 tools, 15 of which are broken, working ends. Elements from both bison and horse were used for tools.

Two medial tibial diaphyses with working ends have the proximal end of the tibia broken in use. One tool (TTU-A12984) had its triangular apex worn and polished. A series of interior thinning flakes was removed along the shaft edge and dorsal side below the working edge. The other chopper (TTU-A4726, 4727) was broken into several sections from heavy use. The discontinuous working edge shows a large damage flake scar on the dorsal side and the ventral side exhibits wear polish and rounded edges (fig. 9.15b).

The proximal ends of three femora (TTU-A6606, 4827, 12917) were treated similarly. Battering resulted in removal of several hinge fractures and a series of small use-damage flake scars along both sides of the working edge. This edge was rounded and shows use polish. One tool (TTU-A12917) had further modification beyond the helical fracture surface. A series of thinning flakes was removed from the diaphyseal lateral side below the trochanter major. The impact blow to disengage the diaphysis occurs on the medial side below the neck (fig. 9.15a).

A distal end of a radius (TTU-A4563) has a discontinuous working edge with several large hinge fractures. The impact fracture is evident on the lateral border.

A proximal end (TTU-A6550) of a rib has a series of small step fractures at the edge that blunted the point. Slight wear polish appears along the adjacent edges. The shaft section (TTU-A12898) of a rib exhibits slight rounding and wear polish on the working edge and ventral side.

Proximal (TTU-A12978) and distal (TTU-A4744) ends of metatarsals exhibit battering. The former has a discontinuous edge from use breakage, with numerous hinge fractures along the remaining surface, slight wear polish, and rounding. The latter shows slight wear polish and a series of hinge fractures along one edge and damage flake scarring on the point.

An ulna (TTU-A12982) exhibits hinge fracturing at the working edge and a highly worn and polished adjacent symphyseal surface. Wear polish, hinge fracturing, and a series of damage flake scars denote the working edge of a scapula section (TTU-A12735).

A long bone diaphyseal segment (TTU-A4534) has three large thinning flakes removed, one along the anterior edge and others from the working edge. Numerous use-damage flake scars occur along the work edge (fig. 9.15c). Two proximal ends of scapulae (TTU-A10932, 12991) exhibit ventral unifacial damage with minimal battering evidence and some wear polish.

A bone awl (TTU-A4593) was made from a section of

mammal bone (fig. 9.13d). The tip was fashioned by a minimum of whittling and grinding. The shaft was worn, rounded, and polished from use, and the apex was rounded and polished. The distal end had cracked midshaft but had not broken during use. The tool measured 65.65 mm in length and 20.05 mm in base width. A sherd (TTU-A8145) of thin-walled, micaceous Apache pottery was recovered.

The bison kill/butchering locale (FA9-3) tool kit was minimal. A utilized flake (TTU-A8712) had use-damage flaking along the left ventral lateral edge. Edwards Formation chert resharpening debris was recovered. A bone expediency tool was represented by the broken working end (TTU-A8801).

A broken bone pendant (TTU-A14900) was cut from a section of mammal bone, ground smooth, and polished. The proximal end still exhibited an incision cut, although the end was ground smooth. The distal end was jagged from breakage. The hole was almost centered and was drilled from the posterior side. The posterior diameter measured 2.1 mm, with the hole spaced 1.5 mm from the right lateral side and 2 mm from the left lateral side. The anterior diam-

eter was 1.7 mm. Maximum length was 11.85 mm, and maximum width 5.7 mm (fig. 9.15e).

The latest living surface (FA8-11) strongly shows European influence and includes heavily patinated green glass (TTU-A12348), brass cartridges (TTU-A12356, 12357), square nails (TTU-A21099), and metal chain parts (TTU-A12346). Green (1962) recovered similar material along with parts of tin cans.

A recovered bone button (TTU-A12342) was circular in form with a stem extension for attachment (fig. 9.15g). The extension piece for the hole was broken. The bone was ground, and the cut edge of the circle was smoothed in finishing. Diameter measured 11.7 mm. The circular extension was centered and a continuous part of the bone. Base diameter was 4 mm, and it projected outward from the flat face by 2 mm.

Several European items were recovered from the uppermost processing stations (FA1-1, FA5-2). The material consisted of a piece of leather (TTU-A1898), oxidized metal pieces that were probably large square nails (TTU-A1890, 1896, 6769), parts of a tin can (TTU-A9368), and both green (TTU-A1579) and brown (TTU-A4617) bottle glass. The latter (TTU-A4617) appeared to have been used, with retouch and damage along two edges.

## CONCLUSIONS

Perhaps the most outstanding feature of the Lubbock Lake lithic collection is the tool reworking as a means of prolonging usefulness and conserving material. Conservation practices undoubtedly were due to the paucity of good lithic resources in the site area. In turn, bone served as an alternate tool material resource to lithics. Lithic and bone materials appear to complement each other to create a more flexible tool kit.

Another notable aspect of the lithic collection is the wide variety, in both quality and type, of material used. This variety appears to reflect the wide range in materials from the general region, but only a single, immediately available source. Poor-quality silicified caliche crops out at the site. The Ogallala Formation gravel was available beginning about 20 km downstream from the site area.

The limited data indicate some general trends in material preference through time. During the Paleoindian occupations an increased preference for silicified caliche and quartzites occurred with a decrease in use of Edwards Formation material. During subsequent occupations this trend reversed, with an increase in preference for Edwards Formation chert. Tecovas jasper and Alibates agate were consistently present in inventories during all occupations but were never dominant. These trends may be cultural preferences, perhaps reflecting different populations or differences in methods of procurement. However, they may also be a function of changing geologic conditions in the source areas or environmental factors affecting travel or trade or may simply be related to sampling biases.

A major technological thrust through time was the production of fracture-based utilitarian tools. Bone quarrying

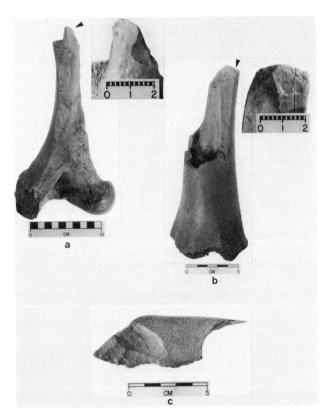

Fig. 9.15. Historic period bone expediency tools (arrows point to location of closeups). a: proximal end of a bison femur (TTU-A12917) with closeup of fractured edge exhibiting use-wear polish, use-damage flaking, and edge rounding; b: distal end of a horse radius (TTU-A10996) featuring a helical fracture surface and closeup of fractured edge exhibiting use-wear polish, use-damage flaking, and edge rounding; c: radial diaphyseal segment (TTU-A4534) exhibiting thinning flake scars and use-damage flake scarring along the edge (photographs by Nicky L. Olson).

was limited to proboscidean remains because of its reliance on thick cortical bone. Elements from a variety of ungulates and similar-sized giant bears were fractured and used as expediency tools. Different elements could be selected in which to produce tools that could perform the same tasks. This flexibility created a broader-based repertoire in terms of tool production by not being limited to a specific species or element. Metapodials were the most common elements selected for tool use during the Paleoindian period, while a wide variety of elements were utilized in the Ceramic through Historic periods.

The frequency of use appeared to vary through time, with two contrasting trends. Expediency tool use appeared to build (increase) during the Paleoindian period, peak, and then decrease significantly by the end of that period. Lithic tools were most numerous when bone-tool frequency was at its lowest. In contrast, during the Ceramic through Historic periods the trend was one of a steady, constant level of use comparable to the frequency of lithic tool use at that time. These contrasting trends may be related more to the different activity types represented than to general cultural trends indicating behavioral changes.

# 10. Cultural Activities and Interactions

## EILEEN JOHNSON

The various cultural activities at Lubbock Lake centered around subsistence and the technology involved in making the implements necessary for the procurement and processing of the food resources. The primary evidence is focused on the meat (protein) and marrow (fat) aspects of the diet. Evidence for plant (carbohydrate) use is limited. Several large game animals and various small animals were used as food sources. A tripartite subsistence pattern for animal-protein procurement was reflected in the quantity and occurrence of remains per species. No one animal was the primary food source during the Clovis-age occupation. Various large game animals, including mammoth, were processed at Lubbock Lake. Bison was the most consistently hunted animal in the post–Clovis-age occupations. In later times pronghorn antelope was a frequent subsidiary source, as was modern horse. Smaller animals formed another steady, supplemental food source.

Evidence of butchering, systematic processing, and other man-induced modifications was seen on the remains of numerous species through time. Butchering patterns were determined by the use of criteria established by Guilday et al. (1962), Johnson (1978a), and Wheat (1979). These determinations are based on repeated action in the same area and an anatomical reason for that action. The man-induced modifications were categorized, and each category represented a different task in carcass processing.

A cut line is a damage mark left on a bone by a tool as its edge struck the cortical surface (cf. Shipman, 1981; Bunn, 1981; Potts and Shipman, 1981). When made by a lithic tool, this type of mark, in general, is short and straight and has a V-shaped morphology under low-power microscopy. Its placement relates to an anatomical reason for its location. Cut lines generally occur in one or more sets, and sets occur with some frequency in a particular location for a given element. A set is composed of two or more parallel, grouped lines. Four classes of butchery-related cut lines are (1) skinning marks, generally found on near-surface bones below the carpal and hock joints, skull, and exterior mandible; (2) defleshing marks, made on long-bone diaphyses and other deeply buried elements from muscle filleting; (3) disjointing marks, made at proximal and distal ends of bones from severing ligaments and muscle insertions; and (4) pry marks, made on articular surfaces from tool insertion during disjointing operations. A class of marrow/technology-related cut lines is that of periosteal removal marks which co-occurs with the category of bone breakage. Because this class of cut lines occurs on metapodials and other long bones, it can be confused with skinning and defleshing marks.

Although the micromorphology of cut lines was defined (Shipman, 1981; Potts and Shipman, 1981), distinctions, if any, in the micromorphology of the different classes has not yet been established. Until the micromorphologies are defined, it is assumed that a mixture of marks occurs on a broken element. For the present, element and anatomical position distinguish skinning from defleshing marks on intact elements. When a marked long bone is broken, the marks are classified by both periosteal removal (because this removal is a step in the sequence of man-induced bone fracture) and the appropriate butchering class (i.e., skinning or defleshing).

Bone comminution is the loss of cortical surface and cancellous bone around the articular surfaces and in areas of heavy musculature. Three classes of comminution damage are (1) bone crushing, (2) blow depression, and (3) muscle insertion plucking. Bone crushing involves the general grinding removal of cortical surface from around the edges of articular surfaces. Blow depressions were inflicted either by a lithic hammerstone (producing a damage morphology of a circular, crushed, inverted cone), or by a bone expediency tool (producing a damage morphology of an ovoid depression with a ruptured central crack that has one or more subsidiary cracks emanating from that central line). Blow depressions in the butchering operation served a different function from blow depressions related to bone fracture, and, therefore, their location on the element is different. The former were designed to loosen ligaments and muscle attachments, while the latter were delivered to open the bone.

Muscle insertion plucking involved the ripping of the muscle bundle end from its attachment point. The damage is localized to that attachment point, generally occurring at the ends of long bones, and the surrounding cortical surface is unaltered. It can be accompanied by blow depressions around the attachment point. The damage morphology is that of a pockmarked area where tiny pieces of cortical surface and underlying traebecular bone were pulled away. This damage is not to be confused with carnivore chewing of epiphyseal ends, which is a crushing activity of a more generalized nature around the ends and usually leaves other traces of damage.

Bone fracturing is another category of man-induced modification (cf. Johnson, 1985, for a detailed discussion on bone-fracture mechanics). Although the basic principles are the same, two different modes were employed in opening an element, depending on the primary reason for its fracture. In marrow processing, a number of blows may be delivered along the diaphysis. This method sets up a series of radial fractures, which allows the diaphysis to be peeled open and exposes the marrow tube intact along the length of the cavity. Characteristically, a number of diaphyseal radial segments are created. In the manufacture of bone expediency tools one or more blows may be delivered to the diaphysis at the same location. This method sets up one main fracture front to split the long bone into two main segments.

Characteristically, few to no diaphyseal radial segments are created. The main segments consist of the proximal end with a diaphyseal extension having a convex fracture surface and a distal end with a diaphyseal extension having the opposing convex fracture surface. The length of diaphyseal fracture can vary from minimal to extensive (Johnson, 1985). Depending on the task at hand, the feature apparently being selected for is the morphology of the convex fracture surface. However, in analysis, the identification of tool use is based on wear pattern and not on fracture morphology.

## ECONOMIC ACTIVITIES

### Paleoindian Period

*Clovis* The processing station (FA2-1; fig. 10.1) is situated within fluvial sediments, and some question was raised about the primacy of cultural deposit (Stafford, 1981). Recent bone orientation data (Kreutzer, 1986) has shown that preferred bone orientation was evident and that fluvial processes played a more significant role within the internal bone bed structure than previously estimated (Johnson and Holliday, 1985; Holliday, 1985b). The stream velocity and competency data, however, indicate that neither the large caliche boulders nor many of the megafaunal limb elements could have been transported in by the stream (Kreutzer, 1986). Carnivore disturbance to the internal structure of the bone bed also occurred, with about 5% of the elements exhibiting carnivore-induced modifications. The internal structure of the bone bed as it reflects human behavior, then, was disturbed and modified by both fluvial and carnivore processes. The degree and extent of the disturbances are

not yet known, and the current discussion is based on an assumption that the spatial patterning still reflects some amount of human activity. Even if all spatial patterning in terms of human activity was destroyed, the individual bones contain data on human behavior (Johnson, 1985).

Three types of activity occurred in the processing station: secondary butchering, marrow processing, and bone quarrying. Hide preparation probably took place, given the circumstance, but little evidence was recovered to substantiate this activity. Localized activity spots representing different activities within the station are evident from the clustering of some materials (fig. 10.1). These areas are superimposed on a widespread scatter of debris.

Seven species of large game animals (nine individuals) were recovered. Although mammoth dominates the station in terms of size and number of animals, other animals include extinct camel, two species of extinct horse, extinct bison, extinct short-faced bear, and extinct giant armadillo. Smaller animals, such as turtles, formed a supplemental dietary component.

Parts of three mammoths (an adult and two young) were recovered. The adult upper molars were aged on the assumption that comparable upper molars erupt at approximately the same time as lower ones (Laws, 1966; Krumrey and Buss, 1968). The teeth ($M^2$; TTU-A17813, 17814) were approximately half-erupted, which indicated that the $M^1$ were still functioning. The exposed laminae were in wear, the first anterior lamina being worn. Such a condition suggested an African age equivalent of between 24 and 26 years with a ± factor of 2 years (Laws, 1966:12, 30).

One of the young is represented by a right mandible (TTU-A5444), maxillae (TTU-A5325, 17658), and an emerging left tusk (TTU-A17659). The mandible is aged at 1 to 1½ years (African age equivalent). The $dP_2$ is well

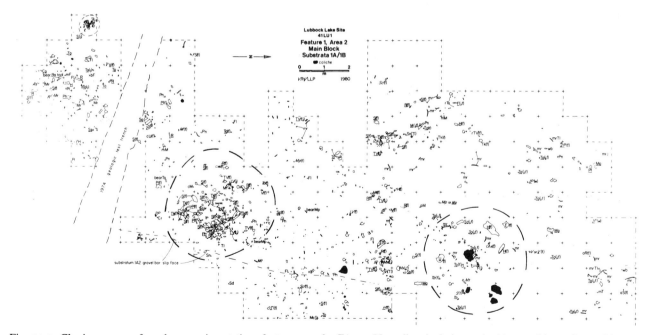

Fig. 10.1. Clovis-age megafaunal processing station, feature map for FA2-1. Note disarticulation and widespread bone disposal in general but concentrations around the caliche boulders and adult mammoth skull.

worn, and $dP_3$ is in wear with enamel loops forming. The maxillae have $dP^2$ in place with full wear. The tusk is within the socket, barely beginning to erupt. This condition is expectable for a yearling (Laws, 1966:27).

The second youth is represented by a right mandible (TTU-A17540), maxillae (TTU-A25402, 25403), and a partial skull (TTU-A25400, 25401). The mandible is aged to about 2 years (African-age equivalent). The $dP_3$ is erupting but lacking wear. The dental wear is the same as that seen on maxillae TTU-A5325 and TTU-A17658 of the first youth, which indicates either a third youth or only a few months of age separating these two. Various postcranial elements and tooth sections are attributable to these two individuals.

The remains of the smaller horse consist of the back of a skull (TTU-A5272), postcranial elements, and a left $P^4$ and $M^3$ (both fully erupted and in wear). This animal was an adult of more than 4 years (Sisson and Grossman, 1953: 405). Remains of the larger horse consist of a right maxilla (TTU-A20214) and postcranial elements. The $M^2$ is in beginning wear, and the $M^3$ is unerupted. These characters would age this juvenile at about 2 years.

An adult camel is represented by various post cranial elements (fused epiphyses). The long bones (TTU-A16963, 20039) recovered are distal ends that were opened through controlled breakage and the cancellous material gouged out for marrow. The medial epicondyle and condyle of the humerus (TTU-A16963) also exhibit battering and crushing. The distal end of a camel tibia (TTU-A24636) from elsewhere in the site was treated the same as these elements. A frist phalange (892-297) exhibits a series of skinning cut lines on the proximal anterior diaphysis and a disjointing set at the distoposterior end (fig. 10.2).

Bone expediency tools were made from bear and ungulate remains. The implements were utilized pieces that show little modification beyond technological breakage features before use. Tools were found both within and away from bone clusters.

A bison is represented by the scatter of a few isolated teeth, an anterior section of a mandible (TTU-A17930), and postcranial elements. The fully erupted $P_2$ with little wear and the erupting permanent incisors indicate an age of $3\frac{1}{2}$ to $4\frac{1}{2}$ years.

Numerous ribs representing the three ungulate species were recovered throughout the station. Many exhibit defleshing cut lines along the shafts.

Short-faced bear material consisted of a few front-paw elements (metacarpals and carpal), a canine (TTU-A20111), and the distal end of a left radius (TTU-A25024). The material was found either in or near bone clusters. Two metacarpals exhibited skinning cut lines along the diaphysis. Metacarpal TTU-A17598 had marks above the condyle along the dorsal ridge and along the ventral surface at the proximal end (fig. 10.3a). Deep cut lines occurred along the lateral diaphysis above the epicondyle (fig. 10.3b) on the other metacarpal (TTU-A17909).

Two types of defleshing cut lines occurred along the radial diaphysis: narrow, single-stroke serial lines, and wide, deep, multiple-stroke lines within one location. The latter

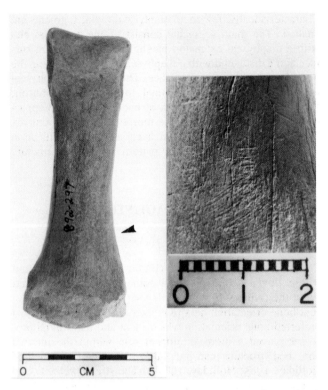

Fig. 10.2 Skinning cut lines on first phalange (TMM 892-297) of *Camelops hesternus* (extinct camel); arrow points to location of closeup of cut lines (TMM 892 artifact access courtesy of Texas Memorial Museum, University of Texas at Austin; photographs by Nicky L. Olson).

type results from a sawing motion. Pry marks occurred on the articular surface, and bone crushing appeared around the edges.

Bear hunting may not have been common during Clovis times, particularly with bears the size of *Arctodus*, but it did occur occasionally. Haynes et al. (1975; Saunders, 1977:51) reported burned remains of a 3-month-old modern bear cub (*Ursus americanus*) from a roasting pit at Lehner.

The use of several turtle species as a food source is indicated by many carapace sections that are broken across suture lines. Soft-shell and pond turtles are edible, and females reach a large size. The extinct box turtle is a much larger form than the modern one.

Extinct box turtle may have been a favored regional food source. Remains of this species from the Clovis level at Blackwater Draw Locality No. 1 (Hughes, 1984) exhibit cut lines on the exterior of plastron sections. At least 18 shells of this turtle were stacked next to a hearth (Johnson, 1977). These turtles are generally solitary animals but gather together during hibernation and the spring mating season. They are easily captured by hand, and the number at Blackwater Draw Locality No. 1 suggests a harvesting technique. Their frequency at both Blackwater Draw Locality No. 1 and Lubbock Lake indicates an abundance of these turtles on the Southern High Plains.

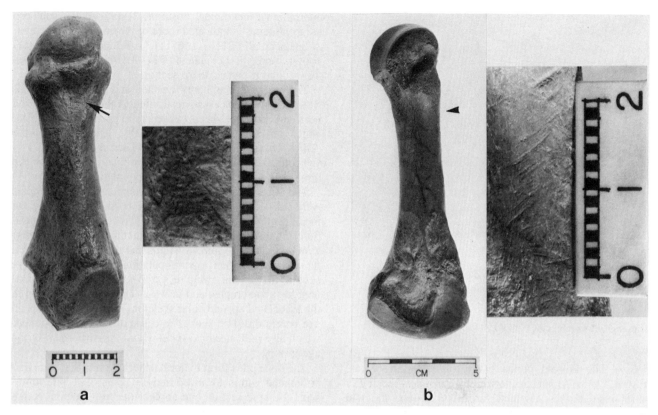

Fig. 10.3. Skinning cut lines on metacarpals of *Arctodus simus* (short-faced bear); arrows point to location of closeup of cut lines. a: left first metacarpal (TTU-A17598); b: right third metacarpal (TTU-A17909) (photographs by Nicky L. Olson).

Wild turkey as a food source is indicated from remains recovered elsewhere in stratum 1. Two short, shallow cut lines occur on the diaphysis of a tibiotarsus (TTU-A1399) above the lateral condyle. Damage in this area was probably the result of severing of tendons and disposal of feet.

Two major clusters of bone and debris that represent localized activity spots are discernible adjacent to the gravel-bar slip face. A cluster of adult mammoth skull and tusk sections occurs in the southern section of the exposed station (fig. 10.1). Much of the skull was in approximate anatomical position, oriented southwest (posterior) to northeast (anterior). The skull was completely broken apart, from either the butchering or the weathering process or both.

The tusks were broken into slab sections that formed a generalized arc pattern from northeast to south. Some tusk-slab movement occurred during sand deposition, although large pieces were in anatomical position, and the displacement appears minimal. Tusk sections and exfoliation are a pattern indicative of weathering. Implements from the cluster include a quartzite stone and a bone expediency tool.

The second localized activity spot, in the northern section (fig. 10.1), is a bone cluster (mainly mammoth) surrounding two large caliche boulders. Although most remains scattered around the boulders show butchering and marrow-extraction damage, the major activity appears to be that of mammoth bone quarrying.

The anterior diaphysis of a mammoth humerus (TTU-A5027) exhibits a blow depression at mid-diaphysis above the supracondyloid ridge and a helical fracture from controlled breakage (fig. 10.4a). A set of cut lines occurs on the posterior diaphysis below the helical fracture surface. Because of the size and density of mammoth bone, an anvil and a very large pounding stone were necessary in controlled breakage. The directed stone had to be delivered with a strong force (cf. Stanford et al., 1981).

A humeral shaft section (TTU-A5198) was formed from intersecting fracture fronts (Johnson, 1985, fig. 5.16B). One side exhibits the remnants of a major impact point and a cone flake that did not completely detach at impact. A juncture of intersecting fracture fronts and an adjacent, smaller impact depression also occur along this side. The posterior side of a left femoral section (TTU-A5191) was helically fractured and split. Neither piece exhibits modification beyond the helical fracturing and technological flaking.

Bone flakes were recovered at the edge of the quarry area and scattered in the station. Flakes from ungulate material were relatively small and thin. A cone flake (TTU-A4140) of thick-walled cortical bone was struck off a mammoth long-bone segment during the initial impact (Johnson, 1985:197, fig. 5.15A). It exhibited an impact point and radial ridges from the radiating fracture fronts.

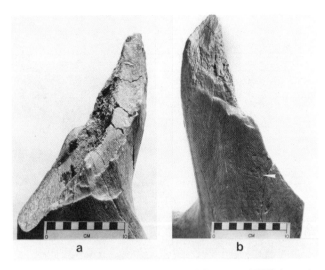

Fig. 10.4. Helically fractured mammoth humerus (TTU-A5027). a: exposed helical fracture surface and impact on anterior mid-diaphysis; b: arrow points to cut lines on posterior diaphysis below the helical fracture surface from periosteal removal or meat stripping (photographs by Nicky L. Olson).

*Folsom* The Folsom period bison kill/butchering locale (FA6-8; fig. 10.5) is characterized by a distinct stacking of bones in small piles, complete carcass processing, minimal marrow processing, and the presence of expediency bone tools and their manufacturing debris, and lithic percussion flake tools. These same characters denote the later Plainview locales. The major differences between the Folsom and the Plainview locales are the treatment of the bone piles, variance within the tool assemblage, and distinctive types of projectile points. Kills involving up to six animals occurred around marshy edges of ponds during both these periods.

Carcass processing for a meat supply appears to have been the major activity in the Folsom locale, although by-products (e.g., hide and tendons) undoubtedly were taken. Marrow processing per se was at a minimum. Most bone breakage is attributable to bone-tool manufacturing. Although marrow may have been taken from the elements used, several are low in marrow content and are not considered prime marrow bones. On the other hand, some elements such as the tibiae may have been chosen both for their durability as tools and for their high marrow content.

Production of bone expediency tools is considered a subsidiary activity performed to expedite carcass processing. Reduction areas where this activity occurred are delineated. Little bone scatter occurs between bone piles, and the tools were found in and at the periphery of these piles.

At least three bison (two adults and a subadult) were killed and processed in the locale. The subadult bison is in the southern section of the locale within one bone pile (fig. 10.5). This pile appears to represent a butchering unit that was incompletely processed. The pile consists of a skull (TTU-A23018) with disarticulated mandibles, articulated cervicals and anterior thoracics, and the scapulae lying in approximate anatomical position. Testing of the southern adjacent deposits indicated more of the carcass in this area. A metacarpal (TTU-A196711), a femur (TTU-A18468/19063), and a first phalange (TTU-A21665) of the subadult were found in the northern section of the locale.

The material was badly crushed and poorly preserved. Butchering evidence was restricted to the mandibles. The head and neck had been twisted to expose the mandibles, which left the skull resting dorsally. The left mandible (TTU-A19351) was used to age and sex the animal as a 3-year-old male. The estimated mandibular width was 87.1 mm, well within the Casper male population.

The second animal is an adult female, whose remains were stacked in several piles in the northern section of the locale (fig. 10.5). Skull (TTU-A2678) size and configuration is that of a female, and the mandibles (TTU-A2765, 2766) measure 79 mm, a length that places them within a female group of the Casper population. The mandibles were aged to the general group of 5.6 to 11.6 years. The permanent teeth are erupted and in wear. The epiphyseal union in the associated appendicular skeleton, however, indicates an age within the sixth year. The cusps of the $M_3$ are pointed, which also indicates placement within the earlier part of the age group.

The bone piles form major butchering units that were disarticulated within localized activity spots. One pile represents the hind section and another the front section of the cow. These units were split at the posterior thoracics. The thoracic cavity formed a third pile. The skull, lying dorsally, was isolated between the hind- and front-section piles. The mandibles were removed in a similar fashion to those of the subadult and placed with the ribs. Stacked incisors were deliberately removed from the mandibles and placed end to end in a small pile about 0.5 m away (fig. 10.5o).

The presence of a second adult female is based on duplicated left elements of a metacarpal (TTU-A19245) and metatarsal (TTU-A2707). From the small size the animal is a female. The distal epiphyses are fused on both metapodials, which indicates an age of 5 years or older. The metatarsal was recovered from one of the bone piles of the first female, while the metacarpal was near the subadult skull group. These elements indicate not only the presence of a third individual in unexcavated deposits but also movement between the localized activity spots (fig. 10.5). Such associations between these areas support their contemporaneity and unity as a single occurrence.

Muskrat remains consist mainly of mandibles and teeth and a few postcranial elements. An adult ilium (TTU-A22817) and a juvenile femur (TTU-A2685) exhibit cut lines (fig. 10.6a). Duck remains are wing and pectoral elements, which lack cut lines or blow marks. However, the consistent breakage pattern of limb elements from both muskrat and duck suggests disjointing. These animals are small enough to be dismembered by breaking through the joints.

Most lithic resharpening flakes were found around the bone piles, which indicated that tool rejuvenation took place in the localized area of activity and not removed from

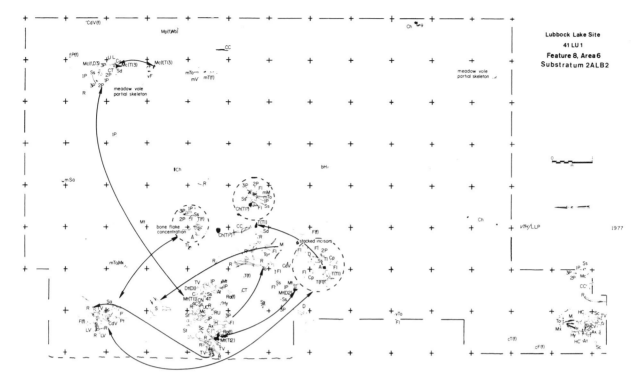

Fig. 10.5. Folsom period bison kill/butchering locale, feature map for FA6-8, with bone expediency tool production areas and butchering articulation nets. Note the stacking of bones in small piles.

it. The presence of Edwards Formation material among the resharpening flakes identified the use of an unrecovered tool in the locale.

A suite of bone expediency tools represents several probable tasks. Most tools appear to be choppers and muscle separators (Johnson, 1982). Proposed choppers exhibit use-damage flake removal along the working edge and wear polish and generally have a helically fractured surface as the working edge. Proposed muscle separators do not exhibit the intensive wear damage of choppers but show wear polish, rounding of working surfaces, and smoothing of inner-cancellous material near the working edge and have a working edge that is a helically fractured surface. Muscle separators may have been used to separate muscle bundles being stripped from a carcass.

Proposed choppers and muscle separators were produced in two related ways, one method being a refinement of the other. The first step involved controlled breakage with the high-velocity impact technique to produce a helical edge. This edge was at times the only purposeful modification necessary before use. Technological flaking is involved in the initial opening of the bone and occurs near a depressed fracture. The second step involved modifying the tool shaft by shaping the sides through flake removal. The manufacturing debris of most tools was recovered in the locale. Movement between localized activity spots is indicated in both tool production and use. Some tools were associated with their debris, while others were removed from it (fig. 10.5).

Each major bone pile from the adult female carcass had at least one bone expediency tool associated with it. Seven of the eight tools were made from elements of this carcass. The eighth is from the metatarsal of the second adult female. Metapodials were favored elements, and all four from the first adult female bison were modified into tools.

Although used for different purposes, metapodials were broken in the same manner during tool manufacture. Controlled breakage occurred with a high-velocity impact blow directed to the distal anterior diaphysis of the metacarpals and lateral diaphysis of the metatarsals. The proximal end of metapodials on four of the five metapodial tools was selected for the tool and purposefully modified before use. A distal end of a metatarsal was used without secondary modification. A cleavage blow was directed to the lateral diaphysis about mid-diaphysis. This procedure caused the distal end to be the longer section, with a convex helical surface. This situation indicates that blow placement in controlled breakage played a role in determining which end of the bone would be used as a tool.

The localized activity in the northeastern section of the locale (fig. 10.5) was involved with the manufacture of tool TTU-A19804/21535. The tool was apparently broken shortly after employment, since wear was slight, but use-damage flake scarring was evident. The localized activity was isolated, and a large gap existed between it and the main concentration of the adult female carcass to which it belonged (fig. 10.5).

Three other localized activity areas were concerned with

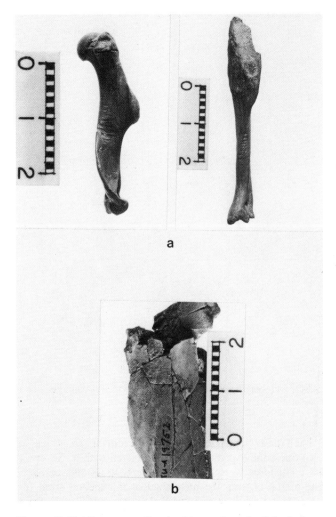

a

b

Fig. 10.6. Cut lines on small-animal bones from the Paleoindian period. a: mid-diaphysis location on muskrat femur (TTU-A2685) and tibia (TTU-A40418) from meat stripping; b: proximal end location on snow-goose humerus (TTU-A19752) from disjointing (photographs by Nicky L. Olson).

bone reduction. They form an arc on the eastern perimeter of the bone piles of the female carcass (fig. 10.5). Caliche cobbles associated with two reduction areas may have been pounding stones. The southern and northernmost reduction areas (1 and 3) are similar in configuration, and both involved the reduction of a tibia to an expediency tool (fig. 10.7). The resulting tool (TTU-A2775, right tibia) from the activity in the southern area (fig. 10.7a) was associated with the adjacent pile of ribs and mandibles. Intersecting fracture fronts produced a tibial diaphyseal segment with two convex helical surfaces that were used. The diaphysis was modified by flake removal (fig. 10.7a; Johnson, 1982, fig. 7d). The debris from the left tibia (TTU-A19493) exhibited in more detail the breakage scatter of sections and bone flakes (fig. 10.7b).

The third bone-reduction area (2) was between the two tibial reduction areas and consisted mainly of bone flakes, debitage, and foot elements around a broken caliche cobble.

It was reminiscent of a lithic chipping station, and the concentration of flakes and debitage around the cobble suggested the cobble's use as the anvil. One large flake (TTU-A19087) exhibited wear polish and use-damage flake scarring from utilization. It had cracked in use, since the three articulating pieces recovered exhibit old breaks.

If hides were processed on the butchering floor, it would be expected archaeologically that areas clear of debris would be found with appropriate tools near and within the vacant areas. A metacarpal tool was found at the northeastern edge of a large vacant area (fig. 10.5), and a lithic utilized flake was found a few meters away within the area. The metacarpal was purposefully brought to that spot for reduction and tool use. This situation suggested an activity occurring in the vacant expanse that was not directly concerned with meat retrieval. Hide processing in the locale would have a similar subsidiary role as bone-tool manufacture in that it occurred as a result of the primary goal of meat procurement.

*Unknown Cultural Affiliation* This bison/kill butchering locale (FA6-15) also yielded the remains of surface-feeding ducks and a snow goose. The goose humerus (TTU-A19752) exhibited two sets of fine cut lines on the proximal end (fig. 10.6b), which probably resulted during disjointing. The duck limb elements were broken in a consistent manner similar to that seen in FA6-8, suggesting wing disjointing.

*Plainview* In addition to the characteristics already discussed, Plainview bison kill/butchering locales are further characterized by the clustering or grouping of bones in distinct concentrations and the resharpening and reuse of Plainview points as knives. A major goal of meat supply continued, with subsidiary bone-tool manufacture and use; hide processing probably occurred.

At least six bison found in four main bone concentrations (fig. 10.8) are indicated in locale FA6-11 (Johnson and Holliday, 1980; Holliday and Johnson, 1981). Each concentration represents an individual animal, additional bison being indicated by surplus elements. The animals include a fetus, two adults, and three subadults. These concentrations, connected with a thin scatter of bone and lithic material, represent localized activity spots within the locale. Although interareas are not as devoid of material as those in the Folsom locale, the interareas also probably reflect hideworking activity. Meat processing is generally complete. Several articulated metapodial-phalange units occur, and metapodial butchering tools are lacking.

An adult female of approximately 7.6 years is represented in the remains from bone concentration 3 (fig. 10.8). Dental characters of the mandibles (TTU-A19350, 19378) indicate that the animal was mature and within the 5.6–11.6-year group. Dental characters of the maxillae (TTU-A19362, 19363) used to refine the estimate appear to age the animal to the 7.6-year group. The lingual styles of $M^1$ and $M^2$ are in wear, while wear on the $M^3$ lingual style is slight. The mandibular measurements are 72.2 mm (TTU-A19350) and 74.2 mm (TTU-A11378). Although some crushing occurred, these measurements are well within the compared female population. The small skull size also indicates a female. The skull (TTU-A19362–19365) had been

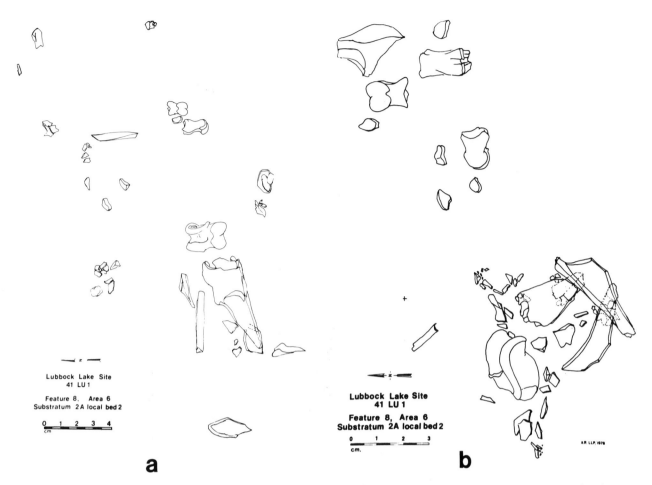

Fig. 10.7. Closeup of Folsom period bone-reduction areas in feature FA6-8 where tibiae from a female bison were made into bone expediency tools for use in processing the carcass; remains in both areas are the production debris. a: southern reduction area; b: northern reduction area.

turned upside down, and the mandibles and maxillary region had been removed.

A right calcaneum (TTU-A22500) in bone concentration 4 indicates an adult male in the locale. Although only a left calcaneum (TTU-A15681) of the adult female in bone concentration 3 was recovered, the right calcaneum represents another bison, as indicated by its much larger size. Other elements in bone concentration 4 that represent the adult male include a sacrum (TTU-A28509), a pelvis (TTU-A7698, 7699), and a right tibia (TTU-A28503). On the basis of epiphyseal fusion, the animal was older than 6 years but younger than 8 years.

The grouped and piled remains of a subadult form bone concentration 1. Skull sections (TTU-A19386, 19387, 19406, 19420) in this concentration indicate that the cranium was broken apart, which is a different treatment from that seen with the adult female in bone concentration 3 or in the Folsom locale. The mandibular dental characters (left mandible, TTU-A19170) indicate an age of 3.6 years. Very slight wear is evident on the $P_3$, $P_4$ is erupting, and the first cusp of $M_3$ has slight wear. The $P_2$ and $P_4$ were broken out of this mandible, and the mandibles could not be measured be-

cause of butchering damage. However, the slender size of the metacarpal (TTU-A19198), although it is unfused, suggests a female.

The remains of a second subadult are grouped in bone concentration 4, most elements being piled on top of each other. The remains include a mandible set (TTU-A18304, 18305) and most of a skeleton. The mandibles were aged to 1.6 years: $M_2$ were erupted to the level of $M_1$, the first cusp in beginning wear and wear lacking on second cusp; $M_3$ were unerupted but visible in the alveolus. Although the $M_3$ were unerupted, the estimated mandibular widths yielded measurements of 83.7 mm (left) and 83.1 mm (right). Such a large size for a very young animal indicates that it was probably a male. The size of the unfused metatarsals (TTU-A22759, 22854) when compared with fused metatarsals designated female, also suggests that this subadult was male.

An isolated mandible (TTU-A19352–19361), broken into a number of pieces, represents the third subadult. Although the mandible could not be measured, dental characters age it to 4.6 years. The premolars are erupted and in wear, $M_1$ and $M_2$ are in regular wear, and the first and second cusps of $M_3$ are in wear with slight wear on the third cusp.

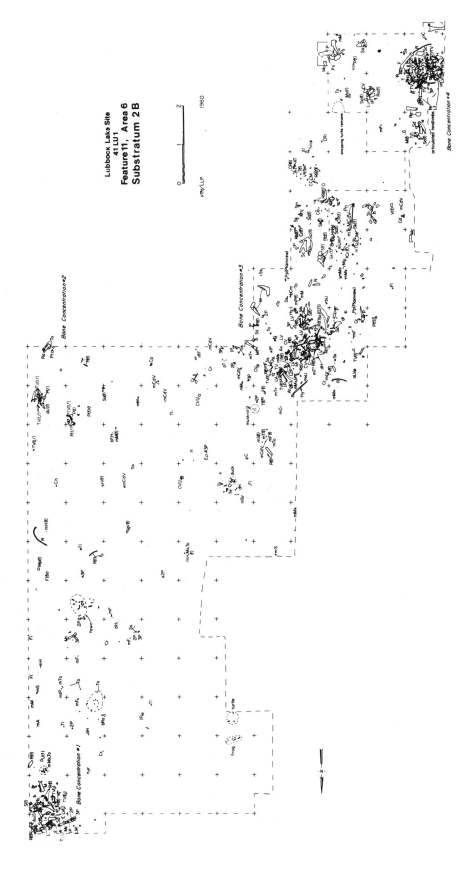

Fig. 10.8. Plainview period bison kill/butchering locale, feature map for FA6-11; note the concentration of elements by carcass.

Fetal remains were grouped into two piles in bone concentration 2, which consisted mainly of ribs, centra, and thoracic vertebral spines (spinal column). The pelvis was in several sections, the right ilium (TTU-A19266) in one pile and four sections (TTU-A18245, 19029, 19032, 19041) of the left innominate in the other pile. Although butchering evidence is lacking, its context within a kill, the complete skeletal disarticulation, and the bone piling imply processing by the Plainview people.

Muskrat remains were numerous, concentrated around the carcasses, and disarticulated, and most long bones were broken in a consistent manner. Four limb elements (TTU-A15658, 15985, 19461, 28349) exhibited defleshing cut lines (fig. 10.6a). Most mandibles were broken in a similar fashion with the ascending ramus removed. The articulated partial skeleton (TTU-A15933) of a juvenile muskrat was recovered near bone concentration 3 (fig. 10.8). The intact and fragile skeleton indicates that little natural disturbance occurred to scatter and break these small carcasses. A skull and maxillae count yielded a minimum of nine muskrats.

Several individual ducks were represented by wing and pectoral elements that were disarticulated and broken. Separate small piles of wing elements were uncovered, while other elements were scattered around the bone concentrations. The consistent breakage and wing units point strongly to disjointing and discarding of wings.

Pronghorn antelope was represented by two vertebrae. A lumbar (TTU-A15875) was found on the western periphery of bone concentration 3, and a thoracic (TTU-A22540) was found in bone concentration 4. Both show butchering damage in the form of crushing and removal of spines and transverse processes.

The deciduous dentition and decayed cranial sections of a fawn (*Odocoileus* sp.) were recovered from a restricted spot in the expanse between bone concentrations 1 and 2. The dentition is unworn, and the fawn may have been a fetus. The partial right maxilla (TTU-A28554, 28555, 29967) of an adult deer (*Odocoileus* sp.), presumably the doe, was recovered on the northeastern periphery of bone concentration 4. Blow depressions are evident along the broken edges with a single skinning mark on the maxillary border between $P^3$ and $P^4$.

Two Plainview points (TTU-A18464, 19941) were found in bone concentration 3. Other lithic tools were scattered throughout the expanse between bone concentrations 1, 2, and 3. Resharpening flakes were found in and around bone concentrations and near the isolated subadult mandible north of bone concentration 3. Tool rejuvenation was occurring at the place of activity. The presence of resharpening flakes in bone concentration 2 strengthens the claim for fetal butchering and indicates the use of an unrecovered lithic tool (made from a white chert of unknown source). The bone expediency tools were associated with bone concentration 3 (Johnson, 1982; Johnson and Holliday, 1980).

The distribution of lithic tools in the open area suggests two possible hide-working areas, one near bone concentration 1 and the other near bone concentration 3 (fig. 10.8). Such a situation indicates that the hides were those of the individuals represented in the concentrations.

Although the other Plainview bison kill/butchering locale (FA9-1; fig. 10.9) did not yield diagnostic artifacts, it has a radiocarbon age of 9900 B.P., which is within the known range of Plainview (Johnson and Holliday, 1980; Holliday and Johnson, 1981; Johnson et al., 1982; Holliday et al., 1983). The locale pattern and location were similar to those of FA6-11. Marrow processing was limited, and most bone breakage was attributable to tool manufacture. Various elements of several bison were stacked within a concentration, rather than the concentration representing a single carcass.

At least five bison were slaughtered. Much of one bison and parts of two others were represented in the main bone concentration. The determination was based on mandible count, age, and sex. Others were represented by a few elements each. Three adult females and a subadult female were indicated by mandibular measurements. The presence of a male was indicated by various very large postcranial remains in the main concentration. These remains age to greater than 6 years on the basis of epiphyseal closure.

The main bone concentration consists of the major part of the appendicular skeleton of a male and parts of two females. Various appendicular elements and a right mandible in the concentration represent an adult female. The mandible (TTU-A13790) measures 77 mm. The permanent teeth are fully erupted and in wear, which ages it between 5.6 and 11.6 years; the degree of wear indicates that the animal was closer to the younger end of the range.

Another right mandible (TTU-A18760) from the concentration is that of a subadult female. The mandibular width measures 80.3 mm, which is near the limits of large females from the Casper population. The dental characters indicate a probable age of 4 years. The first two cusps of $M_3$ are in wear, but the tooth is not fully erupted, and the third cusp is unworn. Various appendicular elements with unfused epiphyses found in the concentration are from this individual.

An isolated right mandible (TTU-A13851) is that of the second mature female. Mandibular width measures 79 mm. The permanent teeth are in full wear, which ages it to the 5.6–11.6-year range. The third adult female is represented by a pair of mandibles in the small bone concentration. The dental characters age the animal to the 5.6–11.6-year category. Mandibular width of the left mandible (TTU-A17333) is 80.3 mm.

An abundance and variety of snakes were recovered in the locale. The coiled skeleton of a racer was found near the main bone concentration (fig. 10.9). On the basis of species count, at least 10 individuals were represented. The situation may represent snakes preying on carrion feeders. On the other hand, the snakes may have been harvested as a food source.

Lithic resharpening debris indicates the use of at least seven tools in the locale, although only one was recovered. More than 160 flakes and debitage were recovered from matrix concentrates and *in situ* throughout the locale. Most bone expediency tools, some with manufacturing debris, were found in the main concentration, one in the small concentration, and one in a small bone pile.

*Firstview* Firstview bison kill/butchering locale location

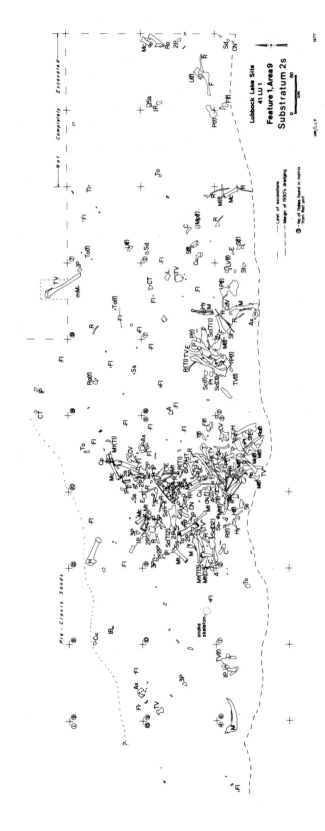

Fig. 10.9. Plainview-age bison kill/butchering locale, feature map for FA9-1; note the concentration of elements.

and pattern are similar to those of the preceding periods. They are at marsh edges, and only a few animals are involved. Bone fracturing is minimal, and, therefore, bone-tool manufacturing is reduced; marrow processing is rare. Lithic tools are more numerous, and bone expediency tools are rare. The stacking of elements and bone concentrations continue, but the amount of carcass processing varies from complete disarticulation to stages of semiarticulation. Selectivity of meat cuts appears to play a larger role during this period.

At least seven bison (two adults, two calves, and three fetuses) were recovered in locale FA6-3 (fig. 10.10). The remains of an adult and a fetus were stacked in respective bone piles. Remains of the other fetuses were found in restricted areas. The other bison were represented by one or more elements, each near or in fetal concentrations.

An adult bison represented by worn teeth ($P_3$; TTU-A13287; $M^1$; TTU-A13055) and a partial left scapula that had been made into an expediency tool (TTU-A21523). These remains were from within the stacked elements of fetal individual 2. The two calves are represented by partial right scapulae (TTU-A19905, 22549) that were found in the concentration of fetal individual 3.

The semiarticulated forequarters and hindquarters, vertebrae, and ribs of an adult female bison were stacked in a pile. The mandibles were lying at the outer edge (fig. 10.10). The mandibular width of both mandibles (TTU-A13048, 13449), 81 mm, indicates a large female. The permanent teeth are erupted and in wear, placing the animal in the 5.6–11.6-year group. From a combination of leg elements the best age estimate is 6 years, on the basis of epiphyseal closure.

Selectivity of meat cuts is suggested by incomplete butchering of the limbs, and foot units (carpals, metacarpal, and phalanges) were articulated. The upper-arm muscle mass was sought, as indicated by butchering damage on the left humerus (TTU-A13417) and the ulna (TTU-A13450). Butchering damage involved in tongue removal is restricted to the left mandible (TTU-A13449). The bison was probably lying on its right side during the limited processing.

Each fetal concentration represents an individual partial carcass. Although butchering damage was not noted on the remains, the piling of elements, complete disarticulation, associated butchering tools, and locale context indicate that they were processed. The scapulae from the calves show butchering damage. The fetuses were approximately the same age, ¾ year to near full term (7 to 9 months). The calves were young of the year.

The butchering tool kit consists of a bone expediency tool, stylized lithic tools, unifacial flake tools, a core scraper, and utilized flakes. Six lithic tools were found with the stacked remains of fetal individual 2, as was the bone expediency tool. Each of the concentrations of fetal individuals 1 and 3 had a lithic tool. Two lithic tools (including a reworked projectile point) were near fetal individual 2, and one was between individuals 2 and 3.

The dependence on quartzites and silicified caliche is apparent (Johnson and Holliday, 1981). Most tools were made

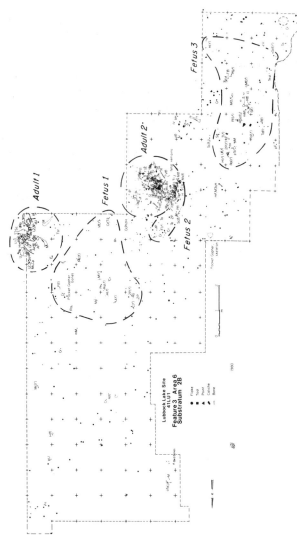

Fig. 10.10. Firstview period complex activity area including a bison kill/butchering locale, feature map for FA6-3; note the concentration of elements by carcass and articulated to semiarticulated units; the northern widespread lithic and bone debris represents the living area or plant-harvesting area.

on percussion flakes, and utilized flakes form a large part of the tool kit. In contrast to other locales, few resharpening flakes were recovered, and the lithic sources in general are represented in retouched tools from the locale. On the basis of color, texture, and grain size, various quartzites were used. Alibates agate and quartzite resharpening flakes came from the concentration of fetal individual 1. A tool made from Alibates agate was recovered in this concentration, but the quartzite flakes indicate an unrecovered second tool used in processing the fetus.

Two resharpening flakes (silicified caliche and Tecovas quartzite) were recovered within the concentration of fetal individual 3. A tool made from silicified caliche was found in the concentration; the Tecovas quartzite flake indicated the use of an unrecovered second tool. A quartzite resharpening flake found with the stacked remains of the adult fe-

male indicated the use of another unrecovered tool.

Minimal data are available from a second bison kill/ butchering locale (FA5-8/10). No bone butchering tools were recovered, but several lithic tools were found. Most are large percussion flakes from a variety of material sources. The distribution pattern of lithic versus bone material shows a partial segregation of the two, and the topographic setting is that of an inclined surface in marsh deposits.

At least two bison (a subadult and a fetus) are represented. A partial skull (TTU-A1596) and parts of a left hind leg are that of a subadult bison, and a left astragalus (TTU-A11933) is that of a fetal bison. The skull consists of occipital and frontal regions with part of the horn cores. On the basis of size it is probably from a female. The metatarsal (TTU-A11928) and calcaneum (TTU-A11931) epiphyseal plates are unfused, which indicates an animal less than 5 years old.

An activity area adjacent to the FA6-3 bison kill/butchering locale was interpreted alternatively as a camp (Johnson and Holliday, 1981) and as a plant-harvesting and processing area (Bamforth, 1985). The area exhibits a widespread scatter of lithics (broken tools, flakes, and debris) and food debris. Tools include bifaces, unifacial flake tools, choppers, and utilized flakes. A variety of cores and different sizes and shapes of flakes were recovered. The pattern from the accumulated lithic material indicates an emphasis on silicified caliche and quartzites with a preference for percussion flakes. Most unifacially retouched items and utilized flakes were made on percussion flakes, although the wear pattern, shape, and material vary (Johnson and Holliday, 1981).

Individual animals are represented by only a few elements. Game sources include pronghorn antelope, jackrabbit, cottontail, mallard, cinnamon teal, gadwall, pintail, and grouse.

Pronghorn antelope is represented by a right calcaneum (TTU-A7525) and a metatarsal shaft fragment (TTU-A2985). The calcaneum is cracked at the exterior base of the distal projection and exhibits a blow depression at that place. The dorsal ridge between the articular surface and the tuber calcis has a series of both shallow and deep cut lines (Johnson and Holliday, 1981, fig. 7).

The major elements of the surface-feeding ducks are consistently broken, either the proximal or the distal ends having been snapped and removed in disjointing. The remains of the grouse are burned.

Although only one jackrabbit humerus (TTU-A13374) and one cottontail ulna (TTU-A21937) were recovered, numerous jackrabbit and cottontail remains were in the WTM collection from upper substratum 2B (Firstview) in association with camping material. Most recovered elements show evidence of having been processed, and identical bones were broken in the same manner. Humeral distal ends exhibited a helical fracture above the distal articular surface. Ulnae were pulled apart from radii, and the olecranon process was removed. Scapular borders were broken out, and pelvic borders were chopped through, at times leaving only the acetabulum.

## Archaic Period

Of the 38 features explored during all excavations, 1 is from the Early Archaic, 28 are from Middle Archaic, and 9 are from Late Archaic. Assemblages from these features were described in detail by Johnson and Holliday (1986). Two major LLP features are summarized.

*Early Archaic* The characteristics of a few slaughtered animals, bone concentrations, minimal marrow processing, and tool rejuvenation continued in the Early Archaic bison kill/butchering locale (FA4-1; fig. 10.11). Meat supply on a selective basis was the goal. The topographic location was different from previous locales in that the activity area was situated on drier ground away from the edge of the marsh. The main bone concentration reflects the partial remains of several individuals in contrast to single carcasses within a concentration.

At least three bison (two adults and one subadult) are indicated in locale FA4-1 (fig. 10.11). Neither lithic nor bone butchering tools were recovered. However, resharpening flakes indicated the use of at least eight lithic tools. The flakes came from within the main concentration and throughout the exposed area, indicating tool rejuvenation both at the activity area and away from it. Edwards Formation chert was the most abundant, followed by other cherts.

The major bone concentration had scattered elements and skulls around it. Subunits within the concentration are butchering units. One was a lower hind leg, and another unit consisted of the anterior section of the spinal column (cervicals and thoracics) and ribs. The near articulation of these units and completeness of vertebrae indicated partial processing. Hump muscles were removed, for each thoracic vertebra had a blow depression at the base of the spine.

The distribution pattern and condition of elements sug-

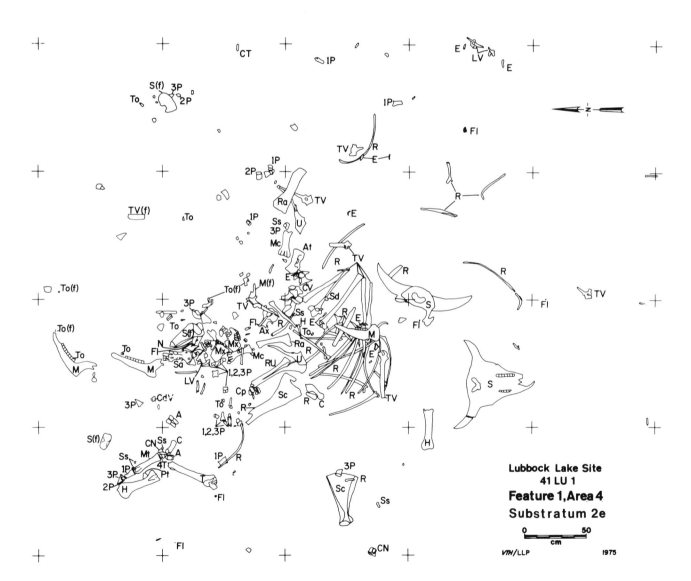

Fig. 10.11. Early Archaic period bison kill/butchering locale, feature map for FA4-1; note the concentration of elements and articulated to semiarticulated units.

gest selectivity for hump, upper arm, and thigh area, that is, the large-muscle masses. This pattern is in contrast to one of near total utilization of muscle resources seen in Folsom and Plainview locales but follows the Firstview pattern suggested in locale FA6-3.

One bison is an adult male, represented by a skull (TTU-A2299) and a right humerus (TTU-A14050). The palatal area of the skull was removed, and no dentition was recovered. The fused proximal end of the humerus indicates an animal older than 6 years.

A second skull (TTU-A2300) is that of an adult female. The permanent maxillary teeth are erupted and in wear. Both mandibles were recovered at the outer fringes of the concentration. Mandibular width measures 71 mm for the right mandible (TTU-A2407) and 72 mm for the left (TTU-A2380). The permanent teeth are erupted and in wear, aging the animal to the 5.6–11.6-year group. However, the third cusp of the $M_3$ is not greatly worn, and the individual is probably closer in age to the younger part of the range. On the basis of element size, the postcranial adult remains are female, and the fused epiphyses indicate that she was older than 6 years.

A smashed skull (TTU-A14151, 14155, 14160) is from a subadult. This animal is represented by radio-ulnae (TTU-A2448, 2485), a few miscellaneous elements, maxillae (TTU-A14155, 14160), and a left mandible (TTU-A2302). Dental eruption and tooth-row wear of the mandible age the subadult to between 2.6 and 3 years. The $P_4$ was just erupting (heavily worn $dP_4$ were recovered), the third cusp of $M_3$ was not yet erupted, and the first cusp of $M_3$ was in beginning wear. The $M^1–M^3$ fall in the 2.6-year age category. Mandibular width is 75 mm. This measurement is larger than that of the adult female, and from its age this subadult is probably a male.

*Middle Archaic* The burned, hardened outline of a pit was ovoid, approximately 1 m across and 40 cm deep. The interior was filled with ash. The pit was capped with burned caliche cobbles (fig. 10.12). A broken, worn sandstone metate (TTU-A3458) was found in the rock covering. A lithic resharpening flake and several unburned, extremely weathered small bison bones were found in the fill among the cobbles. This material probably represents postuse deposition.

The lack of vertebrate material (burned or unburned) within and around the pit; the presence of very fine, pure ash; a rock covering instead of rock lining; and the metate suggest that the pit was used as a baking oven and vegetal processing area.

*Late Archaic* A number of activity areas were exposed in the A horizon of the Lubbock Lake Soil. Most areas represent camping events. None yielded diagnostic artifacts. Because of the possibility of mixing with early Ceramic materials, most cannot be identified unequivocally as Late Archaic or early Ceramic (cf. Johnson and Holliday, 1986).

## Ceramic Period

*Late Ceramic* Two late Ceramic processing stations were found in serially stratigraphic position. Material distribution in both stations followed the same scattered pattern. Game animals included modern bison, pronghorn antelope, coyote, and wolf. Bison remains exhibited the most intense processing damage, and most other animals were represented by one individual each.

The most common bison elements recovered were vertebrae, carpals, tarsals, ribs, and phalanges. Long bones were present, usually in the form of proximal and distal ends or broken diaphyseal sections. Long-bone sections were not as abundant as they should have been, given the minimum number of individuals represented.

Processing station FA1-3 (fig. 10.13a) contained the postcranial remains of an adult bison. No other game animals were recovered, perhaps because of the small excavation area (2 × 5 m). From the size and epiphyseal closure the animal was a female 6 years old or older. No bone expediency tools were recovered. Lithic resharpening debris indicated the use of two unrecovered tools made from Edwards Formation chert and milky quartz, for a minimum of five tools.

The remains of at least three female bison were recovered from processing station FA1-2 (fig. 10.13b), on the basis of skull count and size (TTU-A3743, 3744, 7401). The maxillary and palatal regions were removed from the skulls, but one skull (TTU-A3743) had a remaining $M^2$-$M^3$ in full wear, indicating a mature animal. A left mandible (TTU-A10042) had the posterior style of $M_3$ unworn, which ages it to 4.5 years. Mandibular width is 64 mm, which is within the Glenrock female population. A right mandible (TTU-A7252) had all teeth in heavy wear, which ages the animal to between 10.5 and 13.5 years. The mandible measures 68 mm and represents another female.

The recovered tool kit contained both lithic and bone butchering tools. Lithic resharpening debris indicated the use of three unrecovered tools made from Alibates agate, chert of unknown source, and silicified caliche. This count increased the lithic tool inventory to eight.

The scattered lithic and food debris recovered from small test units in Area 8 indicates probable camping activity. The lower feature (FA8-8) yielded only resharpening flakes indicating two tools. The higher feature (FA8-5) yielded mainly food debris (fig. 10.14) representing two adult bison and a coyote. The bison remains reflect a male (large size of humerus, TTU-A12351) and a female (small size of metacarpal, TTU-A21079) older than 4 years (fused epiphyses). Most bison material exhibits marrow-processing damage. The coyote radius (TTU-A21027) was struck mid-diaphysis to expose the marrow cavity. Two large pieces of burned caliche, probably hearthstones, and a small piece of burned silicified caliche indicate the presence of a nearby, unlocated, hearth.

## Protohistoric Period

This time period is marked by numerous occupation levels attesting to intense and repeated use of the area. These levels are characterized by a particular point type known as

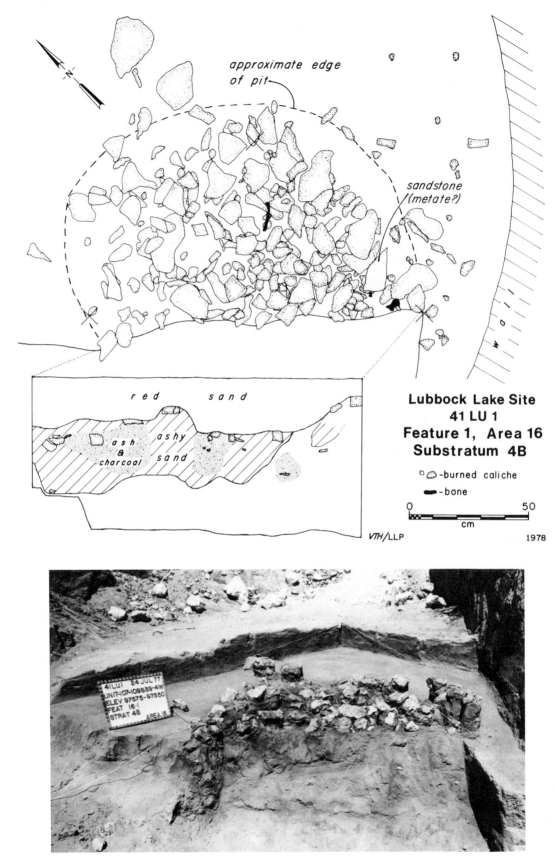

Fig. 10.12. Middle Archaic period caliche-capped pit, feature map (plan and profile), and field photograph for FA16-1.

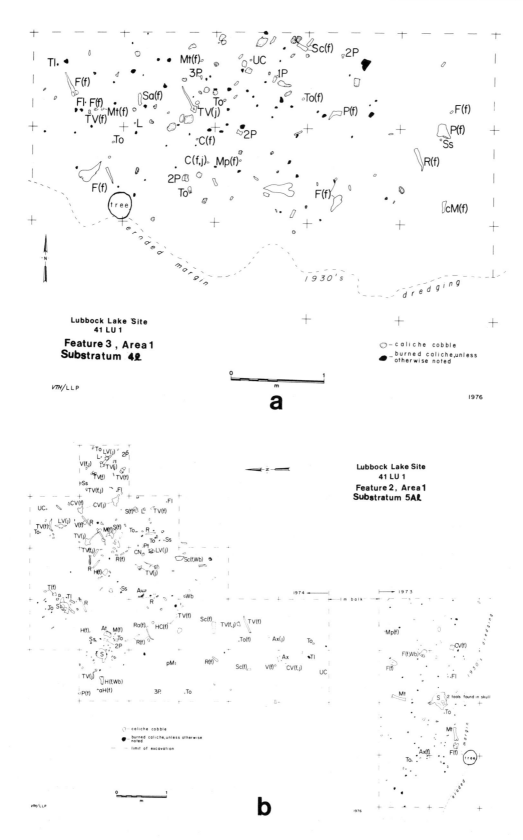

Fig. 10.13. Later Ceramic period processing stations. Note the disarticulation and widespread disposal of bone. a: feature map for FA1-3; b: feature map for FA1-2.

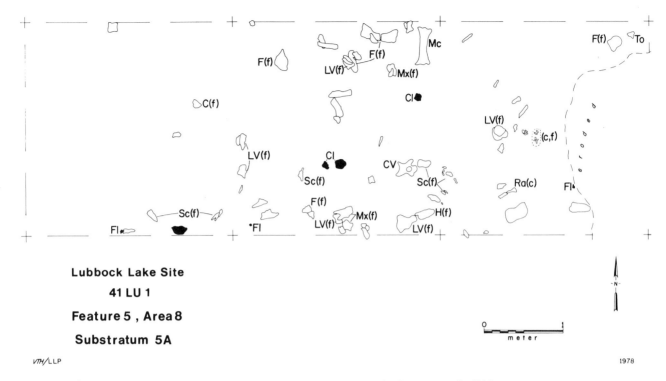

Fig. 10.14. Later Ceramic period living floor with mainly scattered food debris, feature map for FA8-5.

Garza. The activities represented may be those of an Apache group. Radiocarbon dates fall within the known time span of Apache on the Southern High Plains, Apache pottery (a thin-walled micaceous ware) was recovered from the activity areas, and the Garza point has a spatially and temporally limited distribution (Johnson et al., 1977).

Most of the material from this period was described by Johnson et al. (1977) and is summarized here. The features exposed from this time period (either hearths or living floors) represent camping and processing activities.

Hearths FA14-1 and FA19-2 were basin-shaped and filled with ash and charcoal. Hearth FA14-1 was unlined, while FA19-2 was lined with cobble-size pieces of caliche. Hearth FA15-1 is more appropriately termed a kettle-shaped pit. The unlined pit was filled with ash and charcoal along with burned and unburned lithic and bone debris (Johnson et al., 1977, fig. 2). The fourth hearth (FA8-6) was a caliche-lined pit that was used twice, with an intervening, relatively clean zone between charcoal concentrations. A fifth hearth (FA4-3) was an unlined basin filled with charcoal and ash.

A series of living floors was defined, and two floors (FA8-4, FA8-2; fig. 10.15) indicated intensive utilization. Green (1962) also identified these two major living surfaces (Johnson et al., 1977).

The living surface of the earlier occupation (FA8-4) was strewn with both lithic and bone debris (fig. 10.15a). Green (1962) excavated a shallow, unlined basin hearth within the living surface. Knapping debris indicated the use of two unrecovered tools, and several knapping stations were delineated, suggesting various production or resharpening events.

At least eight different food sources were utilized by people in the camp. Meat acquisition was not the main goal with the bison remains in the camp. That goal had been accomplished at a processing station, and selected bones had been brought back to camp. The further aims were secondary processing, marrow and brain extraction, and grease production. The carcasses of the smaller game were brought back to camp for preparation.

Postcranial bison material was scattered around the hearth and throughout the surface. A cluster of 16 bison skulls was uncovered by Green (1962:119). He suggested that their somewhat circular arrangement may be ritually significant; however, reanalysis showed that the skulls were processed for marrow and brain extraction (Kaczor, 1978).

The maxillae were removed, and the few skulls remaining in the collection could not be aged. On the basis of a field drawing at least two young were represented. The recovered skulls (TTU-A595 to 599) appeared to be female, and a horn core (TTU-A593) appeared to be that of a male. The material was brought to camp for continued marrow processing and bone-grease production (Kaczor, 1978).

The remains from a variety of game animals were concentrated around or in the hearth. A completely disarticulated partial wolf skeleton was scattered east of the skull cluster. Some carnivore disturbance of the skeleton was indicated by a cone-shaped depression on the lateral side below the condyle of a left tibia (TTU-A671). Human-induced processing evidence was preserved on other elements.

An edentulous left mandible (TTU-A568) had the $P_3–P_1$ broken out. Pounding blows had removed part of the ascending ramus, the mandibular condyle and angle were chopped through, and the mandible pair had been split at the symphyseal surface. The mandible is weathered, although other wolf material did not exhibit weathering characteristics.

The wings of the atlas (TTU-A677) and transverse process of the cervicals showed crushing damage. A thoracic vertebra (TTU-A675) had the spine removed and exhibited cut lines at the base of the spine.

A right ulna (TTU-A539) exhibited a mid-diaphysis helical fracture, and the olecranon had been removed. One metacarpal (TTU-A676) had a short series of skinning cut lines on the diaphysis above the distal condyle. The left tibia (TTU-A671) was struck mid-diaphysis to expose the marrow cavity; the distal end (TTU-A566) was found elsewhere in the scatter.

Material from the hearth area was burned to calcined. Remains of two pronghorn antelope represented a young animal and an adult. The young animal was aged on the basis of the unfused distal epiphysis of a left radius (TTU-A24950). The distal end of a right radius (TTU-A24705) is fused and represents the adult.

Some pronghorn antelope remains showed butchering evidence; all were broken apart for marrow processing and perhaps bone-grease production. An unburned left posterior mandible (TTU-A34711) with $M_2$-$M_3$ is from the adult. A blow to the exterior ramus below $M_2$ removed the anterior section and exposed the marrow cavity below the tooth row. The fused radial end had the ulna diaphysis snapped. A blow was delivered laterally above the epiphyseal area to open the diaphysis. A distal end of a metatarsal (TTU-A24705) exhibits cut lines along the diaphysis from severing of the tendons of various exterior muscles. A mid-diaphyseal blow on the anterolateral edge opened the diaphysis for marrow extraction. Several metapodial sections exhibited step fracturing and pounding marks from breakage. A rib (TTU-A24705) had defleshing cut lines on the proximal end of the shaft, and the distal end had been removed by pounding.

A burned adult coyote ulna (TTU-A24707) exhibited a mid-diaphysis helical fracture. An unburned juvenile (unfused proximal epiphysis) tibia (TTU-A628) was struck mid-diaphysis to expose the marrow cavity. The lateral condyloid crest of a badger humerus (TTU-A24704) was removed in the severing of the muscle attachment.

A wolf metatarsal (TTU-A24709) was in the burned debris. Other charred remains include the proximal end of the right radius (TTU-A24701) of a jackrabbit, and the distal end of the tibia (TTU-A24702) and innominate (TTU-A24702) of a cottontail, and a vertebra (TTU-A24703) of a large rattlesnake.

The later, intensively occupied living surface (FA8-2) was similar in pattern to the earlier one but lacked the variety of food resources and skull cluster (fig. 10.15b). Similar activities were occurring on both living surfaces. Another caliche-lined shallow hearth (probably basin-shaped) was uncovered by Green (1962). Several knapping stations were definable. Edwards Formation chert was the preponderant lithic source, and most tools are of this material.

Food resources were represented by scattered and processed remains of bison, pronghorn antelope, and wolf. Most remains are from an adult and a subadult bison. The two mandibles recovered could be aged though not sexed owing to processing damage. A left mandible (TTU-A5893) with a fully erupted and in-wear $M_3$ aged between 5.5 and 9.5 years. A right mandible (TTU-A5644) is from a 3.5-year-old. The $M_3$ was erupting, the first two cusps being in wear and the third cusp unworn.

One wolf cervical (TTU-A5645) had the transverse processes removed. The pronghorn antelope remains did not show direct butchering evidence.

Processing station FA5-6 (fig. 10.16) contained an overrepresentation of bison vertebrae, ribs, carpals, tarsals, and phalanges. Most bison long bones were represented by proximal and distal ends. The pattern of faunal and tool distribution was a widespread scatter. One localized activity spot was discernible from faunal material, and several activity spots were discernible from resharpening debris (Johnson et al., 1977). Both lithic and bone butchering tools were relatively numerous, and Apache pottery and a Garza point were recovered. Game animals included bison, pronghorn antelope, coyote, and wolf.

Numerous different material sources in resharpening debitage indicated that at least six more lithic tools were used than were recovered. Concentrations of resharpening debitage indicated probable work areas that overlapped and were shifted.

Various elements of the bone expediency tool kit and lithic keeled scrapers suggested hide preparation as a processing-station activity. Tanning material was available. Skull sections in the station indicated complete processing for brain extraction. These tools clustered in a linear fashion along the eastern edge of the exposed station. However, the area was also littered with faunal debris and other tools, which made a claim for a specific work area tenuous.

A localized activity spot in the southernmost exposed section was composed of a small pile of bison long bones and other elements capped by a skull (TTU-A1917). The anterior cranium was removed. A large cobble chopper (TTU-A1783) was found next to the pile. Few elements were broken, although some showed butchering damage. More than 70 resharpening flakes, mainly of Edwards Formation chert, were recovered from the pile. The various material sources indicated the additional use of at least eight tools that were not recovered. Stacking and lack of marrow processing are the antithesis of the pattern seen in the main section of the station. This isolated activity spot may represent part of an adjacent, unexposed kill/butchering locale.

Direct butchering evidence for pronghorn antelope, coyote, and wolf was minimal, and the remains indicated one individual per species. A coyote axis (TTU-A11740) and lumbar (TTU-A11739) had transverse processes and spines removed through pounding. Blows were noticeable along the broken areas. A wolf left innominate (TTU-A11658) had the pubis and ilium removed to the acetabulum and the ischial blade eliminated by pounding.

Remains of at least six bison segregate into four adults, a

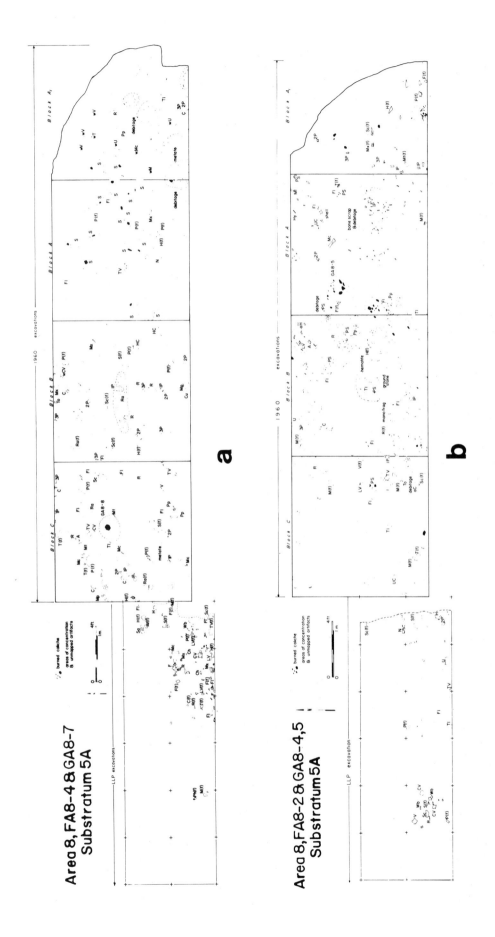

Fig. 10.15. Protohistoric period living floors. a: feature map of FA8-4 correlated with GA8-7 of the same surface excavated by F. E. Green (from files at The Museum, Texas Tech University). Note the concentration of bison skulls, widespread bone debris, and unlined hearth (dotted circle); b: feature map for FA8-2 correlated with GA8-4&5 of the same surface excavated by F. E. Green (from files at The Museum, Texas Tech University).

subadult, and a fetus. The fetus was about three-fourths term. Its partial remains were grouped in a small area. Although butchering damage was not noted on the material, its disarticulation and the grouping of disparate elements indicated processing.

An adult male is represented by a skull (TTU-A1917) and tibiae (TTU-A1782, 1848) on which it rested. On the basis of epiphyseal closure the bison was older than 4.5 years. The other three adults are female and age in the 5.5–9.5-year category. The permanent teeth of the recovered mandibles were erupted and in wear. Wear was not extensive, and the animals were probably closer to the younger end of the age range. Mandibular width on the right (TTU-A9034) and two left mandibles (TTU-A9019, 11652) measured 65, 67 and 67 mm, respectively. These measurements fall well within those of the Glenrock female population.

A subadult was indicated by a skull (TTU-A9310) and epiphyseal plates from the distal end of a radius (TTU-A11556) and proximal end of a humerus (TTU-A11522). The skull and horn cores are small with unfused sutures. On the basis of epiphyseal closure the animal is less than 6

years old, and the skull condition indicates an animal considerably younger.

## Historic Period

The Historic period is marked by the appearance of European trade goods and modern horse. Historic features include camps, processing stations, and a kill/butchering locale. Most are aboriginal in origin.

Apache and Comanche are known to have occupied the Southern High Plains successively during this time period. Evidence at Lubbock Lake is strongest for Apache occupation. Comanche occupation may be represented in features where diagnostic artifacts were not recovered but date within the known Comanche period in the area.

Historic features date between the mid-1600s and 1900. Apache on the Southern High Plains are known to have had horses by the early 1600s from trade in New Mexico (Oliver, 1962). The Comanche acquired horses by 1700, invading the Southern High Plains and displacing the Apache

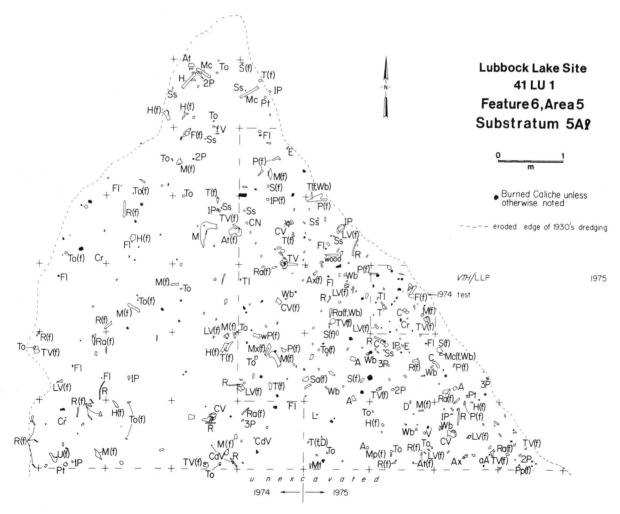

Fig. 10.16. Protohistoric period processing station, feature map for FA5-6. Note the disarticulation and widespread disposal of the bone.

by 1750. The particular band of Comanche who occupied the Southern High Plains, the Kwahadies, or Antelope, band, had approximately 15,000 horses and 300 to 400 mules in 1867 (Wallace and Hoebel, 1952:39). This Comanche group had entered the reservation at Fort Sill, Oklahoma, by 1875. In the early 1880s, George Singer established a trading store at the site, which marks the beginning of Anglo settlement (Holden, 1962a) in the area.

Processing stations are similar to stations of the preceding periods. They are, however, distinctive in the inclusion of modern horse as a game animal. The earliest documented use of horse by the Apache was as a food resource (Worcester, 1944). Comanche war parties ate their horses when they did not have time to hunt, and feral horses were hunted as a food supply (Newcomb, 1961:163).

Coyote and wolf continued to be sought as game animals. Although the Comanche had a taboo on eating dog and dog relatives (Wallace and Hoebel, 1952), they did so during periods of starvation (Newcomb, 1961). Individual discretion governed consumption of these animals in some Apache groups (Opler, 1941). Bison and pronghorn antelope persist as game animals. These animals were major food sources for both the Apache and the Comanche.

Four Historic processing stations were exposed. The distribution patterns are similar, and all contained remains of bison, horse, and wolf. Pronghorn antelope and coyote were represented in three processing stations (FA1-1, FA5-2, FA6-1). Their absence from the fourth processing station (FA6-10) is more likely the result of a small area opened than not using the resource. Bison is the most common animal, followed by horse. Axial and foot elements from both species are the most common of the remains recovered.

The FA1-1 processing station contained the partial remains of an adult and subadult bison. The adult is probably a male, from the size of a partial skull (TTU-A3993, 3994) and scattered, fused postcranial elements. The unfused epiphyseal plates from long bones and an unfused proximal end of a tibia (TTU-A4781) indicate a subadult that was less than 5½ years old. Remains from other game animals reflect one individual each. A partial cottontail skeleton (TTU-A4318) and the left mandible (TTU-A4683) of a skunk may indicate casual utilization of these food resources.

At least five bison (four adults and one subadult) were represented in remains at the FA5-2 processing station (fig. 10.17). No measurable or ageable mandibles were recovered. However, several pairs of elements and bone counts such as right calcanea (TTU-A6733, 6925, 6948, 6998) indicated four adults. From the sizes, one was male, and the others were female. A subadult was represented by a radial diaphysis (TTU-A9014) with the distal end unfused and an unfused calcaneum (TTU-A1736). This animal was 4 years old or younger.

Parts of four horses (three adults and one yearling) were recovered. The adult number was based on counts of atlases (TTU-A6602, 6745, 6929) and sacra (TTU-A6580, 6648, 6861). Most of the teeth of the two mandible sets were broken. One set (TTU-A1980) had an erupted and in-wear $M_2$. The $M_3$ socket condition indicated a well-developed tooth, which suggests an age of 3 years or older. Postcranial

material had fused epiphyses, indicating animals older than 3½ years. An isolated unworn $P_2$ (TTU-A6728) represented the yearling since these teeth erupt at 2 years.

The distal ends of right humeri (TTU-A1664, 8003) indicated two adult pronghorn antelope. Adult wolf and coyote were represented by a partial right mandible (TTU-A1825) and a calcaneum (TTU-A6511), respectively. The wolf was an old individual, for the $M_1$ is very worn.

Two processing stations in Area 6 may represent one intensively used area. Some stratigraphic separation exists, and the processing stations were considered as two events. The horse remains may be from one individual, since the counts on different elements yield the same minimum number, with unduplicated elements between the defined levels.

The lower processing station (FA6-10) yielded the remains of six bison: four adults, one subadult, and one calf (fig. 10.18a). The calf was represented by several vertebrae (TTU-A12844, 12883, 12859, 12860). A partial skull (TTU-A12601, 12705) and the distal end of a radius (TTU-A10996) represented the subadult. The unfused radius indicated a subadult of less than 6 years, but the small horn cores suggested an animal much younger. The number of adults was identified by four sets of metacarpals. Their size indicated three males (TTU-A12604, 12866, 12942) and a female (TTU-A12869).

An adult horse was indicated by maxillae and a few postcranial elements. The permanent teeth of the maxillae (TTU-A12504, 12593) were erupted and in wear, which indicated an animal of 4 years or more. Two adult wolves were indicated by right humeri (TTU-A12500, 12849), and the difference in size implied a male and a female.

The upper processing station (FA6-1) contained the partial remains of four adult bison and two calves (fig. 10.18b). The adults were indicated by right humeri (TTU-A10987, 12188, 12851, 12952). The humeral head of one adult (TTU-A12188) was in the process of fusing, which indicated that the animal was about 6 years old. From its small size it was probably a female. The other humeri appeared to represent a male (TTU-A10987) and two females (TTU-A12851, 12952). Two calves were represented by left calcanea (TTU-A10799, 12717) and a few postcranial items.

The remains of an adult horse included a partial skull (TTU-A10942) and a mandible (TTU-A19041). The teeth, except $P_4$, were broken out, and the roots of $M_3$ indicated that it had already erupted. The animal was at least 4 years old. The presence of a 4-year-old horse in both processing stations, one represented by maxillae and the other by a skull without maxillae, suggested that the processing station may be one event. Although the maxillae did not fit onto the skull, this lack of fit may be due more to butchering damage than to the presence of two different animals.

Two adult wolves were represented by right tibiae (TTU-A12658, 12659) and other postcranial material, and an adult coyote was represented by a skull (TTU-A10948). Remains from an adult pronghorn antelope (TTU-A10856, 10973, 12528, 12532, 12533) complete the game inventory.

Bone breakage and crushing constituted the major lines of butchering evidence for nonbison remains in the four processing stations, although a few elements had defleshing cut

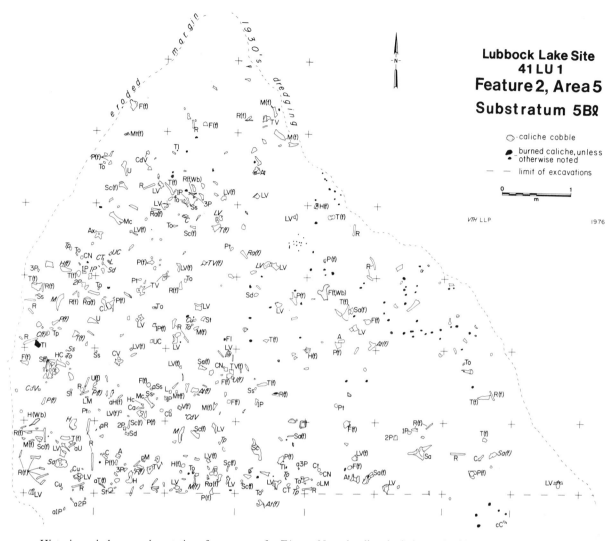

Fig. 10.17. Historic period processing station, feature map for FA5-2. Note the disarticulation and widespread disposal of the bone.

lines. Pronghorn antelope ulnae were snapped off radii, and the olecranon process was removed through blows. The medial tuberosity of the humeral head was partly removed by a chopping action. A series of defleshing and periosteal removal cut lines appeared on humeral (TTU-A1664, 4621, 8003) and radial diaphyses (TTU-A8133, 12529). The distal and proximal ends of long bones exhibited helical fracturing from controlled breakage.

Wolf and coyote carcasses were treated in a similar manner. The back of the coyote skull (TTU-A10948) was broken, and the occipital region (found elsewhere in the station) was removed. The wolf mandible (TTU-A1825) exhibited blow depressions along the broken edge that resulted in removal of the ascending ramus, angle, and ramus anterior to $M_1$. Scapular (TTU-A4783, 12950) blades and spines were pounded, and disjointing cut lines appeared on the ventral side below the glenoid cavity. The head and medial tuberosity of humeri (TTU-A4783, 12501, 12849) exhibited crushing, and defleshing cut lines occur on the humeral diaphyses. Disjointing cut lines occur on the ischial ridge

(TTU-A29788). A wolf tibia (TTU-A12402) has a series of defleshing cut lines along the diaphysis.

The combined tool kits from all four stations were extensive. Edwards Formation chert was the predominant lithic source, but resharpening debris indicated the additional use of purple quartzite. Elements from both bison and horse were used in making expediency tools.

The bison kill/butchering locale (FA9-3) represents an end of a continuum toward high selectivity of meat cuts. Three females were slaughtered. Neither skulls nor mandibles were located. Two carcasses were well represented, and front and hind limb bones were recovered articulated and in anatomical position. None of the long bones showed butchering evidence, although the axial skeleton did. Apparently the hunters took the hump and shoulder muscles but did not utilize the large leg-muscle bundles. The third animal was indicated by a duplicated metatarsal (TTU-A13533). Its disarticulation from the carcass may suggest a greater resource use.

A series of living surfaces was delineated in Area 8 in the

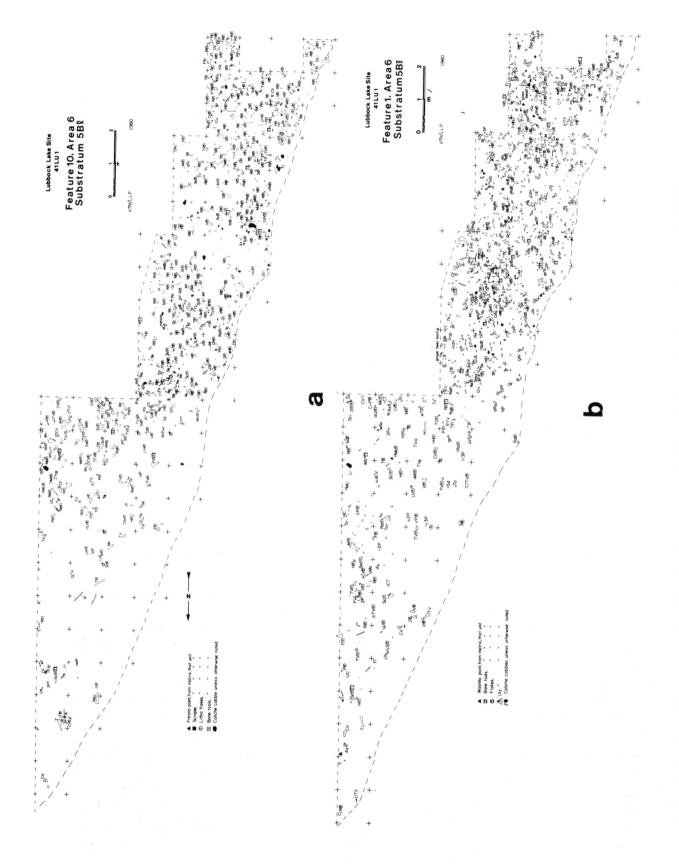

Fig. 10.18. Historic period processing station. Note the disarticulation and widespread disposal of the bone. a: feature map for FA6-10; b: feature map for FA6-1.

Historic deposits. Aboriginal material is limited to a few food remains and lithic items. Scattered, processed remains of bison and pronghorn antelope indicate continued hunting in the area. Lithic tools were made from Edwards Formation chert. Retouch and resharpening flakes indicate the additional use of Tecovas jasper and chalcedony as lithic sources. This limited pattern suggests a continued aboriginal camping style and resource utilization despite a growing Anglo influence.

## BUTCHERING PATTERNS

Carnivores produce a wide variety of alterations owing to chewing, crushing, scooping, splintering, and partial digestion. They usually attach the soft, spongy epiphyseal ends first, which leaves such features as tooth perforation holes, scratches, chewed and jagged edges, and scoop marks. Carnivore tooth scoring and abrasion are distinguished from human-induced butchering cut lines made by lithic tools through morphology, size, length, and orientation (cf. G. Miller, 1969; Sutcliffe, 1970; Walker and Long, 1977; Bonnichsen, 1979; Bunn, 1981; Shipman, 1981; Potts and Shipman, 1981). Carnivore tooth perforation holes are distinguished from human-induced blow marks made by lithic or bone tools through morphology and size (cf. Morlan, 1980; Wan, 1980; Johnson, 1985). A further discussion of the subject can be found in Johnson (1985).

A butchering pattern consists of several parts or processes: skinning, meat extraction, secondary by-product retrieval, bone disposal, and tool assemblage. The tool type and its use influence bone damage and carcass dismemberment. Certain kinds of bone damage are caused by bone expediency tools (e.g., Frison, 1974; Wan, 1980); other damage is caused by lithic tools (e.g., Bunn, 1981; Shipman, 1981; Potts and Shipman, 1981; Walker and Long, 1977). General categories of butchering evidence (bone damage) were constructed with the focus on technique (the method or procedure employed in carrying out the operation). Limited experimental butchering (artiodactyls, elephant) was conducted.

In the butchering process a particular area was acted upon for a particular anatomical reason: to skin the carcass, sever muscle and ligament attachments, or deflesh meat from bones. Bones were broken open for secondary processing or for tool manufacture. Although a butchering action could be accomplished in several ways, evidence suggests that it was accomplished within a very limited number of ways. This behavior creates a pattern in carcass treatment that is seen in the bone damage. Most or all bones of the same element have similar damage areas caused by the same action repeated on both sides of the carcass and on each carcass processed.

Several muscles attach either in the same place or in the same general area. Several things occurred during the butchering process. First, action in one area of the body precipitated action in another to free both ends of a muscle mass. This motion in turn freed more than one muscle attachment at either end. Second, unit butchering occurred in which the carcass was segmented during the initial phase. Because of muscle arrangement segmentation necessitated following a sequential order during processing to free muscle ends and expose areas. Third, muscle masses were taken off the carcass whole. Carcass units were filleted, and the bone was left as waste. Disarticulated units and broken elements were the result of secondary processing and tool manufacture.

The basic anatomy of an animal must be understood to comprehend the causes and results of butchering actions. A brief synopsis (table 10.1) of the major ungulate musculature (Sisson and Grossman, 1953), its origin, and insertions is presented as a simplified model and guide to the understanding of butchering practices in general. Ungulates vary in size, and some muscle bundles are of relatively different proportions. Variations in procedure and bone damage are expected to have occurred because of these differences among ungulates.

Several sets of ligaments in the hind leg are important to the butchering process. The femur is bound to the acetabulum by three short ligaments: the cotyloid, the transverse acetabular, and the round. These ligaments attach on the femoral head. Another set of ligaments binds the patella to the tibial tuberosity. These patellar ligaments govern access to the femoral-tibial joint. Various ligaments bind the hock joint. Several ligaments attach to the calcaneum and control its freedom from the joint. The planter ligament covers the posterior of the calcaneum and binds it to the metatarsal. Various annular ligaments bind the lateral side of the calcaneum to the tibia and metatarsal.

### Bison

Two elements of the butchering pattern are the amount of processing a carcass receives and bone disposal. Two distinct and contrasting patterns are found at Lubbock Lake, one in the Paleoindian period and the other in the Ceramic through Historic periods. In the Paleoindian period the main objective was meat retrieval, and little attention was paid to marrow extraction. Bones were disposed of in distinct piles or concentrations, the makeup of which helps in determining a butchering sequence. During the Ceramic through Historic periods the pattern is one of intense secondary processing for marrow and grease and a widespread bone disposal. Much of the bone damage during initial butchering was obliterated on bones in the processing station. Certain elements were missing, and it was assumed that they were left at the kill area, although they could also have been processed beyond recognition.

For the Paleoindian period an early attempt (Johnson, 1978) at a regional butchering pattern presented processing points at the pelvic and pectoral girdles (down the leg) or at metapodials (up the leg). Butchering experience modified this view to a selection of effective and efficient butchering units that were stripped after disassociation from the carcass. Seven units could be formed: the skull, the pectoral girdle (two forequarters), the pelvic girdle (two hindquarters), the thoracic region, and the lumbar region. At times the cervical region may have been an eighth unit.

Table 10.1. Ungulate Anatomy

| Anatomical Area | Muscle/Tendon | Origin | Insertion |
|---|---|---|---|
| Skull | Masseter tendon | Zygomatic arch | Ascending ramus of mandible |
| | Temporales | Temporal fossa and crest | Coronoid process of mandible |
| | Brachiocephalicus | Mastoid process, nuchal crest, wings of atlas vertebra, transverse processes of cervical vertebrae | Deltoid tuberosity and humerus (proximal end) |
| | Mylohyoideus | Medial surface of mandibular border | Mandibular symphysis and hyoid apparatus |
| | Tongue | | Hyoid apparatus |
| Neck | Ligamentum nuchae | Nuchal crest | Tops of vertebral spines |
| | Sternocephalicus complex | Sternum | Mandibular ramus and mastoid process |
| Shoulder girdle | Trapezius complex | Ligamentum nuchae along cervical and thoracic vertebrae | Scapular spine |
| | Rhomboideus complex | Ligamentum nuchae along cervical and thoracic vertebrae | Cartilaginous distal border of scapula |
| | Omotransversarius | Wings of atlas vertebra and transverse processes of axis vertebra | Scapular spine |
| | Serratus complex | Transverse processes of cervical vertebrae and lateral surfaces of ribs | Cartilaginous distal border of scapula |
| | Latissimus dorsi | Lumbar and thoracic spines | Humeral teres tuberosity |
| | Deep pectoral complex | Sternum | Humeral tuberosities |
| Shoulder | Deltoid | Scapular posterior border spine | Humeral deltoid tuberosity (proximal end) |
| | Supraspinatus, infraspinatus, teres minor and major, subscapularis, and coracobrachialis | Various scapular areas | Several humeral tuberosities (proximal end) |
| Arm | Biceps brachii | Tuber scapulae | Radial tuberosity (proximal end) |
| | Tensor fasciae antibrachii | Scapular posterior border | Ulnar olecranon (proximal end) |
| | Triceps brachii complex | Scapular posterior border and humeral shaft | Ulnar olecranon |
| | Brachialis | Humeral shaft | Medial border of radius below radial tuberosity |
| Forearm | Exterior carpi radialis | Humeral lateral condyloid crest and coronoid fossa (distal end) | Metacarpal tuberosity (proximal end) |
| | Common digital extensor | Coronoid fossa, radial lateral tuberosity (proximal end), and along radial shaft | Phalanges |
| | Lateral digital extensor | Radial lateral tuberosity and along radial and ulnar shafts | Phalanges |
| | Medial digital extensor | Humeral lateral epicondyle (distal end) | Phalanges |
| | Extensor carpi obliquus | Radial shaft | Proximal end of metacarpal |
| | Flexor carpi radialis, flexor carpi ulnaris, ulnaris lateralis | Humeral epicondyles, olecranon, and radial shaft | Proximal end of metacarpal and carpals |
| | Superficial digital flexor, deep digital flexor | Humeral epicondyles, olecranon, and radial shaft | Phalanges |
| Pelvic girdle | Poas major | Bodies and transverse processes of last few thoracic and lumbar vertebrae | Femoral trochanter minor |
| | Poas minor | Bodies and transverse processes of last few thoracic and lumbar vertebrae | Ilial shaft |
| | Iliacus | Ilium and sacral wing | Femoral trochanter minor |
| | Quadratus lumborum | Ventral surface of last ribs and transverse processes of lumbar vertebrae | Sacral wing |
| Thigh | Rectus abdominus | Cartilage of lower sternal ribs and sternum | Pubis |
| | Obliquus abdominis internus | Pelvic tuber coxae | Cartilage of lower sternal ribs |
| | Transversus abdominis | Nonsternal ribs and transverse processes of lumbar vertebrae | Sternal xiphoid cartilage |
| | Longissimus complex | Ilium, sacrum, and lumbar and thoracic spines | Vertebral transverse processes posterior and borders of ribs |
| | Tensor fasciae latae | Tuber coxae | Tibial crest and patella |
| | Gluteus medius | Fourth lumbar vertebra to gluteal surface and tubera of ilium | Femoral trochanter major (proximal end) |
| | Gluteus profundus | Tuber coxae | Femoral trochanter major |
| | Biceps femoris | Sacral spines and tuber ischii | Patellas, tibial crest, and tuber calcis of calcaneum |

Table 10.1. *Continued*

| Anatomical Area | Muscle/Tendon | Origin | Insertion |
|---|---|---|---|
| | Semitendinosus | Ischium | Tibial crest and tuber calcis of calcaneum |
| | Semimembranosus | Ischium | Femoral medial epicondyle (distal end) and tibial medial condyle (proximal end) |
| | Sartorius | Ilial shaft | Tibial tuberosity (proximal end) |
| | Gracilis | Pelvic symphysis and surface of pubis | Medial tibial surface |
| | Pectineus | Pubis | Femoral medial epicondyle (distal end) |
| | Adductor | Ventral surface of pubis and ischium | Posterior surface of femur (proximal end) |
| | Quadratus femoris | Ventral surface of ischium | Posterior surface of femur near trochanter minor |
| | Rectus femoris | Ilial shaft anterior to acetabulum | Patella |
| | Vastus subcomplex | Femoral trochanter major, neck, and shaft (proximal end) | Patella |
| | Obturator externus | Ventral surfaces of pubis and ischium and margin of obturator foramen | Femoral trochanteric fossa (proximal end) |
| | Obturator internus | Pelvic surfaces of pubis and ischium around obturator foramen and sacral wing | Trochanteric fossa |
| Foreleg | Gemellus | Lateral border of ischium | Trochanteric fossa and ridge |
| | Long digital extensor | Distal femoral articulating surface | Phalanges |
| | Lateral digital extensor | Proximal tibial shaft | Proximal metatarsal shaft |
| | Peroneus complex | Distal femoral articulating surface and tibial lateral condyle | Proximal end of metatarsal |
| | Gastrocnemius | Medial and lateral supracondyloid femoral crests | Posterior of tuber calcis |
| | Superficial digital flexor | Femoral supracondyloid crest | Tuber calcis and phalanges |
| | Deep digital flexor | Tibial lateral condyle and border (proximal end) | Third phalange |

Within the pectoral girdle the scapula and large shoulder muscles form a part of the front-leg unit. Initial cuts, blows, and slipping of a hand or bone expediency tool around and under the scapular area would free the unit. Similar but more time-consuming action occurred in the pelvic girdle. Filleting the innominate around the femoral joint exposed the head and binding ligaments. Disjointing freed the hind-leg unit.

Modification of leg-unit processing arose when metapodials were selected for expediency tools. After the skinning but before leg-unit removal, metapodials were stripped of tendons, disjointed, and made into tools. Unit-removal butchering could then proceed with the aid of bone expediency tools.

Cut lines from lithic tools are rare, and much of the butchering reconstruction is based on muscle arrangement, bone comminutions, and bone disposal (fig. 10.19). The reconstruction of butchering practices begins with the skull to place the data in a logical sequence. The presentation order is not necessarily the sequence followed by the various aboriginal groups. Skinning and gutting were probably the first two steps; skinning evidence was limited. Mandibles had a series of short cut lines along the lateral border in various places, such as below the diastema and the premolars. Cut lines on the anterior or posterior mid-diaphyses of metatarsals represented skinning, tendon removal, or periosteal removal before controlled breakage. The lower

leg muscles that attach along metapodials and phalanges are tendinous and provided little muscle mass but abundant sinew by-products.

Skulls were isolated. The nuchal crest and the occipital area beneath it were either battered, with one to several holes evident, or removed. Holes were too small for brain extraction, nor are they carnivore tooth punctures. They more likely were the result of the severing of neck attachments. Angle damage was common on mandibles, and the coronoid process was damaged or snapped off and broken at the symphyseal plate. The ascending ramus was frequently removed through pounding action that left jagged blow fractures. Occasionally a series of cut lines appeared on the mandibular medial border below the tooth row and diastema area. Concomitant with this mandibular treatment, the zygomatic arch and molars were broken from the skull. Hyoid bones were broken. Maxillae, together with the nasals, were frequently broken out of the skull by blows to the maxillary area and nasal base. This procedure was probably the mechanism for brain extraction.

The spines and processes of most vertebrae were damaged or removed. Wings of the atlas were commonly damaged, and the dorsal arch was sometimes broken out. Blow marks at the base of the spine of thoracic vertebrae were common. The acromion and spine of the scapula were consistently removed. The angle of the blade (anterior across to the posterior) was generally damaged. Treatment beyond this point was varied. Most of the scapular borders were removed through pounding; a large blow depression occurred below the glenoid cavity, opposite the acromion, or defleshing marks were present in the blade area. Damage to the humeral proximal end ranged from blow marks and crushing to removal of the tuberosities. Infrequent occurrences included defleshing cut lines along the diaphysis and damage to the distal condyles. The ulna was generally snapped from the radius, and the olecranon was damaged either by a large blow depression or by removal of the posterior border. Cut lines appeared on the radial diaphysis.

Ribs were generally disarticulated, as were sternal sections and costal cartilage, and grouped in piles. Most ribs were nearly whole, many having a series of defleshing cut lines along the midsection. The ilial and ischial borders of pelves were pounded out with numerous blow marks. The wings and spines of sacra were damaged or removed by pounding. The femoral trochanter major was either damaged by blows or removed. Tibiae exhibited crushing of the condyles and tibial crest, with removal of the proximal epiphyseal plate in juveniles. The edges of most patellae were crushed and battered. The distal projections of several calcanea were cracked through blows or removed. The tuber calcis (epiphyseal plate) was missing from immature cal-

canea. Metatarsals exhibited a series of cut lines on the metatarsal tuberosity from skinning, tendon removal, or periosteal removal before controlled breakage.

A schematic drawing of a bison skeleton shows the areas affected by the butchering process (fig. 10.19) during the Paleoindian period. The order of the numbering system is the order in which the actions are discussed and not necessarily the order in which they took place. Several operations were involved in severing the skull from the skeleton and removing the two large muscle masses and the tongue. Two main muscles and the ligamentum nuchae hold the neck to the body; both the ligament and the dorsal neck muscle originate on the nuchal crest of the skull. Battering the skulls in this area would sever the attachments (fig. 10.19, action 1). The ventral neck muscle was detached by pounding on the borders of the mandible (fig. 10.19, action 2). The atlas was exposed by stripping back the dorsal neck muscles, which involved battering the cervical vertebrae. Breaking out the dorsal arch (fig. 10.19, action 3) created easier access to the spinal cord. With the dorsal and ventral neck muscles freed and spinal cord severed, the head could be detached from the body.

Actions 2 and 3 could be reversed, the spinal cord being severed before the ventral neck muscles were detached from

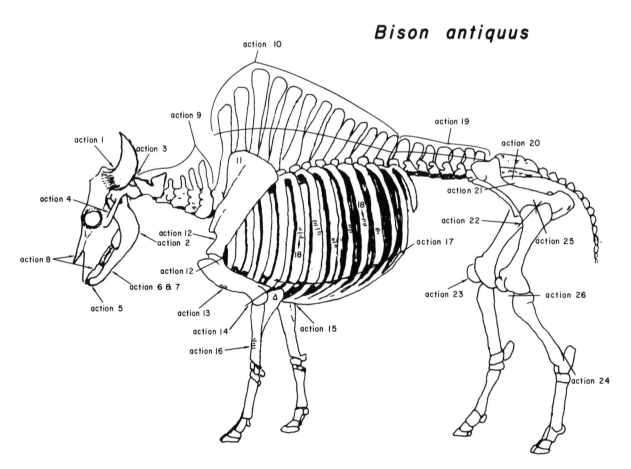

Fig. 10.19. Bison skeleton depicting butchering and bone treatment during the Paleoindian period. The actions are labeled sequentially as discussed and not necessarily as performed in the actual operation.

the mandibles. The large head muscles attach to the coronoid process and the zygomatic arch. Blows to this area (fig. 10.19, action 4) would sever those attachments. Tongue extraction was accomplished by breaking the mandibles at the symphyseal area (fig. 10.19, action 5) and cutting back the mylohyoideus muscle (fig. 10.19, action 6). The tongue could then be pulled out, which would break the hyoid bones (fig. 10.19, action 7). The brain was removed by breaking into the side and front of the skull (fig. 10.19, action 8).

To strip neck muscles and detach the ligamentum nuchae along the vertebral column, attachments on the cervical vertebrae were severed (fig. 10.19, action 9). The tops of the thoracic spines were removed (fig. 10.19, action 10). This action also severed hump-muscle attachments. Battering the spines released superficial muscles extending from the vertebrae to the scapula, as well as providing long strips of ligament for sinew.

The pectoral girdle (scapula) and front leg could be removed as a unit for further processing. Most of the deeper muscles are attached to the scapula. Freeing this unit involved loosening and undercutting scapular muscle fasciae by hand or bone expediency tool and battering the cartilaginous scapular distal end (fig. 10.19, action 11).

This detached unit included muscles extending from the scapula to various front leg bones. These muscles could be stripped back to expose the shoulder joint. The joint was severed by pounding or chopping through the acromion and large humeral tuberosities (fig. 10.19, action 12). Several scapular muscles were freed, and the scapula was disposed. Various shoulder, scapular, and arm muscles were filleted from the humerus (fig. 10.19, action 13). The humerus was disarticulated (fig. 10.19, action 14) from the radio-ulna, which also severed attachments for flexor and extensor tendons. A blow to the olecranon (fig. 10.19, action 15) severed attachments of several overlapping muscle masses and aided in disjointing. The lower leg muscles would then be stripped from the radius (fig. 10.19, action 16). If it was not detached initially for tool use, the metacarpal could then be detached.

The sternum was chopped from the rib cage (fig. 10.19, action 17), which freed the ends of several masses, including the ventral neck muscle. Pounding on transverse processes and on the base of the spine helped detach ribs from thoracic vertebrae. The muscle sheet covering the ribs was filleted from the bone (fig. 10.19, action 18), and the ribs were discarded. Thoracic vertebrae were generally discarded as a unit. Lumbar vertebrae were found both scattered and disposed of as a unit. Pounding on the lumbar vertebrae (fig. 10.19, action 19) detached several back muscles. Some of these muscles extend to the sternal area, and they could then be removed.

The pelvic girdle and the hind leg form processing units similar to the pectoral girdle and front leg. Two variations occurred. The unit could consist of the pelvic acetabular triangle and hind leg or the hind leg detached from the pelvis. Battering sacral wings and spines (fig. 10.19, action 20) released several back muscles and severed attachments of others at one end. Major leg muscles originate on various areas of the pelvis, and heavy pounding on the areas released these ends (fig. 10.19, action 21). Further action freeing this unit involved the loosening and undercutting of femoral muscle fasciae by hand or bone expediency tool. If the hind-leg unit was sought, then the femoral joint was disarticulated by severing of the encapsulating ligaments of the femoral ball (fig. 10.19, action 22).

Both the patella and the calcaneum provided good handles for stripping superficial hind-leg muscles. Freeing them may have been the first step in processing the hind leg (Frison, 1970). They were detached by blows to the patellar capsule (fig. 10.19, action 23) and distal projection of the calcaneum (fig. 10.19, action 24). Stripping superficial muscles exposed deeper muscles and the femoral trochanter major. The trochanter was battered to detach several muscle masses (fig. 10.19, action 25). Disjointing the tibia and severing the remaining muscle attachments were the next step (fig. 10.19, action 26).

Meat was undoubtedly stripped from the femur and tibia, although direct evidence on the diaphyses was lacking. Once the leg unit was detached, it was possible to remove a major segment of the thigh muscles intact as a unit instead of stripping individual bundles. The use of a bone expediency tool along the shaft would not leave defleshing lines. Damage to articular surfaces was a result of detaching muscle ends and disjointing efforts.

In terms of bone damage, the method of butchering a bison during the Ceramic through Historic periods was about the same as in the Paleoindian period. Two differences were noted. First, defleshing or periosteal removal cut lines on the diaphyses of long bones and cut lines in general were more evident during the Ceramic through Historic periods. This increase implied a greater use of lithic tools or a less careful approach. Second, more damage was done to certain elements, such as the calcaneum, the scapula, and the distal end of the humerus, in terms of bone crushing and removal of parts of the element. The general impression given when bones from the two types of activity areas were compared was that of much rougher treatment during the later periods. This treatment reflected intense secondary by-product processing. Few long bones were whole. The number of long bones was underrepresented in the stations, and, of those present, more were distal than proximal ends. The ends of long bones were treated differently. The areas of spongy bone were generally chopped apart, whereas ends with denser bone were fractured through controlled breakage. Most large elements recovered, including skulls and mandibles, were broken into or chopped apart during secondary marrow processing.

For the Ceramic through Historic periods the treatment of bison carcasses was reconstructed from bone damage resulting from a combination of butchering and secondary marrow processing. Marrow processing could have been done after the carcasses were butchered or during butchering as various bones became available.

During initial butchering, the skull and mandibles were treated in a manner similar to that noted previously. Skinning marks appeared on the mandibular lateral border (a series of cut lines below the molars) and on the ascending ramus. On both mandibles with intact ascending rami and isolated ascending rami the coronoid process was damaged or snapped. The angle was occasionally damaged. Mandibles were broken at the symphyseal area, and the mylohyoideus muscle was cut to remove the tongue. A series of defleshing cut lines appears on the mandibular medial border below the molars. Further processing of the mandible exposed the marrow cavity below the teeth. Various parts of the mandible were removed, including the border, the ascending ramus, the angle, the diastema area, and part of the tooth row.

The occipital area was damaged by pounding, and the zygomatic arch and molars were missing from most skulls. Further processing resulted in skull reduction, with the removal of either the back half of the skull or the back, nasals, and maxillary area, which left the horn cores and frontals. An additional step involved splitting the latter section in half, which resulted in a horn core and frontal section. The hyoids were broken, and some showed a series of cut lines from tongue removal.

The transverse processes and spines of the vertebrae were damaged or removed. Blows at the base of spines and below the rib articulation on thoracics were common. Cut lines occasionally appeared on thoracic spines, and a few lumbar vertebrae had blows to the base of their spines. Wings of the atlas were either damaged or removed, and blow depressions occurred in the arch area.

Most of the scapular borders and blades were broken out to the extent that at times only the glenoid cavity remained. The acromion and spines were removed, and the tuber scapulae were damaged. A series of defleshing marks appeared on both sides of the scapula.

Cut lines from meat filleting or periosteal removal appeared on humeral diaphyses. Most humeri are distal ends. Both helical fracturing and jagged breaks occurred.

Ulnae had sets of long cut lines across the bodies. Radii were represented primarily by proximal and distal ends. Defleshing or periosteal removal cut lines appeared along the diaphyses with impact depressions from controlled breakage on the sides. Several ends broken through helical fracturing were then split longitudinally. Metacarpals had cut lines along their shafts as a result of either tendon or periosteal removal.

Pelvic material consisted mainly of acetabular sections with blow depressions on the remaining branches. Defleshing marks appeared around the ischial ridge near the acetabulum and along the ilial shaft. On occasion the acetabulum was chopped in half, and the borders were pounded out. The femoral trochanter major was consistently removed or damaged, and the trochlea and condyles of the distal end were damaged. At times the femoral ball was chopped off, which detached the femur from the acetabulum. Femora were represented by proximal and distal ends.

Tibial crests and condyles were damaged. Defleshing lines appeared on the diaphyses of two nearly complete immature specimens. Twice as many distal ends as proximal ends were recovered. Some of the proximal ends were chopped off, but distal ends exhibited controlled breakage, with the impact depression on the side (posterior or anterior

diaphyseal placement was rare). Some of the distal ends were split longitudinally after detachment.

Either the distal projection of the calcaneum was removed, with a blow depression above it, or the area was intact but cracked. The tuber calcis was damaged, as was the sustentaculum (the area of attachment for the deep flexor tendon). Several calcanea had a series of short, shallow cut lines on the anterior ridges from freeing the calcaneum from the hock capsule. Metatarsals had a series of cut lines along their diaphyses from tendon or periosteal removal.

The broken and fragmentary nature of the bone attested to intense processing. Most bone was broken to an extent much greater than was necessary for marrow collection. Skulls were reduced to sections. Many ends were further split, and diaphyses were shattered. This breakage pattern was similar to that seen in bone-grease production from the Calling Lake Cree (Bonnichsen, 1973) and in bison remains from camping areas of this general time period at Lubbock Lake (Kaczor, 1978).

## Horse

Muscle names and arrangements are the same in horse as in bison, although a few muscles are present in horse that are absent from bison. Horses were butchered and utilized during both Clovis-age and Historic times. Since the butchering process is more evident in the Historic material, bone damage and the butchering reconstruction are discussed for Historic remains. This presentation forms a background for interpreting evidence on horse remains from the Clovis-age feature.

The posterior sections of skulls had blow depressions along the broken edges. The nuchal crests and occipital areas of skull sections were damaged, and the paramastoid and mastoid processes were broken. The left side and nasals had been removed from one skull, with blow depressions around borders. The zygomatic arch on the right side was battered, and the malar was removed. The palatines were broken out by blows to the area. In one maxilla a series of cut lines appeared on the palatine posterior to the $M^3$, which was probably the result of removing the three small soft-palate muscles. Maxillae were broken out of the skull by pounding at and above the facial crest and infraorbital foramen.

Mandibles, atlas, and lumbar vertebrae were treated similarly to those of bison, No other cervicals or thoracics were recovered. The medial and lateral tuberosities of one humerus were damaged; defleshing marks occurred along the diaphysis. The distal end of another humerus was fractured mid-diaphysis at the deltoid tuberosity and exhibited split line interference. Radio-ulnae were treated similarly to those of bison.

Sacra and pelves were also treated similarly to those of bison. Pelvic treatment generally resulted in an acetabular triangle. Variations included the removal of the ilium and ischium, the pubis being left intact, or the removal of the ilium and pubis, and partial removal of the ischium. The trochanter major and minor of the proximal end of a femur were pounded out, with blow depressions in the damaged areas. Only the distal ends of tibiae were recovered. Defleshing or periosteal removal cut lines appeared along the lower diaphyses, and the fracture edges exhibited split line interference. Slight damage occurred to the tuber calcis of the calcaneum.

A schematic drawing (fig. 10.20) depicts the various areas of the horse skeleton that received damage. The numbering is in the order the actions are discussed and not necessarily the order in which they occurred. No skinning marks were found on appropriate bones.

Severing the head and removing the large-muscle masses involved several steps. Along with the mastoid and paramastoid processes the nuchal crest and occipital were battered to release attachments for the dorsal neck muscle and ligamentum nuchae (fig. 10.20, action 1). Pounding the mandibular ascending ramus and angle detached one of the masseter (fig. 10.20, action 2). Neck muscles and the ligament could then have been stripped back, battering the atlas and other cervical vertebrae. The dorsal arch was pounded out of the atlas, and the spinal cord was severed (fig. 10.20, action 3).

A quick blow or battering of the zygomatic arch, breaking the coronoid process, released attachments of the large skull muscles (fig. 10.20, action 4). A blow to the area of the mandibular mental foramen of the symphyseal area freed the main body of the mandible (fig. 10.20, action 5) and allowed for cutting back of the mylohyoideus muscle in preparation for tongue extraction (fig. 10.20, action 6). The palatines and then the maxillae and nasals were pounded and detached from the skull, which exposed the tongue base and the muscles of the soft palate (fig. 10.20, action 7). Further battering to frontal and temporal regions broke open the cranium for brain removal (fig. 10.20, action 8).

Pectoral and pelvic girdles formed butchering units separate from the thoracic and lumbar regions. Once released from the trunk, scapular muscle bundles were stripped, and muscle attachments on the proximal end of the humerus were pounded free (fig. 10.20, action 9). The humerus was probably severed from the scapula, and meat filleting continued (fig. 10.20, action 10). Blows to the olecranon (fig. 10.20, action 11) released muscle attachments for both upper- and lower-arm bundles.

In the disarticulation of the pelvic girdle from the trunk the sacrum was removed, which freed several back and hind-leg muscles (fig. 10.20, action 12). Battering and pounding of the pelvic areas released several large leg muscles (fig. 10.20, action 13) and the hind-leg unit. A blow to the tuber calcis (fig. 10.20, action 14) detached the planter group of superficial muscles and large lateral muscles. These bundles could then be stripped up the tibia and femur. Battering the femoral trochanters would detach the ends of deeper muscles (fig. 10.20, action 15). The tibia-femur unit was probably disjointed after removal of su-

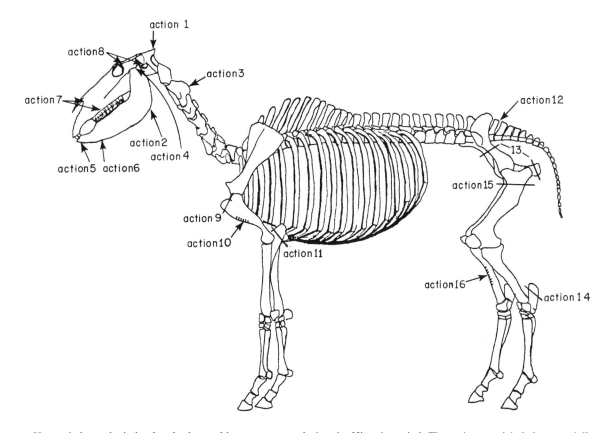

Fig. 10.20. Horse skeleton depicting butchering and bone treatment during the Historic period. The actions are labeled sequentially as discussed and not necessarily as performed in the actual operation.

perficial muscles. Deeper muscles could then be filleted from the tibia (fig. 10.20, action 16).

The damage on elements of both horse species in the Clovis-age material appeared consistent with that seen in modern horse remains. Similar butchering units were probably employed.

The occipital-basioccipital area of one skull exhibited a battered nuchal crest and paramastoids. Battering would release attachments for the brachiocephalicus muscle and ligamentum nuchae as well as provide access to the brain. The maxillae were pounded around the facial crest, which detached them from the skull and exposed the marrow cavity.

The entire blade and tuber scapulae of the scapulae were removed through pounding and chopping action. Several scapular and arm muscles were loosened by this procedure. Defleshing or periosteal removal cut lines appear on the posterior distal diaphysis of a humerus. Three sets of defleshing cut lines occur along the diaphysis of an intact radius. Postbutchering carnivore damage occurred at the proximal end. The distal end of a metapodial exhibited a helical fracture. A first phalange exhibited a series of skinning or tendon-removal cut lines in a chevron pattern along the anterior diaphysis.

The evidence suggests a butchering process similar to that used on bison during the Paleoindian period and that seen with modern horse. A greater emphasis was placed on marrow processing. This emphasis is concordant with the pattern for modern horse but contrasts with that seen in extinct bison. The reduction pattern associated with bone-grease production prevalent during later periods is not noticeable with extinct horse remains or with those of any other game animals from the Paleoindian period.

## Mammoth

The anatomy of modern elephant species is incompletely known. Musculature arrangement and explanations of bone damage were based on Miall and Greenwood (1877) and Sikes (1971). The major bones recovered showed evidence of the butchering process, but, particularly for the limb bones of the two youths, carnivore modification also occurred (fig. 10.21). Carnivore action focused on the ends of long bones, which left primarily diaphyseal cylinders of these young mammoth limb elements.

From experimental experience the same seven to eight major butchering units as those in ungulates were practical. A schematic drawing of an elephant skeleton (fig. 10.22) indicates areas affected in the butchering process recorded in the recovered elements. The order indicated does not imply the order in which the butchering proceeded.

Although the adult skull lay in approximate anatomical order, skull pieces were lying on the gravel bar, indicating that destruction occurred before burial. The condition of the tusks indicates weathering for some time before burial. Some to all skull degradation may have occurred through this natural process. The skull may also have been smashed to pieces.

Destruction on such a large element would have had to be carried out with heavy-duty pounding stones. The small quartzite pebble found in the skull-and-tusk cluster could not have broken the massive bone. Breaking into the skull would serve several purposes, such as freeing muscle attachments, removing the tongue, exposing the maxillary marrow cavity, extracting the brain, and severing the trunk.

Zygomatic arches missing from the cluster were found elsewhere in the station. The lambdoidal crest and frontal area received the major concentration of damage. These areas are regions of major-muscle attachments as well as entryways to the brain and marrow cavities. In addition, the coronoid process and mandibular condyle lie underneath the zygoma. The condyle articulates with the mandibular fossa of the skull. Breakage of the zygomatic arch (fig. 10.22, action 1) released facial-muscle ends, both those attached to the zygoma (masseter) and those on the ascending ramus (temporalis), and freed the mandibles from the skull.

The frontal area supports the base of both trunk musculature and the tusks. Various longitudinal, transverse, and radiating muscles compose the trunk, with major muscles arising from the frontals and premaxillae. Battering in this region (fig. 10.2, action 2) severed the trunk, released the tusks, and exposed maxillary marrow cavities. The lambdoidal crest is a prominent, rounded area of the back skull for attachment of large muscles that raise the front of the head and tusks. Battering (fig. 10.22, action 3) in this area freed various muscle ends and allowed access to the brain cavity.

Skulls of the youths were treated in a similar manner. Maxillae were broken apart with pounded edges, and tusks were removed from the premaxillae through pounding action (fig. 10.22, action 4). Mandibles were broken at the symphyseal area (fig. 10.2, action 5), and the ascending ramus was pounded out, the lateral border was removed, and the tooth cavity was exposed (fig. 10.22, action 6). The

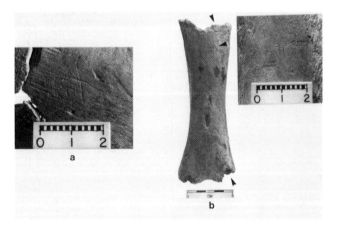

Fig. 10.21. Young mammoth elements from the Clovis-age processing station (FA2-1) exhibiting modifications. a: closeup of skinning cut lines on exterior of ramus (TTU-A17540) from human activity; b: femoral shaft exhibiting complex life history; closeup of cut lines by human activity during meat-retrieval operations; arrows at either end point to carnivore chewing damage (photographs by Nicky L. Olson).

angle and the horizontal ramus are areas of muscle attachment for both facial (platysma and buccinator) and neck (sternomaxillaris) muscles. Mandibular battering would free them from the skull, allow tongue access, sever assorted muscle ends, and expose the mandibular marrow cavity. Skinning evidence is limited to a series of cut lines (fig. 10.21a) on the dorsolateral margin below the premolar alveolar (fig. 10.22, action 7).

The cranial and vertebral (anterior and posterior) borders of a scapula had been pounded out (fig. 10.22, action 8). Blow depressions were apparent along the edges. Various scapular and upper-arm muscles (subscapularis, teres complex, deltoideus, and triceps) originate along the blade and various prominences. Several of these muscles insert on humeral tuberosities. The glenoid cavity of the scapula was probably removed during shoulder disjointing. Elephant fasciae are not readily torn by slipping a hand between muscle bundles, as is possible with ungulates, and bone expediency muscle separators may not have sufficed for the task when a mammoth was butchered. A sharp-edged tool used in a cutting fashion was necessary.

The medial epicondyle of the adult humerus was battered (fig. 10.22, action 9), and a small amount of battering on the proximal section of the supracondyloid crest occurred (fig. 10.22, action 10). Defleshing or periosteal removal cut lines appear on the diaphysis (fig. 10.22, action 11). These occurrences are the result of severing muscle attachments, such as part of the brachialis complex, the pronator radii teres, and the flexor carpi radialis, or of defleshing or bone fracturing.

The olecranon of the ulna bears a blow depression (fig. 10.22, action 12). The olecranon is a major area of muscle attachment for the insertion of both shoulder and upper-arm bundles (triceps, dorsoepitrochlearis) and origination of a lower-arm mass (flexor carpi ulnaris).

Adult ribs were broken into sections, and proximal ends and rib heads were battered (fig. 10.22, action 13). Tips of thoracic spines were removed or battered, or the spine was separated from the centrum (fig. 10.22, action 14). Several large-muscle masses attach along the processes and spines of these vertebrae, including the trapezius, the rhomboideus major, and the serratus posticus. Long strips of sinew can also be taken along the column in this area.

Tips of sacral spines were removed through battering (fig. 10.22, action 15), which released part of the longissimus dorsi complex and freed the ligamentum nuchae in the lower-back region. Of numerous muscles attaching along the pelvic girdle, major ones include the iliacus, the glutaeus complex, the biceps femoris, and the adductor complex. Branches of acetabular triangles were removed through pounding (fig. 10.22, action 16), and blow depressions were evident along the broken edges. These actions loosened muscle attachments and allowed for their stripping.

The base of the femoral head (adult) was battered along the circumference, with several blow depressions evident. Both the poas magnus and the iliacus insert in this area. Freeing these muscles permitted severing of several encapsulating ligaments that bind the head to the acetabulum and action performed during disjointing the hind leg from the pelvis (fig. 10.22, action 17). A proximal femoral di-

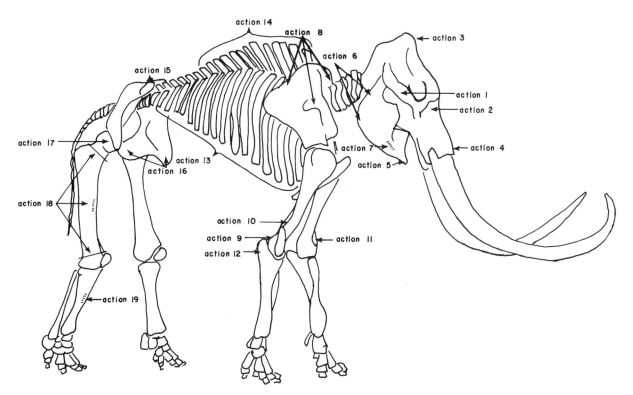

Fig. 10.22. Mammoth skeleton depicting butchering and bone treatment during the Clovis period. The actions are labeled sequentially as discussed and not necessarily as performed in the actual operation.

aphyseal section exhibited battering and crushing. At least one muscle (sartorius) originates in this area, and another (glutaeus maximum) inserts mid-diaphysis.

Defleshing cut lines (fig. 10.21b) occurred on the anteroproximal side (fig. 10.22, action 18) of a femur. A tibial diaphyseal section exhibited defleshing (or periosteal removal) cut lines (fig. 10.22, action 19) made during removal of the popliteus. Pry marks occurred on the astragalar articulating facets of a calcaneum (fig. 10.22, action 20). Isolated metapodials and phalanges further indicate that leg units were disarticulated. Several large-muscle bundles run the length of the foot from hock to phalanges. These bundles include various flexor and abductor muscles, lumbricales, and interossei. A similar bundle set occurs in the forefoot. These muscle bundles end in long, strong tendons. Complete foot disarticulation points to intensive meat retrieval and tendon stripping.

## BONE TECHNOLOGY

The Lubbock Lake faunal remains were examined closely to determine the role of bone as a material resource and the frequency of tool use and production. The controversy surrounding man-induced bone modifications and arguments presented by the critics were reviewed by Johnson (1985). The fracture-based utilitarian traditions of bone quarrying and bone expediency tools are minimally modified implement categories (Johnson, 1985). Bone quarrying involved the use of proboscidean carcasses as a resource supply for cores and blanks for tool production. Bone expediency tools were based on the employment of ungulate postcranial bone.

Isolating the categories of man-induced modifications and identifying specimens within those categories were based on (1) key characters that indicated dynamic loading of fresh bone (e.g., helical fracture, impact point, and hackle marks), in contrast to carnivore action characters, and (2) characters that point to subsequent use. Use wear constitutes localized and restricted postfracturing bone removal along the fractured edge. Use-wear characters were compared with the kinds and location of damage produced by carnivores, and specimens designated as tools generally lack carnivore damage (Johnson, 1985).

The production of fracture-based utilitarian tools was a major technological thrust at Lubbock Lake. The concept of expediency governed the technological pattern whereby tools were made quickly and efficiently regardless of their performance or material. Both the concept and the technological procedures were applicable to bone and lithic resources that resulted in a transfer technology (cf. Bonnichsen and Young, 1980; Bonnichsen, 1982). The interplay of transfer technology and expediency created a flexible repertoire in production of tools of a wide variety of sizes, shapes, and functions.

Bone quarrying, which involved the reduction of proboscidean long bones, was another technological behavior pattern. Two trajectories were available in the reduction process (Johnson, 1985). Blanks were the beginning point

of a highly formalized trajectory that ended with a highly modified and stylized product (cf. Lahren and Bonnichsen, 1974; Haynes and Hemmings, 1968). Cores appeared to be governed by the expediency concept with unmodified flakes as the product (cf. Stanford et al., 1981; Bonnichsen, 1979; Miller, 1984; Hannus, 1984a, b; Carlson et al., 1984).

### Bone Expediency Tools

The expediency concept reflects local manufacture and use of the tools exclusively for a specialized economic task. These tools were made in the activity area during butchering from bones of animals being processed, were used in the processing, and then were discarded in the activity area with the rest of the faunal debris. With such an immediate abundant resource only the knowledge of how to produce these tools need be brought to a locality. The associated manufacturing debris and bone-reduction areas in the Lubbock Lake kills support this interpretation (e.g., fig. 10.5).

The same task could be performed with tools made from different elements. The differences in assemblages involved the frequencies of occurrence of elements selected for tool use. Metapodials, particularly metatarsals, had a high use frequency at Lubbock Lake, whereas at Bonfire (Johnson, 1982) and Casper (Frison, 1974) their use was minimal. Although scapulae were used as butchering tools at Lubbock Lake, they were not used as such at the latter localities.

A basic technological construct concerns the creation of the fractured edge. In the production of bone expediency tools the high-velocity impact technique was applied to both long and flat bones, which produced two types of fracture morphology. This technique, when applied to fresh long bones, produces a spiral morphology. The morphology is helical in nature and is the shape of a curve through a series of planes as it circles around the diaphysis. The compact bone is exposed through a helical fracture. When the high-velocity-impact technique is applied to fresh, flat bones (e.g., ribs, scapulae, and pelves) a right-angle morphology results. This morphology has a cleavage plane and configuration that are perpendicular to the external cortical bone surface. The compact bone is exposed through a right-angle fracture. Because of the tubular nature of certain sections of flat bones, both fracture patterns can be produced during the process (Johnson, 1985).

As a second technological construct, two general classificatory categories of manufacturing technique were created. Function could be the same within each category. These morpho-units are manufactured and utilized. A manufactured expediency tool is an item intentionally shaped before use. The presence of redundant, serially overlapping flake scars, generally away from the working edge, is the main criterion. A utilized item is an implement that was unmodified before use and takes advantage of the fractured edge. The lack of modification before use is the main entry criterion for this category. Each morpho-unit exhibits one or more wear characters, such as microflaking, differential polishing, or rounding of surfaces.

These constructs were applied to the Folsom and Plainview assemblages. Of the 30 tools classified, 11 (37%) were manufactured tools. This situation indicates a high selectivity for a tool edge, requiring minimum preparation time before use.

A resultant major question centered around the function of a helical fracture. Controlled breakage can be an aspect of either marrow processing or tool manufacture. With long bones either event is likely. At times both events may have been equally important, and long bones may have been selected for use because of their durability and high marrow content. Some data indicate a difference in treatment of elements slated for marrow processing versus tool use in terms of number and placement of blows and number and size of diaphyseal radial segments created. Such treatment difference implies a manufacturing template.

At Lubbock Lake the disposal pattern of bone expediency tools followed that of bone disposal at the activity area. In Paleoindian locales tools were generally found with bone piles. During the Ceramic through Historic periods they were scattered throughout the processing stations. Many tools were broken or cracked from heavy use, and some were recovered in cojoining pieces. Isolated sections of broken tools were also found, a situation common in processing stations.

The area of impact and rebound can often be determined from surface features (intersecting fracture fronts and hackle marks) and blow depressions or from reassembly of the tool and its debris. Generally blows were to the side diaphysis; infrequently impact was on the posterior diaphysis. Blow placement was an important aspect, for it influenced the ease with which the bone was opened. Other influencing factors were speed, strength, and angle of blow; the presence or absence of periosteum; and use of a single- or double-anvil mode (Johnson, 1985).

Retouch and utilization flaking occurred on tools (Johnson, 1985:213–14). Retouch is purposeful flaking for modification before use or for rejuvenation of an angle (Johnson, 1985, fig. 5.15C). Utilization flaking is unintentional posttechnological flaking that occurred along the working edge during use (Johnson, 1985, figs. 5.15B, 5.16A, 5.27C). A wedge flake is a technological feature, a large exterior pressure flake removed on the cortical side opposite to the point of impact. It represents an unintentional flaking event that occurred during bone breakage and is associated with bending failure when the bone flexes (Johnson, 1985:197, figs. 5.6C, 5.16A). Modification by both man and natural agency can produce wedge flaking.

Wear polish frequently occurs along the working edges and adjacent ventral and dorsal sides. The location, amount, and degree of wear polish appears to be correlated with the amount of tool use and the type of use. Rounding of the working edge and smoothing of rough areas such as inner-cancellous bone structure are other wear results. Johnson (1985:214–17) discussed and categorized the various types of recognized use wear.

A functional construct based on wear patterns, morphology, technique, and use experimentation includes four proposed categories. Category A contains tools with pointed tips (which vary from squared to narrow circular; Johnson,

1985, fig. 5.5). The major wear character is microflaking along the working edge. These tools appear to represent choppers. Category B contains tools with broad circular working edges. The major wear characters are worn inner-cancellous structure, rounded working edge, and absence of microflaking. From the wear pattern these tools may have been used in separating (stripping and defleshing) muscle bundles and are thus called muscle separators.

Category C contains tools with scalloped margins created by right-angle breakage. The major wear characters are rounding and polishing of the working edge; microflaking occasionally occurs. Scapulae are the only elements exhibiting this combination, and they may have been used as knives. Category D contains tools with blunted tips produced through right-angle breakage. The major wear character is a rounded, pitted, and eroded working surface; microflaking occasionally occurs. Ribs are the only elements in this category, and they may be scrapers.

At Lubbock Lake no particular element was selected preferentially for expediency tools in the processing stations. In Paleoindian kill/butchering locales tools produced from metatarsals dominated. More than 100 bone expediency tools were recovered from various features at the site from 1973 to 1979. Seventy were from Ceramic through Historic processing stations, and 37 were from Paleoindian activity areas.

The bone expediency tool kits for Paleoindian, Protohistoric, and aboriginal Historic occupations were distinctive and reflect differences in activity-area orientation. The Paleoindian kit was a varied one, consisting of tools from all four functional categories. Although Category A predominated (42%), proposed choppers did not form as high a percentage in the Paleoindian assemblage as in the other two periods (ca. 66%).

The Paleoindian assemblage was predominantly composed of meat-processing tools. Proposed choppers, muscle separators, and scapula knives accounted for 86% of the assemblage, while rib tools totaled 14%. Skeletal disarticulation and complete meat processing took place in the locales. Where meat processing was incomplete, the articulated units were left intact, which indicates that secondary butchering or marrow processing did not take place elsewhere.

No tools for meat processing other than choppers were seen in the processing-station assemblages. In addition, differences occur in element distribution, bone disposal, and breakage pattern. These variances between the two types of activity areas support the claim for secondary processing as the major goal of the stations.

Proposed choppers (Category A) accounted for two-thirds of the bone expediency tools from Protohistoric (64%) and aboriginal Historic (67%) assemblages. These assemblages were less varied in their composition than was the Paleoindian assemblage. The rest of the Protohistoric assemblage was made up of rib tools (Category D). If these tools were scraping implements, they may indicate a hide-working process.

The aboriginal Historic assemblage was similar to the Protohistoric assemblage. Although the proposed choppers were performing the same tasks (e.g., disjointing and muscle detachment) as those of the Paleoindian period, they were doing so in a different context. Initial butchering units were brought to the station for secondary butchering (disjointing and final stripping of muscles).

Choppers may also have been used in secondary processing of bones. Although not suitable for breaking open prime marrow bones, bone choppers were appropriate for processing ribs and vertebrae for bone-grease production (Bonnichsen, 1973; Frison, 1974). Furthermore, once bones were broken and the marrow was collected, choppers may have functioned in further breakage of these sections for bone-grease production.

Variation existed within the proposed chopping assemblage (Category A) of the tool kit of each period. Metatarsals dominated the Paleoindian kit, and metapodials accounted for 57% of the proposed choppers. Three other kinds of elements were used, and of these, tibiae are the most common. This situation is in direct contrast to the Casper assemblage, where tibia choppers dominate, and the use of metapodials for tools is minimal (Frison, 1974).

A wider variety of elements was used for proposed choppers in the Protohistoric and aboriginal Historic processing stations. Seven different elements appeared in Protohistoric, and six in aboriginal Historic proposed chopper assemblages. No particular element dominated, and metapodial use was limited. Metacarpals used in the Protohistoric station accounted for 22% of the proposed chopper assemblage. Metatarsal use during the aboriginal Historic period was restricted to 15% of the proposed chopper assemblage.

The frequency of broken tool sections appeared to increase through time, perhaps reflecting that more heavy-duty processing occurred in stations than in locales. Broken sections in Paleoindian locales accounted for 17% of the total recognized items that indicated tool use. The frequency in the Protohistoric processing station was 26% and increased to 63% in the aboriginal Historic. Some tools from all periods exhibited cracked and broken edges and shafts, with occasional continued use of a broken edge. This situation reflects intensive use of particular tools and momentary conservation. Even though bone expediency tools were left with the faunal debris and a skeleton provided ample resource for tool production, it may have been more efficient (less time-consuming) to reuse a broken tool until it was exhausted and then create a new one.

The manufacturing debris from several tools was found in Lubbock Lake Paleoindian locales. The debris permitted reconstruction of some details of the manufacturing process and the creation of articulation nets. This matching procedure defined the boundaries of activity areas and related subareas to one another.

Several articulation nets were created in FA6-8 (fig. 10.5) for tool/debitage and anatomical relationship sets. Both compressed and widespread nets existed. Bone expediency tools were made and used in the same pile or were made elsewhere in the activity area and brought to a pile. Three bone-reduction areas occurred at a distance from their original butchering units. A tool made from one of the reductions was used elsewhere in the activity area. Another net reaches across an empty space (possibly a hide-working area) to bind a tool/debitage net to the main group. These nets created a picture of motion that served to relate the work areas into a single unit.

## Bone Quarrying

Another bone procedure, the quarrying of mammoth bone, was confined to the late Pleistocene. Quarry preparation produced a core from which additional flakes could be struck and used in camp or a blank from which flaking or other technological procedures produced the desired object or objects. The Lubbock Lake quarrying assemblage is interpreted as that of blank production leading eventually to such formalized tools as bone foreshafts (Lahren and Bonnichsen 1974:148) and bone wrenches (Haynes and Hemmings, 1968).

Strength, proper leverage, and suitable anvil(s) and hammerstone were required to open fresh mammoth bones in a controlled manner. The bone-quarrying debris was situated around large caliche boulders. A double-anvil mode was used in breaking open the humerus (Johnson, 1985:207–10, fig. 5.22). The break spiraled at the narrowest part of the diaphysis above the supracondyloid ridge. The preserved point of impact is on the posterior mid-diaphysis with a wedge flake situated on the anterior mid-diaphysis just above the supracondyloid ridge (fig. 10.4).

The humeral diaphyseal section (TTU-A5198) had convex helical fractures at both ends. Four different fracture fronts interacted to form the piece. The initial impact blow depression and the characteristic underlying chevron from radiating fracture fronts occurred on one side. The initial left fracture front (front 1) spiraled quickly and intersected another front (front 2) about 15 cm from the point of impact. The initial right fracture front (front 3) spiraled and both dissipated into the interior of the piece and merged with another front (front 4) that formed part of the opposite diaphyseal edge. Front 4 intersected front 2 about midway, front 2 forming the other part of the opposite diaphyseal edge.

The posterior side of a femoral diaphyseal section (TTU-A16605) exhibited a large blow depression on the distal posteromedial side below the helical fracture surface (the proximal end was badly eroded).

A third diaphyseal segment (TTU-A3006) exhibited helical fracture surfaces on both side margins. Both ends had blunted edges, one broken after the fracturing event. The other edge was purposefully blunted, and numerous hinge fractures and flake scars occurred along the surface.

Several flakes had been removed from one tibial diaphyseal section (TTU-A17666), including four adjacent hinge fractures in a perpendicular line across the diaphysis.

In the Clovis period bone quarrying and expediency tools represented two contemporaneous technological traditions based on an abundant skeletal resource of large game animals. These traditions represented different aspects of bone technology. Although expediency tools and the bones from which they were made were portable, they were made, used, and discarded in the same locale. Production is dependent on a carcass but is not tied to a particular species. Although tools from bison elements predominated, elements from other ungulates were also used. Element reduction was carried out for tool production; flakes were a secondary, waste product.

Quarrying operations and the production of large diaphyseal segments and cores were limited to proboscideans. The techniques were designed for problems in dealing with such a massive resource. The large-scale operation required at least two people to move and position a limb bone. The items being produced were in an initial stage, and the final product was finished elsewhere. Bone quarrying becomes defunct at the close of the Pleistocene with the extinction of proboscideans and the reduction of choices in a transforming ecosystem. Bone expediency tools (a versatile concept with a broader strategy base) appear to become the major technological utilitarian tradition in the early Holocene.

## PROCUREMENT SYSTEMS

Plant resources contributed most of the food supply of ethnographically known hunting and gathering groups. While plant materials undoubtedly played a large role in Paleoindian economy, little is known about their procurement. On the basis of microwear polishes Bamforth (1985) interpreted part of the Firstview lithic assemblage as a plant-harvesting and processing tool kit. Whether the plants had dietary or other economic uses is speculative. Widespread evidence exists for animal-procurement systems at this time.

### Mammoth

Some type of band organization composed of nuclear or extended families is generally accepted as the working model for Paleoindian social structure (Hemmings, 1970; Wheat, 1971; Gorman, 1972; Wilmsen, 1974). Large herd animals, such as mammoth and bison, were considered migratory animals that were available during only part of the year. However, under favorable to optimal conditions little long-distance migration probably took place. With mild to frost-free winters and extensive grasslands on the Southern Plains and in the Southwest, herd animals would not have had to move far for maintenance.

Little is known of the seasonal behavior of other game animals. The short-faced bear may have hibernated, but hibernation was a mechanism to survive winters. Given mild winters during Clovis times, hibernation may not have been necessary. If some or all of the game animals were available year round, hunting patterns may have been geared to aspects of seasonality other than availability. Other seasonality factors could include the prime condition of a herd and the period of greatest manageability.

Modern African elephants live in a matriarchal society consisting of kinship groups composed of family units. These units in turn consist of adult females, immature females and males, and satellite young mature males. Family units range from 4 to 22 members but average 10 to 12 cows and calves. The simplest family unit consists of 3 members, an adult female and 2 immature offspring. A simple matriarchal group is a minimum of 4 individuals, a mother, a mature daughter, and 2 immature offspring (Douglas-Hamilton and Douglas-Hamilton, 1975; Laws et al., 1975).

Strong family bonds ensure protection for individuals. The family unit or the entire kinship group gathers to defend an elephant in trouble. This protection extends to the young satellite bulls. Occasionally cows may defend mature bulls or bulls may defend other bulls, but they are usually on their own.

Intense care and protection are afforded calves by the family unit or kinship group. In times of danger calves are herded into the middle of the group and surrounded by adults. Calves are kept close to their mothers throughout daily activities. Babies of a year or more often shelter between the mother's legs. When an animal collapses, numerous attempts are made to raise it, and the family gathers around for protection. Calves and adolescents do not wander far from the herd, and the slightest squeal or bellow instantly brings the herd to their defense.

Modern ranges are small (their restricted size may be due to human pressures), and current home ranges are about 52 km² (20 square miles) (Douglas-Hamilton and Douglas-Hamilton, 1975; Laws et al., 1975). The home ranges of family units overlap extensively. The family unit covers most of its range every month, traversing several habitats. There are no territorial boundaries or displays defining a group's range, and elephants move through it freely and feed with other herds of elephants.

Mammoth sites have been categorized on the basis of the nature of tools recovered and bone disposition (Judge, 1974; MacDowell, 1979). Kills have been classed as successful, with projectile points in vital areas and tools recovered from a disarticulated skeleton, or unsuccessful, with the recovery of one or a few points in nonvital to vital areas in an articulated skeleton. The Domebo mammoth (Leonhardy, 1966) typified the former category, and Naco (Haury, 1953) and Escapule (Hemmings and Haynes, 1969) the latter. A third category was mammoth-carcass scavenging characterized by the absence of points (unless they were used as knives) and lack of hunting evidence (MacDowell, 1979:27).

The traditional view of mammoth hunting involves a small number of Clovis hunters ambushing or surrounding an isolated mammoth at a watering area (Wheat, 1971:24) If mammoth and modern African elephant behavioral patterns are similar, then isolated individuals were an infrequent occurrence. Cows and calves were in family units or kinship groups. An attack on one would bring instant reprisal. If most of the mammoths recovered at Clovis sites were bulls, then it could be hypothesized that isolated individuals occurred more frequently than they do today and that a systematic procurement pattern centered on hunting the isolated animals.

Several single, individual localities were excavated, and some animals were sexed. Naco (Lance, 1953) and Escapule (Hemmings and Haynes, 1969) kills are bulls. The kill at

Domebo was probably a female (Mehl, 1966). The Cooperton mammoth was a young bull of 17 to 18 years (Mehl, 1975). The bull was young enough to be either part of a family unit or a satellite (Laws et al., 1975:153) and had been protected and defended by the unit, as had the Domebo female. Isolating an animal from the protecting herd was a problem. Hunters could not approach a cow or young bull and attack it without being trampled by the entire herd.

Clovis hunters may have tried to wound a mammoth on the periphery of the group and then retreat to a safe distance as the herd gathered for defense and wait for the mammoth to die. If wounds were fatal, the herd would eventually leave the carcass, and it could be claimed by the hunters. This passive hunting scene was based on safety and patience to accomplish the goal.

If indeed Clovis hunters had to wait to claim a carcass, little difference would exist between it and the carcass of an animal that had died of natural causes within a few hours to a day of being found. Meat and by-products would still be usable. Scavenging a recently dead carcass would accomplish the same goal as hunting and with much less danger.

A pattern is beginning to emerge of large-scale kills of family units at various multiple individual localities. Saunders (1977, 1980) demonstrated that the 13 mammoths killed at both Lehner and Dent were female-calf groups exhibiting the age, sex, and size structure of a family unit. Two bone stacks of three mammoths each at Colby (Frison, 1976, 1977, 1978) indicated either a one-time kill or two smaller kills. The question arises how Clovis hunters could quickly, efficiently, and safely dispatch an entire family unit, particularly the larger ones.

With African elephants the matriarch is the key. During an alert the unit gathers around her. If she is alarmed, she either runs or defends. In either situation the rest of the family follows suit. If the matriarch is hurt, the unit gathers around in an attempt to revive and protect her (Laws et al., 1975:162).

The strategy of wounding an animal and retreating until it died would not work on a large scale. The rest of the mammoths would be alerted to danger, aggravated, and dangerous to approach. However, by first attacking the matriarch and potential leaders, a family unit could be dispatched. With a favorable wind Clovis hunters could stalk close to appropriate targets, make their thrusts, and remove themselves quickly. Immature animals would mill around the dead matriarch and could be taken in the confusion.

The immense task of hunting and slaughtering an entire family unit was undoubtedly a band-level activity. Such an activity would involve a well-coordinated group, advanced planning, and detailed attention to herd behavior. But the question of how Clovis hunters actually went about the kill is still unanswered.

The age structure of the Lubbock Lake mammoth is not appropriate for a family unit, indicating that the deaths were not a single catastrophic event, that remains of a second adult female are in the unexcavated deposits, or that the second adult female escaped. Initial taphonomic data, however, indicate a single-event deposit. If a second adult female was involved, the unit would reflect a simple matri-

archal group. If the deaths were accumulative, they could be scavenging events or could indicate that an isolation mechanism was involved in hunting that separated the young from the unit. One youth was young enough to be kept between its mother's legs, and both youths would have been sheltered between the females. An initial attack on a youth would have alerted the females of the unit and made them dangerous.

## Bison

The bison-procurement system—its hunting and butchering patterns—appears to have its origin in the Clovis period. The hunting patterns were of small-scale kills involving a small group of people and large-scale kills involving a large number of people. Clovis bison kills were small-scale kills. The coordinated group effort necessary for large-scale kills was confined to hunting mammoths. This effort probably formed the rudiments of the large-scale kill technique later applied to bison.

With the extinction of most large game animals at the close of the Pleistocene and concurrent increase in grasslands during the early Holocene, bison herds increased in the expanded niche. With reduced large-game choices, bison procurement became the major economic system during Folsom times and continued in existence into the Historic period. Sophisticated methods of jumps and traps were introduced by ca. 10,000 B.P. (Dibble and Lorrain, 1968; Wheat, 1972; Frison, 1974). Increased herd size, greater knowledge of herd management, and improved hunting techniques appear to have led to increased numbers of animals per kill through time. The lowest number of bison that indicates a large-scale kill is debatable. However, the large-scale kill appears first as a scaled-down version of the later scores-of-bison-killed event.

Social organization may have developed further with a changing economy. Scheduling, seasonality, and other mechanisms in the society continued to operate. The society remained a hunting one. The basic structure of a band society composed of nuclear or extended families of Folsom and later Paleoindian groups has been proposed several times (Dibble, 1970; Wheat, 1971, 1972; Wilmsen, 1974). Families joined forces to form task groups. Population or band size may have increased during Paleoindian times. An alternative to increased band size was cooperative hunting by two or more bands, which indicates a more complex social order and a higher degree of fusion.

On the Southern Plains points were reused as knives. The final disposition of a point was a result more often of butchering practice than of hunting technique. A point's placement in a carcass thus could not be used to indicate a kin-group claim, a kin-oriented hunt, or a death blow (cf. Wendorf and Hester, 1962; Gorman, 1972).

Seasonality and scheduling mechanisms appear to have been operative in the bison-procurement system. These mechanisms were reflected in the small- and large-scale kill sites and hunting patterns that were a part of the system. Large-scale kills appeared to reflect communal, band activity generally during either spring (Wheat, 1972; Sellards et al., 1947) or late fall (Frison, 1974, 1978; Agenbroad, 1978). These periods were also favored times for large-scale hunts by historic Plains Indians (Oliver, 1962). The communal kills generally involved a trap of some sort, a forced jump over a cliff or an arroyo, a drive up an arroyo, or possibly a corral or surround. Occasionally some carcasses (particularly those on the bottom of the pile) were not butchered (Sellards et al., 1947; Dibble and Lorain, 1968; Wheat, 1972).

Group scheduling decisions would be aimed at maximum efficiency and utilization of resources that composed a broad-based economy. Scheduling and seasonality practices were probably different during Clovis and post-Clovis times because of climatic and faunal (choice reduction) changes. By Folsom times the scaled-down version of large-scale bison kills was beginning to occur. Twenty-three animals each were recorded at Folsom (Wormington, 1957) and Lipscomb (Schultz, 1943), and a larger number from Bonfire Shelter (Dibble and Lorrain, 1968). The kill at Lake Theo (Harrison and Smith, 1975; Harrison and Killen, 1978) appears to be another smaller version of the large-scale kill. Such kills continued into post-Folsom times, exemplified by Jurgens (Wheat, 1979) with 35 bison.

During late Paleoindian times large-scale kill techniques were known throughout the plains. Undetermined large numbers of animals were killed in the combined Plainview levels at Bonfire Shelter (Dibble and Lorrain, 1968). Up to 100 bison were killed at each site in drives at Plainview (Sellards et al., 1947) and at Casper (Frison, 1974). At Olsen-Chubbuck (Wheat, 1972) an estimated 190 bison were driven across an arroyo. The numbers for Hudson-Meng (Agenbroad, 1978) and Jones-Miller (Stanford, 1974) were even larger. Communal hunts resulting in Hudson-Meng (Agenbroad, 1978), Casper (Frison, 1974), Jones-Miller (Stanford, 1974; Frison, 1978), Folsom (Frison, 1978), Olsen-Chubbuck (Wheat, 1972), and Plainview (Sellards et al., 1947) took place during late fall, winter, spring, and spring to early summer.

In contrast to communal large-scale kill sites, a number of localities represent activities of either family or task groups in which a few animals were killed. Most animals were killed around the edges of marshes or ponds as bison came to water. These task-group small-scale kill sites occur throughout the Southern High Plains into northern New Mexico, Colorado, and Oklahoma and extending to Arizona. The Rex Rodgers kill site (Speer, 1978) yielded a minimum of six bison. At least eight bison were slaughtered at Perry Ranch (Saunders and Penman, 1979). Linger (Hurst, 1943) and Zapata (Wormington, 1957) apparently were one-time kills of at least five animals each. Lindenmeier (Roberts, 1936; Wilmsen and Roberts, 1978) had a minimum of nine bison, which may or may not have been killed at one time. Murray Springs (Hemmings, 1970) contained the remains of six bison.

Two localities on the Southern High Plains reflected repeated small-scale kills over a period of time. The total number of bison killed around ponds at Blackwater Draw Locality No. 1 (Hester, 1972) during the Paleoindian period

is unknown, but up to six at a time seems to have been the pattern. The same pattern holds at Lubbock Lake. Numerous Lubbock Lake bison kill/butchering locales attest to intensive use of the site area during Paleoindian times by a residential unit or task group.

Seasonality information was lacking for most small-kill sites. Data at Lubbock Lake were tenuous. Only a few specimens could be aged, and the ages indicated early spring and fall kills. These time periods were the same as those of communal large-scale kills. Task-group small-scale kills might be expected in the off seasons, summer and winter. Rex Rodgers (Speer, 1978) and Murray Springs (Frison, 1978:149) were winter small-kill sites. Kills at Lubbock Lake may represent activities before and after communal hunts.

Similarities and differences existed in the patterns seen at communal large-scale and task-group small-scale kill sites on the Southern Plains. The butchering techniques used to process carcasses in both kill types were the main similarities. The striking differences were the bone-disposal patterns and the amount of secondary processing. At Lubbock Lake bones from individual carcasses were placed in discrete piles, with little random scattering of elements. Marrow extraction was minimal. Bone damage was a result of butchering technique, and most bone breakage was a by-product of tool manufacture.

At Plainview (Sellards et al., 1947) bones from dismembered carcasses were scattered randomly across the kill floor. The jumbled mass appeared as a thick bone bed in a restricted area and without distinct piling. Disarticulated limbs were broken to obtain marrow. Intense marrow processing took place at Bonfire Shelter (Dibble and Lorrain, 1968) and Olsen-Chubbuck (Wheat, 1972).

A form of bone piling occurred at both Olsen-Chubbuck (Wheat, 1972) and Bonfire Shelter (Dibble and Lorrain, 1968), although the nature of the piles was different from those at Lubbock lake. At Olsen-Chubbuck (Wheat, 1972) piles were concentrated areas consisting of similar butchering units and individual elements. At Bonfire Shelter (Dibble and Lorrain, 1968) a pile of scapulae was found.

Lithic tool kits appeared standardized to contain points and unifacially retouched percussion flake tools. Points were modified for use as knives (Wheat, 1976, 1977, 1979) in both small- and large-scale kills. Within the bone expediency tool assemblages some implements were common in large-scale kills (e.g., tibia choppers), and others (e.g., scapula knives) appeared only at small-scale kills (Lubbock Lake). The frequency of occurrence of bone expediency tools differed, as did the selection of elements used for tools.

## Horse and Camel

Individual horse and camel kills were probably family or task-group activities, in keeping with the general economic patterns at Lubbock Lake. Horses and camels were attacked along the Clovis-age stream when they came to water. Blackwater Draw Locality No. 1 (Hughes, 1984) and Lehner

(Haynes et al., 1975) recorded individual camel or horse kills recovered in similar circumstances along stream banks. Other sites in Wyoming (Frison et al., 1978) indicated individual camels accidentally trapped along with bison herds that were being driven into a contained area. The probable horse kill at Murray Springs (Hemmings 1970), along a stream, was interpreted as a task-group pursuit (Hemmings, 1970:186). The small horse was a fast runner, while the large horse was slower-moving. Two different hunting techniques may have been required to kill these animals.

A seemingly strictly task-group orientation of the horse-procurement system in the New World is in contrast to the patterns seen in Old World sites, where both small-scale (Berke, 1984, 1986) and large-scale (Vereshchagin, 1967; Stern, 1969) horse kills are known. Large-scale kills appear to have been more common. The drive and the jump were the hunting techniques used by Middle and Late Paleolithic horse hunters, with obvious parallels to techniques used in communal bison hunts in the New World.

Camels, horses, and bison are ungulate herd animals. Why camels and horses were not hunted on a large scale in the New World is unknown, although population density (related to niche competition) may have been a factor. During the Clovis period bison were hunted on a similar small scale. Ungulate hunting may have been a task-group specialty. Large herds of any one species may not have existed owing to the variety of grassland forms and concomitant competition (although an equal variety existed in the Old World).

## HABITAT UTILIZATION

The major ecological zones of the draw and site can be placed in two or three groups, each of which was exploited to varying degrees by human beings in their hunting activities. Zones fall into three groups during the Clovis period: watercourse, grasslands, and tree groves. During other periods the draw's environs were made up of the watercourse and grasslands. The grasslands zone was the principal habitat utilized by human beings. However, given the narrowness of the draw and the compressed zones, they undoubtedly traversed all available habitats in their daily activities and utilized them to some extent.

While the small animals of the riparian community may not have been a food resource, the area around streams and ponds was utilized by humans for campsites, kill/butchering locales, and processing stations. Two types of habitat utilization took place: hunting of animals that occurred in a particular habitat and use of physical space within a habitat for a cultural pursuit.

The bison-hunting pattern was a further possible difference in the utilization of these two habitats at Lubbock Lake by Paleoindians and Ceramic through Historic peoples. While both groups were hunting bison in the grasslands habitat and using the riparian habitat to process carcasses, the Paleoindians apparently did not go out into the open grasslands to hunt bison. Instead, they killed bison around ponds and marshes and butchered them there. Paleoindian economic pursuits were centered around the riparian habitat. The peoples of the Ceramic through Historic periods killed bison elsewhere (perhaps on the open grasslands) and brought units to processing stations for further processing. This pattern entails a more physical use of the grasslands habitat during the Ceramic through Historic periods than in the previous period.

During Clovis times a wide variety of animals served as food sources, most of which inhabited the grasslands. Mammoths, horses, camels, bison, coyotes, wolves, and jackrabbits were obtained from this habitat. Bear and turkey hunting could be considered evidence of utilization of wooded habitat. Muskrats, turtles, surface-feeding ducks, and geese represented aquatic resource utilization. The ratio of utilized grasslands to genera to wood to aquatic genera, 3.5:1:2.5, demonstrates both a restricted faunal exploitation of wooded areas and the broad-based economy of Clovis peoples.

The other periods presented a contrast between grasslands and aquatic habitats. While bison was the major game animal for various post-Clovis Paleoindian cultures at the site, various other grassland forms were occasionally hunted, including pronghorn antelope, deer, jackrabbits, cottontails, and grouse. The exploitation of the aquatic habitat included surface-feeding ducks, geese, and muskrats. The utilization ratio of grasslands to aquatic genera for the combined post-Clovis Paleoindian periods was 2:1.

Grassland exploitation continued into the Historic period, an expectable pattern given the dominant grasslands habitat in the draw. The exploitation of grasslands habitat included both large and small animals. The Ceramic period ratio of 4:0 increased during the aboriginal Historic to 5:0 with the addition of modern horse as a food resource. The intensity of utilization per genera, however, was not equal, and bison was the major exploited animal.

# 11. Summary

EILEEN JOHNSON AND VANCE T. HOLLIDAY

Lubbock Lake was discovered in 1936 during dredging operations in Yellowhouse Draw for a city reservoir. Four major archaeological projects have investigated the site, the most recent being the Lubbock Lake Project through The Museum, Texas Tech University (Lubbock). Data from these various excavations demonstrate that Lubbock Lake contains detailed and interdependent histories of the cultural and natural records of the past 11,000+ years.

Five major stratigraphic units and five soils provide the physical framework for the cultural and natural-history records. Stratum 1 represents a graded, meandering stream that terminated abruptly at ca. 11,000 B.P. Stratum 2 represents a series of ponds and an aggrading marsh from 11,000 to 8600 B.P. The impounding of stratum 2 waters may have been due to eolian sediments choking the more constricted reaches of the draw and locally damming the valley. The Firstview Soil represents a period of landscape stability from ca. 8600 to 6400 B.P. The depositional environments of upper stratum 2 and stratum 3 indicate a warming and drying tend. Strata 3 (6400 to 5500 B.P.) and 4 (5000 to 4500 B.P.) eolian sediments point to increased amounts of blowing dust and long-term reduction in the vegetation cover. These deposits represent two periods of relatively intense drought (Altithermal) separated by a brief return (5500 to 5000 B.P.) to moisture and stable land conditions (Yellowhouse Soil). Xeric conditions end ca. 4500 B.P., and the return to mesic conditions is denoted by the Lubbock Lake Soil. Stratum 5 signals another warming and drying trend with a cyclical drought pattern, beginning with deposition from about 1000 B.P. to the present.

The vertebrate and invertebrate faunas and flora reflect communities existing in the local environs at a particular time. These records represent living communities, not simply death assemblages, and reflect an evolving community responding to changing environmental conditions. A number of species are good climatic or environmental indicators, occur outside their modern ranges, or constitute fossil temporal or spatial records. The flora reflects primarily the riparian environ, and bullrush seeds are the most common floral macrofossil through time. Netleaf hackberry persists in the earlier and later parts of the record, with an increase in the variety of deciduous trees in stratum 5. A replacement pattern is evident for this evolving community as climatic trends wax and wane with decrease or increase in available moisture, annual temperature fluctuation, seasonal differentiation, and amount and distribution of grasses and trees or shrubbery.

This physical framework provides for a first approximation of a detailed regional cultural chronology. Five major cultural periods are recognized: Paleoindian (11,500–8500 B.P.); Archaic 8500–2000 B.P.); Ceramic (2000 B.P.– A.D. 1450); Protohistoric (1450–1650s); Historic (1650s–

1930s). The three earlier periods are subdivided.

The cultural record reflects the economic system in a variety of environmental settings through time. Various cultural activities centered around subsistence and the technology employed to carry out those pursuits. Both lithic and fracture-based utilitarian bone tools were used throughout the time span. At bison kill/butchering locales an inverse relationship of lithic to bone expediency tools existed, whereas in processing stations quantities of tools from these two media were about equal. Resharpening and reuse of projectile points as knives were prevalent during Paleoindian times and appear to have been part of a general conservancy of lithic tools. During the Paleoindian period there occurred a trend away from fine-grained cherts toward locally available quartzites and silicified caliche. This trend was reversed in the Archaic. Edwards Formation chert attains dominant use, along with a greater use frequency of obsidian, during the last 1,000 years.

The most common tool kits were those of expediency tools, both lithic and bone. In the kill/butchering locales emphasis was on lithic percussion flake tools and unmodified fracture-based utilitarian tools. Stylized tools formed a minor component. In processing stations and camps a greater emphasis was on stylized tools, although expediency tools remained a component of the processing-station tool kit. A wide variety of lithic material sources recovered in resharpening debris indicated a greater number of tools used in the pursuits than recovered. On a smaller scale the same pattern occurred with bone expediency tools, with the recovery of broken working edges.

The various data sets available permit the reconstruction of the late Quaternary environments, speculation on the nature of the climate and climatic changes, and study of cultural adaptation to the environment and those changes. In turn, these data can be used to establish a model of the late Quaternary history of the region. Wide-ranging cultural and environmental correlations are fraught with risks, but such correlations are probably more realistic for the Southern High Plains than many other areas owing to the flat topography, low modern environmental gradients, and uniform regional geology.

Throughout the past 11,000+ years the resources available to aboriginal occupants of the Lubbock Lake area were considerable. Water was always present, and because of the water plants and animals were always present. The relief along Yellowhouse Draw, considerable during the earlier stages of occupation, also provided the only natural shelter of any sort on the otherwise open High Plains surface. Abundant skeletal resources were available for tool and decorative production. Lithic materials were the only fundamental resource in short supply. A poor-quality silicified caliche was the only lithic resource in the immediate vicinity. Higher-quality materials were a minimum of 20 km away, and abundant supplies were considerably farther.

During the earliest aboriginal occupations at the site, in Clovis times, a competent stream flowed along the floor of the relatively deep valley. Wet-meadow sedge beds grew along the waterway and graded into a parkland. Stands of netleaf hackberry grew along the stream and valley floor. Tortoises, box turtles, and a variety of herd herbivores grazed the open prairie. Mild, frost-free winters and cool summers provided a more equitable climate of less temperature fluctuation and seasonality and more effective precipitation and available moisture.

The Clovis-age feature at Lubbock Lake was unlike Clovis features elsewhere in that it was not primarily a mammoth kill, but instead a wide variety of game animals were represented. Secondary butchering, marrow processing, and bone quarrying were the dominant activities along point bars of the stream. Bone expediency tools were made from ungulate and giant bear elements. Elements were disarticulated and disassociated from carcasses. The appendicular skeleton was underrepresented, and recovered limb elements were represented by ends. Elements of the axial skeleton were more common. Bone quarrying of mammoth limb elements produced blanks of diaphyseal radial segments and production and technological debris such as cone flakes. These blanks appear to have been slated for use in the production of highly modified formal tools dependent on thick cortical bone.

At about 11,000 B.P. a number of changes occurred in the area. Seasonality became more pronounced with a general warming and drying trend, probably representing a trend in a changing climate that began long before the Clovis-age occupation. Various large mammals became extinct, and other animals were extirpated. Water ceased to flow along the floor of the draw, and the valley slowly began to fill, first with diatomaceous sediments from freshwater ponds and then, starting about 10,000 B.P., with freshwater marsh sediments. A decrease in runoff probably contributed to this condition as well as creation of impoundments along the valley, possibly by wind scouring the surface of stream sediments and choking the more constricted reaches of the draw with eolian deposits. Eolian sediments began to aggrade in the draw by 9000 B.P., suggesting some destruction of the grasslands on the High Plains surface. Faunal extirpation continued as the warming and drying trend accelerated, changing the character of the pluvial-related fauna toward a more modern one by 8600 B.P.

During Folsom through Plainview times the valley setting was one of axial ponds within a savanna. Scattered hackberry and cottonwood grew along the marshy banks. Mild winters persisted with occasional periods of below-freezing conditions; summers were warming. By Firstview times the area was a scrub grasslands that was transitional from the mixed prairie of the preceding period and desert-plains grasslands of the following period. The axial wet-meadow-marshland was surrounded by open prairie. Although conditions were still mesic, they reflected a marked acceleration of the warming and drying trend. Yearly precipitation or effective moisture was decreasing. On the basis of inter-

preted grassland association, a probable shift occurred in the rainfall pattern away from spring-summer to summer-winter rains.

Task-group-oriented small-scale bison kills around the marshy edges of ponds (Folsom and Plainview) and marshes (Firstview) were the main subsistence activity. The focus was on meat procurement, and bison were supplemented by puddle ducks and muskrats. Marrow processing was minimal to nonexistent. The dietary protein from the bison meat appeared to be supplemented by fat from puddle ducks and muskrat meat (high-fat meat sources) and not bone marrow to provide a balanced diet and avoid a lean-meat–low-energy situation (cf. Speth, 1983; Speth and Spielman, 1983). Elements were disarticulated from carcasses but were generally kept associated with the carcass by carcass-specific bone piling. Meat stripping was extensive, and bone fracturing was oriented toward expediency tool production. This production was a subsidiary activity conducted to carry out processing of the bison carcasses.

Some controversy surrounds the reconstruction of the Folsom paleoecology of Lubbock Lake and the Southern High Plains. Hafsten (1961) and Oldfield and Schoenwetter (1964) proposed that a pine parkland existed in the area. Wendorf (1970:23, 32) proposed the Lubbock Subpluvial, a period of cool, moist conditions and a time of dense pine and spruce forestation. The Subpluvial dated from about 10,600 to 10,300 B.P. Some of these interpretations were based on pollen from Lubbock Lake (substratum 2A). Oldfield and Schoenwetter (1975) later modified their paleoecological reconstructions, but the interpretation remained that of a pine parkland. These interpretations were questioned on several grounds including reproduceability (Holliday et al., 1985b; Holliday, 1986). Considerably more geochronological data are now available at Lubbock Lake, as well as at other Southern High Plains sites. Pollen diagrams of Oldfield (1975) and Schoenwetter (1975) apparently do not reproduce one another or those from other sites, and more recent work failed to reproduce any of the previous records (Bryant and Schoenwetter, chap. 5). The significance of increases and decreases in pine pollen was questioned owing to the problems of long-distance transport of pine and differential preservation (Holliday et al., 1985b; Bryant and Holloway, 1983). Furthermore, morphological and chemical data from regional soils do not provide any indications that the area ever supported a coniferous forest or pine parkland. While the Folsom and Plainview faunal assemblages (10,800 to 10,000 B.P.; tables 6.1, 6.2, 7.1, 8.1) indicate relatively cool, moist conditions, strictly woodland-dependent forms are lacking. Moreover, the snail fauna, in particular, is indicative of a grasslands.

By Firstview times selection of certain meat cuts instead of total meat stripping was occurring. Semiarticulated units were still grouped in carcass-specific piles close to anatomical position. Long-bone elements were whole, and bone expediency tool production and use were minimal. The marsh was boglike with waterlogged spongy ground. Shallow surface water may have puddled in small areas. Muskrats were rare, small catfish were present, and waterfowl were available. Marsh-plant harvesting was occurring. Although the purpose of the harvesting is speculative, marsh plants are a ready source of carbohydrates. Because supplemental fat sources were dwindling, plant carbohydrates may have taken the place of fatty meat to provide the high-energy source needed in the diet.

Small-scale task-group-oriented bison hunting continued throughout the Archaic with a greater reliance on plants as a food source during the Middle Archaic. Warming and drying intensified during the Early Archaic occupations, with a decrease in available moisture and humidity level. Eolian sediment accumulation increased with eolian sediments draped across the valley margin and encroaching on the marsh. A gradual decrease in the vegetative cover was occurring. The bison kill/butchering locale was situated away from the boglike marsh (although nearby) toward the drier ground of a sandy eolian drape. The grasslands fauna was a modern one that could withstand xeric conditions. The invertebrates were a depauperate fauna of heat- and drought-tolerant species. A treeless dry prairie surrounded a restricted axial freshwater marsh.

Selectivity of meat cuts continued with carcass grouping and articulated to semiarticulated associated units. Bone fracturing was nonexistent, neither marrow processing nor bone expediency tool production or use being evident. Aquatic resources at best would be minimal and may have been nonexistent. Extensive marsh-plant resources were available, although direct evidence of their use as a food source was lacking. Their use may be inferred from the lack of fatty meat sources and selectivity of bison meat cuts. Without dietary fat carbohydrates would have been necessary to counterbalance the effects of a lean meat diet.

At about 6400 B.P. a geochemical and sedimentological change occurred along the valley floor and the freshwater marsh was replaced by an alkaline marsh. Xeric conditions were prevalent, and eolian sedimentation became more common. Between 6400 and 4500 B.P. several meters of eolian sediment filled the draw, indicating considerable destruction of the regional grasslands by drought. The depauperate microvertebrate and invertebrate faunas were xeric-adapted. Since water was still available in the draw, the area may have acted as a local refugium. During the first drought the brackish marsh was surrounded by a treeless prairie, probably a desert plains grasslands. During the respite interval a small freshwater stream flowed in the valley axis. An increase in precipitation reactivated spring discharge. The landscape was stable. Although conditions were not as harsh as during the drought intervals, the climate still was dry and warm. A scrub grasslands dominated the draw. The second drought interval was marked by a decrease in precipitation and renewed vegetation denuding. A restricted freshwater marsh was surrounded by another treeless prairie, again probably a desert plains grasslands.

During the Middle Archaic occupations climatic conditions were the harshest of any time in the late Quaternary. Despite the length and intensity of the two-drought Altithermal, the area was not abandoned by humans or game herd animals. Disarticulated remains indicated a return to muscle stripping and more thorough utilization of the meat resource than in the Early Archaic. Bone fracturing was

minimal, and bone expediency tools were lacking. Lithic percussion tools were rare in the locale. Range conditions were poor, the bison herd size was probably reduced, and marrow was not being processed. The oven indicated a systematic use of desert plant resources, which implied a greater reliance on dietary carbohydrates than previously. More meat may have been taken per animal because it would have been of poorer quality than previously owing to the harsh conditions. The meat may have been the supplement to counteract a diet that was carbohydrate-rich but lacked complete essential amino acids. Numerous camping events were recorded on the valley margin. Retouched tools were relatively common.

Data from other localities corroborate the interpretation of harsh environmental and climatic conditions during the Middle Archaic, as local manifestations of the Altithermal (Antevs, 1955). Similar cycles of middle Holocene droughts are known from various parts of the central United States, although the timing varies from region to region (Benedict, 1978, 1979; Dean et al., 1984; Gaylord, 1982; Winkler et al., 1986).

Beginning around 4500 B.P. climatic conditions ameliorated. Cooler, more mesic conditions prevailed with a return to a stable vegetative cover. Moisture availability increased significantly. A mixed-grasslands prairie surrounded the freshwater marsh. Modern climatic conditions and probably a modern rainfall pattern were established, and a modern fauna inhabited the area. This situation prevailed until about 1000 B.P. During the Late Archaic into the earlier Ceramic, small-scale bison hunting continued, and camping events were recorded. Little is known of these cultural periods during this time span because of the lack of deposition and possible admixture of materials.

During the past 1,000 years several climatic departures toward drought conditions occurred but apparently were not severe enough to affect adversely the faunal and floral communities. The presence of slopewash and eolian sediments along the valley floor indicates that vegetation along the valley margin and on the High Plains surface was reduced during episodes of drier and warmer climate. Nevertheless, the recurrence of netleaf hackberry and additional hardwoods indicates a greater availability of moisture and less arid conditions overall than during the mid-Holocene droughts. From about 1000 to 300 B.P. a spring-fed stream and wet meadow-marshland complex was surrounded by an open mixed-grasslands habitat. By 500 B.P. and extending into the twentieth century the draw environs was that of a mesquite savanna grading into an extensive freshwater marshlands and open-water complex.

From later Ceramic through aboriginal Historic times the subsistence focus was on secondary by-product retrieval in these processing stations. Small-scale, task-oriented hunting continued, but a broader meat subsistence base developed through the 1,000 years. Elements were disarticulated and disassociated from carcasses. Long bones were fractured and underrepresented, while axial elements were overrepresented. Marrow processing was minimal in the later Ceramic but increased through time, and grease production also intensified. A much more nearly complete to exhaustive use of bone nutritional resources indicates an orientation toward increasing dietary-fat production. Metates indicate plant processing, and both mesquite and marsh-plant resources were readily available. Both fat and carbohydrates appear to have had a role in balancing the diet.

Camping events are numerous, and prepared hearths may indicate extended stays. Mesquite was the common firewood during the Protohistoric and Historic, probably favored over the other hardwoods owing to its hot- and long-burning qualities. Food refuse indicates that a large variety of meat sources was hunted. Small-animal carcasses were brought back to camp, while only selected parts of large-animal carcasses were transported back. Marrow processing and grease production also occurred in camp. Lithic tool production occurred in camp, and stylized tools were more common. "Keeled scrapers" were frequent in both camps and processing stations, indicating hide preparation. Bone expediency tools were absent from the camps but were common in the processing stations. Most were proposed choppers, and the common lithic tools were choppers and scrapers. A probable anvil underscores the heavy-duty orientation of the processing-station tool kit.

The Lubbock Lake record is one of intensive and repeated use of the area through time by a small group of people involved in task-oriented economic activities. Because only a few bison mandibles could be aged, seasonality determinations are very tenuous, but activities appeared to have occurred in the fall (more common) or spring. Given the emphasis on obtaining fatty meats and plants, a late-winter or early-spring pattern may have been more expectable.

A number of trends or patterns are emerging. In bison butchering, the main objective during the Paleoindian period was meat retrieval with little attention paid to marrow. Completely disarticulated to semiarticulated carcasses were the trend through the period, with distinct bone piling. Fractured elements were utilized for fracture-based utilitarian tools. The trend of semiarticulated units and the lack of marrow processing were carried into at least the Early Archaic. During the Ceramic through Historic the focus of the activity areas was on intense processing of bone for marrow and grease production. Complete disarticulation, disassociation, and bone fracturing and reduction with a wide-spread bone disposal were the pattern. Whole elements were rare. Bone expediency tools were used, but their manufacturing debris was not recovered probably because it was further processed. This difference in handling the bone resource may account for the difference in element selection for tool use between the Paleoindian and Ceramic through Historic periods. Metapodials dominated the Paleoindian assemblage, whereas a large variety of elements was used in the Ceramic through Historic assemblage. The frequency of broken tool sections increased through time, perhaps reflecting the greater amount of heavy-duty processing in stations than in locales.

The general Paleoindian tool assemblage is predominantly a meat-retrieval assemblage for muscle-bundle stripping, although hide preparation may also have occurred as a subsidiary activity. The Ceramic through Historic tool assemblage is primarily a processing assemblage for disjointing, bone reduction, and hide preparation. A major technological thrust in these activities is that of production of fracture-base utilitarian tools. These tools were minimally modified implement categories. Both categories were employed in the late Pleistocene, but bone expediency tools emerge as the tradition throughout the Holocene. Bone quarrying, focused on the use of thick cortical bone, ceased at the end of the Pleistocene with proboscidean extinction. The bone expediency tool tradition employed a wider range of resources, using elements of middle to large-sized mammals, and that flexibility permitted its continued use from a wide-based procurement setting through a focused setting to a mixed economy.

The excellent geologic sequence at Lubbock Lake holds evidence of successive cultures and changing lifeways from Clovis times continuing through to the founding of the Lubbock community in the latter part of the nineteenth century. This remarkable sequence is further enhanced by the excellent age control available, which establishes the site as one of the best dated in the New World. Analysis, integration, and interpretation of generated data have progressed to varying degrees, and vast amounts of data are yet to be recovered. Nevertheless, the site has produced one of the most nearly complete late Quaternary records in the New World and serves as a model for the late Quaternary history of the Southern High Plains.

# References Cited

Agenbroad, Larry D. 1978. *The Hudson-Meng Site: An Alberta Bison Kill in the Nebraska High Plains.* Washington, D.C.: University Press of America.

Alexander, Herbert L., Jr. 1978. The Legalistic Approach to Early Man Studies. In Early Man in America from a Circum-Pacific Perspecitve, ed. Alan Lyle Bryan. *Occasional Papers of the Department of Anthropology, University of Alberta* 1:20–22. Edmonton: Archaeological Researches International.

Allred, B. W. 1956. Mixed Prairie in Texas. In *Grasslands of the Great Plains, Their Nature and Use,* ed. John Ernest Weaver and F. W. Albertson, pp. 267–83. Lincoln, Nebr.: Johnson Publishing Co.

Anderson, Adrian D., ed. 1975. The Cooperton Mammoth: An Early Man Bone Quarry. *Great Plains Journal* 14(2):130–64.

Anderson, Elaine. 1974. A Survey of the Late Pleistocene and Holocene Mammal Fauna of Wyoming. In Applied Geology and Archaeology: The Holocene History of Wyoming, ed. Michael Wilson, Geological Survey of Wyoming, *Report of Investigations* 10:79–87. Laramie: Geological Survey of Wyoming.

———. 1984. Who's Who in the Pleistocene: A Mammalian Bestiary. In *Quaternary Extinctions: A Prehistoric Revolution,* ed. Paul S. Martin and Richard G. Klein, pp. 40–89. Tucson: University of Arizona Press.

Antevs, Ernest. 1955. Geologic-Climatic Dating in the West. *American Antiquity* 20(4):317–35.

Applegarth, John Stirling. 1979. Herpetofauna (Anurans and Lizards) of Eddy County, New Mexico: Quaternary Changes and Environmental Implications. Ph.D. diss., University of New Mexico.

Ayer, Mary Youngman. 1936. The Archaeological and Faunal Material from Williams Cave, Guadalupe Mountains, Texas. *Proceedings of the Academy of Natural Sciences of Philadelphia* 88:599–618.

Bamforth, Douglas B. 1985. The Technological Organization of Paleo-Indian Small-Group Bison Hunting on the Llano Estacado. *Plains Anthropologist* 30(109):243–58.

Barbour, Erwin Hinckley, and C. Bertrand Schultz. 1941. The Lipscomb Bison Quarry, Lipscomb County, Texas. *Bulletin of the University of Nebraska State Museum* 2(7):67–68.

Barkley, A. 1934. The Statistical Theory of Pollen Analysis. *Ecology* 15(3):283–89.

Benedict, James B. 1978. The Mount Albion Complex and the Altithermal. In The Mount Albion Complex, ed. James B. Benedict and Byron L. Olson. *Center for Mountain Archeology, Research Report* 1:139–80.

———. 1979. Getting Away from It All: A Study of Man, Mountains, and the Two-Drought Altithermal. *Southwestern Lore* 45(3):1–12.

Bequaert, Joseph Charles, and Walter B. Miller. 1973. *The Mollusks of the Arid Southwest, with an Arizona Checklist.* Tucson: University of Arizona Press.

Berke, Hubert. 1984. The Distribution of Bones from Large Mammals in the Magdalenian Site Petersfels (Engen/Hegau) in the Archaeological Horizon (AH) 3, Site Pl. In *Upper Palaeolithic Settlement Patterns in Europe,* ed. Hubert Berke, Joachim Hahn, and Claus-Joachim Kind, pp. 103–108. Tübingen: Archaeologica Venatoria.

———. 1986. Butchering Marks on Horse Bones from the Magdalenian Site of Petersfels, Southwestern Germany. *Program and Abstracts of the Annual Meeting of the Society for American Archaeology* 51:57.

Binford, Lewis R. 1980. Willow Smoke and Dogs' Tails: Hunter-Gatherer Settlement Systems and Archaeological Site Formation. *American Antiquity* 45(1):4–20.

Black, Craig C., ed. 1974. History and Prehistory of the Lubbock Lake Site. *Museum Journal* (West Texas Museum Association) 15:1–160.

Blackstock, Dan A. 1979. *Soil Survey of Lubbock County, Texas.* Washington, D.C.: Soil Conservation Service, U.S. Department of Agriculture.

Bleything, Dennis. 1972. *Edible Plants in the Wilderness.* Vol. 1. Beaverton, Ore.: Life Support Technology.

Bonnichsen, Robson. 1973. Some Operational Aspects of Human and Animal Bone Alteration. In *Mammalian Osteo-Archaeology: North America,* ed. B. Miles Gilbert, pp. 9–24. Columbia: Missouri Archaeological Society.

———. 1979. Pleistocene Bone Technology in the Beringia Refugium. National Museum of Man, Ottawa, *Archaeological Survey of Canada Paper* 89:1–280.

———. 1982. Bone Technology as a Taphonomic Factor: An Introductory Statement. *Canadian Journal of Anthropology* 2(2):137–44.

Bonnichsen, Robson, and David E. Young. 1980. Early Technological Repertoires: Bone to Stone. In The Ice-Free Corridor and Peopling of the New World, ed. N. W. Rutter and C. E. Schweger. *Canadian Journal of Anthropology* 1(1):123–28.

Brattstrom, Bayard H. 1964. Amphibians and Reptiles from Cave Deposits in South-Central New Mexico. *Bulletin of Southern California Academy of Sciences* 63(2):93–103.

Bryan, Alan, ed. 1986. *New Evidence for the Pleistocene Peopling of the Americas.* Orono, Maine: Center for the Study of Early Man.

Bryant, Monroe D. 1945. Phylogeny of Nearctic Sciuridae. *American Midland Naturalist* 33(2):257–390.

Bryant, Vaughn, Jr. 1969. Late Full-Glacial and Postglacial Pollen Analysis of Texas Sediments. Ph.D. diss., University of Texas at Austin.

———. 1978. Palynology: A Useful Method for Determining Paleoenvironments. *Texas Journal of Science* 30(1): 25–42.

Bryant, Vaughn M., Jr., and Richard G. Holloway. 1983. The Role of Palynology in Archaeology. In *Advances in Archaeological Method and Theory,* ed. Michael Schiffer. 6:191–224. New York: Academic Press.

Bryant, Vaughn, Jr., and Harry J. Shafer. 1977. The Late Quaternary Paleoenvironment of Texas: A Model for the Archaeologist. *Bulletin of the Texas Archeological Society* 48:1–25.

Bunn, Henry T. 1981. Archaeological Evidence for Meat-eating by Plio-Pleistocene Hominids from Koobi Fora and Olduvai Gorge. *Nature* 291(5816):574–76.

Burch, John Bayard. 1962. *The Eastern Land Snails.* Dubuque, Iowa: William C. Brown.

Burt, William B., and Richard P. Grossenheider. 1964. *A Field Guide to the Mammals.* 2d ed. Boston: Houghton Mifflin Co.

Carlson, David L., D. Gentry Steele, and A. G. Comuzzie. 1984. Mammoth Excavations at the Duewall-Newberry Site on the Brazos River in Texas, 1983. *Current Research in the Pleistocene* 1:63–64.

Cassells, E. Steve. 1983. *The Archaeology of Colorado.* Boulder, Colo.: Johnson Books.

Cheatum, E. P., and R. W. Fullington. 1971. The Aquatic and Land Mollusca of Texas, Part 1. *Bulletin of the Dallas Museum of Natural History 1(1):1–74.*

———. 1973. The Aquatic and Land Mollusca of Texas, Part 2. *Bulletin of the Dallas Museum of Natural History* 1(2):1–67.

Chrapliwy, P. S., and A. J. Ward. 1963. New Records of the Western Hook-nosed Snake, *Ficimia cana* (Cope), in West Texas. *The Southwestern Naturalist* 8:52–53.

Clarke, Arthur H. 1973. The Freshwater Molluscs of the Canadian Interior Basin. *Malacologia* 13:1–509.

Clarke, W. T., Jr. 1938. List of Mollusks from Drift Debris of Paladora Creek, Texas. *Nautilus* 52:14–15.

Clausen, C. J., A. D. Cohen, C. Emiliani, J. A. Holman, and J. J. Stipp. 1979. Little Salt Spring, Florida: A Unique Underwater Site. *Science* 203:609–14.

Collins, Michael B. 1971. A Review of Llano Estacado Archaeology and Ethnohistory. *Plains Anthropologist* 16(52):82–104.

Compton, Joe L. 1975. Diatoms of the Lubbock Lake Site, Lubbock County, Texas. Master's thesis, Texas Tech University.

Conant, Roger. 1975. *A Field Guide to Reptiles and Amphibians of Eastern and Central North America.* Boston: Houghton Mifflin Co.

Conkling, Roscoe P. 1932. Conkling Cavern: The Discoveries in the Bone Cave and Bishop's Gap, New Mexico. *West Texas Historical and Scientific Society Bulletin* 4:7–19.

Connor, Seymour V. 1962. The First Settlers. In *A History of Lubbock,* ed. Lawrence L. Graves, pp. 45–67. Lubbock: West Texas Museum Association.

Correll, D. S., and M. C. Johnston. 1970. *Manual of the Vascular Plants of Texas.* Renner: Texas Research Foundation.

Cushing, J. E., Jr. 1945. Quaternary Rodents and Lagomorphs of Jan Josecito Cave, Nuevo Leon, Mexico. *Journal of Mammalogy* 26(2):182–85.

Dalquest, Walter W. 1962a. A Human Skull and an Associated Fauna from Foard County, Texas. *Transactions of the Kansas Academy of Science* 65(1):76–79.

———. 1962b. The Good Creek Formation, Pleistocene of Texas, and Its Fauna. *Journal of Paleontology* 36(3): 568–82.

———. 1964. A New Pleistocene Local Fauna from Motley County, Texas. *Transactions of the Kansas Academy of Science* 67(3):499–505.

———. 1965. New Pleistocene Formation and Local Fauna from Hardeman County, Texas. *Journal of Paleontology* 39(1):63–79.

———. 1967. Mammals of the Pleistocene Slaton Local Fauna of Texas. *The Southwestern Naturalist* 12:1–30.

Dalquest, Walter W., and Frederick B. Stangle, Jr. 1984. Late Pleistocene and Early Recent Mammals from Fowlkes Cave, Southern Culberson County, Texas. In Contributions in Quaternary Vertebrate Paleontology: A Volume in Memorial to John E. Guilday, ed. Hugh H. Genoways and Mary R. Dawson. *Special Publication of Carnegie Museum of Natural History* 8:432–55.

Dalquest, Walter W., Edward Roth, and Frank Judd. 1969. The Mammal Fauna of Schulze Cave, Edwards County, Texas. *Bulletin of the Florida State Museum* 13(4): 205–76.

Davis, R. B., C. F. Herrid II, and H. L. Short. 1962. Mexican Free-tailed Bats in Texas. *Ecology Monograph* 32:311–46.

Davis, William B. 1974. The Mammals of Texas. *Bulletin of the Texas Parks and Wildlife Department* 41: 1–294.

Dean, Walter E., J. Platt Bradbury, Roger Y. Anderson, and Cathy W. Barnosky. 1984. The Variability of Holocene Climatic Changes: Evidence from Varved Lake Sediments. *Science* 226:1191–94.

Dibble, David S. 1970. On the Significance of Additional Radiocarbon Dates from Bonfire Shelter, Texas. *Plains Anthropologist* 15(50):251–54.

Dibble, Davis S., and Dessamae Lorrain. 1968. Bonfire Shelter: A Stratified Bison Kill Site, Val Verde County, Texas. *Texas Memorial Museum Miscellaneous Papers* 1:1–138.

Dice, Lee Raymond. 1922. Some Factors Affecting the Distribution of the Prairie Vole, Forest Deer Mouse, and Prairie Deer Mouse. *Ecology* 3(1):29–47.

Dillehay, Tom D. 1974. Late Quaternary Bison Population Changes on the Southern High Plains. *Plains Anthropologist* 19(65):180–96.

Douglas-Hamilton, Iain, and Oria Douglas-Hamilton. 1975. *Among the Elephants.* New York: Viking Press.

Doutt, J. Kenneth, Caroline A. Heppenstall, and John E. Guilday. 1973. *Mammals of Pennsylvania.* Harrisburg: Pennsylvania Game Commission.

Drake, Robert J. 1975. Fossil Nonmarine Mollusks of the 1961–1963 Llano Estacado Paleoecology Study. In *Late Pleistocene Environments of the Southern High Plains,* ed. Fred Wendorf and James J. Hester, pp. 201–45. Dallas: Fort Burgwin Research Center, Southern Methodist University.

Edmund, A. Gordon. 1985. The Armor of Fossil Giant Armadillos (Pampatheriidae, Xenarthra, Mammalia). *Pearce-Sellards Series* (Texas Memorial Museum) 40:1–20.

Emory, William H. 1857–59. *Report on the United States Boundary Survey.* Vols. 1 and 2. 34th Cong. 1st sess. H. Exec. Doc. 135. Washington, D.C.

Evans, Glen L. 1949. Upper Cenozoic of the High Plains. In Guidebook, Field Trip No. 2, Cenozoic Geology of the Llano Estacado and Rio Grande Valley, ed. Glen L. Evans et al. *West Texas Geological Society Guidebook* 2:1–22.

Evans, Glen L., and Grayson E. Meade. 1945. Quaternary of the Texas High Plains. University of Texas, *Contributions to Geology* 4401:485–507.

Fenneman, Nevin M. 1931. *Physiography of Western United States.* New York: McGraw-Hill.

Figgins, Jesse D. 1933. A Further Contribution to the Antiquity of Man in America. *Proceedings of the Colorado Museum of Natural History* 12(2):4–10.

Findley, James S. 1954. Competition as a Possible Limiting Factor in the Distribution of *Microtus. Ecology* 35(3):418–20.

Findley, James S., Arthur H. Harris, Don E. Wilson, and Clyde Jones. 1975. *Mammals of New Mexico.* Albuquerque: University of New Mexico Press.

Frank, Ruben M. 1964. The Vertebrate Paleontology of Texas Caves. *Texas Speleological Survey* 2(3):1–43.

Frison, George C. 1970. The Glenrock Buffalo Jump, 48CO304. *Plains Anthropologist* 15(50):1–66.

———. 1974. *The Casper Site: A Hell Gap Bison Kill on the High Plains.* New York: Academic Press.

———. 1976. Cultural Activity Associated with Prehistoric Mammoth Butchering and Processing. *Science* 194:728–30.

———. 1978. *Prehistoric Hunters of the High Plains.* New York: Academic Press.

———. 1983. The Western Plains and Mountain Region. In *Early Man in the New World,* ed. Richard Shutler, Jr., pp. 109–24. Beverly Hills, Calif.: Sage Publications.

Frison, George C., Danny N. Walker, S. David Webb, and George M. Zeimens. 1978. Pelo-Indian Procurement of *Camelops* on the Northwestern Plains. *Quaternary Research* 10(3):385–400.

Frye, John C., and A. Byron Leonard. 1957. Studies of Cenozoic Geology Along Eastern Margin of Texas High Plains, Armstrong to Howard Counties. University of Texas, Bureau of Economic Geology, *Report of Investigations* 32:1–62.

———. 1963. Pleistocene Geology of the Red River Basin in Texas. University of Texas, Bureau of Economic Geology, *Report of Investigations* 49:1–48.

———. 1965. Quaternary of the Southern Great Plains. In *The Quaternary of the United States,* ed. H. E. Wright, Jr., and David A. Frey, pp. 203–16. Princeton, N.J.: Princeton University Press.

Fullington, Richard W., and William Lloyd Pratt, Jr. 1974. The Aquatic and Land Mollusca of Texas, Part 3. *Bulletin of the Dallas Museum of Natural History* 1(3):1–48.

Gaylord, David R. 1982. Geologic History of the Ferris Dune Field, Southcentral Wyoming. In Interpretation of Windflow Characteristics from Eolian Landforms, ed. Ronald W. Marrs and Kenneth E. Kolm. *Geological Society of America Special Paper* 192:65–82.

Gazin, C. Lewis. 1955. Identification of Some Vertebrate Fossil Material from the Scharbauer Site, Midland, Texas. In *The Midland Discovery,* ed. Fred Wendorf, Alex D. Krieger, and Claude C. Albritton. App. 2:119. Austin: University of Texas Press.

Gehlbach, Frederick R., and J. Alan Holman. 1974. Paleoecology of Amphibians and Reptiles from Pratt Cave, Guadalupe Mountains National Park, Texas. *The Southwestern Naturalist* 19(2):191–98.

Genoways, H. H., and J. R. Choate. 1972. A Multivariate Analysis of Systematic Relationships among Populations of the Short-tailed Shrew (genus *Blarina*) in Nebraska. *Systematic Zoology* 21:106–16.

Gile, Leland H. 1979. Holocene Soils in Eolian Sediments of Bailey County, Texas. *Soil Science Society of America Journal* 43(4):994–1003.

———. 1985. *The Sandhills Project Soil Monograph.* Las Cruces: Rio Grande Historical Collections, New Mexico State University.

Goertz, J. W. 1964. The Influence of Habitat Quality upon Density of Cotton Rat Populations. *Ecological Monograph* 34:259–381.

Gorman, Frederick. 1972. The Clovis Hunters: An Alternate View of Their Environment and Ecology. In *Contemporary Archaeology,* ed. Mark P. Leone, pp. 206–21. Carbondale: Southern Illinois University Press.

Gould, Frank W., and Robert B. Shaw. 1983. *Grass Systematics.* 2d ed. College Station: Texas A&M University Press.

Graham, Russell W. 1974. Guidebook to the Vertebrate Paleontology of Friesenhahn, Fyllan, and Laubach Caves. Fifth Annual Meeting of the Society of Vertebrate Paleontology, Austin, Texas.

———. 1976. Pleistocene and Holocene Mammals, Taphonomy, and Paleoecology of the Friesenhahn Cave Local Fauna, Bexar County, Texas. Ph.D. diss., University of Texas at Austin.

Graham, Russell W., and Holmes Semken. 1976. Paleoecological Significance of the Short-tailed Shrew (*Blarina*) with a Systematic Discussion of *Blarina ozarkensis. Journal of Mammalogy* 57(3):433–49.

Green, F. Earl. 1962. The Lubbock Reservoir Site. *Museum*

*Journal* (West Texas Museum Association) 6:83–123.

——. 1967. The Lubbock Reservoir Site. Manuscript, The Museum, Texas Tech University, Lubbock.

Greiser, Sally Thompson. 1977. Micro-Analysis of Wear-Patterns on Projectile Points and Knives from the Jurgens Site, Kersey, Colorado. *Plains Anthropologist* 22(76):107–16.

Guilday, John E., Harold W. Hamilton, and Allen D. Mc-Crady. 1971. The Welsh Cave Peccaries (*Platygonus*) and Associated Fauna, Kentucky Pleistocene. *Annals of Carnegie Museum* 43:249–320.

Guilday, John E., Paul S. Martin, and Allen D. McCrady. 1964. New Paris No. 4: A Late Pleistocene Cave Deposit in Bedford County, Pennsylvania. *Bulletin of the National Speleological Society* 26(4):1–94.

Guilday, John E., Paul W. Parmalee, and D. P. Tanner. 1962. Aboriginal Butchering Techniques at the Eschelman Site (36 La 12), Lancaster County, Pennsylvania. *Pennsylvania Archaeologist* 32:59–83.

Gunnerson, D. A. 1956. The Southern Athabascans: Their Arrival in the Southwest. *El Palacio* 63:346–65.

Gunnerson, James H. 1969. Apache Archaeology in Northeastern New Mexico. *American Antiquity* 34(1):23–29.

Gustavson, Thomas C., and Vance T. Holliday. 1985. Depositional Architecture of the Quaternary Blackwater Draw and Tertiary Ogallala Formations, Texas Panhandle and Eastern New Mexico. University of Texas, Bureau of Economic Geology, Open File Report, OF-WTWI-1985-23, pp. 1–92.

Guthrie, R. D. 1970. Bison Evolution and Zoogeography in North America during the Pleistocene. *Quarterly Review of Biology* 45(1):1–15.

Haas, Herbert, Vance T. Holliday, and Robert Stuckenrath. 1986. Dating of Holocene Stratigraphy with Soluble and Insoluble Organic Fractions at the Lubbock Lake Archaeological Site, Texas: An Ideal Case Study. *Radiocarbon* 28(2A):473–85.

Hafsten, Ulf. 1961. Pleistocene Development of Vegetation and Climate in the Southern High Plains as Evidenced by Pollen Analysis. In *Paleoecology of the Llano Estacado,* ed. Fred Wendorf, pp. 59–91. Santa Fe: Museum of New Mexico Press.

Hall, E. Raymond. 1981 *Mammals of North America.* 2 vols. New York: John Wiley & Sons.

Hall, E. Raymond, and Keith R. Kelson. 1959. *The Mammals of North America.* New York: Ronald Press Co.

Hall, Stephen A. 1982. Late Holocene Paleoecology of the Southern High Plains. *Quaternary Research* 17(3):391–407.

Hannus, L. Adrien. 1984a. Flaked Mammoth Bone from the Lange/Ferguson Site, White River Badlands Area, South Dakota. *Abstracts of the International Conference on Bone Modification* 1:16–17.

——. 1984b. The Lange/Ferguson Site. An Event of Clovis Mammoth Butchering with the Associated Bone Tool Technology: The Mammoth and Its Track. Ph.D. diss., Utah State University.

Haragan, Donald R. 1983. *Blue Northers to Sea Breezes:*

*Texas Weather and Climate.* Dallas: Hendrick-Long Publishing Co.

Harbour, Jerry. 1975. General Stratigraphy. In *Late Pleistocene Environments of the Southern High Plains,* ed. Fred Wendorf and James J. Hester, pp. 33–55. Dallas: Fort Burgwin Research Center, Southern Methodist University.

Harrington, H. D. 1972. *Western Edible Wild Plants.* Albuquerque: University of New Mexico Press.

Harris, Arthur H. 1970. The Dry Cave Mammalian Fauna and Late Pluvial Conditions in Southeastern New Mexico. *Texas Journal of Science* 12(1):3–27.

——. 1977a. Wisconsin Age Environments in the Northern Chihuahuan Desert: Evidence from the Higher Vertebrates. In Transactions of the Symposium on the Biological Resources of the Chihuahuan Desert Region, United States and Mexico. ed. R. H. Wauer and D. H. Riskind, pp. 23–52. *National Park Service Transactions and Proceedings Series* 3:23–52.

——. 1977b. Biotic Environments of the Paleoindian. In Paleoindian Lifeways, ed. Eileen Johnson. *Museum Journal* (West Texas Museum Association) 17:1–12.

——. 1980. The Paleoecology of Dry Cave, New Mexico. *National Geographic Society Research Reports* 12:331–38.

——. 1984. Neotoma in the Late Pleistocene of New Mexico and Chihuahua. In Contributions in Quaternary Vertebrate Paleontology: A Volume in Memorial to John E. Guilday, ed. Hugh H. Genoways and Mary R. Dawson. *Special Publication of Carnegie Museum of Natural History* 8:164–78.

——. 1985a. Preliminary Report on the Vertebrate Fauna of U-Bar Cave, Hidalgo County, New Mexico. *New Mexico Geology,* November, pp. 74–84.

——. 1985b. *Late Pleistocene Vertebrate Paleoecology of the West.* Austin: University of Texas Press.

Harris, Arthur H., and James S. Findley. 1964. Pleistocene-Recent Fauna of the Isleta Caves, Bernalillo County, New Mexico. *American Journal of Science* 262:114–20.

Harris, Arthur H., and Linda S. W. Porter. 1980. Late Pleistocene Horses of Dry Cave, Eddy County, New Mexico. *Journal of Mammalogy* 61(1):46–65.

Harrison, Billy R., and Kay L. Killen. 1978. Lake Theo: A Stratified, Early Man Bison Butchering and Camp Site, Briscoe County, Texas: Archeological Investigations Phase II. *Panhandle-Plains Historical Museum Special Archeological Report* 1:1–108.

Harrison, Billy R., and Henry C. Smith. 1975. Excavations at the Lake Theo Site, PPHM-A917, Briscoe County, Texas. *Panhandle-Plains Historical Review* 48:70–106.

Haury, Emil W. 1953. Artifacts with Mammoth Remains, Naco, Arizona: Discovery of the Naco Mammoth and Associated Projectile Points. *American Antiquity* 19:1–14.

Hawley, John W., G. O. Bachman, and K. Manley. 1976. Quaternary Stratigraphy in the Basin and Range and Great Basin Provinces, New Mexico and Western

Texas. In *Quaternary Stratigraphy of North America,* ed. W. C. Mahaney, pp. 235–74. Stroudsburg, Pa.: Dowder, Hutchinson, and Ross.

Haynes, C. Vance. 1971. Time, Environment, and Early Man. *Arctic Anthropology* 8(2):3–14.

———. 1975. Pleistocene and Recent Stratigraphy. In *Late Pleistocene Environments of the Southern High Plains,* ed. Fred Wendorf and James J. Hester, pp. 57–96. Dallas: Fort Burgwin Research Center, Southern Methodist University.

———. 1980. The Clovis Culture. In The Ice-Free Corridor and Peopling of the New World, ed. N. W. Rutter and C. E. Schweger, *Canadian Journal of Anthropology* 1(1):115–21.

Haynes, C. Vance, and E. Thomas Hemmings. 1968. Mammoth-Bone Shaft Wrench from Murray Springs, Arizona. *Science* 159:186–87.

Haynes, C. Vance, L. D. Agenbroad, and Emil W. Haury. 1975. New Data from the Lehner Clovis Site. Paper presented at the Annual Meeting of the Society for American Archaeology, Dallas.

Hemmings, Ernest T. 1970. Early Man in the San Pedro Valley, Arizona. Ph.D. diss., University of Arizona.

Hemmings, Ernest T., and C. Vance Haynes. 1969. The Escapule Mammoth and Associated Projectile Points, San Pedro Valley, Arizona. *Journal of the Arizona Academy of Science* 5(3):184–88.

Hester, James J. 1972. *Blackwater Locality No. 1: A Stratified Early Man Site in Eastern New Mexico.* Dallas: Fort Burgwin Research Center, Southern Methodist University.

Hibbard, Claude W. 1949. Techniques of Collecting Microvertebrate Fossils. *Contributions from the Museum of Paleontology, University of Michigan* 8(2):7–19.

———. 1960. An Interpretation of Pliocene and Pleistocene Climates in North America. *Michigan Academy of Sciences, Arts, and Letters* 62:5–30.

Hibbard, Claude W., and George C. Rinker. 1942. A New Bog Lemming (*Synaptomys*) from Meade County, Kansas. *University of Kansas Science Bulletin* 28(2):25–35.

Hibbard, Claude W., and D. W. Taylor. 1960. Two Late Pleistocene Faunas from Southwestern Kansas. *Contributions from the Museum of Paleontology, University of Michigan* 16:1–223.

Hill, Frederick. 1982. The Paleoichtyofauna of Lubbock Lake, Texas. Report on file, The Museum, Texas Tech University, Lubbock.

Hill, William H. 1971. Pleistocene Snakes from a Cave in Kendall County, Texas. *Texas Journal of Science* 22(2-3):209–16.

Hillerud, John M. 1966. The Duffield Site and Its Fossil Bison, Alberta, Canada. Master's thesis, University of Nebraska.

Hoffmeister, D. F. 1969. The Species Problem in *Thomomys bottae-Thomomys umbrinus* Complex of Pocket Gophers in Arizona. University of Kansas, Museum of Natural History, *Miscellaneous Publications* 51:75–91.

Holden, Jane. 1952. The Bonnell Site. *Bulletin of the Texas Archeological and Paleontological Society* 23:78–132.

Holden, W. Curry. 1962a. Indians, Spaniards, and Anglos. In *A History of Lubbock,* ed. L. L. Graves, pp. 17–44. Lubbock: West Texas Museum Association.

———. 1962b. The Land. In *A History of Lubbock,* ed. L. L. Graves, pp. 1–16. Lubbock: West Texas Museum Association.

———. 1974. Historical Background of the Lubbock Lake Site. In History and Prehistory of the Lubbock Lake Site, ed. Craig C. Black. *Museum Journal* (West Texas Museum Association) 15:11–14.

Holliday, Vance T. 1982. Morphological and Chemical Trends in Holocene Soils, Lubbock Lake Site, Texas. Ph.D. diss., University of Colorado.

———. 1983. *Guidebook to the Central Llano Estacado.* Friends of the Pleistocene South-Central Cell Field Trip. ICASALS, and Lubbock: The Museum, Texas Tech University.

———. 1985a. Holocene Soil-Geomorphological Relations in a Semi-Arid Environment: The Southern High Plains of Texas. In *Soils and Quaternary Landscape Evolution,* ed. J. Boardman, pp. 325–57. New York: John Wiley & Sons.

———. 1985b. Archaeological Geology of the Lubbock Lake Site, Southern High Plains of Texas. *Geological Society of America Bulletin* 96:1483–92.

———. 1985c. Early and Middle Holocene Soils at the Lubbock Lake Archeological Site, Texas. *Catena* 12:61–78.

———. 1985d. Morphology of Late Holocene Soils at the Lubbock Lake Archeological Site, Texas. *Soil Science Society of America Journal* 49(4):938–46.

———. 1985e. New Data on the Stratigraphy and Pedology of the Clovis and Plainview Sites, Southern High Plains. *Quaternary Research* 23:388–402.

———. 1986. Late Pleistocene Vegetation of the Southern High Plains: A Reappraisal. *Current Research in the Pleistocene* 3:53–54.

Holliday, Vance T., and Eileen Johnson. 1981. An Update on the Plainview Occupation at the Lubbock Lake Site. *Plains Anthropologist* 26:251–53.

———. 1986. Re-evaluation of the First Radiocarbon Age for the Folsom Culture. *American Antiquity* 51(2):332–38.

Holliday, Vance T., and Curtis Welty. 1981. Lithic Tool Resources of the Eastern Llano Estacado. *Bulletin of the Texas Archeological Society* 52:201–14.

Holliday, Vance T., Eileen Johnson, Herbert Haas, and Robert Stuckenrath. 1983. Radiocarbon Ages from the Lubbock Lake Site, 1950–1980: Framework for Cultural and Ecological Change on the Southern High Plains. *Plains Anthropologist* 28(101):165–82.

———. 1985a. Radiocarbon Ages from the Lubbock Lake Site: 1981–1984. *Plains Anthropologist* 30(110):277–91.

Holliday, Vance T., Eileen Johnson, Stephen A. Hall, and Vaughn M. Bryant. 1985b. Re-evaluation of the Lubbock Subpluvial. *Current Research in the Pleistocene* 2:119–21.

Holloway, Richard G. 1981. Preservation and Experimental Diagenesis of the Pollen Exine. Ph.D. diss., Texas A&M University.

Holman, J. Alan. 1962. A Texas Pleistocene Herpetofauna. *Copeia,* pp. 255–61.

———. 1963. Late Pleistocene Amphibians and Reptiles of the Clear Creek and Ben Franklin Local Faunas of Texas. *Journal of the Graduate Research Center* (Southern Methodist University) 31(3):152–67.

———. 1964. Pleistocene Amphibians and Reptiles from Texas. *Herpetologica* 20:73–83.

———. 1965a. A Small Pleistocene Herpetofauna from Houston, Texas. *Texas Journal of Science* 17(4): 418–23.

———. 1965b. Pleistocene Snakes from the Seymour Formation of Texas. *Copeia,* pp. 102–104.

———. 1966a. The Pleistocene Herpetofauna of Miller's Cave, Texas. *Texas Journal of Science* 28:372–77.

———. 1966b. A Huge Pleistocene Box Turtle from Texas. *Quarterly Journal of the Florida Academy of Sciences* 28(4):345–48.

———. 1968. A Pleistocene Herpetofauna from Kendall County, Texas. *Quarterly Journal of the Florida Academy of Sciences* 31(3):167–72.

———. 1969a. Herpetofauna of the Pleistocene Slaton Local Fauna of Texas. *The Southwestern Naturalist* 14(2):203–12.

———. 1969b. The Pleistocene Amphibians and Reptiles of Texas. *Publications of the Museum, Michigan State University, Biological Series* 4(5):161–92.

———. 1969. Pleistocene Amphibians from a Cave in Edwards County, Texas. *Texas Journal of Science* 21(1): 63–67.

———. 1970. A Pleistocene Herpetofauna from Eddy County, New Mexico. *Texas Journal of Science* 22(1): 29–39.

———. 1975. Neotenic Tiger Salamander Remnants. In *Late Pleistocene Environments of the Southern High Plains,* ed. Fred Wendorf and James J. Hester, pp. 193–96. Dallas: Fort Burgwin Research Center, Southern Methodist University.

Honea, Kenneth. 1980. Mark's Beach, Stratified Paleoindian Site, Lamb County, Texas: Preliminary Report. *Bulletin of the Texas Archeological Society* 51:243–69.

Hooper, Emmel T. 1952. A Systematic Review of the Harvest Mice (genus *Reithrodontomys*) of Latin America. University of Michigan Museum of Zoology *Miscellaneous Publications* 77:1–255.

———. 1957. Dental Patterns in Mice of the Genus *Peromyscus.* University of Michigan Museum of Zoology, *Miscellaneous Publications* 99:1–59.

Hubendick, B. 1951. *Recent Lymnaeidae, Their Variation, Morphology, Taxonomy, Nomenclature and Distribution.* Stockholm: Almqvist and Wicksells.

Hughes, Elaine. 1984. Blackwater Draw Locality #1: A Case Study of Conservation, Collection Management,

and Site Data Reconstruction Techniques. Master's thesis, Texas Tech University.

Hughes, Jack T., and Patrick Willey. 1978. Archeology. In Archeology at MacKenzie Reservoir, ed. Jack T. Hughes and Patrick S. Willey. Texas Historical Commission, Office of the State Archeologist, *Archeological Survey Report* 24:24–31.

Hunt, Charles B. 1974. *Natural Regions of the United States and Canada.* San Francisco: W. H. Freeman & Co.

Hurst, C. T. 1943. A Folsom Site in a Mountain Valley of Colorado. *American Antiquity* 8(3):250–53.

James, Gideon T. 1957. An Edentate from the Pleistocene of Texas. *Journal of Paleontology* 31(4):796–808.

Johnson, Charles A., II. 1974. Geologic Investigations at the Lubbock Lake Site. In History and Prehistory of the Lubbock Lake Site, ed. Craig C. Black. *Museum Journal* (West Texas Museum Association) 15: 79–105.

Johnson, Eileen. 1974. Zooarchaeology and the Lubbock Lake Site. In History and Prehistory of the Lubbock Lake Site, ed. Craig C. Black. *Museum Journal* (West Texas Museum Association). 15:107–22.

———. 1976. Investigations into the Zooarchaeology of the Lubbock Lake Site. Ph.D. diss., Texas Tech University.

———. 1977. Animal Food Resources of Paleoindians. In Paleoindian Lifeways, ed. Eileen Johnson, *Museum Journal* (West Texas Museum Association) 17:65–77.

———. 1978. Cultural Modification and Bone Technology in the Late Quaternary: Lubbock Lake, Bonfire Shelter, and 41VV162a. Paper presented at the annual meeting of the Plains Conference, Denver.

———. 1982. Paleoindian Bone Expediency Tools—Lubbock Lake and Bonfire Shelter. *Canadian Journal of Anthropology* 2(2):145–57.

———. 1983. The Lubbock Lake Paleoindian Record. In *Guidebook to the Central Llano Estacado,* ed. Vance T. Holliday, pp. 81–105. Friends of the Pleistocene South-Central Cell Field Trip. ICASALS, and Lubbock: The Museum, Texas Tech University.

———. 1985. Current Developments in Bone Technology. In *Advances in Archaeological Method and Theory,* ed. Michael B. Schiffer, 8:157–235. New York: Academic Press.

Johnson, Eileen, and Vance T. Holliday. 1980. A Plainview Kill/Butchering Locale on the Llano Estacado—The Lubbock Lake Site. *Plains Anthropologist* 25(88): 89–111.

———. 1981. Late Paleoindian Activity at the Lubbock Lake Site. *Plains Anthropologist* 26(93):173–93.

———. 1985. A Clovis Age Megafaunal Processing Station at the Lubbock Lake Landmark. *Current Research in the Pleistocene* 2:17–19.

———. 1986. The Archaic Record at Lubbock Lake. In Current Trends in Southern Plains Archaeology, ed. Timothy G. Baugh. *Plains Anthropologist Memoir* 21:7–54.

Johnson, Eileen, Vance T. Holliday, and Raymond W. Neck. 1982. Lake Theo: Late Quaternary Paleoenvironmental

Data and New Plainview (Paleoindian) Date. *North American Archaeologist* 3(2): 113–37.

Johnson, Eileen, Vance T. Holliday, Michael J. Kaczor, and Robert Stuckenrath. 1977. The Garza Occupation at the Lubbock Lake Site. *Bulletin of the Texas Archeological Society* 48:83–109.

Jones, J. Knox, Jr., Dilford C. Carter, Hugh H. Genoways, Robert S. Hoffmann, Dale W. Rice, and Clyde Jones. 1986. Revised Checklist of North American Mammals North of Mexico, 1986. The Museum, Texas Tech University *Occasional Papers* 107:1–22.

Judge, W. James. 1974. Projectile Point Form and Function in Late Paleo-Indian Period Assemblages. In History and Prehistory of the Lubbock Lake Site, ed. Craig C. Black. *Museum Journal* (West Texas Museum Association) 15:123–32.

Kaczor, Michael John. 1978. A Correlative Study of the West Texas Museum Excavations at the Lubbock Lake Site, 1959–61: An Example of Applied Museum Collection Management Techniques within a Research Analysis Design. Master's thesis, Texas Tech University.

Kelley, Jane Holden. 1964. Comments on the Archaeology of the Llano Estacado. *Bulletin of the Texas Archeological Society* 35:1–18.

———. 1974. A Brief Resume of Artifacts Collected at the Lubbock Lake Site Prior to 1961. In History and Prehistory of the Lubbock Lake Site, ed. Craig C. Black. *Museum Journal* (West Texas Museum Association) 15:43–78.

Kreutzer, Lee Ann. 1986. Cultural vs. Natural Bone Disposition in Feature Area 2–1, Lubbock Lake Site. Master's thesis, University of Washington.

Krumrey, William A., and Irven O. Buss. 1968. Age Estimation, Growth, and Relationship between Body Dimensions of the Female Elephant. *Journal of Mammalogy* 49(1):22–31.

Kurtén, Björn. 1963. Fossil Bears from Texas. *Pearce-Sellards Series* (Texas Memorial Museum) 1:1–15.

———. 1967. Pleistocene Bears of North America 2. Genus *Arctodus,* Short-faced Bears. *Acta Zoologica Fennica* 117:1–60.

Lahren, Larry, and Robson Bonnichsen. 1974. Bone Foreshafts from a Clovis Burial in Southwestern Montana. *Science* 186:147–50.

Lance, John F. 1953. Artifacts with Mammoth Remains, Naco, Arizona. III. Description of the Naco Mammoth. *American Antiquity* 19(1):19–22.

Laws, R. M. 1966. Age Criteria for the African Elephant, *Loxodonta a. africanus. East African Wildlife Journal* 4:1–35.

Laws, R. M., I. S. C. Parker, and R. C. B. Johnstone. 1975. *Elephants and Their Habitats: The Ecology of Elephants in North Bunyoro, Uganda.* London: Oxford University Press.

Leonard, A. Bryon. 1950. A Yarmouthian Molluscan Fauna in the Mid-Continent Region of the United States. University of Kansas Paleontological Contributions, *Mollusca* 3:1–48.

———. 1959. Handbook of Gastropods in Kansas. University of Kansas Museum of Natural History *Miscellaneous Publications* 20:1–224.

Leonard, A. Byron, and John Chapman Frye. 1962. Pleistocene Molluscan Faunas and Physiographic History of Pecos Valley in Texas. University of Texas, Bureau of Economic Geology, *Report of Investigations* 45:1–42.

Leonhardy, Frank C. 1966. Domebo: A Paleo-Indian Mammoth Kill in the Prairie-Plains. *Contributions of the Museum of the Great Plains* 1:1–53.

Libby, Willard. 1952. *Radiocarbon Dating.* Chicago: University of Chicago Press.

Littlejohn, M. J., and R. S. Oldham. 1968. *Rana pipiens* Complex: Mating Call Structure and Taxonomy. *Science* 162:1003–1004.

Logan, Lloyd. 1977. The Paleoclimatic Implications of the Avian and Mammalian Faunas of Lower Sloth Cave, Guadalupe Mountains, Texas. Master's thesis, Texas Tech University.

Logan, Lloyd, and Craig C. Black. 1979. The Quaternary Vertebrate Fauna of Upper Sloth Cave, Guadalupe National Park, Texas. In Biological Investigations in the Guadalupe Mountains National Park, Texas, ed. Hugh H. Genoways and Robert J. Baker. *National Park Services Proceedings and Transaction Series* 4:141–58.

Lundelius, Ernest L., Jr. 1967. Late Pleistocene and Holocene Faunal History of Central Texas. In *Pleistocene Extinctions: The Search for a Cause,* ed. P. S. Martin and H. E. Wright, Jr., pp. 287–319. New Haven, Conn.: Yale University Press.

———. 1972a. Vertebrate Remains from the Gray Sand. In *Blackwater Locality No. 1: A Stratified Early Man Site in Eastern New Mexico,* ed. James J. Hester, pp. 148–63. Dallas: Fort Burgwin Research Center, Southern Methodist University.

———. 1972b. Fossil Vertebrates from the Late Pleistocene Ingleside Fauna, San Patricio County, Texas. University of Texas, Bureau of Economic Geology *Report of Investigations* 77:1–72.

———. 1974. The Last Fifteen Thousand Years of Faunal Change in North America. In History and Prehistory of the Lubbock Lake Site, ed. Craig C. Black. *Museum Journal* (West Texas Museum Association) 15:141–60.

———. 1979. Post-Pleistocene Mammals from Pratt Cave and Their Environmental Significance. In Biological Investigations in the Guadalupe Mountains National Park, Texas, ed. H. H. Genoways and R. J. Baker. *National Park Service Proceedings and Transactions Series* 4:239–58.

———. 1984. A Late Pleistocene Mammalian Fauna from Cueva Quebrada, Val Verde County, Texas. In Contributions in Quaternary Vertebrate Paleontology: A Volume in Memorial to John E. Guilday, ed. Hugh H. Genoways and Mary R. Dawson. *Special Publication of Carnegie Museum of Natural History* 8:456–81.

Lundelius, Ernest L., Jr., and Margaret S. Stevens. 1970. *Equus francisci* Hay, a Small Stilt-legged Horse,

Middle Pleistocene of Texas. *Journal of Paleontology* 44(1):148–53.

Lundelius, Ernest L., Russell W. Graham, Elaine Anderson, John Guilday, J. Alan Holman, David W. Steadman, and S. David Webb. 1983. Terrestrial Vertebrate Faunas. In *Late-Quaternary Environments of the United States*, ed. H. E. Wright, Jr., 1:311–53.

MacDowell, April. 1979. Mammoth Hunting Patterns of Early Man in North America. Master's thesis, University of Wisconsin.

McHugh, Tom. 1958. Social Behavior of the American Buffalo (*Bison bison bison*). *New York Zoological Society Zoologica* 43:1–40.

Mack, Richard N., and Vaughn M. Bryant, Jr. 1974. Modern Pollen Spectra from the Columbia Basin, Washington. *Northwest Science* 48:183–94.

McLaughlin, Diane. 1978. Preliminary Thoughts on the Canyon Lakes 6 Core. Manuscript, The Museum, Texas Tech University, Lubbock.

Marcy, R. B. 1850. *Report of the Exploration and Survey of the Route from Fort Smith, Arkansas, to Santa Fe, New Mexico, Made in 1849.* 31st Cong., 1st sess. H. Exec. Doc. 45, Pub. Doc. 577. Washington, D.C.

Martin, Paul S. 1963. *The Last 10,000 Years: A Fossil Pollen Record of the American Southwest.* Tucson: University of Arizona Press.

Martin, Robert A. 1968a. Further Study of the Friesenhahn Cave *Peromyscus. The Southwestern Naturalist* 13(3): 253–66.

———. 1968b. Late Pleistocene Distribution of *Microtus pennsylvanicus. Journal of Mammalogy* 49(2): 264–71.

Mattox, Richard B., and Vestal L. Yeats. 1984. *Physical Geology Laboratory Manual: Geology 1101.* Minneapolis: Burgess Publishing Co.

Mawby, John E. 1967. Fossil Vertebrates of the Tule Springs Site, Nevada. In Pleistocene Studies in Southern Nevada, ed. H. M. Wormington and Dorothy Ellis. *Nevada State Museum Anthropological Papers* 13: 105–29.

Meade, Grayson E. 1942. A New Species of *Capromeryx* from the Pleistocene of West Texas. *Bulletin of the Texas Archeological and Paleontological Society* 14: 88–96.

Meade, Grayson E., Glen L. Evans, and John P. Brand, eds. 1974. *Guidebook to the Mesozoic and Cenozoic Geology of the Southern Llano Estacado.* Lubbock: Lubbock Geological Society.

Mecham, J. S. 1959. Some Pleistocene Amphibians and Reptiles from Friesenhahn Cave, Texas. *The Southwestern Naturalist* 3:17–27.

———. 1969. New Information from Experimental Crosses on Genetic Relationships within the *Rana pipiens* Species group. *Journal of Experimental Zoology* 170: 169–80.

Mecham, J. S., M. J. Littlejohn, R. S. Oldham, L. E. Brown, and J. R. Brown. 1973. A New Species of Leopard Frog (*Rana pipiens* Complex) from the Plains of the Central United States. The Museum, Texas Tech

University, *Occasional Papers* 18:1–11.

Medsger, Oliver Perry. 1966. *Edible Wild Plants.* New York: Macmillan Co.

Mehl, M. G. 1966. The Domebo Mammoth: Vertebrate Paleomortology. In Domebo: A Paleo-Indian Mammoth Kill in the Prairie-Plains, ed. Frank C. Leonhardy. *Contributions of the Museum of the Great Plains* 1:27–30.

———. 1975. Vertebrate Paleomortology of the Cooperton Site. In The Cooperton Mammoth: An Early Man Bone Quarry, ed. Adrian D. Anderson. *Great Plains Journal* 14(2):165–68.

Merriam, John C., and Chester Stock. 1921. Notes on Peccary Remains from Rancho La Brea. *Bulletin of the Department of Geological Sciences, University of California Publications* 13(2):9–17.

———. 1925. Relationships and Structure of the Short-faced Bear, *Arctotherium,* from the Pleistocene of California. *Carnegie Institution of Washington Contributions to Paleontology* 347:1–35.

Miall, L. C., and F. Greenwood. 1877. Anatomy of the Indian Elephant, Part I and Part II. *Journal of Anatomy* 12:261, 287, 384–400.

Miller, George J. 1969. A Study of Cuts, Grooves, and Other Marks on Recent and Fossil Bone. I. Animal Tooth Marks. *Tebiwa* 12(1):20–26.

Miller, Susanne J. 1984. Characteristics of Mammoth Bone Reduction at Owl Cave, the Wasden Site, Idaho. *Abstracts of the International Conference on Bone Modification* 1:25.

Miller, Wade E. 1971. Pleistocene Vertebrates of the Los Angeles Basin and Vicinity (Exclusive of Rancho La Brea). *Science Bulletin of the Los Angeles County Museum of Natural History* 10:1–119.

Milstead, William W. 1967. Fossil Box Turtles (*Terrapene*) from Central North America, and Box Turtles of Eastern Mexico. *Copeia* 1:168–79.

———. 1969. Studies on the Evolution of Box Turtles (genus *Terrapene*). *Bulletin of the Florida State Museum, Biological Series* 14(1):1–113.

Mohlhenrich, J. 1961. Distribution and Ecology of the Hispid and Least Cotton Rats in New Mexico. *Journal of Mammalogy* 42:13–24.

Moodie, Kevin B., and Thomas R. Van Devender. 1979. Extinction and Extirpation in the Herpetofauna of the Southern High Plains with Emphasis on *Geochelone wilsoni* (Testudinidae). *Herpetologica* 35(3):198–206.

Morlan, Richard E. 1980. Taphonomy and Archaeology in the Upper Pleistocene of the Northern Yukon Territory: A Glimpse of the Peopling of the New World. National Museum of Man, Ottawa, *Archaeological Survey of Canada Paper* 94:1–398.

Murry, Robert E., Jr. 1982. Charcoal and Wood Identifications from the Lubbock Lake Excavations. Manuscript, The Museum, Texas Tech University, Lubbock.

National Oceanic and Atmospheric Administration. 1974. *Climates of the States.* Vols. 1, 2. Port Washington, N.Y.: Water Information Center.

———. 1982. *Climate of Texas.* Asheville, N.C.: NOAA Environmental Data Service, National Climatic Center.

Newcomb, W. W., Jr. 1961. *The Indians of Texas from Prehistoric to Modern Times.* Austin: University of Texas Press.

Newcomb, W. W., Jr., and Forrest Kirkland. 1967. *The Rock Art of Texas Indians.* Austin: University of Texas Press.

Niethammer, Carolyn. 1974. *American Indian Food and Lore.* New York: Macmillan Co.

Oberholser, Harry C., and Edgar B. Kincaid, Jr. 1974. *The Bird Life of Texas.* Vols. 1, 2. Austin: University of Texas Press.

Oldfield, Frank. 1975. Pollen-Analytical Results, Part 2. In *Late Pleistocene Environments of the Southern High Plains,* ed. Fred Wendorf and James J. Hester, pp. 121–47. Dallas: Fort Burgwin Research Center, Southern Methodist University.

Oldfield, Frank, and James Schoenwetter. 1964. Late Quaternary Environments of Early Man on the Southern High Plains. *Antiquity* 38(151):226–29.

———. 1975. Discussion of the Pollen-Analytical Evidence. In *Late Pleistocene Environments of the Southern High Plains,* ed. Fred Wendorf and James J. Hester, pp. 149–79. Dallas: Fort Burgwin Research Center, Southern Methodist University.

Oliver, Symmes C. 1962. Ecology and Cultural Continuity as Contributing Factors in the Social Organization of the Plains Indians. *University of California Publications in American Archaeology and Ethnology* 48(1):1–90.

Opler, Morris Edward. 1941. *An Apache Life-Way.* Chicago: University of Chicago Press.

Packard, Robert L., and J. Hoyt Bowers. 1970. Distributional Notes on Some Foxes from Western Texas and Eastern New Mexico. *Texas Journal of Science* 14(4):450–51.

Patton, James L. 1973. An Analysis of Natural Hybridization between the Pocket Gophers, *Thomomys bottae* and *Thomomys umbrinus,* in Arizona. *Journal of Mammalogy* 54:561–84.

Patton, James L., and Ross E. Dingman. 1968. Chromosome Studies of Pocket Gophers, Genus *Thomomys.* I. The Specific Status of *Thomomys umbrinus* (Richardson) in Arizona. *Journal of Mammalogy* 49(1):1–13.

Patton, T. H. 1963. Fossil Vertebrates from Miller's Cave, Llano County, Texas. *Bulletin of the Texas Memorial Museum* 7:1–41.

Pettus, David. 1956. Fossil Rabbit (*Lagomorpha*) of the Friesenhahn Cave Deposit, Texas. *The Southwestern Naturalist* 1(3):109–15.

Pierce, Harold G. 1975. The Blanco Beds. In *Guidebook to the Mesozoic and Cenozoic Geology of the Southern Llano Estacado,* ed. Grayson E. Meade, Glen L. Evans, and John P. Brand. Lubbock: Lubbock Geological Society.

———. 1975. Diversity of Late Cenozoic Gastropods on the Southern High Plains. Ph.D. diss., Texas Tech University.

Pilsbry, Henry Augustus. 1948. Land Mollusca of North America (North of Mexico). *Philadelphia Academy of Natural Sciences Monograph* 3(2):521–1113.

Pope, J. 1855. Report of the Explorations near the Thirty-second Parallel of North Latitude from the Red River to the Rio Grande, vol. 2. *Report of the Exploration and Survey from the Mississippi River to the Pacific Ocean.* 33d Cong., 2d sess., S. Exec. Doc. 78. Washington, D.C.

Potts, Richard, and Pat Shipman. 1981. Cut Marks Made by Stone Tools on Bones from Olduvai Gorge, Tanzania. *Nature* 291:577–80.

Preston, Robert C. 1966. Turtles of the Gilliland Faunule from the Pleistocene of Knox County, Texas. *Papers of the Michigan Academy of Science, Arts, and Letters* 51:221–39.

Prewitt, Elton R. 1981. Cultural Chronology in Central Texas. *Bulletin of the Texas Archeological Society* 52:65–89.

Raun, Gerald G., and Frederick R. Gehlbach. 1972. Amphibians and Reptiles in Texas. *Bulletin of the Dallas Museum of Natural History* 2:1–61.

Ray, C. E., C. S. Denny, and M. Rubin. 1970. A Peccary, *Platygonus compressus* Le Conte, from Drift of Wisconsinan Age in Northern Pennsylvania. *American Journal of Science* 268:78–94.

Rea, Amadeo M., Robert Chandler, and Eileen Johnson. N.d. Late Quaternary Paleoavifaunas from the Southern High Plains, USA. Manuscript, The Museum, Texas Tech University, Lubbock.

Reeves, C. C., Jr. 1970. Some Geomorphic, Structural, and Stratigraphic Aspects of the Pliocene and Pleistocene Sediments of the Southern High Plains. Ph.D., diss., Texas Tech University.

———. 1972. Tertiary-Quaternary Stratigraphy and Geomorphology of West Texas and Southeastern New Mexico. In *Guidebook of East-Central New Mexico,* ed. Vincent C. Kelley and Frederick D. Trauger. 23:108–117. Socorro: New Mexico Geological Society.

———. 1976. Quaternary Stratigraphy and Geologic History of the Southern High Plains, Texas and New Mexico. In *Quaternary Stratigraphy of North America,* ed. W. C. Mahaney, pp. 213–34. Stroudsburg, Pa.: Dowden, Hutchinson, and Ross.

Reeves, C. C., Jr., and W. T. Parry. 1965. Geology of West Texas Pluvial Lake Carbonates. *American Journal of Science* 263:606–15.

Reichman, O. J., and R. J. Baker, 1972. Distribution and Movements of Two Species of Pocket Gophers (Geomyidae) in an Area of Sympatry in the Davis Mountains, Texas. *Journal of Mammalogy* 53:21–33.

Roberts, Frank H. H., Jr. 1936. Report on the Second Season's Investigations at the Lindenmeier Site in North Colorado. *Smithsonian Miscellaneous Collections* 95(10):1–37.

———. 1942. Archaeological and Geological Investigations in the San Jon District, Eastern New Mexico. *Smithsonian Miscellaneous Collections* 103(4):1–30.

Robinson, Michael D., and Thomas R. Van Devender. 1973. Miocene Lizards from Wyoming and Nebraska. *Copeia* 4:698–704.

Robinson, Ralph. 1982. Phytoliths from the Lubbock Lake Landmark. Report on file. The Museum, Texas Tech University, Lubbock.

Runkles, Frank A. 1964. The Garza Site: A Neo-American Campsite near Post, Texas. *Bulletin of the Texas Archeological Society* 35:101–26.

Russell, Robert J. 1968. Evolution and Classification of the Pocket Gophers of the Subfamily Geomyinae. *Museum of Natural History, University of Kansas, Publications* 16:473–579.

Russell, Stephen M. 1966. Status of the Black Rail and the Gray-breasted Crake in British Honduras. *Condor* 68:105–107.

Saunders, Jeffrey John. 1970. The Distribution and Taxonomy of *Mammuthus* in Arizona. Master's thesis, University of Arizona.

———. 1977. Lehner Ranch Revisited. In Paleoindian Lifeways, ed. Eileen Johnson. *Museum Journal* (West Texas Museum Association) 17:48–64.

———. 1980. A Model for Man-Mammoth Relationships in Late Pleistocene North America. In The Ice-Free Corridor and Peopling of the New World, ed. N. W. Rutter and C. E. Schweger. *Canadian Journal of Anthropology* 1(1):87–98.

Saunders, Roger A., and John T. Penman. 1979. Perry Ranch: A Plainview Bison Kill on the Southern Plains. *Plains Anthropologist* 24(83):51–65.

Schleiser, Karl H. 1972. Rethinking the Dismal River Aspect and the Plains Athapaskans, A.D. 1692–1768. *Plains Anthropologist* 17(56):101–103.

Schmidly, David. 1977. *The Mammals of Trans-Pecos Texas.* College Station: Texas A&M University Press.

———. 1983. *Texas Mammals East of the Balcones Fault Zone.* College Station: Texas A&M University Press.

Schoenwetter, James. 1975. Pollen-Analytical Results, Part I. In *Late Pleistocene Environments of the Southern High Plains,* ed. Fred Wendorf and James J. Hester, pp. 103–20. Dallas: Fort Burgwin Research Center, Southern Methodist University.

Schultz, C. Bertrand. 1943. Some Artifact Sites of Early Man in the Great Plains and Adjacent Areas. *American Antiquity* 8:242–49.

Schultz, C. Bertrand, and Edgar B. Howard. 1935. The Fauna of Burnet Cave, Guadalupe Mountains, New Mexico. *Proceedings of the Academy of Natural Sciences of Philadelphia* 87:272–98.

Schultz, Gerald E. 1967. Four Superimposed Late-Pleistocene Vertebrate Faunas from Southwest Kansas. In *Pleistocene Extinctions: The Search for a Cause,* ed. Paul S. Martin and H. E. Wright, Jr., pp. 321–36. New Haven, Conn.: Yale University Press.

———. 1978. Supplementary Data on the Rex Rodgers Site: Micromammals. In Archeology at MacKenzie Reservoir, ed. Jack T. Hughes and Patrick S. Willey. Texas Historical Commission, Office of the State Archeologist, *Archeological Survey Report* 24:114.

Schultz, Gerald E., and Elmer P. Cheatum. 1970. *Bison occidentalis* and Associated Invertebrates from the Late Wisconsin of Randall County, Texas. *Journal of Paleontology* 44:836–50.

Secoy, Frank Raymond. 1953. Changing Military Patterns on the Great Plains. *Monographs of the American Ethnological Society* 21:1–112.

Sellards, E. H. 1938. Artifacts Associated with Fossil Elephant. *Bulletin of the Geological Society of America* 49:999–1010.

———. 1952. *Early Man in America.* Austin: University of Texas Press.

———. 1955a. Fossil Bison and Associated Artifacts from Milnesand, New Mexico. *American Antiquity* 20(4):336–44.

———. 1955b. Further Investigations at the Scharbauer Site. In *The Midland Discovery,* ed. Fred Wendorf, Alex D. Krieger, and Claude C. Albritton, pp. 126–32. Austin: University of Texas Press.

Sellards, E. H., Glen L. Evans, and Grayson E. Meade. 1947. Fossil Bison and Associated Artifacts from Plainview, Texas. *Bulletin of the Geological Society of America* 58:927–54.

Semken, Holmes A., Jr. 1974. Micromammal Distribution and Migration during the Holocene. *American Quaternary Association Abstracts* 3:25.

———. 1983. Holocene Mammalian Biogeography and Climatic Change in the Eastern and Central United States. In *Late Quaternary Environments of the United States,* ed. H. E. Wright, Jr., 2:182–207. Minneapolis: University of Minnesota Press.

Shipman, Pat. 1981. Applications of Scanning Electron Microscopy to Taphonomic Problems. In The Research Potential of Anthropological Museum Collections, ed. Anne-Marie E. Cantwell, James B. Griffin, and Nan A. Rothschild. *Annals of the New York Academy of Sciences* 376:357–86.

Shotwell, J. Arnold. 1955. An Approach to the Paleoecology of Mammals. *Ecology* 36(2):327–37.

———. 1958. Inter-Community Relationships in Hemphillian (Mid-Pleistocene) Mammals. *Ecology* 30(2):271–82.

Sikes, Sylvia. 1971. *The Natural History of the African Elephant.* London: Weidenfeld and Nicolson.

Sisson, Septimus, and James Daniels Grossman. 1953. *The Anatomy of the Domestic Animals.* Philadelphia: W. B. Saunders Co.

Skinner, Morris F., and Ove C. Kaisen. 1947. The Fossil Bison of Alaska and Preliminary Revision of the Genus. *Bulletin of the American Museum of Natural History* 89:127–256.

Slaughter, Bob H. 1961. A New Coyote in the Late Pleistocene of Texas. *Journal of Mammalogy* 42:503–509.

———. 1966a. The Vertebrates of the Domebo Local Fauna, Pleistocene of Oklahoma. In Domebo: A Paleoindian Mammoth Kill in the Prairie Plains, ed. Frank C. Leonhardy. *Contributions of the Museum of the Great Plains* 1:31–35.

———. 1966b. The Moore Pit Local Fauna: The Pleistocene of Texas. *Journal of Paleontology* 40:78–91.

————. 1966c. *Platygonus compressus* and Associated Fauna from the Laubach Cave of Texas. *American Midland Naturalist* 75:475–94.

————. 1975. Ecological Interpretation of Brown Sand Wedge Local Fauna. In *Late Pleistocene Environments on the Southern High Plains,* ed. Fred Wendorf and James J. Hester, pp. 179–92. Dallas: Fort Burgwin Research Center, Southern Methodist University.

Slaughter, Bob H., and B. R. Hoover. 1963. Sulphur River Formation and the Pleistocene Mammals of the Ben Franklin Local Fauna. *Journal of the Graduate Research Center* (Southern Methodist University) 31: 132–48.

Slaughter, Bob H., and William L. McClure. 1965. The Sims Bayou Local Fauna: Pleistocene of Houston, Texas. *Texas Journal of Science* 18(4):404–17.

Slaughter, Bob H., and Ronald Ritchie. 1963. The Pleistocene Mammals of the Clear Creek Local Fauna, Denton County, Texas. *Journal of the Graduate Research Center* (Southern Methodist University) 31:117–31.

Slaughter, Bob H., W. W. Crook, Jr., R. K. Harris, D. C. Allen, and Martin Seifert. 1962. The Hill-Shuler Local Faunas of the Upper Trinity River, Dallas and Denton Counties, Texas. University of Texas, Bureau of Economic Geology, *Report of Investigations* 48: 1–75.

Smartt, Richard A. 1972. Late Pleistocene and Recent *Microtus* from Southcentral and Southwestern New Mexico. Master's thesis, University of Texas at El Paso.

Smith, Hobart M. 1956. Handbook of Amphibians and Reptiles of Kansas. University of Kansas Museum of Natural History *Miscellaneous Publications* 9:1–356.

Sneath, Peter H., and Robert R. Sokal. 1973. *Numerical Taxonomy.* San Francisco: W. H. Freeman and Co.

Soil Survey Staff. 1975. Soil Taxonomy. In *Agricultural Handbook* 436:1–754. Washington, D.C.: U.S. Department of Agriculture, Soil Conservation Service.

Spaulding, W. Geoffrey, Estella B. Leopold, and Thomas V. Van Devender. 1983. Late Wisconsin Paleoecology of the American Southwest. In *Late Quaternary Environments of the United States,* ed. H. E. Wright, Jr., 1: 259–93. Minneapolis: University of Minnesota Press.

Speer, Roberta D. 1978. Fossil Bison Remains from the Rex Rodgers Site. In Archeology at MacKenzie Reservoir, ed. Jack T. Hughes and Patrick S. Willey. Texas Historical Commission, Office of the State Archeologist, *Archeological Survey Report* 24:68–105.

Spenrath, Curtis A., and Richard K. LaVal. 1974. An Ecological Study of a Resident Population of *Tadarida brasiliensis* in Eastern Texas. The Museum, Texas Tech University, *Occasional Papers* 21:1–14.

Speth, John D. 1983. *Bison Kills and Bone Counts: Decision Making by Ancient Hunters.* Chicago: University of Chicago Press.

Speth, John D., and Katherine Spielmann. 1983. Energy Source, Protein Metabolism, and Hunter-Gatherer Subsistence Strategies. *Journal of Anthropological Archaeology* 2(1):1–31.

Stafford, Thomas W. Jr. 1977. Late Quaternary Alluvial Stratigraphy of Yellowhouse Draw, Lubbock, Texas. In Cultural Adaptation to Ecological Change on the Llano Estacado: Preliminary Report of the 1976 Field Season of the Lubbock Lake Project, ed. Eileen Johnson and Thomas W. Stafford, Jr. Report submitted to the National Science Foundation, Washington, D.C.

————. 1978. Late Quaternary Alluvial Stratigraphy of Yellowhouse and Blackwater Draws, Llano Estacado, Texas. In Cultural Adaptation to Ecological Change on the Llano Estacado: Preliminary Report of the 1977 Field Season of the Lubbock Lake Site, ed. Eileen Johnson. Report submitted to the National Science Foundation, Washington, D.C.

————. 1981. Alluvial Geology and Archaeological Potential of the Texas Southern Plains. *American Antiquity* 46(3):548–85.

Stanford, Dennis. 1974. Preliminary Report of the Excavation of the Jones-Miller Hell Gap Site, Yuma County, Colorado. *Southwestern Lore* 40(3–4):29–36.

Stanford, Dennis, Robson Bonnichsen, and Richard Morlan. 1981. The Ginsberg Experiment: Modern and Prehistoric Evidence of a Bone-Flaking Technique. *Science* 212:438–40.

Stebbins, Robert C. 1966. *A Field Guide to Western Reptiles and Amphibians.* Boston: Houghton Mifflin Co.

Stephens, J. L. 1960. Stratigraphy and Paleontology of a Late Pleistocene Basin, Harper County, Oklahoma. *Bulletin of the Geological Society of America* 71(11): 1676–1702.

Stern, Philip Van Doren. 1969. *Prehistoric Europe.* New York: W. W. Norton and Co.

Stock, Chester. 1928. *Tanupolama,* a New Genus of Llama from the Pleistocene of California. *Carnegie Institution of Washington Publications* 393:29–37.

Stock, Chester, and Francis D. Bode. 1936. The Occurrence of Flints and Extinct Animals in Pluvial Deposits Near Clovis, New Mexico, Part III. Geology and Vertebrate Paleontology of the Late Quaternary near Clovis, New Mexico. *Proceedings of the Academy of Natural Sciences of Philadelphia* 88:219–41.

Strahler, Arthur N., and Alan H. Strahler. 1983. *Modern Physical Geography.* 2d ed. New York: John Wiley & Sons.

Suhm, Dee Ann, Alex D. Krieger, and Edward B. Jelks. 1954. An Introductory Handbook of Texas Archeology. *Bulletin of the Texas Archeological Society* 25: 1–299.

Stucliffe, Antony J. 1970. Spotted Hyaena: Crusher, Gnawer, Digester and Collector of Bones. *Nature* 227:1110–13.

Taylor, D. W. 1960. Late Cenozoic Molluscan Faunas from the High Plains. United States Geological Survey *Professional Papers* 337:1–94.

Tedford, Richard H. 1970. Principles and Practices of Mammalian Geochronology in North America. In *Proceedings of the North American Paleontological Convention,* ed. Ellis L. Yochelson. 1:666–703. Lawrence, Kans.: Allen Press.

Thaeler, Charles S., Jr. 1980. Chromosome Numbers and Systematic Relations in the Genus *Thomomys* (Rodentia: Geomyidae). *Journal of Mammalogy* 61(3): 414–22.

Thompson, Daniel Q. 1965. Food Preferences of the Meadow Vole (*Microtus pennsylvanicus*) in Relation to Habitat Affinities. *American Midland Naturalist* 74(1): 76–86.

Torrey, John, and Asa Gray. 1855. Report of the Botany. In Report of the Exploration near the Thirty-second Parallel of North Latitude from the Red River to the Rio Grande, ed. J. Pope, vol. 2. *Report of the Exploration and Survey from the Mississippi River to the Pacific Ocean.* 33d Cong., 2d sess., S. Exec. Doc. 78. Washington, D.C.

Tunnell, Curtis D. 1977. Fluted Point Production as Revealed by Lithic Specimens from the Adair-Steadman Site in Northwestern Texas. In Paleoindian Lifeways, ed. Eileen Johnson. *Museum Journal* (West Texas Museum Association) 17: 140–68.

Tunnell, Curtis D., and Jack T. Hughes. 1955. An Archaic Bison Kill in the Texas Panhandle. *Panhandle-Plains Historical Review* 28: 63–70.

Turner, Sue Ellen, and Thomas R. Hester. 1985. *A Field Guide to Stone Artifacts of Texas Indians.* Austin: Texas Monthly Press.

Van Devender, Thomas R., and W. Geoffrey Spaulding. 1979. Development of Vegetation and Climate in the Southwestern United States. *Science* 204: 701–10.

Van Devender, Thomas R., and Richard D. Worthington. 1977. The Herpetofauna of Howell's Ridge Cave and the Paleoecology of the Northwestern Chihuahuan Desert. In Transactions of the Symposium on the Biological Resources of the Chihuahuan Desert Region, United States and Mexico, ed. R. H. Wauer and D. H. Riskind. *National Park Service Transactions and Proceedings Series* 3: 85–106.

Van Devender, Thomas R., Paul S. Martin, A. M. Phillips III, and W. G. Spaulding. 1977. Late Pleistocene Biotic Communities from the Guadalupe Mountains, Culberson County, Texas. In Transactions of the Symposium on the Biological Resources of the Chihuahuan Desert Region, United States and Mexico, ed. R. Wauer and D. Riskind. *National Park Service Transactions and Proceedings Series* 3: 107–13.

Vaughn, Terry A. 1961. Vertebrates Inhabiting Pocket Gopher Burrows in Colorado. *Journal of Mammalogy* 42(2): 171–74.

Vereschagin, N. K. 1967. Primitive Hunters and Pleistocene Extinction in the Soviet Union. In *Pleistocene Extinction: The Search for a Cause,* ed. Paul S. Martin and H. E. Wright, pp. 365–98. New Haven, Conn.: Yale University Press.

Walker, Phillip L., and Jeffrey C. Long. 1977. An Experimental Study of the Morphological Characteristics of Tool Marks. *American Antiquity* 42(4): 605–16.

Wallace, Ernest, and E. Adamson Hoebel. 1952. *The Comanches: Lords of the South Plains.* Norman: University of Oklahoma Press.

Wallen, I. E., and Paul Dunlap. 1953. Further Additions to the Snail Fauna of Oklahoma. *Proceedings of the Oklahoma Academy of Sciences* 34: 76–80.

Wan, Mei. 1980. Basic Archaeological Collection Management Considerations and Research into Bone Technology: A Case Study of the 1975 Canyon Lakes Project, Lubbock, Texas. Master's thesis, Texas Tech University.

Weaver, W. F., Jr., and Francis L. Rose. 1967. Systematics, Fossil History, and Evolution of the Genus *Chrysemys. Tulane Studies in Zoology* 14: 63–73.

Webb, Robert G. 1970. *Reptiles of Oklahoma.* Norman: University of Oklahoma Press.

Webb, S. David. 1965. The Osteology of Camelops. *Science Bulletin of the Los Angeles County Museum* 1: 1–54.

Wendorf, Fred. 1961a. *Paleoecology of the Llano Estacado.* Santa Fe: Museum of New Mexico Press.

———. 1961b. An Interpretation of Late Pleistocene Environments of the Llano Estacado. In *Paleoecology of the Llano Estacado,* ed. Fred Wendorf, pp. 115–33. Santa Fe: Museum of New Mexico Press.

———. 1961c. Invertebrate Collections. In *Paleoecology of the Llano Estacado,* ed. Fred Wendorf, pp. 105–13. Santa Fe: Museum of New Mexico Press.

———. 1970. The Lubbock Subpluvial. In *Pleistocene and Recent Environments of the Central Great Plains,* ed. Wakefield Dort and J. Knox Jones Jr., pp. 23–36. Lawrence: University Press of Kansas.

———. 1975. Summary and Conclusions. In *Late Pleistocene Environments of the Southern High Plains,* ed. Fred Wendorf and James J. Hester, pp. 257–70. Dallas: Fort Burgwin Research Center, Southern Methodist University.

Wendorf, Fred, and James J. Hester. 1962. Early Man's Utilization of the Great Plains Environment. *American Antiquity* 28(2): 159–71.

———. 1975. *Late Pleistocene Environments of the Southern High Plains.* Dallas: Fort Burgwin Research Center, Southern Methodist University.

Wendorf, Fred, Alex D. Krieger, Claude C. Albritton, and T. D. Stewart. 1955. *The Midland Discovery.* Austin: University of Texas Press.

Wetzel, Ralph M. 1955. Speciation and Dispersal of the Southern Bog Lemming, *Synaptomys cooperi* (Baird). *Journal of Mammalogy* 36(1): 1–20.

Wheat, Joe Ben. 1955. Two Archaeological Sites near Lubbock, Texas. *Panhandle-Plains Historical Review* 28: 71–77.

———. 1971. Lifeways of Early Man in North America. *Arctic Anthropology* 8(2): 22–31.

———. 1972. The Olsen-Chubbuck Site: A Paleo-Indian Bison Kill. *Society for American Archaeology Memoirs* 26: 1–179.

———. 1974. First Excavations at the Lubbock Lake Site. In History and Prehistory of the Lubbock Lake Site, ed. Craig C. Black. *Museum Journal* (West Texas Museum Association) 15: 15–42.

———. 1976. Artifact Life Histories: Cultural Templates, Typology, Evidence, and Inference. In *Primitive Art and Technology,* pp. 7–15. Alberta: Archaeological Association, Department of Archaeology, Univeristy of Calgary.

———. 1977. Technology, Typology, and Use Patterns at the Jurgens Site. In Paleoindian Lifeways, ed. Eileen Johnson. *Musem Journal* (West Texas Museum Association) 17:48–64.

———. 1979. The Jurgens Site. *Plains Anthropologist* 15: 1–153.

Willey, Patrick S., and Jack T. Hughes. 1978. The Deadman's Terrace Site. In Archeology at MacKenzie Reservoir, ed. Jack T. Hughes and Patrick S. Willey. Texas Historical Commission, Office of the State Archeologist, *Archeological Survey Report* 24:205–25.

Wilmsen, Edwin N. 1974. *Lindenmeier: A Plesitocene Hunting Society.* New York: Harper & Row.

Wilmsen, Edwin N., and Frank H. H. Roberts, Jr. 1978. Lindenmeier, 1934–1974: Concluding Report on Investigations. *Smithsonian Contributions to Anthropology* 24:1–187.

Wilson, Michael. 1974a. History of the Bison in Wyoming, with Particular Reference to Early Holocene Forms. In *Applied Geology and Archaeology: The Holocene History of Wyoming,* ed. Michael Wilson. 10:91–99.

———. 1974b. The Casper Local Fauna and Its Fossil Bison. In *The Casper Site: A Hell Gap Kill on the High Plains,* ed. George Frison, pp. 125–72. New York: Academic Press.

Winans, Melissa Constance. 1985. Revision of North American Fossil Species of the Genus *Equus* (Mammalia: Perissodactyla: Equidae). Ph.D. diss., University of Texas at Austin.

Winkler, M. G., A. M. Swain, and J. E. Kutzbach. 1986. Middle Holocene Dry Period in the Northern Midwestern United States: Lake Levels and Pollen Stratigraphy. *Quaternary Research* 25(2):235–50.

Womochel, Daniel. 1977. Taphonomy and Paleoecology of the Slaton Local Fauna (Pleistocene, Texas). Ph.D. diss., Texas Tech University.

Wood, A. E. 1935. The Evolution and Relationship of Heteromyid Rodents. *Annals of the Carnegie Museum* 24(7):73–262.

Worcester, D. E. 1944. The Spread of Spanish Horses in the Southwest. *New Mexico Historical Review* 19:225–32.

Wormington, H. Marie. 1957. Ancient Man in North America. *Denver Museum of Natural History Popular Series* 4:1–322.

Wyckoff, Don G. 1984. The Foragers: Eastern Oklahoma. In *Prehistory of Oklahoma,* ed. Robert E. Bell, pp. 119–60. New York: Academic Press.

Yapp, Crayton J., and Samuel Epstein. 1977. Climatic Implications of D/H Ratios of Meteoric Water over North America (9500–22,000 B.P.) as Inferred from Ancient Wood Cellulose C-H Hydrogen. *Earth and Planetary Science Letters* 34:333–50.

Young, David E., and Robson Bonnichsen. 1984. *Understanding Stone Tools: A Cognitive Approach.* Orono: Center for the Study of Early Man, University of Maine.

# Contributors

B. L. Allen, Professor, Department of Plant and Soil Science, Texas Tech University, Lubbock, Texas

Vaughn M. Bryant, Jr., Professor, Department of Anthropology, Texas A&M University, College Station, Texas

Vance T. Holliday, Lubbock Lake Landmark Project Geologist and Assistant Professor, Department of Geography, University of Wisconsin, Madison, Wisconsin

Eileen Johnson, Director of Lubbock Lake Landmark and Curator of Anthropology, The Museum, Texas Tech University, Lubbock, Texas

Harold G. Pierce, Consulting Geologist, O'Neill, Nebraska

James Schoenwetter, Professor, Department of Anthropology, Arizona State University, Tempe, Arizona

Jerome L. Thompson, Property Development Specialist, Iowa State Historical Department, Des Moines, Iowa

# Index

*Acris* cf. *crepitans*, 63–64
activity areas: Clovis Period, 123; Folsom Period, 124, 125–26;
  Historic Period, 141–42; Protohistoric Period, 137
age (of soil deposits), 17, 19, 20, 120
*Agkistrodon contortrix*, 70, 98
A-horizon, 19
Altithermal, two-drought, 99, 161
*Ambystoma tigrinum*, 49
amphibians, fossil, 49, 63–64, 65
anatomy, butchery and, 143
Anglo-Europeans, 139, 140
antelope, 84–85, 92, 93, 94, 96, 106, 133, 140, 158
antelope, pronghorn, 129, 131, 137, 141
*Antilocapra americana*, 85
Apaches, 136, 139
Apache Soil, 19, 20, 24, 136, 137
Archaic Period, 19, 23, 33, 46, 94–95, 96, 111, 132–33, 161
*Arctodus simus*, 79–80, 88
*Argemone* sp., 33
armadillo, giant, 71, 88, 90, 121
*Armiger crista*, 45
artifacts, bone: Ceramic Period, 112, 133; Clovis Period,
  101–102, 122, 160; Firstview Period, 110–11, 130; Folsom
  Period, 105, 125; Historic Period, 117–18; Plainview Period,
  108–109, 129; Protohistoric Period, 114–15
artifacts, ceramic and shell, 115
artifacts, lithic: Archaic Period, 111; Ceramic Period, 112–13,
  133; Clovis Period, 101, 104; Firstview Period, 109–10,
  130–31; Folsom Period, 104–105, 107; Historic Period, 115,
  117; Plainview Period, 107–108, 129; Protohistoric Period,
  113–14

bat, 71, 96
bear, giant, 79–80, 90, 121, 122, 158
bison, 85–86, 145–48; in Archaic Period, 94, 95; bone concentrations, 126; butchering patterns, 143–48; butchering
  site, 124, 129, 130–31, 132–33, 137–39, 140, 141; in Ceramic Period, 96; in Clovis Period, 121; in Firstview Period,
  93; in Folsom Period, 92; hunting of, 158; in Plainview Period, 92; procurement systems, 156–57
*Bison antiquus*, 85–86, 97
*Bison bison*, 86
*Blarina* sp., 70–71, 97
bobcat, 80, 93
bone: concentrations, 126–27, 129, 132; quarrying, 122, 123,
  160; piling, 124. *See also* artifacts, bone; tools
*Bufo woodhousei bexarensis*, 64
*Bufo woodhousei woodhousei*, 64
butchery, 120, 143. *See also* bone; *specific animals*

camel, 122, 157–58
camelids, 83, 90, 121, 157–58
*Camelops hesternus*, 83
canids, 78–79, 91, 92, 93, 94, 96, 133, 136–37, 140, 141, 158
*Canis latrans*, 78
*Canis lupus*, 78
*Capromeryx* sp., 84, 88

*Carphophis amoenus*, 68, 97
*Carychium exiguum*, 43
*Celtis reticulata*, 32
Ceramic Period, 19, 20, 24, 34, 46–47, 96–99, 112–13, 133,
  161
*Chara* sp., 33, 43, 45
*Chelydra serpentina*, 65
*Chenopodium* sp., 33
*Chlamydotheca* n.s.?, 45, 46, 47, 48
chronology (of cultural periods), 22–24
*Chrysemys scripta*, 66
clams, sphaeriid, 43, 45
Clovis Period, 17, 22, 32, 45, 90–91, 97–98, 158, 160
*Coluber constrictor*, 68, 98
Comanches, 139–40
cotton rat, 75, 86, 92, 93, 94
coyote, 131, 133, 137, 141
*Cratogeomys castenops*, 74, 88
cricket frog, 63–64
*Crotalus atrox*, 70
cultures, chronology of, 22–24
*Cynomys ludovicianus*, 73

deer, 83–84, 129, 158
deposition, soil strata, 16, 17, 19–20
deposition environments, 20–21
*Deroceras laeve*, 43, 44, 46
*Dipodomys ordii*, 74
*Discus cronkhitei*, 44
drought cycle, 96, 99, 161
duck, 124, 129, 131

*Elaphe guttata*, 44
*Eleocharis* sp., 32
*Equisetum* sp., 33
*Equus caballus*, 82
*Equus mexicanus*, 81
*Euconulus fulvus*, 44
*Eumeces obsoletus*, 68

fauna: communities of, 88–89, 90, 91, 92, 93, 159; sympatry
  area of, 97–98, 99
*Felis* cf. *rufus*, 80
*Ferrissia rivularis*, 45
Firstview Period, 17, 19, 23, 38–39, 93, 98–99, 109–11,
  130–31, 145–47, 156–57
Firstview Soil, 17, 19
flora, fossil, 32, 33, 34
Folsom Period, 17, 22–23, 33, 37–38, 45, 46, 92, 98, 99,
  124–26, 158, 160
fossils: amphibians, 49, 63, 64, 65; flora, 32, 33, 34; gastropods, 44, 45, 46–47; limpets, 45; mammals, 70–88, 97,
  98, 99; reptiles, 65–70, 86, 97, 98, 99; seeds, 32–34, 43, 45
frogs, 64–65, 90, 92, 93, 94, 96; cricket, 63–64

game animals, 136–37, 140, 155–58
*Gastrocopta cristata*, 43, 45, 46

*Gastrocopta pellucida hordeacella,* 46
*Gastrocopta pentodon,* 43, 45
*Gastrocopta procera,* 43, 45, 46
gastropods, 41–43; and climate, 47–48; correlation with other, 44; fossil, 43–47; modern, 47; statistical analysis of, 42, 47
*Gaura* sp., 32
*Geochelone* sp., 66, 98
*Geochelone wilsoni,* 65–66, 86, 98
*Geomys bursarius,* 74
gophers, pocket, 73–74, 88, 92, 93, 94, 96
ground squirrels, 72–73, 90, 91, 92, 93, 96
*Gyalopion canum,* 68, 97
*Gyraulus circumstriatus,* 45, 46, 47
*Gyraulus deflectus,* 45
*Gyraulus parvus,* 46

habitat exploitation, 158
*Hawaiia minuscula,* 46
hearths, 136, 137
*Heliocodiscus eigenmanni,* 45, 46
*Helicodiscus parallelus,* 44, 45
*Helicodiscus singleyanus,* 46
*Helisoma anceps,* 43, 45
*Helisoma trivolvis,* 43, 45
*Hemiauchenia* sp., 83
*Heterodon nasicus,* 68
Historic Period, 19–20, 24, 33–34, 46–47, 96, 99, 120, 139, 140, 141–42, 161
*Holmesina septentrionalis,* 71, 88, 98
horned lizard, 68, 93, 96
horses, 81–82, 90, 121, 122, 140, 148–50, 157–58

Indians, 136, 139–40

kangaroo rat, 74, 92, 94
*Kinosternon flavescens,* 65

*Laevapex fuscus,* 45
*Lampropeltis getulus,* 68–69
*Lampropeltis triangulum,* 69
lemming, bog, 77, 87, 92
*Lepus californicus,* 72
limpets, fossil, 45
*Lithospermum* sp., 32
lizard, horned, 68, 93, 96
Lubbock Lake: described, 3; fauna (local), 96–99; flora (historic), 29, 31–33; flora (modern), 26, 29; gastropods (modern), 47; history and discovery of, 4–8, 159; importance of, 4; stratigraphy of, 14, 15, 16, 17, 19, 20, 159
Lubbock Lake Project, 3, 8, 10–11, 49, 100, 121
Lubbock Lake Soil, 19, 23
Lubbock Subpluvial, 37, 160
*Lymnaea bulimoides,* 45
*Lymnaea palustris,* 45, 46, 47

mammals, fossil, 70–88, 97, 98, 99
mammoth, 80–81, 90, 121–22, 150–52, 155–56, 158
*Mammuthus columbi,* 80–81
*Mephitis mephitis,* 80
mice, 74–75, 91
*Microtus ochrogaster,* 76–77, 87, 98, 99
*Microtus pennsylvanicus,* 76, 87, 98, 99
muskrat, 77, 87, 90, 92, 93, 124, 129, 158
mustelids, 80, 93, 96

*Neotoma* cf. *albigula,* 76
*Neotoma* cf. *micropus,* 75–76
*Nerodia* cf. *cyclopion* or *N. rhombifera,* 69, 98
*Nerodia erythrogaster,* 69
*Nesovitrea hammonis electrina,* 44
*Notiosorex crawfordi,* 71
*Nymphaea* sp., 33

*Odocoileus* sp., 83–84
*Ondatra zibethicus,* 77, 87, 98, 99
*Onychomys leucogaster,* 75
Ostracods, fossil, 45, 46, 47, 48
*Oxyloma* cf. *O. retusa,* 45, 46

paleoenvironment, 94–95; in Archaic Period, 46, 94–95, 96, 161; in Ceramic Period, 96; in Clovis Period, 45, 90–91, 98, 160; in Firstview Period, 93, 98–99, 160; in Folsom Period, 46, 92, 98, 160; in Historic Period, 47, 96, 161; in Plainview Period, 46, 92, 98, 160; species indicators of, 43, 44, 45, 46, 86, 87–88, 98
peccary, 82, 90
*Perognathus* cf. *hispidus,* 74
*Peromyscus* cf. *eremicus,* 75, 97
*Phrynosoma cornutum,* 68
*Physa anatina,* 46
*Pituophis melanoleucus,* 69
Plainview people, bone processing by, 129
Plainview Period, 17, 19, 23, 33, 34–35, 45, 46, 92, 98, 99, 145–47, 158
plants, economic uses of, 34–35
*Platygonus compressus,* 82
pluvial conditions, 99
pocket gophers, 73–74, 88, 92, 93, 94, 96
pocket mice, 74, 92
pollen record, 36–39
*Proboscidea* sp., 33
*Promenetus exacuous,* 45
*Promenetus umbilicatellus,* 45
pronghorn antelope, 129, 131, 137, 141
*Prosopis* sp., 33
Protohistoric Period, 19, 20, 23, 34, 46–47, 96, 99, 113–15, 136, 137, 161
*Punctum minutissimum,* 45
*Pupilla muscorum,* 43
*Pupilla muscorum sinistra,* 43
*Pupoides albilabris,* 46

rabbits, 72, 92, 93, 94, 96, 131, 137, 158
radiocarbon dating, 8
*Rana catesbeiana,* 64
*Rana palustris,* 65, 97
*Rana pipiens,* 65
rats: cotton, 75, 86, 92, 93, 94; kangaroo (fossil), 74, 92, 94; wood, 75–76, 93, 94
*Reithrodontomys montanus,* 74–75
reptiles (fossil), 65–70, 86, 97, 98, 99
*Rhinocheilus lecontei,* 69

salamander, tiger, 49, 90, 94, 96
*Salvadora* sp., 69, 97
*Scaphiopus bombifrons* or *S. hammondi,* 63
*Scaphiopus couchi,* 62–63
*Scirpus* sp., 32
seeds, fossil, 32–34, 43, 45
shrews, 70–71, 90, 92

*Sigmodon hispidus,* 75, 86, 98
Singer Soil, 19, 20, 24, 96, 115, 139–40
Singer Store location, 5, 140
skink, 68, 93
snakes, 68–70, 90–96, 137
soil development, 17, 19, 20
*Solanum rostratum,* 33
*Solanum* sp., 34
*Sonora semiannulata,* 69, 97, 98
Southern High Plains, 3, 4, 14–15
spadefoot toad, 62–63, 94
*Spermophilus mexicanus,* 73
*Spermophilus richardsonii,* 72, 97
*Spermophilus tridecemlineatus,* 72–73
sphaeriid clams, 43, 45
squirrels, ground, 72–73, 90, 91, 92, 93, 96
stratigraphic units, 17, 19–20
*Strobilops labyrinthica,* 45
*Suaeda* sp., 32
cf. *Succinea* sp., 46
*Sylvilagus* cf. *audubonii,* 72
*Sylvilagus* sp., 72
*Synaptomys cooperi,* 77–78, 87–88, 98

*Tadarida brasiliensis,* 71
*Taxidea taxus,* 80
*Terrapene carolina putnami,* 66–67, 86, 97
*Terrapene ornata,* 67, 86
*Thamnophis* cf. *marcianus,* 69
*Thamnophis proximus,* 70

*Thamnophis* cf. *sirtalis,* 70, 97, 98, 99
*Thomomys bottae,* 73–74, 97
tiger salamander, 49, 90, 94, 96
toads, 62–63, 64, 90, 94
tools, 152; assemblages of expediency, 153–54; bone, 125–26; bone quarrying, 101, 123, 152, 154–55; expediency, 101–102, 105, 108–109, 110, 112, 114–15, 117, 122, 125, 152, 154; manufacture of bone, 120–21, 125–26, 154
*Trionyx* sp., 67, 97
*Tropidoclonion lineatum,* 70, 97, 98
turkey, wild, 122, 123
turtles, 65–67, 90, 91, 92, 93, 94, 96, 121, 122, 158

*Vallonia cyclophorella,* 43
*Vallonia gracillicosta,* 43
*Vallonia parvula,* 46
*Vallonia,* sp., 43
*Valvata tricarinata,* 45
*Vertigo gouldi basidens,* 43
*Vertigo ovata,* 43, 45
*Virginia* cf. *striatula,* 70, 97
voles, 76–77, 86–87, 90, 92, 93
*Vulpes macrotis,* 78–79, 97

wolf, 136–37, 141
wood rats, 75–76, 93, 94

Yellowhouse Soil, 19, 23, 94, 99

*Zonitoides arboreus,* 45